Joe Hightower's Hitch in Hell

A Soldier's Story Through World War II

Based on Five Personal Journals

Joe Hightower

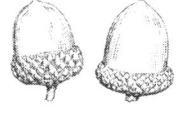

Hog Press

Hog Press
an imprint of Culicidae Press®
PO Box 5069
Madison, WI 53705-5069
USA
hogpress.com
culicidaepress.com
editor@culicidaepress.com

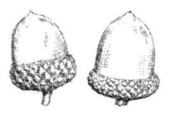

HOG PRESS

JOE HIGHTOWER'S HITCH IN HELL: A SOLDIER'S STORY THROUGH WORLD WAR II BASED ON FIVE PERSONAL JOURNALS
Copyright © 2024 by Joe Hightower

No part of this book may be reproduced in any form by any electronic or mechanized means (including photocopying, recording, or information storage and retrieval) without written permission, except in the case of brief quotations embodied in critical articles and reviews. For more information, please visit culicidaepress.com

First Hardcover Edition

ISBN: 978-1-941892-90-9

Library of Congress Control Number: 2024945236

Our books may be purchased in bulk for promotional, educational or business use. Please contact your local bookseller or the Culicidae Press Sales Department at +1-515-462-0278 or by email at sales@culicidaepress.com

x.com/culicidaepress – facebook.com/culicidaepress
threads.net/culicidaepress – instagram.com/culicidaepress

Designed by polytekton ©2024
Painting on back cover by Charles Bickel

Table of Contents

Introduction by Marijo Starnes	5
Fort Des Moines, Des Moines, Iowa	9
Leaving Fort Des Moines	12
The Voyage Overseas to Brisbane, Australia	43
Fiji	48
Welcome to Australia	52
Moving to Rockhampton, Australia—A 24 Hour-Train-Ride	57
1943, Triangle Camp, Townsville, Australia	73
New Guinea: "A Hitch in Hell"	75
Still in New Guinea	196
The Mansion Furlough Aug. 2 – 25, 1944	240
The Last Leg of The Journey, Back from Furlough	254
Heading to Subic Bay	317
Biographies	405
Joseph Carl Hightower (1913-1998)	405
Marijo Starnes	405
Charles Bickel	405

Introduction

BY MARIJO STARNES

The accounts in the contents of my father's diaries expose the raw truth about the sacrifices, trauma, and the intense drive that drove our soldiers to fight and to win World War II. My father realized our God-given freedoms were being threatened and in harm's way. I've heard him say: "There was a mission at hand and any sacrifices I made were all worth the fight to save this country from all the evil that was trying to overtake us."

He was also very explicit about how he felt toward those enemies. Some excerpts and entries in his diaries and letters are *not* politically correct. I did not soften any of his descriptions. Our fighting men and women witnessed many horrific actions committed against their fellow soldiers. My father had no sympathy or respect for the enemies he considered to be heathens. I was not aware until I read his journals that he took part in four major battles in the Philippines (the battles of Papus, Luzon, New Guinea, and Southern Philippines). He received a Bronze Star and was on a ship that was involved in one of the greatest enemy air attacks in the Southwest Pacific (SWPC). His duties provided vital radio communication channels required by General Headquarters.

I've sorted through hundreds of old photographs and have tried to correctly match them up with the entries mentioned. Since most of his black-and-white snapshots were not marked, there is a chance some have been mismatched. With this said, all the entries make a statement as to what the ravages of this war were all about.

My parents were married on June 15, 1941. Eight months later my father enlisted and was inducted into the Army on February 24, 1942. He shipped overseas from Angel Island (California) in September of that same year. From this point on my parents would wait five long years before celebrating their wedding anniversary together. My father's letters to my mother were loving and beautiful. And my mother's return letters reflect how much she, too, loved and missed him.

As a child I knew about the diaries. However, I never saw them or knew where they were kept. The only thing my father shared with me about his time in the U.S. Army was a sit-down with a world globe, and he would show me the progression of his travels from Fort Des Moines (Des Moines, Iowa) to Camp Crowder (Missouri) to Tyler (Texas) to Angel Island (California) and from there his routes overseas.

This mission was quite a journey for me. I became aware of the extreme loneliness, the unhealthy living conditions, sometimes food not fit to be consumed, and going months without mail service.

I would love to have one moment with my father, who passed away in 1998, to tell him how much I now understand what he went through, and to say: "THANK YOU!"

Book one

Memories are strange things. We have so many of them. Many good—some bad—We retain them all.—Yet so few come back to us unless we are reminded by a written word, a friend or a landmark—So many fine memories are stored away each day that can be recalled in later years by a simple word or two—

☆

Fort Des Moines, Des Moines, Iowa

Tuesday, February 24, 1942 My entrance into the Army started today after many weeks of trying to decide what would be best to do as to enlist or to wait and be drafted. I decided to enlist as this would give me a chance to get into aviation as a mechanic or some other branch.

As the whole war picture looks now things are very dark for the United Nations. The British have been pushed back across Libya the Japs took Singapore about two weeks ago and are now spreading south toward Australia. The only bright spot is Russia where they are closing in on Smolensk but the general opinion is that Germany's might, will not be known until this summer.

Wednesday, February 25, 1942 I have been spending most of my time sitting around the day room. I took my physical examination today and sailed right through. Marian came out last night and we talked a couple of hours.

Thursday, February 26, 1942 Up at 4:45 A.M. (3:45 regular time) I took my shots around 9 AM this morning. We had two in the right arm besides a blood count and a vaccination, and a blood test in the left arm.

We took our I.Q. test this afternoon. It was quite an ordeal. My arm had become sore and I had an awful headache. It took from about 1 PM till 9:30 PM.

Mother, Dad, Aunt Effie and Marian came out last night. I felt awful punk but it was good to see them. Aunt Effie gave me a deck of playing cards.[1]

---

[1] Mother = Florence Dykstra Hightower, Father = Carl Baines Hightower, Aunt Effie = Effie Hightower Walker – Carl's sister, Marian = Marian Forney Hightower – Joe's wife

Friday, February 27, 1942 Our bunch from Co. D started out on our last leg of becoming soldiers in the United States Army. We were informed before we left that we were to have an interview which would have a big bearing on our chances on getting the branch of service we desire. After taking the test yesterday I was quite down hearted about my chances for getting in as an air core mechanic, but by a big lucky break I happen to know Captain Phil Starbuck who gave me my job at Meredith Publishing Company five years ago. He recognized me and told me he was quite sure I would make the grade. Boy this was certainly good news. I was issued my uniform just before noon and couldn't help but feel that the terrible strain that has hung over my head for the past months would almost shove me down. And to make things worse I was put on guard duty tonight so didn't get to see my folks or Marian.

Saturday, February 28, 1942 Mopped the floor this morning and helped clean up around the barracks. This was all that I did all day. Guard duty wasn't so bad but my dislike to walking didn't make it very desirable. Marian and Mom came out this evening and we sat around the reception center and talked until around 9:30 P.M. and then they left.

Sunday, March 1, 1942 I thought sure I would have to go on K.P. today but was lucky and didn't have to. Elwin Jones (my buddy) and I made a rush trip to town to get a check cashed for him at Herdon's Drug store.[2] I called Marian and she drove the car down and met us at 9th and University, and then she rode on out to the Fort with us. Marian and I were together this evening and Jay came out and drove her home at 9:30 P.M.

Monday, March 2, 1942 We are on shipment today and are to be ready by 7 P.M. tonight. I would like to have Marian and the folks come out today but they would know it would be the last time before I leave. I called them up and told them I was leaving and I couldn't see them. Boy how low I feel when I would like to see Marian and the others just once more, and I could but it would not be best.

They took us into an empty horse barn and backed the trucks up to the door to load us up. We didn't leave the post until dark. Just before we pulled out of the

---

[2] Herdon is a cousin (Effie Walker's son) Effie is my dad's aunt on his dad's side. Jay is my mother's dad – would be my Grandpa Forney.

Fort, a fire call came through and the fire truck tore out. I am sure this was just a decoy because the fire truck just drove up Main Street a ways and stopped. We drove towards town and then turned off on a little side road that took us into the yards. We were loaded in the coaches and assigned a berth. Around midnight a switch engine pulled us over to the main line where a through troop train came and picked us up and we and we left town. I didn't sleep much all the rest of the night

Leaving Fort Des Moines

Tuesday, March 3, 1942 We left Des Moines I believe on the Great Northern Railroad and seemed to travel west all night. When day light came (6AM) we came into some large city that I found out later was St. Jo Missouri. We arrived in Kansas City around 8 A.M. and didn't leave till nearly noon. Not about an hour after we left Kansas City did I know where we were going, which is Camp Crowder about 25 miles from Joplin, Missouri. I have been told, and am beginning to realize that I am not going into aircraft mechanics, but some branch in the Signal Corps. I sure feel about half sick and wish I knew just where I am going to end up.

We didn't do much all day, we were not permitted to leave the coach windows open. Bob Martin, Elwin Jones (my friends I met in Fort Des Moines) and a fellow who made out my enlistment papers in Des Moines played cards a while this afternoon.

The food we have had on the train has been nothing but cold dry sandwiches a few cookies and a little fruit. We arrived at Camp Crowder around 3:30 P.M. and what a place. It is just a new camp, and a large one (64,000 acres) all you can see for miles and miles are new buildings and dirt roads. When I think of what an aircraft mechanic would have been and what I got, words can't describe how I feel. An attempt of any one at humor at this time would certainly fall flat. Of 150 fellows on this troop train I don't think there is a one that doesn't feel terrible. A bunch of large Army trucks took us to our new barracks. I was separated from my friends the first thing, but am in the barracks next door. We had supper around 6 P.M. The first meal ever served in the new mess hall. All we had was canned meat, un-peeled potatoes, bread butter and coffee. I wrote my first letter home this evening and sure did unload my feelings. It was far from being cheerful. Bob, Elvin, and I went down to the P.X. (post- exchange trading center) tonight and have talked things over. They don't feel any better about things than I do, but we have decided to make the best of things and pick radio as a branch to go into. I am convinced that choosing what you want is a lot of bologna in this Army. What a day. Signal Training Battalion Company B. Camp Crowder, Missouri 34th Battalion.

Wednesday, March 4, 1942 Today we arose at six A.M. to find our fine new camp a mire of mud. It rained all night.

I feel a little better about things as I have found that the Signal Corps offers quite a few opportunities and when I find to what I am assigned I am going to work to beat Hell to make the grade. We took two tests today, one in wireless receiving, and the other in electricity. I got a good grade in both tests. I have been assigned to Aircraft Warning Dept. The fellows assigned to this branch will go to school for around two or three weeks and at that time you will know if you can continue in that branch for the remainder of the course of 13 weeks.[3]

Thursday, March 5, 1942 We didn't do anything but lay around all morning. This afternoon we put on our fatigues clothes (work clothes) and went out in the mud and picked up sticks and piled lumber. The food is a little better than it was but it is still bad. Bob, Elwin and I went over to the P.X. (Post Exchange and Store) last night and then came back to the Barracks.

Friday, March 6, 1942 Nothing to do this morning. The lieutenant was up in our barracks for inspection. I guess everything was O.K. because he didn't say anything. Elwin, Bob and I took a walk to a couple of other P.X.es. We walked about five miles. I wasn't so tired tonight even though we picked up rocks and made a sidewalk this afternoon.

Saturday, March 7, 1942 We didn't do so much today. We went over to the infirmary this morning and got another shot in the arm for typhoid fever. We were issued overshoes this afternoon. My arm is starting to get stiff from the shot

---

[3] As I am writing about his days of preparation for "who knows what," I feel as though I have stepped back in time, and I am right there with my dad.

I took. I received my first letter from Marian today and I was sure glad to get it. Marian's boss, Chafee, is starting to raise Hell again and if I was home I think I would sure do something about it.

One thing I am thankful for is that when I get home we will be able to start out and have a home of our own and Marian won't have to work either. I am just about down with the flu and that shot I took has made me sure feel terrible.[4]

Sunday, March 8, 1942

I was sure sick last night. I hardly slept at all. All I have done today is lay around. If I had been put on a detail, I doubt if I could have done it at all. I went up to the P.X. this afternoon for a little while with Bob and Elwin. They wanted me to go to a show with them tonight, but I feel too punk. I wrote Jack, Vince & Alice, and Marian letters today.[5]

I was issued my gas mask today. We start to school tomorrow and from what I hear it will be quite a long walk. A mile and a half four times a day besides an hour of drill from 5:30 till 6:30.

Monday, March 9, 1942

We start to school today. We all lined up at seven AM this morning and started to march. I never did see so many fellows in my life in one bunch. There must have been at least 15 or 20,000. At least there was column of four men wide and at least 1 ½ miles long, and other troops coming in the opposite direction besides. We took up study of gas mask and articles of war this morning. This afternoon we studied the pistol. We also had drill tonight for an hour. Boy it sure has been tough today. I felt a lot better after mail call, as I received a letter from Marian and also a big surprise from Meredith of a check for $64.00 vacation money. I think I will send the check home to Marian. I went up to the P.X. tonight with Bob and Elwin. I still don't feel so hot.

Tuesday, March 10, 1942 To school again this morning. We studied about gases and their uses and affects in chemical warfare. We were shown some motion pictures on first aid. We had mail call this noon. No mail.

---

[4] My mother worked at the F.W. Grand a Dime Store in Des Moines. I remember her talking about how terrible this man was to work for.
[5] Vince was a cousin, Alice his wife. My mother always referred to Vince as too "yellow" to fight in the war. His excuse was that he had to stay home and take care of his elderly parents on the farm.

This afternoon we had more instruction on the pistol and also pistol drill. We will have to put in quite a few hours study and practice on the pistol before we go out on the range. We had drill again tonight and our bunch, (Platoon) seem to be picking up a little. There was mail call again tonight and I received no mail. It sure made me feel lonesome tonight.

Wednesday, March 11, 1942 Up at 5:45 A.M. as usual. Made our beds, ate breakfast and started to school on schedule.

We had more study on gasses and saw a motion picture on conduct alertness and efficiency of a soldier. After noon chow we had another class on the operation of the pistol. Mail call was pretty good to me today. I received six letters and two newspapers. I had to sign up to go and hear a speech about the Far East tonight.

March, 12 – April 13, 1942 My service record in this book has been going away behind as you can see by the number of days I have missed. Everything has been going along in pretty close routine. We get up at 5:45 A.M. stand revelry at 5:00 A.M. We come back in make our beds and clean up a bit. We eat breakfast at 6:00 A.M. and then go to school at 7. We are back for noon meal at 11:30 A.M. We usually have mail call and eat dinner at noon. We go back to school (marching as a platoon) at 1 P.M. We have been having pistol instruction in the afternoon. We start back to the barracks at 3:30 P.M. and clean up a little and are ready for drill at 4 P.M. We usually drill until about 5:15 P.M. We then have afternoon mail call and then have chow at 6 P.M. Our time is usually our own from now till 11 P.M. We are usually busy washing out clothes, taking showers, shaving and writing letters. I have been writing.

Tuesday, April 14, 1942 I finally lost out on my diary all together. For the last three and a half weeks I have been so busy I hardly had time even to write home. A couple of weeks ago I was taken out of Aircraft Warning and assigned to radio operator. Here at Camp Crowder we have not been permitted any more than an eleven-o clock pass. I wanted to meet Marian in Kansas City but I was unable to receive enough time off to make the trip.

Neosho is the closest town to this camp. It is quite a small place in comparison with the size of Camp Crowder, Neosho being about 5000 population. It is hardly possible to see any civilians at all with the sidewalks packed with soldiers.

(Note) From here on this book continues in my small black diary as I hope to keep this to fill in a final condensed record. It is my last day in Camp Crowder, after spending one month and three weeks here.

Wednesday April 15, 1942 Today the bottom sure dropped out from under things. I am on the shipping list, and am to leave on Friday. As Marian was planning on being here at Camp Crowder on Friday, I won't get to see her if she comes then. I called Marian by phone and she is starting on her way now so we can be together Thursday. I was scheduled for K.P. tomorrow and the Co. Commander is gone and the first Sgt. is in Joplin so after weighing the facts of my chances of getting off tomorrow I got a[n] 11 P.M. pass and went to Neosho, Missouri intending on going A.W.O.L. This is the only way I can see my way to Marian.

Thursday April 16, 1942, I stayed in a hotel last night. At 11P.M. last night I was charged with missing bed check at 6 A.M. this morning I was A.W.O.L. I sure don't feel very good about the whole thing, but there was no other way. I hung around the streets of Neosho all morning waiting for Marian, and wondering if the M.P.s would pick me up. Marian finally arrived at 1 P.M. She had called camp and they told her I was A.W.O.L. She was quite broken up about it, but it

16

was sure swell to be together again. Scott came over to Neosho about 6 P.M. and told me I had better call camp, so I did. Got back to camp at 11 P.M.

Friday, April 17, 1942 This morning at 7 A.M. I was on the carpet before the Co. Commander. He sure ripped it into me, and said my reasons for A.W.O.L. were none at all. He was a pretty understanding sort of fellow, so he told me to have Marian come out to Camp until I was to leave. Marian and I were together until 12:30 P.M. when I had to get into the truck to travel. I will never be able to explain how low I felt waving goodbye to Marian from the back of the truck, not knowing where I am headed or when we will meet again. Outside of camp on a siding we entered our coaches. A streamliner hooked on to us and we headed south into Arkansas. We arrived into Texarkana around 9 P.M.

Saturday, April 18, 1942 We stayed in Texarkana all night on a siding and pulled out headed south at 8:30 A.M. We can't imagine where we are to be sent. Our ration money of $2.00 shouldn't carry us very far. Well we finally arrived in Tyler Texas at 2:00 P.M. and have been informed we are to attend radio school for 13 weeks. We eat in a cafeteria and stay at the Blue Bonnet Auto Court about 1 ½ miles from town. Boy this set up is too good to be true. Note: left Neosho at 12:30 PM on April 17 stayed overnight in Texarkana left at 8:30 AM arrived Tyler, TX. at 2:00 PM on April 18 by train.

Sunday, April 19, 1942 "What do you know." I got a weekend pass for this weekend. The people here in Tyler sure treat us royally. This town is 30,000 and there are but 300 soldiers here, this is truly a soldier's paradise. The "Military Miss" Organization is giving a reception for us tomorrow night. There are four of us in each cabin. Ours is cabin 3 containing Martin Herring of Cleveland Ohio, Ray Fleshman of Toledo Ohio, Eddie Johnston of St. Cloud Florida and myself. I messed around town today and went to a show.

Monday April 20, 1942 We started to radio school today. It is the same as we had at Crowder. I am starting over from scratch and I think the review will do me good. The tests here are a lot stricter th[a]n at Crowder. We had the reception at the Blackstone Hotel tonight and it was a formal dance. The music was furnished by a nickelodeon. Tyler is more like living, than Crowder.

Tuesday April 21, 1942 I am beginning to realize how little I learned at Camp Crowder, as far as this code is concerned. Our code school is in the Tyler Commercial College. The class is one large room and will accommodate around three hundred soldiers.

They say a hundred more soldiers will arrive here in a couple of weeks. That will make three companies of a hundred each or company's A, B, and C.

I haven't received any mail from home as yet. I kinda wonder what the folks and Marian will think about my new location.

Wednesday, April 22, 1942 School as usual I am now in class three Z, boy am I ever getting off to a slow start. Tyler is built like any county seat town with the courthouse in the middle of the square and the stores and other business establishments surrounding it as the business district. Almost all the buildings are quite small except for a couple, the tallest of which is seventeen stories. As the surrounding country is comparative level, this building is visible for miles.

Thursday, April 23, 1942 I am now in class four Z and climbing slow but sure. This code sure gets on your nerves, at the end of the day it seems every "dit" and "daah" hits you in the head like a hammer.

Friday, April 24, 1942 Code School as usual. I have been in the army two months today. Tyler is truly a wonderful place. The people here treat you as a human rather than a little machine as they did at Crowder. This code is sure tough for me to get. I am no farther now than I was at the same length of time at Crowder. Passing a test is sure different here.

Saturday, April 25, 1942 Went to school this A.M. we get from noon till Sunday night to ourselves. I received a weekend pass after finishing the first week in code school. I find I don't know much about it and what I learned in "Crowder" hasn't helped much. Here it takes 100 consecutive correct characters to pass a test and in Crowder but 50. They opened the recreation center tonight and had a party and a dance. The newspaper took pictures of which will appear in tomorrow's paper.

Sunday, April 26, 1942 Slept late this morning and went to town around noon to get some dinner. The people here pick you up in their cars without you asking. I went to a show this afternoon and down to the recreation center this evening. I am writing to Jack at Camp Barkly to see if it is possible for us to meet some weekend.[6]

Monday, April 27, 1942 Code school today. It seems to me of all the assignments handed out in this Army, they gave me one that couldn't be any harder to get. Ability to memorize is important and that is one place where I definitely don't shine. I am trying my best, but a lot of fellows pass me just the same. You can hand in two tests per day. If you make a mistake you are out of luck for that day.

Tuesday, April 28, 1942 The fact that I was in class seven "W" at Crowder doesn't seem to help me much as I supposed it would. In fact, I think I would get along better if I had never had code at all. My knowledge of the code is in my mind in an altogether different order than I am taking them in here.

Wednesday, April 29, 1942 The code that we take here is sure on a stricter basis than at Camp Crowder. There out of fifty characters you could make a mistake or two and still pass into the next class. Here if a letter is not printed absolutely clear no go and you can only hand in two tests per day.[7]

---

[6] Jack Hightower is Joe Hightower's brother.
[7] My dad will realize how important this accuracy will be when he gets to the battlefield.

Thursday, April 30, 1942 School is a routine occurrence now. This code school is run by civilian instructors but directed by the army. Our Commanding officer is Major Caldwell. All of we soldiers like him fine. He sure has the ability to handle men. After school I spend my time in numerous ways. Such as going down to the recreation center, eating ice cream, writing letters or once in a while going to the show.

Friday, May 1, 1942 School as usual. I wrote and suggested to Marian that if possible, plan to come down to Tyler to see me. All the folks could go to see Jack in the same trip. One thing about the army and that is to make any plans work, you must carry them out on a moment's notice.

Saturday, May 2, 1942 Code school this morning as usual. Went to the show this afternoon and out to a dance tonight. I thought I knew how to dance back in Des Moines but I find that style don't work so good here.

Sunday, May 3, 1942 Slept late this morning and went to town around noon for dinner. If we sign off for meals of three in a row we receive a dollar refund. I usually sign off for meals over the week end as with all the hospitality there is here, you stand a good chance of being invited out for dinner. Went to the show this afternoon.

Monday, May 4, 1942 Back to school this code usually goes easier the first part of the week. Boy this code and I sure don't match. I sure earn all I get. I am now out of the "Z" class and starting to work on speed of seven words per min.

Tuesday, May 5, 1942 School as usual. I receive letters from Marian every day. Lately they haven't contained much news that benefits me and my unaccustomed military life. It seems she and the folks don't get along so good. The car seems to be the reason. I have been afraid all along that this might occur.

Wednesday, May 6, 1942 School as usual today. Wrote letters and went to bed early.

Thursday, May 7, 1942 The same routine today. Was down at the recreation center a while tonight. Boy I sure have been hung up in this 7.W. speed for a while.[8]

---

[8] 7 words per min.

Friday, May 8, 1942 I finally passed into code speed 8.W. For some reason I sailed right through this class and now I am in 10.W. I have a feeling I will be stuck here for a while.

Saturday, May 9, 1942 School this morning. I went to a show this afternoon and then decided going to the dance tonight.

Sunday, May 10, 1942 Went to town this noon and had dinner at the Black Stone hotel. This is about the best place in town to eat. Hung around the recreation center this afternoon. Went to bed early tonight.

Monday, May 11, 1942 Another weekend and code school again today. The Sgt. asked me to be right guide for Co. B. There are one hundred soldiers in our Co. Right guide takes a position at the front and to the right of the company. He is required to set the cadence (step or stride) for the company. The Co. following his steps.

Tuesday, May 12, 1942 Code school as usual I am still stuck in 10.W. I guess maybe I try too hard as it seems the fellows who don't give a damn, get along the best. I was asked today to enter the Signal Corps Glee Club. It is called the Signal Choirsters. Tonight we practiced up at the Black Stone Hotel tonight for the broadcast that is to be given tomorrow night.

Wednesday, May 13, 1942 School as usual. Boy I am sure getting tired of this "dit" and "daw" business. Went to the Black Stone tonight and our bunch put on a radio program. It was pretty good. There is sure a lot of talent in our Signal bunch.

Thursday, May 14, 1942 The American Legion gave us a barbeque. We had all we could eat. We talked with some of the Veterans of the last war, trying in a round-about way, what to expect. Of course we all pretty well know. The picnic was over rather early so I went to town to the show.

Friday, May 15, 1942 School as usual today. This code is sure hard for me to get. I still have a lot of time to improve though. Today Marian and I have been married eleven months. It looks like we will spend our first anniversary apart. I have wrote to Marian and the folks to come and see Jack and I as an opportunity, as this may blow up any time.

Saturday, May 16, 1942 I went to Fort Worth this afternoon, where I met Jack. It was sure good to see him. We made arrangements for a room and then sat down and had a long talk. We went to a show this evening and then stopped in a picture studio and had our picture taken for the folks. It was rather expensive, but I know they will sure appreciate getting it.

Sunday, May 17, 1942 Jack and I slept rather late this morning. We went down to a restaurant and had a good meal. We then went to the show. By the time it was over it was nearly time for me to catch the bus so we went to the depot. It always gives me a sick feeling to say "good bye".

Monday, May 18, 1942 School as usual. I received many letters from home. It seems they may decide it is more worthwhile to argue about coming down than to actually come.[9]

Tuesday, May 19, 1942 Code school is still a hard pull. I am now in ten words per min. My main trouble is being under such a strain when I try to pass a test. I can copy this stuff fairly well but to be able to pass a test. No.

Wednesday, May 20, 1942 Well I received many letters from home, but they don't shed much light on whether they intend to come and see Jack and I. Sometimes yes. Sometimes no. ??? Today yes. We have been drilling for the victory parade, of which Dorothy Lamore is to take part. I have been acting as right guide for Co. B. School as usual. I guess the folks are not coming. Marian is now sore at me about a letter I should have written to her rather than Sally.[10]

Friday, May 22, 1942 "Ah" good news today. They are coming. ???

Saturday, May 23, 1942 Well perhaps the folks may come down to see us. Perhaps. As of today it stands yes. I am sure catching it from Marian. I sure missed the boat, when I wrote that letter. I didn't think it was that important.

Sunday, May 24, 1942 As for code is concerned, last week was nil. As long as you can expect the war to last I am sick of this whole business, right now. Civilians say they know there is a war going on but I wonder.

---

[9] It seemed as though there was always someone in the family at odds with someone else. I never understood, even as a child and later on as an adult, why the families had such a difficult time getting along. The diaries reflect some concerns my father had when he would receive letters from my mom reflecting her frustrations with my father's family.

[10] Sally was Joe's sister – she and Marian never did get along. There seemed to be a "power struggle" between the two of them. There was always discord / jealousy between them up until the day she (Sally) passed away.

Wednesday, May 27, 1942 We had the victory parade today. I was right guide for Co. B. To march was impossible as the Military Cadence is far different than a bunch of high school marchers. They furnished the music. Dorothy Lamour was here and in the parade. I was appointed as one of a group as a military guard for Dorothy Lamour. I rode down in the elevator with her.[11] Have been looking forward to the arrival of the folks. I received a telegram from Marian today.

Thursday, May 28, 1942 The folks, Sally, Dick, Buddy, and my wife Marian came to Tyler today. I met them out at the Blue Bonnet at 6 P.M. You will never know what a feeling it is to see all the folks from home. It is at such a time as this, I feel giving up our home and having to stay away for so long. I got some cabins up the hill from the Blue Bonnet for the folks. Marian and I had a cabin to ourselves. It was so wonderful to be together again. I was not permitted to stay with Marian, but I did so any way. To heck with them.

---

[11] Dorothy Lamour was an American actress and singer, for her contribution to the radio and motion picture industry, Lamour has two stars on The Hollywood Walk of Fame.

Friday, May 29, 1942 The folks all went to Fort Worth today to meet Jack. Marian stayed in Tyler with me. I went out to the cabins after school as soon as I could. It is so wonderful to be together again. It doesn't seem quite fair we should have to sacrifice so much but I guess there is a job and we have to do it.

Saturday, May 30, 1942 As we only have a half day of school on Saturdays, I was able to meet Marian at noon. We just walked around and took a few pictures. Being together made the day just perfect. We went to a show this afternoon and I showed Marian the school. She got a little jealous when a girl called me by my first name. I sure love her for the way she acts.

Sunday, May 31, 1942 Marian and I didn't get up till late this morning. We ate dinner at the Blackstone hotel. Everything seems so perfect now. We didn't get out to the cabins until a little late. I was surprised to find the folks had gotten back from Fort Worth. As I am writing this in quite a while after the above date, I will make this very brief as to what occurred when Marian and I got back from town. It makes me sick to think of it now. We had a bad dispute over the car. Whose fault it might have been was not important. I have felt bad about it ever since. I felt so sorry for mom. If Marian and I are indebted to the folks, which I know we are, our hands are tied now as we will have to wait till after the war.

Florence Hightower / Cousin Rick / Mom & Dad

Monday, June 1, 1942 Stayed with Marian last night. Up early to catch the bus to school. Met the folks after school. Mom had a good home cooked meal out at the cabin. The car deal kinda has blown over, but there is a feeling there, that I am so afraid will always stay. The folks are talking of leaving tomorrow. Dick thinks the car should have some work done on it, so this way keeps them here a little longer. The fellows are kinda raising heck about me missing bed check. Sometimes I can't hardly keep my hands off of d. j.[12]

Tuesday, June 2, 1942 I stayed at the cabin last night and arose early and went up to where Marian is. She drove me to school. I came directly to the cabin tonight where I sat down to one of moms delicious meals. As the car isn't fixed yet, the folks can't leave until the repairs are made.

Wednesday, June 3, 1942 I stayed with Marian last night and she drove me to school early this morning. The folks had not left when I got home this evening. I had supper with them. We talked a little while and then they packed the car to depart. I went to bed about 6pm as no one can explain how I feel after saying good bye and seeing them drive away. I wonder when and if I will see any of them again.

Thursday, June 4, 1942 Went to school as usual. Since saying good bye and seeing Marian and all the folks leave Tyler yesterday I can't be interested in anything. I feel like going off in a corner by myself. It is a horrible feeling. To say goodbye to the ones you love, and feeling per-

---

[12] I'm not sure but I think my dad is referring to Dick Johnson, Sally's husband. The family didn't think he was treating his wife and family with the respect they deserved.

haps it will be forever. I know I must not let it get me down, but it will take a little time to get any interest in the code again.

Friday, June 5, 1942 Code school today. I am seemingly at a stand- still. I received a telegram from Marian that they arrived home O.K. It is a relief to know they made it O.K. Went up to the Recreation Hall and wrote some letters. The weather is beginning to get quite hot now. Major Caldwell has canceled our drill period from three thirty till four thirty because of the heat.

Saturday, June 6, 1942 Didn't do much this afternoon. Laid around most of the time. Decided to walk out to the dance this evening. I met David and Nell Hughes and also most of the fellows in the band. I left rather early as I haven't felt like staying in one spot very long since I last saw Marian and the folks.

Sunday, June 7, 1942 A friend and myself went to town and ate dinner at the Blackstone hotel. It has been just a week since Marian and I ate here. We went down to the recreation hall and wrote some letters, after which we went to the show. The war doesn't look so good for us at the present time. The Germans are getting the upper hand in Russia and the Japs are still showing an awful lot of strength.

Monday, June 8, 1942 Major Caldwell today passed application blanks around for officers candidate school. I took some blanks but I am undecided if I will fill them out.

Tuesday, June 9, 1942 One minute I think I will apply for O.C.S. and then I think not. I am afraid if a fellow were an officer he would have to stay in the army longer, and I sure don't want to have a career out of this.

Friday, June 12, 1942 This should be June 12 put it on wrong page. Well today is my birthday as far as I know I am the only one in this town that knows. Everything went as usual. Went to school today and up to the recreation center tonight. For my birthday, the folks sent me some handkerchiefs, also one from Aunt Effie. I have a swell camera Marian gave me.[13]

---

[13] Memo entered by Joe — wrote today's record on July 12 by mistake. found in July.

Monday, June 15, 1942 Today is our wedding anniversary of one year. What a heck of a way to spend it. I sent Marian some roses. Roses are very plentiful here and also cheap – two dozen for twenty-five cents. As they cost around three dollars per dozen at home. I bet Marian will be surprised to get ten dozen.

Wednesday, June 24, 1942 Went to school today. We had minstrel practice tonight. We were not on the usual radio program tonight due to minstrel practice. I have been in the army five months today.

Thursday, June 25, 1942 Had the minstrel dress rehearsal tonight. The first time we went through it, "boy" were we ever "lousy" We did better the second time through, but it still needs a lot of improvement or it will sure flop tomorrow night.

Friday, June 26, 1942 We had the Signal Corps Minstrel show tonight. It really went over big and everyone sure turned out to see it. We took in over $1,000.00 to be spent for a farewell dance and banquets for Companies A, B, C. Eddy Johnston and I went down to Marty's girl's house for a surprise on Marty as it is his birthday.

Saturday, June 27, 1942 Had school this morning but everyone is pretty tired and not much code is being copied. Went to a show this afternoon and wrote some letters this evening, and went to bed rather early.

Sunday, June 28, 1942 My friends Mr. & Mrs. Hughes picked me up this morning and took me to church with them. My friend and I went to a show this afternoon. He had to pick up his wife so I went down and spent some time at the recreation hall writing letters.

Monday, June 29, 1942 Starting another week and it won't be long until we will be leaving Tyler. Most fellows are not putting forth the effort in code now as when they first started, as for me I have had to keep plugging all the way to even come up to standard.

Tuesday, June 30, 1942 The typing class here has helped me in typing quite a bit. Since coming to Tyler this is the first I have used a typewriter in ten years. Had Signal Choristers practice tonight for the broadcast tomorrow night.

Wednesday, July 1, 1942 School as usual. I went back to our cabin early after supper as we put on the broadcast at seven p.m. Since we first arrived in Tyler we have given a broadcast each Wednesday since. We really have some professional performers. Our announcer use to announce for N.B.C. and many others have had radio experience.

Thursday, July 2, 1942 The end of the week is starting to roll around and as usual my code practice is becoming more annoying and difficult. We are all beginning to wonder where we might be sent from Tyler.

Friday, July 3, 1942 Had the Signal Corps graduation dance tonight it was sure a gala affair. Everyone was pretty well canned up. Another soldier and I tried to sober up another fellow. He was just too far gone. We finally took him to the Alamo Courts - (his home.)

Saturday, July 4, 1942 We get all day today off. I was at the Depot to see a bunch of Co. A. friends leave at 1 P.M. and the rest at 5 P.M. It was sure a sad sight to see them go. They had all made many friends in Tyler, especially girl friends. Some had gotten married. Being married is sure lucky for me as my leaving Tyler won't make any difference. I said my good-byes in Des Moines.

Sunday, July 5, 1942 A bunch of new soldiers came in as Co. A. left. They walk around town about the same as we did when we first arrived. Tyler is sure far removed from what a soldier could ordinarily expect. I went to the show this afternoon, and then I wrote some letters at the recreation center.

Monday, July 6, 1942 School as usual this morning. Our radio school is quite large now with this new bunch now as Co. D. They have now equipped the school with a section consisting of typewriters and speed keys or "bugs" for fix station training. I will never make the grade enough to be eligible for that section. It seems I have had to work twice as hard as anyone else to get this stuff.

Tuesday, July 7, 1942 The same routine today. In one day's work we usually copy code in the morning, have an hour of typing in the afternoon and the rest of the time sending. We get a ten min. rest every hour. During this rest we drink cokes and talk things over.

Wednesday, July 8, 1942 School and the same old grind. If it wasn't for getting Saturday and Sunday off I don't see how I could stand this code at all. Towards the end of each week I usually get a headache and I don't see how I can listen to another "dit" "daah".

Thursday, July, 9 1942 It is usually a mad scramble at noon to get in the first line of the chow line. As I am on the side of the room next to the exit, I usually get to the café in good time. Whenever it rains we usually stay in ranks long enough to run to the café in a mob. The fastest runner getting there first.

Friday, July 10, 1942 School as usual today. It is sure hard to keep interested in this code. If I had desired learning it I would have had it a long time ago. I turned one page too many this time so look for Saturday on the other side of the previous "page.[14]

Saturday, July 11, 1942 Another soldier and I hitchhiked to Dallas today. We had very good luck. Getting a ride in a new Buick. I left my friend in Dallas and caught a bus over to Fort Worth. I met Jack there about 5 P.M. at the U.S.O. club. It sure is swell that I am able to see brother Jack so far from home. It sure is a coincidence that we can get together so far from home. We ate supper and talked and talked. We went to a U.S.O. dance up in the top of the Texas Hotel. We then went to the midnight show. We slept pretty late Sunday morning and then got up and went to a show. I left to come back to Tyler at 3 P.M. I will never forget how I felt when I left Jack. This is the last time till fate knows when I will get to see Jack as both of us are to be moved.

Sunday, July 12, 1942 This day Jack and I spent together, as stated on the previous (*) page of July 9. The bus arrived at the Blue Bonnet Courts at 9:30 p.m.

Monday, July 13, 1942 Well it won't be long until we leave Tyler. As yet no one knows where we are to be sent. The past couple of weeks have certainly gone by in a hurry. Even though it has been swell here in Tyler, I will be glad to leave, and taking up my duties.

Tuesday, July 14, 1942 School as usual today. I am trying to make one last supreme effort to accomplish as much as I can in this code. They gave us a special

---

[14] The diary entries were mixed up by date – with entries on the wrong day for the events taking place.

test today. Only four out of the twenty of us who took it passed. I think I was one of the ones who made it.

Wednesday, July 15, 1942 School as usual. We are all wondering where we are to be sent. I guess for military reasons, they don't want us to know. I passed today. I sure had a heck of a time doing it. They changed tapes on the machines, and I had to get use to it into class eighteen all over. Marian and I have been married a year and one month.

Thursday, July 16, 1942 Went to school as usual today. I think if I had a couple of more weeks I could copy twenty. I have worked hard to try and get as much as I could in the past couple of weeks. As yet Major Caldwell hasn't told us where we are to be sent. You can guess almost anywhere in the world and you may be right.

Friday, July 17, 1942 This is our last day in Tyler. We are not sure where we are going. I am almost afraid to ask as I guess I am afraid of the truth. I hate to think what this is going to do to Marian and the rest of the folks. I am to be sent to the 32nd Division. Where that is we don't know but it looks very much like Australia. I feel weak and kinda sick about the whole thing. How I am going to break the news to Marian I don't know, but she sure must know. I wrote Marian and the folks tonight. We had a farewell banquet. It was quite nice with Major Caldwell and others giving speeches. There was also a floor show.

Saturday, July 18, 1942 I hung around town getting a few things and saying good bye to my friends. This has sure been a perfect 3 months. All but one thing and that was Marian was not with me. We left Tyler about 5:30 by bus to go to Mineola, TX. to catch the train. The train pulled in at 6:30 p.m. and we headed West. We were sure disappointed that we did not get a Pullman, and therefore we had to sit up all night. I couldn't sleep at all and boy am I ever tired.

Sunday, July 19, 1942 We passed through Abilene TX. about 5 A.M. this morning. I saw a soldier on the platform and gave him a note to Jack. As Camp Berkley is near here. I don't think much of anything could have happened to dishearten me as much as what my future will hold for me as I learned yesterday and I am on my road today. Marian should get my letter tomorrow. Oh how I hate to think she will take it. All of we soldiers feel the same way though. We are sure a tired bunch of soldiers today. We have been traveling through the dessert country all day. It is not much as far as scenery is concerned. We arrived in El Paso where we had a 2 ½ hour layover. To our surprise we met 13 other fellows of our Co. who left Tyler ahead of us. We will travel on to Los Angeles together. We will go different directions there. We left El Paso around 7:45 P.M. and we got a Pullman. Boy, are we glad of that.

Monday, July 20, 1942 The country on to the coast is more boring than ever and we are now in the mountains. We travel in between the ranges all the time. I have been sending post cards home every day. We arrived in Los Angeles at 6:30 pm, left for S.F. at 7:00 pm. This is sure a beautiful station. We have to travel with the shades down after sundown.

Tuesday, July 21, 1942 Arrived in San Francisco at 10 pm. Crossed the bay by ferry and then to Angel Island by naval boat. Issued full field equipment today. Awful tired tonight.[15]

Last Barracks Angel Island

Wednesday, July 22, 1942 Not much to do today. I repacked my barracks bags and helped clean up the barracks and had to stay and keep fellows from

---

[15] The soldiers boarded the train in Texas at 6:30 the 18th after being bused from Tyler – arrived in S.F. 3 days later with very little sleep on a train that had no comfortable accommodations.

taking showers for a couple of hours. Ted and I took a walk up around the island. We can see the Golden Gate Bridge, Oakland and Frisco very well from here. It sure is a beautiful night. Lots of fog here though. Wrote three letters home and sent a package. I wonder how Marian and the rest of the folks have taken all this. I try not to think about how I feel.

Thursday, July 23, 1942 Still no news as to where or when we depart to. I was on detail today. This is the first time in three months I have had on my fatigue uniform. I helped sort blonces and pants that have been taken from soldiers who have gone over seas. They say they always take your blonces and a pair of your o.d. pants when they inspect your equipment. I have been told before coming here we probably would go to Australia. We have been inspected and all they took was my winter cap? I could tell Marian this but I suppose it is best to wait. I suppose she is sick over this. I know I am. No mail today yet.[16]

Friday, July 24, 1942 Today has been pretty tough. I was one of a bunch of 10 who got dysentery (diarrhea) at the mess hall. I was pretty sick last night and have felt pretty punk all day. I received my first word from Marian today. A telegram and a letter. Her letter was more cheerful than I thought it would be. It makes me feel a lot better to Know she can keep her chin up. I know It must have been quite a shock to her of my future prospects. I am scheduled to go on K.P. in the morning.

Saturday, July 25, 1942 Well I have been running a day behind. I thought today was Friday. I caught my first K.P. duty here today. I had a pretty soft job. I nearly got caught up on an extra days K.P. when I went over to the barracks, and was late getting back. I received two letters today from Marian, 2 from her folks and a card from her aunt whom I met last summer, who lives here in San Francisco. I missed by two fellows of getting a pass for tomorrow. I was kinda disappointed after working 16 ½ hours today on K.P. Marian's folks sent me $6.00. This will sure come in handy.

Sunday, July 26, 1942 I was lucky and got a pass today. Roy, Ted and I went into San Francisco this morning. The boat stopped at Alcatraz prison to let off some supplies. The trip takes about 20 minutes. I called Marian's cousin, Mrs. Dorothy Allen. Mr. Allen picked us up and took us to their house for a waffle supper. I

---

[16] Blonces are an item to make their pants fit better into their boots and "O.D" is olive drab.

Ted and Joe

sure had a good time. Mr. Allen brought us back to the dock where we caught the boat back to camp. I hope I get another pass, so we can go to China Town.[17]

Monday, July 27, 1942 I was quite busy today. This morning we had to take a hike around the island of 7 ½ miles with our full pack. We got back and had about an hours' rest before dinner. This afternoon we put on our fatigues and had a job until supper time of moving some peer piling and placing it in washout. I have spent the evening writing letters to Marian, the folks, Marian's folks, and David Hughes of Tyler.

Thursday, July 28, 1942 The usual 7 ½ mile march today with our packs. When we got back the Sarge was burned up about the barracks being dirty so we had to close order drill for an extra hour. We went to hear a couple of lectures on chemical warfare and sexual diseases. This afternoon another bunch is being shipped out today but nothing about us 30 radio operators. We did not sign the Jay role as many others did. I wonder if I could get a furlough. I know though if I would, when I would leave Marian and the rest of the folks it will be for a long long time.

Wednesday, July 29, 1942 Fatigue duty all day. We went out and worked on the washout the same place as the other day. This afternoon two other soldiers and myself went out to help with some wiring. We just laid around and watched the ships in the bay and airplanes fly over. We still haven't signed the Jay role. I see we are scheduled for K.P. tomorrow. Received a letter from Marian and all the folks today.

---

[17] Dorothy Allyn met Art Allyn while she was working in the dime store in Des Moines. He was very wealthy and eventually ended up living in Chicago – owning the Chicago White Sox baseball team– had diamond mines in Africa—and many business dealings in Chicago. Dorothy called herself a real-life Cinderella — they had a good marriage. She passed away in the 1960s from MS.

18 Eddie Stanky and Arthur Allyn of the Chicago White Sox circa December, 1965. (Photo by Sporting News via Getty Images via Getty Images)

Thursday, July 30, 1942 About all there is for today is a great big K.P. from 4A.M. till 6:30 pm. 800 extra soldiers from the Philippines and Hawaiian Islands came in so we had two extra dinners and an extra supper. I wasn't able to get away to get my letters from Marian today so no mail today. A painter spilled about a quart of paint in the meat stew tonight so they called it called it Turkish beef for supper. I didn't eat any. I turned out a washing tonight. Boy am I tired. I bought Marian a handkerchief today.

Friday, July 31, 1942 Not so much to do today. We went over to the drill hall and signed some forms in regard to the "dependents" allotment plan of which I give Marian $22 and the government puts $28 with it. She will get the total of $250 in November and $50 per month thereafter. My mistake we signed that yesterday. Today we were paid $20 and then found our pass for tonight as canceled as we are on K.P. again tomorrow. Dam it. Twice in three days that takes the cake. They can't ship me out of here quick enough.[18]

---

[18] Eddie Stanky and Arthur Allyn of the Chicago White Sox circa December, 1965. (Photo by Sporting News via Getty Images via Getty Images).

Saturday, August 1, 1942 Up at 3:45 AM and on K.P. Boy I am sure fed up with this place. All we are is a bunch of flunkies for the non com. There are about 20 of them to each prvt. (private) We were told we could have a Sunday pass, but now that has been canceled. As no one gets to leave the island when information is out about troop movements. I wish I were leaving this hell hole of creation tomorrow. I suppose we will get more K.P. Monday or Tuesday. I could fill the rest of this book with cuss words.[19]

Sunday, August 2, 1942 Well not much to do today as our passes were taken away. This thing about troop movement was a lot of hooey because we saw a bunch of non coms. get on the boat. Evidently with our passes. I am sure dam disgusted with everything. Today I wrote a few letters, but didn't receive any as we get no mail on Sunday. Walked up the road around the point this afternoon. Talked with a couple of fellows from the Hawaiian Islands, how some flew some P38 and a light bomber in a mock dog fight.

Monday, August 3, 1942 We were on fatigue duty all day today. I helped run a tar spraying machine this morning and help paint this afternoon. Today was fairly easy. I sure received a lot of mail today. Letters from Marian, Sally & Dick, Vince and Cliffee. I wrote letters this evening to Marian, Cliffie and Sally & Dick. I see we are on K.P. tomorrow. "Dam". The Sarg gave us special instructions in case of an air raid or black out here.[20]

Tuesday, August 4, 1942 Well we were up at 4 A.M. and marched over to the mess hall for K.P. I got a pretty lucky assignment working in the butcher shop. We finished our job early tonight and came over to the barracks. I heard they took role call after we had gone. I hope I am not stuck for an extra days' K.P. I put out a big washing tonight. I didn't hear from Marian today. I got a letter from Aunt Effie.

Wednesday, August 5, 1942 On fatigue duty all day. Worked on the road gang this morning. I kept away from the tar spraying. This afternoon I worked in the quarter master salvage supply. A Sarge came around at 3:00 P.M. and asked me if I was going on a pass. I told him yes. I wasn't, but I did get to go back to the barracks early.

---

[19] Non Com, non commissioned officers.
[20] Cliffie (Clifford Ott) was the preacher who married my mom and dad.

Thursday, August 6, 1942 More fatigue duty today. I worked on a truck this A.M. and helped unload supplies from the boat. This afternoon I worked in a paint shop. Got off at 3:30 to go on a pass. Went to Frisco. Ted, another fellow and I messed around together. About all we did that was of interest to me was we walked down through China Town, San Francisco is sure hard to get around in. I didn't get to write to Marian tonight.

Friday, August 7, 1942 I had a big surprise this morning at 4 A.M. Someone shook my bed and said K.P. today. I wasn't expecting it today. Boy what a day. I hit the hay early tonight after writing Marian a letter. I sent the pictures of our trip from Tyler to Frisco, to Denver where Marian should be by the time the letter reaches there.[21]

Saturday, August 8, 1942 We had to fall out for personal inspection as well as gas mask inspection this morning. Besides that we haven't done anything today. A report came through the barracks that they were looking for fellows for fatigue duty so a bunch of us picked up and came down to the beach. I finished writing a letter to Marian and this page.

Sunday, August 9, 1942 No pass today so I was stuck on this island all day. I spent most of my time writing letters this morning. This afternoon I walked down along the beach, read a few magazines and then went to the show tonight. We don't have any duties here on Sunday except maybe K.P.

Monday, August 10, 1942 We were on fatigue duty today. I had it pretty soft this morning, spending about 15 minutes sweeping out a truck court and then sat around the rest of the morning. This afternoon I had to help shovel dirt on a truck. Not so soft. Hazelwood went on pass last night and never came back. AWOL.

Tuesday, August 11, 1942 Our company (Co. E.) made K.P. again today. Up at 4 A.M. There isn't so many here to feed so K.P. isn't as bad as it was. It still is not good. I didn't get any mail from Marian today or anyone. Wrote Marian two letters tonight. Some of we fellows (30 from Tyler) were wondering when we would get our back money from Tyler. I have around $6.00 coming. No sign of our moving yet. Have been here 3 weeks today.

---

[21] I am not sure why my mother was headed to Denver – perhaps the answer is in future entries.

Wednesday, August 12, 1942 Most of our company was on fatigue duty today. I was lucky and missed this but we had to march around the island with our packs on, which wasn't so soft after all. This afternoon we went over to the drill hall to listen to a lecture on gas. We waited a couple of hours, finally a doctor came and talked to us about ten minutes and that was all. I received a letter today from Marian.

Thursday, August 13, 1942 Well my trying to take a chance on a pass for Saturday, ended up big, I am quite sure of being on K.P. that day. Maybe I can get a pass for Sunday. I did want to get my watch fixed though. We marched around the island again today. This afternoon we had some close order drill and gas mask drill and instruction. I received letters from Marian, the folks, a card from Virginia F. also a nice card from Marian.

Friday, August 14, 1942 Fatigue duty today. Worked up to the Colonel's house this morning putting a fence around his tomatoes to keep the deer out that run around on this island. This would be a hunter's paradise with the amount of game that is here. Quail Ducks, fish etc. This afternoon I had to shovel dirt into a truck. I was sure surprised when I got back to the barracks to find we are not on K.P. tomorrow after all. Maybe I will get that pass after all, I hope.

Saturday, August 15, 1942 Not much to do today. We fell out for personal inspection this morning. I loafed around this afternoon and was burned up when I found out I couldn't get a pass because of being on K.P. tomorrow. This place gets worse and worse. I took a walk down along the beach this afternoon and wrote letters this evening. Today Marian and I have been married 14 months. Marian called me by long distance this morning. It was sure good to hear her voice over the phone and it made me kind of homesick.

Sunday, August 16, 1942 This is the first time since I have been in the Army that I have caught Sunday K.P. I was lucky and got assigned to the dishwasher. This afternoon I got stuck though and had to help open eight cases of eggs. I went to the show tonight the name of it was "Moontide," There is not mail today. I wrote Marian after the show. I think I will get a pass tomorrow. I have sure gained a lot of weight here. From 148 to 163 the most I have ever weighed.

Monday, August 17, 1942 We went on another one of those hikes around the island this morning. This afternoon we listened to a chemical warfare lecture, which I had a hard time keeping awake in. I went on pass tonight with nothing much in mind. When I got to Frisco I called Dorothy & Art Allen. Art came after me and I ate supper at their house. I didn't know it before until dad gave me his address that Don Stone is stationed in Frisco. Art helped me and I got in touch with Don. He and his wife came over to Allen's and picked me up and took me to the boat. This is the best time I have had since my arrival here. I sure hope I get to see them again.

Tuesday, August 18, 1942 On fatigue duty all day. I got a soft job up at the finance office washing windows. The Sarg in charge asked for us back this afternoon. All we did was to mess around and clean a few more windows and polish an old fire extinguisher. I am getting behind on my mail writing again but all I did was to write to Marian tonight and went to bed early. Our bunch from Tyler has been here at McDowell four weeks now.

Wednesday, August 19, 1942 Took the usual march around the island this morning. Had gas mask drill this afternoon. Things went pretty good today. Went to the show tonight.

Thursday, August 20, 1942 Marched around the island again today. This afternoon we had close order drill for a while and was dismissed at 2:30 P.M. I rather expect K.P. for tomorrow. I signed the pass slip for a pass tomorrow. I am quite sure of K.P. instead of a pass tomorrow but what I really want is a pass the next day Saturday. I hope it works.

Friday, August 21, 1942 Well just as I thought K.P. today. I helped the baker today with baking 400 pies and 20 cakes. Boy that was quite a job. I didn't get any mail today from Marian or any of the folks.

Saturday, August 22, 1942 It seems in this "Hell hole of creation" just when you get to the place where you feel you can take it they pull something. Today my name was up for pass. I went to look at the list a little later on and the Sgt. had scratched my name and put down one of his stand ins name instead. Boy was I hot I went into the office and told them what I thought. A little later on I got a note from Don Stone for me to get in touch with him. I managed to get my pass back. Boy I am sure fed up with this place. I got my watch fixed and then caught a Street car out to Don's and found it without any trouble. We sat around and talked till quite late and then went to bed.[22]

Sunday, August 23, 1942 As my pass was only good till 8:30 A.M. I had to catch the early boat. We got up early and Don and Lee took me down to the boat. I didn't do much in camp all day. I ironed my summer uniform and then took a blanket and went down to the beach. I tried to write a letter to Marian but it was too windy so I came back to the barracks. I went to the show tonight. That is the only good thing they have here. Some of us fellows have been wondering when Major Caldwell will send us our lunch allowance.

Monday, August 24, 1942 Today has been pretty close to routine all day. This morning we marched around the island. This afternoon we had another lecture on chemical warfare. The same one we have had for the fourth time. We then had gas mask drill and was through for the day at 3 P.M. I received three letters from Marian today. I have been in the Army six months today. Seems like six years.

Tuesday, August 25, 1942 We caught K.P. again today. Most of our bunch are getting to be experts at this K.P. game. Table waiting wasn't so bad today. A report came over from headquarters, and for once was authentic that we are to move over to north garrison tomorrow. I can't guess what is cooking for us out here. Maybe they need some experienced K.P.s who knows. We have been here at McDowell 5 weeks today. Went to the show tonight. Had to give up our seat again to the permanent party. This place is sure a miscarriage to a democracy and a hell hole of creation. Didn't get any letter from Marian. Got one from Jack.

Wednesday, August 26, 1942 Well today we moved about 1 mile up the road to north garrison. I think it will be better at our new place as we only catch fatigue duty and no K.P. As we will still eat at the same mess hall we won't get K.P. unless they open the north garrison mess hall. This morning we moved in. This afternoon we were on fatigue duty cleaning out poison oak. I have some of it on my legs. poison oak is just thick on this island. Went to the show tonight.

---

[22] I believe Don Stone was a cousin of my dad's.

Lost the crystal out of my watch.

Thursday, August 27, 1942 We were on fatigue duty all day today. The jobs we are given on fatigue duty are not so important, but just to keep us busy. We were on the poison oak detail today. I went to the show this evening. I was disappointed in it as it wasn't much good. The name of it was Nelson Eddy and Janette McDonald in "I Married an Angel." I received a box of caramels from Marian today. Signed the pay role today. We do not get our full amount of pay here. I only received $20 last month.

Friday, August 28, 1942 Fatigue duty again today. Worked in the poison ivy this morning and shoveled dirt this afternoon. In all we didn't do much but mess around today. I received my cameo ring from Marian this morning. Went to the show tonight as usual.

Saturday, August 29, 1942 We were not on fatigue duty today. We changed sheets after breakfast and then got paid. I bought four souvenir pillow cases and sent them to my folks, Sally& Dick, Marian and Marian's folks. I got back to the barracks too late for a pass. Just as well because we have been put on the alert again. Looks like no pass Sunday too. I wrote some letters and took a hike up over the island. The underbrush is so thick you can hardly get through. I went to the show again tonight.

Sunday, August 30, 1942 Our orders came official today that we are to be shipped tomorrow. We are to be ready at 7:45 A.M. tomorrow. I slept rather late this morning. I spent most of the afternoon writing letters home. Under the circumstances it was sure hard to find a way to end my letters, as these are the last I will probably write for quite a while. Some of the fellows we may be shipped back inland. I sure hope they are right. I spent most of the evening getting my things ready to go. I took a few pictures tonight.

Monday, August 31, 1942 We were up early this morning doing our last minute packing. We ate breakfast and then stood on the parade grounds most of the rest of the day having our bags checked and rechecked. I was issued a new pair of shoes. We have been told we would not leave until tomorrow. The usual atmosphere of where we may be going prevails and the rumors are flying high. I had hopes for a while maybe I would be sent back inland but now I have the

41

feeling for sure I am going overseas. I went to the show tonight ("United We Stand") I feel awful down hearted tonight. I got two letters from Marian today. Hard to tell when I will ever see her again.

The Voyage Overseas to Brisbane, Australia

Tuesday, September 1, 1942 Up at the usual time this morning. We didn't do anything all day. This evening we fell out with our equipment to leave Fort McDowell. My spirits hit a low ebb as we were brought over to the Army peer and we embarked on a troop ship. We kinda think we may be going to Australia. We were assigned berths in the forward hold of the ship. I think, originally used for cattle, but we are classed and packed in about the same. Put yourself in my place and you will know how I feel about the future date I will get home. Good bye U.S.A.

Wednesday, September 2, 1942 Our bunks are stacked four deep. Mine is the second from the top and I am about five feet from the floor. We were tied to the dock all night as the ship was loaded. The middle of the morning the ship pulled out and went up the bay. We were at anchor there all day. We pulled anchor and passed through the Golden Gate around five p.m. this evening. The ocean seemed rather rough and quite a few of the fellows feel kinda sick, including me. We passed a large school of porpoise and saw a couple of whales this evening.

Thursday, September 3, 1942 I just finished supper and the meal tonight was pretty good. We get two meals a day. We eat breakfast at 10 A.M. For breakfast this morning I got 3 eggs, bread, butter and jam. For supper, beef (?) corn, cabbage, bread, coffee and peaches. I hope to get my sea legs in a short time, but right now I don't feel so good. My stomach is ok but I am awful light headed. There are four transports plus one heavy cruiser in our convoy. I have no way of knowing how far we are from San Francisco but we have been heading south west all day. We are now about 24 hours out of Frisco. I received my last mail from Marian and home today.

Friday, September 4, 1942 Up at 8:30 A.M. Our time is 6 hours later now than back home. It is sure crowded we haven't much to do, but we stand in line most of the time either for water (we get two canteens full per day) chow or the P.X. I got into the P.X. for the first time today after a long wait in line. A strange boat was sighted and we had "abandon ship" drill. The strange boat proved to be a United Nations freighter. Ted and I sat out on the deck tonight for a while. It was clear and the sea was quiet. The weather is getting warmer as we get farther south. I have felt pretty good all day. I think I will be O.K. now from sea sickness.

Saturday, September 5, 1942 Today was rather uneventful. I have had a headache most all day so I spent most of my time in my bunk. Our bunks are not too comfortable being made of canvas stretched tightly with rope. The voyage so far has been quite enjoyable with sunny skies and clear nights. The ocean takes the same color as the sky, on a clear day it is a dark blue looking as if it had been colored. Tonight the sunset was very beautiful, with one of our convoy ships silhouetted against the sky. Some say we should arrive at the Hawaiian Islands by tomorrow Sunday night. I don't hardly think we have come that far. The weather is getting a lot warmer as we get farther south.

Sunday, September 6, 1942 Up at 6 A.M. as I had to go on my first detail. Ten of us had to carry a bunch of supplies up to the P.X. This was sure a hard job as I am about half sick and the rocking of the boat makes it difficult to walk. The ocean has been quite rough today. There were church services on deck this morning, outside of that it has been just another day. The voyage now is becoming rather monotonous and being as crowded as we are is far from pleasant. It is getting hotter in our quarters each day and the greasy smell in the mess hall sure takes away your appetite. I sat up on deck a while this evening and talked to an Australian.

Monday, September 7, 1942 As each day seem to get warmer, trying to sleep is getting harder all the time. Our bunks are pretty hard and the air gets awful stale. I was up at 5 A.M. It was rather cloudy this A.M. and by afternoon it rained. I saw some flying fish this morning. The first I have ever seen. I haven't felt so very good the past couple of days.

Tuesday, September 8, 1942 I am feeling a little better today but still feel a little light headed. The glamour of this voyage is warring off fast and as crowded as we are it is getting more of an ordeal every day. The discontent of the men is growing every day. Enlisted men are losing respect for officers fast as the officers are traveling first class and enlisted men something like cattle. It begins to look like we may go on by the Hawaiian Islands without stopping. We had a hard rain this afternoon. Many of the fellows took a bath in it.

Wednesday, September 9, 1942 I slept on the deck last night. As almost everyone had the same idea the only place I could find to sleep was on a small deck box where I had to let my legs rest on the rail. All in all it was more comfortable than down in the hold. It rained off and on most of the day and by tonight it looked as if we would run into some bad weather. Some of the waves were high enough till the spray flew over the railing. We get the latest news by radio and it is sent to us by the ships daily paper the "Yankee Clipper".

Thursday, September 10, 1942 I slept in my bunk last night as the weather is still a little threatening. I felt pretty good this morning and was on deck most of the day. I spent quite a lot of time up at the P.X. This was my undoing as I ate candy, crackers and drank pop. By evening I was in real misery. I didn't eat any supper tonight. It rained again most of the afternoon. We are rationed two canteens of water each day. As the weather gets hotter this is none too much as we also have to use some of it to shave in. All water except for drinking and cooking is salt water. We signed pay role today.

Friday, September 11, 1942 Today has been a gala day aboard as we crossed the Equator around 11 A.M. The morning was spent initiating persons who were crossing the line for the first time. Soldiers posing as King and Queen Neptune, wearing quite remarkable costume directed the ceremony. For there were far too many to initiate one at time except the officers they turned a hose on the whole crowd. The route we have to take to the other end of the ship is long and narrow with sharp turns and stairs to climb. We call it the "Burma Road". I feel a little better tonight but still a little washed out.

Saturday, September 12, 1942 I slept rather late this morning. I am sure weak after being sick the other day. I was too late for breakfast this morning so had to go all day before evening meal. We should arrive at the Fiji Islands before long as they seem to be making preparation for some of the troops to leave. Co. 10 was called for a special meeting this afternoon, a bunch were selected as gun tenders. I was not included. I don't mind. Just so I don't pull K.P. instead. It looks kinda rainy tonight. I think I will sleep on deck anyway.

Sunday, September 13, 1942 It rained last night so I had to sleep below. It was so hot in our quarters, that it was impossible to get much rest. Had church services today. There is as much difference between the way the officers and enlisted men live on this boat as night and day. There will be plenty said about this someday. I sure hope we get a breathing spell when we reach our destination. I started to sleep on deck tonight and had a pretty good spot. The ocean was rather rough, but not too bad. All at once the ship struck a wave that came clear over the front. I my blanket, and life jacket were just soaked. I slept below.

Monday, September 14, 1942 Breakfast wasn't so bad for a change, although the bread and butter are now uneatable, was fresh when we left San Francisco. We were told today we may have mail service when we reach the Fiji Islands. I spent most of the day writing and reading. There were some boxing matches on the sports deck today. We didn't get supper until late tonight and then we didn't get much. Our Co. is the last on the meal line and sure get the leftovers if there are any. It is hard to move around the deck after dark as the convoy is blacked out.

Tuesday, September 15, 1942 Crossed the 180* meridian so today was skipped and did not exist. Seems a coincidence being the same date as my wedding. 1 year and 3months.

Wednesday, September 16, 1942b We crossed the 180th meridian last night so Tuesday never did exist as on crossing the timeline traveling west you skip a day. I saw land this afternoon, the first since leaving San Francisco. I don't know what island it was but it must be one of the Fiji group, where we should be in a short time. I finally got a haircut today. I missed breakfast though. It rained hard tonight.

Thursday, September 17, 1942 We traveled all day today and no sign of more land. Someone yesterday said the name of the island we passed was Friendly Island. I thought sure we would arrive at Fiji today. The largest island of the Fiji group is about the size of Connecticut and the capital is Suva. The ocean has been rather calm today and I have felt the best today since leaving Frisco. The weather is getting cooler as we go farther south from the Equator. Seasons are just reversed down here. They say Xmas is one of the hottest days of the year.

Friday, September 18, 1942 I felt pretty good today and the food wasn't so bad. The P.X. has been closed now for a couple of days. I guess to cut down on fellows hording cigarettes. A Navy plane pulling a target flew over the ship for gun practice. We are to arrive at Fiji tomorrow. We are to get shore leave tomorrow. We were given instructions and regulations we are to follow on shore leave. We are to go in groups of 30 men with a Non. Com. And lieutenant in charge. They say things are very cheap here. Our ship and another left the convoy at sundown tonight. We are on our way now and have increased speed.

Fiji

Saturday, September 19, 1942 We reached the Fiji Islands at 9 A.M. I was all ready to go to shore with a group but to our disappointment there was no dock space and so we anchored in the harbor all day, no one leaving the boat. The bay here at Suva is very beautiful with the town on the east shore running along the bay and back in the hills. It does not look so large even though it is the capital. The other side of the bay is mountainous and apparently rather rugged but covered with palm trees and thick vegetation. It is hard to tell the height of these mountains. There are some air craft here both modern and obsolete. Slept on deck tonight. Rained a lot today.

Sunday, September 20, 1942 Our ship sat at anchor until nearly noon, before it moved into port. We went ashore about 1 P.M. It started to rain about this time and has been pouring down ever since. Nevertheless it seemed good to get off the boat. The natives here, men and women alike wear skirts. The police uniform is white skirt blue jacket with brass buttons. The natives have big bushy heads of hair. What automobiles there are, are old American types and small foreign models. Traffic travels on the left. Most business places were closed today. We walked around through town and stopped at the New Zealand Club. Something like the U.S.O. We ate sandwiches and drank pop. Note: Boarded ship on Tuesday, September 1, 1942, at Angel Island, Camp McDowell arrived Fiji Sunday, September 20, 1942.

Monday, September 21, 1942 Got shore leave again today. The Captain in charge of our group turned us loose. Three of we soldiers walked around the town together. We stopped in the museum where we saw a lot of Fiji relics. We then went for a walk around town going through the city park that was very beautiful. The white population's homes look quite modern but are rather simple. An automobile here cost five times as much as in the U.S. These natives are not so dumb. They saw the soldiers coming and everything went up sky high. I was able to get a fairly good meal of steak and eggs but it was far from the equal of the U.S. A lot of the soldiers came back drunk some didn't come back at all. This town is wide open.

Tuesday, September 22, 1942 Went ashore again today. Another fellow and I went together. Suva is only about 15,000 so we saw most of it yesterday. We stopped in at a small café and had dinner. The meal of ham and eggs was pretty was good. I bought Marian a handkerchief and a post card folder. We walked around town for a while and then started out to the N.Z. Club on the way we stopped and shot baskets on an outdoor basketball court. We ate cookies, sandwiches and drank pop at the N.Z. club.

Wednesday, September 23, 1942 Went on shore leave at 10 A.M. I left the gang and was by myself. There wasn't much to do except look around at the shop windows. I ate some ham and eggs and bought some little trinkets. We had to be back to the boat by 1:30 as we are leaving this afternoon. We pulled out of the harbor at sundown. We are to travel the rest of the way to Australia without escort. As rumors go they say they are trying to find a sub outside the harbor. Had a pleasant surprise tonight. Met a friend from Des Moines and Meredith's (Bill Duce.) He with others changed to our boat at Fiji. We sure did have a lot to talk about. For more reasons than one, I slept on deck tonight. We are sure in hostile waters now, and a full moon.

Thursday, September 24, 1942 Today has been rather uneventful. Had abandon ship drill and gun practice. Don't know if we are going to New Zealand before Australia or not. We are taking a "zig- zag" course. I haven't seen Bill Duse all day. It is hard to find anyone. The boat now is not nearly so crowded as quite a few hundred stayed at Fiji. I spent most of the day reading and resting. Supper was the best it has been tonight.

Friday, September 25, 1942 For a while this morning the ocean was smooth as glass but I guess it was just the calm before the storm. By afternoon the wind rose to a gale and the waves were going clear over the prow. I was assigned to a 50 cal. machine gun crew today. We were paid five dollars today, so we should arrive in port in a couple of days. We are now in the Coral Sea and the most hazardous part of the voyage is at hand. An airplane was sighted today but proved to be friendly. Boy is it ever rough. Ropes have been strung along the decks to hold on to. A lot of the fellows are getting sick.

Saturday, September 26, 1942 The ocean is still on a rampage and so many fellows are sick, there is hardly enough for the gun crews. I managed to get up on deck for gun drill, but I have been in my bunk all day. I ate both meals today and managed to keep them down, but "oh" the weather has been getting very cool and we have put on our winter clothes. The climate is about the same as March at home.

Sunday, September 27, 1942 I am getting a little more use to my bunk even though it is very hard to sleep on as yet. The ocean has calmed down today and I feel pretty well again. We were told we would reach port tomorrow and to get our equipment ready to leave. Later this evening we were told to disregard this order. No one knows the reason but the ship has changed courses and is "zig zaggin". Perhaps they suspect enemy sub. This afternoon toward dusk we saw some patches of steam rise mysteriously from the water about 200 yards to port.

Monday, September 28, 1942 The sergeant finally caught up with me today for room orderly. I have been dodging him for the past three days. We have been told we are to reach port tomorrow. Everyone is busy getting things ready to leave. Since we have been on this boat for nearly a month we are all anxious to reach land and our destination. As last night was very clear I saw the Southern Cross for the first time. I saw a large school of tuna fish today. Some of the fellows say name of the ship is the Cliff Fontaine. I guess no one knows for sure what the name is.

Tuesday, September 29, 1942 Land was sighted this morning 6:15 from the crow's nest. Brisbane harbor is skirted by reefs and I rather suppose mine fields. We had to go far out of our way to reach the mouth of the Brisbane River, which took us most of the morning. We traveled some 8 or 10 miles up the river to reach Brisbane, Australia. This river seemed very narrow for as large a boat as ours. As it is spring here at this time, the scenery along the river was very beautiful. In many ways it seemed like the U.S. As we progressed slowly and drew nearer to port we passed many factories and plants with people hanging out the windows waving at us. We disembarked at 5:30 P.M. marching up the ave. for a mile or so to a fair ground where there is a tent camp. We were tired and hungry and not much for supper, but the P.X. filled in.

Wednesday, September 30, 1942 There are eight of us in each tent. We have large sacks filled with straw for mattresses and this makes for a better bed than the bunks on the boat. This is a rather simple camp of which is in the middle of a race track. We eat out of our mess kits the food being served outdoors. I was able to take a shower and get really clean for the first time in a month. The railroads here are not at all like the ones in the U.S. being very lightly built and looking quite frail. It would be impossible going from coach to coach and the locomotive looks like a small American Switch Engine. Our camp is about four miles from downtown Brisbane. I went on pass tonight. The dance I attended was not any different in any way from those of the U.S.[23]

---

[23] And so brings my father from the Golden Gate Bridge to Brisbane, Australia. — To a mattress that is much better than the one on the boat, because it is a sack filled with straw (To) a tent that will accommodate 8 soldiers, AND finally, the best part of all — the shower and being clean – really clean – after a month aboard ship, rough waters, sea sickness, sleeping on deck, with the only chance of a shower IF it rained. I cannot begin to describe my emotions after completing this much of his diaries, and knowing what lies ahead. My heart absolutely aches right now.

Welcome to Australia

Thursday, October 1, 1942 I turned out a big washing this morning and then went over to see the doctor as I have a little rash on my neck. Three of us ate dinner outside of camp this noon, and enjoyed a plate of steak and eggs. It seems quite simple to get out of camp. Pass or no pass and as I had no pass last night Ted and I went to town by the way of the camp fence, no pass. We went to a show which had mostly old American films. Between shows the ushers sell ice cream and persons may smoke at any time. All traffic travels on the left and the street cars are quite modern being half open and half closed. The fare is two pence (5 cents). We got back in camp by climbing the fence.

Friday, October 2, 1942 We have it quite easy here as there is very little detail and fatigue duty. They are getting a little stricter on guarding the fence. Our Signal Corps bunch went over to a radio station and took code speed test this afternoon. On an average we all did about the same, between 14 and 16 words per minute. Another fellow and I talked to a dispatch rider. He said it was a good thing and we might be able to get on as they needed motorcycle riders. I think I will at least check up on it as my idea of radio operating is at a low ebb. Ted and I went to town by way of the fence again tonight. We went to the city hall where there was an Australian dance. It was entirely different from U.S. The auditorium was sure a beautiful place. We got back in camp o.k.

Saturday, October 3, 1942 We were told to stick close to our area this morning as we are to be moved to a different camp about a mile from our original camp. Our new camp is called Camp Doomden. Our new place is not quite as good as it is rather swampy and the mosquitoes are quite bad. I believe we have seen our last barracks for the duration. This place seems to be better fenced and will be harder to leave without a pass. Ted and I had passes tonight. He went to the skating rink and I to the dance at the Coco Nut Grove. The dance wasn't much good and my neck still bothers me so we came back to camp early. There is an airport about a block from here and there are many P.38 and P.40 pursuit ships.

Sunday, October 4, 1942 Was too late to get a pass this morning. Ted and I walked around camp to find a possible exit. At lunch this noon we happened to get acquainted with the Corporal of the Guard and he said he would let us out this evening. We went to the dance at the city hall. Brisbane is about 350,000 in population. There are many modern buildings none of which are very tall. Australian soda fountains are similar to U.S. The ice cream has a different flavor but is good. The cold drinks are similar to ours except a few Australian original flavors. Got by again tonight without a pass.

Monday, October 5, 1942 All we are doing here at Camp Doomden is sitting around waiting for orders. We have no fatigue duty to speak of. Some of our bunch has caught K.P. As rumors go they say the Air Corps and Signal Corps are having a dispute as to where we shall go, as radio operators are needed urgently. We are as likely to be sent to New Guinea or the Solomon Islands as anywhere, and it looks like we may see action quite soon. Took a walk this afternoon and found that the sewer runs under the fence across the road and is a good way of getting out of camp. Went to town on a pass tonight. Didn't have a very good time. Shows are old, dances are no good.

Tuesday, October 6, 1942 Was on fatigue duty this morning. All we did was police up around the grounds. This afternoon we signed the pay role for $21.00. Another fellow and I went over to the airport and watched the ships take off and land. Ted and I cleaned up and was able to get a pass and went to town. We went to the city hall to the dance. It was a 50 – 50 dance, half American and half Australians. The Australian "Gypsy Tap" old time dance and others I can't do and the rhythm is too fast for the rest. They go for what we call Tunisian. "Waltzes" they call them, jazz waltzes. We came back to camp early.

Wednesday, October 7, 1942 Not much doing today. Co. 10 is starting to split up as some of the engineers are being shipped. It looks like we Signal Corps men will be here till the last ones again. I don't mind waiting here as I rather like this place. We were paid $21.00 today which amounted to quite a lot more in Australian money. I have a fair sum saved as Ted paid me what he had borrowed. Went to town again tonight. I ate super at the American Red Cross. I sent Marian a cablegram this evening. She should get it in two or three days.

Thursday, October 8, 1942 Had to go on K.P. today. My job was washing pots and pans (called changing oil.) When I get home I will be able to eat anything, anywhere. Two Sgts. argued if some lettuce was garbage or food. We have named our way of leaving camp without a pass as "Going down the drain" as the place we go through is a long large sewer. It is quite clean however. Went to town tonight. The Australian soldiers are becoming more difficult. What we call "moochers." They think all Americans are rich.

Friday, October 9, 1942 We were put on the alert today, but it turned out with someone else leaving. Not much doing today, all we did was lay around. Our group of tents are near a large area of swamp ground and the mosquitoes have nearly eaten us up. Got a pass tonight and went to town. Ted and I walked around most of the evening. We were stopped by some three or four drunk Australians who asked for money. An American soldier stabbed an Australian soldier to death tonight. Ted and I talked to an Aust. Soldier who was at the scene of the crime. He said there were ten or more Australians on this American.

Saturday, October 10, 1942 Thought sure I would catch guard duty for tonight but I am still down the list quite far. The stabbing in town last night nearly has resulted in a riot. It was a case of self defense, over the refusal of the American to give the Aust. money. The Aust. are very jealous of us and resent our being here, even though it is we Americans who will save their hydes. All you see is American supplies here. A fight always results with four or five Aust. on one American. They do not attack more than one Yank at a time. We have been told to travel in two's or more. Went to town on pass tonight.

Sunday, October 11, 1942 It poured down all day today and there wasn't much to do but stay in the tent and get ate up by misquotes. I was just walking out the tent to go to town when I was told to report for guard duty. I was on and off guard all night. My post was to guard supplies in a kitchen. I got a little amusement out of not allowing the cook sergeant to enter the kitchen in the middle of the night. I was sure burned up because of getting guard tonight.

Monday, October 12, 1942 Still is raining a little today. Wasn't much doing today. I spent my time in the guard tent as I didn't get off duty till 4:30 P.M. The Yanks are rapidly disliking the Aussie soldiers more and more. One Aussie soldier will approach you for money, if you are alone and give, you are to understand there are so many others, backing him up. If you refuse, it is just too bad. They have to have odds of ten to one or they will stay away. Ted and I went to the show tonight. We also had a steak supper at the American Red Cross (P.X.)

Tuesday, October 13, 1942 Laid around all morning. Walked over to the airport and watched a Flying Fortress take off. There were also some Liberators there. Ted and I took a bunch of laundry outside the gate. We are taking a chance of having to take it with us wet, as we may move from here anytime. Went to town tonight. Had supper and got my watch as I had a crystal put in it. There was the usual Australian dance at the City hall tonight. I just about missed the last car to camp tonight. You have to catch them like you would a fast freight. The Australians call streetcars "Trams."

Wednesday, October 14, 1942 We are still waiting to be moved somewhere and the fellows are getting a little restless laying around waiting. I look forward to everyday to getting letters from Marian and home, but so far no letters. It has been a month and a half since the last letters. I went to town early today. I have been spending more money perhaps than I should but we all feel we probably will go up front and we might as well have a little pleasure while we can. I got mixed up on street cars (trams) tonight and was late getting back to camp— got in O.K. though.

Thursday, October 15, 1942 I reported for sick call this morning to get my teeth fixed. I rode over to the hospital in an ambulance but took the Tram back. I can't get anything done to my teeth until Sat. and I suppose we will move before then. Ted and I went to town tonight. There isn't much to do but it is better than staying in camp. The weather is getting quite a bit warmer although the nights are quite cool. Today I have been married a year and four months.

Friday, October 16, 1942 Over slept this morning and was late getting the K.P.s up. As I was C.Q. today I had to hang pretty close to quarters. We were put on the alert today and told we would move tomorrow. I played a little fast ball this afternoon. I stayed in camp tonight and went to the show. The show is up in the grandstand. The name of the one tonight was Bette Davis in "The Letter", Ted and I went outside after the show and bought a lunch and some fruit.

Saturday, October 17, 1942 We fell out at 10:30 A.M. to receive our ration money for the trip which is to take us one days' travel. Our bunch from Tyler is now being split up in groups of from three to seven fellows. I have a feeling it won't be long till we all see a lot of action. Ted is going one direction and I another. Went into Brisbane for the last time this evening. The Japs are making an all out attempt to regain the Solomon Islands. The Germans are putting everything into a final attempt to take Stalingrad. The Allies are pushing the Japs back into New Guinea.

Moving to Rockhampton, Australia—A 24 Hour-Train-Ride

Sunday, October 18, 1942 Said goodbye to Ted and all but eleven of what remains of Co. B. This morning we stayed close to camp all day and at six pm. we were taken to the railroad station. We boarded the train at 9. P.M. and learned we are to go to the 41st signal Co. at Rockhampton, a trip of around 600 miles. These trains are narrow gage (3'3") and can travel about a hundred miles every four hours. We will have to sleep sitting up tonight. Our coach is divided into two compartments with the lavatory separating. It is used by men and women alike.

Monday, November 1, 1942 Had to get up early this morning to get ready to move. We took down our tent and packed our bags and traveled the distance of six miles in the truck. Our new camp is in a rather wooded flat patch of country. We 6 have a good location for our tent being near the mess hall and showers. I feel kinda low tonight as I heard today that my bunch is going to the air corps but I am not going. Why? I don't know. Maybe it is best. I worked hard today so I didn't think about it too much.

Monday, November 2, 1942 I went on the net (radio station) this morning for my first try as a radio operator. I sure have a lot yet to learn. I think I will like it O.K. when I get some experience. I am the first of our bunch to go on as an operator. I took another shot for cholera today. It didn't bother me much. Since our bunch has arrived here at Rockhampton one of our tent mates is trying for a discharge from the Army because of a bad ankle. He the same as says it is an excuse. We are all very bitter toward him, what we think of a slacker etc. I heard today it is not I who is going to stay here. Now what to think?

Tuesday, November 3, 1942 Went back on the net (radio station) this morning. I am sure at a loss what to do, and sure need a lot of practice. The operator who is showing me how left me alone for a little while this noon. We are on duty six hours and off eighteen hours. The weather is beginning to get very hot. It must be more than) 100° today. I haven't received any mail from home since September 2nd. I hope Marian and the folks have heard from me before now. I am staying home and writing them some letters tonight.

Wednesday, November 4, 1942 The camp went on a march this morning down to the beach. I did not go with them as I went back on the "net" this afternoon. It rained very hard and the reception was bad, so I could hardly copy code. I think I am getting a little better all the time and will be able to handle the job alone in a short length of time. I spent a little time this afternoon getting my fatigue clothes and "web" equipment ready to be dyed. They will be a dark green to be used in jungle warfare). It looks like we will go north before long.

Thursday, November 5, 1942 Went on K.P. this morning. I will be off the "net" for a couple of days, but to go back on Saturday. Received word this noon that we are to be transferred to the air corps. No one knows where we are to go. I tried to get released from K.P. to turn in my rifle and other things and get ready, but no luck so I left anyway. Our bunch is to be split up again. Two of the ten left, stay here and some of the rest of us go opposite directions.

Friday, November 6, 1942 This morning we received our orders. Another soldier and myself went to town to make arrangements for each of our groups we are in charge of. My group goes to Townsville. There are four of us going north and four south. We caught our train around 2 P.M. We Americans as usual got what was dished out, and had to sit up all night in a day car. It was very crowded with small children laying in the isles asleep, and with the dirt from the locomotive blowing in the windows it is sure disagreeable.[24]

---

[24] Once again, the soldiers are on the move. Travel accommodations are miserable, dirty, and exhausting. They spent from 2 pm on the 6th until noon the next day on a narrow gauge train – 3' x 3" wide. And my own personal comment – "And we won this war."

Saturday, November 7, 1942 Sleep last night was impossible to get with the narrow gauge train lurching from side to side. All of us are tired and covered with cinders and soot. As usual between towns which are about forty miles apart the country was very wild and covered with timber. As we traveled farther north the country became quite flat and the timber was not quite so thick. We arrived in Townsville around noon. We went to a café and ate dinner and then I called up our commanding officer that we are to report to. We were taken in a truck outside of town to Camp Armstrong, where we were assigned to a tent. "Boy" am I tired.

Sunday, November 8, 1942 Had to go back to town last night to report for our bunch to the Signal officer. Myself and another soldier of our group are to move up town today as we are to be stationed here for a while. The other two are to go to Port Moresby in New Guinea. I hear we may go to Darwin in a short time. I have become acquainted with a soldier who was stationed at Darwin for a time and was bombed quite a few times. He showed me a switch he got from a Jap bomber that was shot down.

Monday, November 9, 1942 Got up at 6:30 A.M. Our new camp is in a vacant lot a few blocks from town. We eat at a hotel that has a mess hall regular Army style which is a couple of blocks. We started to code school today. We have the job now of learning to take code on the type writer as we are to be in fixed station jobs. I sure have a lot to learn. Lee, my new friend and Jaresky and I went to town to a show tonight. This town is sure dead and don't seem to have much for soldiers.

Tuesday, November 10, 1942 Went to code school today. I ate in town this noon as I wanted to get a haircut. We go to code school from 8am till noon and then from one till five P.M. These are sure long hours to take code. The radio station here is quite large being operated by remote control from transmitters and receivers outside of town. We went to town tonight and ate a large amount of ice cream. We stopped in to a Vaudeville house for a short time. It was very "Corny" so we left.

Wednesday, November 11, 1942 Code school as usual today. I am beginning to pick up a little speed on the typewriter. The Sgt. took us out to the transmitting and receiving station outside of town this afternoon. I ate in town this afternoon as I wanted to get some Christmas cards and airmail stamps. I wrote to Marian today and told her my new address. I have received no mail from home as yet. It makes me feel very lonely. Stayed in Camp tonight and addressed Christmas cards.

Thursday, November 12, 1942 Code school today again. I am practically starting over again learning to take it on the typewriter. We go to school in a basement that is rather dark and dirty. There are seventeen of us. Went to town tonight. Lee, Jaresky and I stopped in at a show for a little while. It was a vaudeville very much like a 1890 production. We then ate some ice cream and walked back to camp, about a half mile. It was interesting to watch the search lights spot our aircraft that were flying over Townsville.

Friday, November 13, 1942 Code school again today. I understand we are going to school eight hours a day seven days a week. We were issued flash lights this afternoon also a new summer cap. Lee, Jarsky and I went out to Camp Armstrong to see Heitte and Miller this evening. We all came back to town and looked for a couple other fellows of our gang who are supposed to be in town.

We didn't find them so we all went to a show. I bought some post cards and a map today. The Eighth Army is marching westward across Libya with Rommel in retreats. The U.S. troops have taken Algiers.

Saturday, November 14, 1942 School today. We all took a code test today. I didn't do so well. Some of the fellows are going up stairs on the net tomorrow. We ran into Balone, Dahl, and Anderson this noon and we all ate at the American Red Cross. It was rather like a family reunion. We talked about the gang and exchanged notes as to where some of the fellows are stationed. We were told today we are to go to school the full number of hours plus from 6:30 P.M. till 10:30 P.M. 84 hours per week. "Boy"

Sunday, November 15, 1942 Code school again this morning. The Sgt. gave us a break and let us have this afternoon off. I decided to stay in the tent and write some letters, but I was tired and slept all afternoon. Today Marian and I have been married a year and a half. I have been in the Army as long as I have been home. Went to town tonight. Saw Balone and Dahl at the Red Cross, we were there most all evening. Lee and I thought we would buy a watermelon. They asked us 8 shillings, or $1.28 for one. "Boy" do they ever see the Americans coming.

Monday, November 16, 194 Code school all day today as well as from 6:30 P.M. till 10:30 P.M. "Boy" they are sure piling us up. The book says a normal amount of code is three hours per day. We now have to take 12. I took enough time to write letters to Marian, Sally and Dick and the folks today. No mail from home yet. There must be some around Australia somewhere for me. I am sure tired tonight.

Tuesday, November 17, 1942 Code school again twelve hours today. You hardly have time to wash and shave "not alone" take a shower. Townsville is about the same size as Rockhampton or around 30,000. It is on the coast and surrounded by a number of small mountains. One street running for about a mile and a half contains the business district. I think most anything you buy has two prices. One for the Americans and the cheaper price for the Australians. A dozen scrawny apples cost two shilling, or about .35 cents.

Wednesday, November 18, 1942 Spent all day at code school and went back after supper. We took code tests today. I made one of the highest scores of fifteen words per min. on the typewriter. The tension between Australians and American soldiers is growing. There was a fight on main street tonight. Quite a few soldiers were beat up, including an American major. When you are in town you must travel in twos or threes. My flash light is a handy thing to carry at night and not to see with either.

Thursday, November 19, 1942 I am sure getting tired of code school twelve hours per day and seven days per week. You have no time for anything else. I have been writing my letters at school. The Sgt. in charge is fed up with school also. He let us leave early tonight. I went to the show ("Roxie Heart"). There was another fight tonight. The Aussies are as yellow as they come. They have to have odds of ten to one or they are meek as lambs. One of these days the Americans will put them where they belong.

Friday, November 20, 1942 It looks like I won't be paid this month as my records haven't arrived from Rockhampton as yet. Being we have clothing inspection tomorrow, we got off a little early tonight to get ready for it. The Aussies are sure dumb. They actually think the "Yanks" are of no help. All you see are U.S. trucks and supplies, airplanes, guns and all other war materials that have saved their necks. The newspapers talk up what the Aussies are doing in New Guinea. They actually say the "Yanks" are doing nothing.

Saturday, November 21, 1944 Our commanding officers came down to school this morning and raised "H" because he didn't think we were working hard enough. Before this we thought of asking him for the afternoon off. I am getting so I can take code pretty well on the typewriter, but I am sure going stale on it. One of my tent mates was attacked by two Aussie soldiers as he came home tonight. Another American came by and helped him out. They held them until the Aussie M.P.s came and got them. They probably turned them loose around the corner.

Sunday, November 22, 1942 I went on the net this morning. I worked the circuit between here and Sydney. I got along fairly well but got caught up a number of times on some of the individual procedure they use. Before long our Tyler bunch should be operating together from Sydney to Port Moresby. I went to the show tonight "Eagle Squadron." While we were there, there was an air raid alert. Nothing came of it. All war news is in favor of the United Nations now. At Stalingrad, Libya and New Guinea, the enemy is being trapped and driven back.

Monday, November 23, 1942 I am back in school today. I worked yesterday on the net to enable two Sgts. to change shifts. This afternoon the Master Sgt. came down and told me I was to go on the four P.M. shift tomorrow. I didn't go to school tonight but went to the show instead. I saw Wayne Keith today. He is to leave for Port Moresby in a day or so.

Tuesday, November 24, 1942 Messed around town all day, went up to the Red Cross. Went to the post office and got some "V" mail stationary. Went on the net tonight, got along fairly well, but froze up on my first message. Lee came in and told me we are to move tomorrow to another camp area. I wrote Marian a letter today. It seems I should get some mail. I sure miss her letters and the mail from home.

Wednesday, November 25, 1942 Walked around town today doing not much of anything. I relieved one of the operators so he could eat dinner. A truck came down and moved all our equipment to a new tent area today. We are about the same distance from the mess hall and town. We are sure getting a bad deal by being moved. This area is a vacant lot, containing five tents, full of rubbish, high grass and mosquitoes. We have no floor in our tent as we did have at the other place. I wrote the folks a letter today.

Thursday, November 26, 1942 I went into a show until time to go to work today. This radio is getting easier for me as I learn more of the routine. I took my first message today. Our new tent doesn't only contain a lot of mosquitoes but the ants are nearly walking away with the place. The Aussies are calming down now a little. The Americans leave them alone, and don't care to be around them. In fact we hate their guts. I wrote Sally and Dick a "V" mail letter today. Today was also Thanksgiving. It was the same as any other day except we did have a turkey dinner which was sure good.

Friday, November 27, 1942 A fellow who lives in the house next to our tent allows us to use his shower. Otherwise we would have to walk up to the hotel which is two blocks. The reason for our being moved out of the other camp was because the personnel there couldn't tell us to do anything, such as close order drill or fatigue duty, being we are attached to Headquarters Co., so they shoved us down here in this hole. I bought Marian a handkerchief today for her collection.

Saturday, November 28, 1942 I thought some of going swimming today. I went to every store in town to try and get a pair of swimming trunks. Some of the fellows have bought girls suits and cut the tops off. I went to the show until time to go to work. All the stores close on Saturday afternoon and night. The weather is really getting hot, around 100° today.

Sunday, November 29, 1942 Went to work at 8 A.M. this morning. I will be off from 4 P.M. till midnight Monday. I am getting so I need no more help on my circuit. About all I need now is some speed (plenty) and to learn the "Z" signals better. I went to the show tonight. It wasn't so bad, "Night in Reo". Went up to the Red Cross and ate hamburgers. If I am here in this Co. Det. for very long maybe I will get a rating after-while. I hope. I hear my service records arrived up here from Rockhampton. I heard a girl twelve years old was killed by a crocodile the other day near here.

Monday, November 30, 1942 Laid around all day, not much of anything to do. Today was pay day but not for me. Maybe I will get in on the supplementary pay on the thirteenth. They told me today up at the hotel that I and another fellow are under their jurisdiction. I sure hope they are wrong and our Sgt. says they are. If not we are in for a rough time as they have it in for us, and if they can, will hand us a lot of B.S. because they couldn't tell us what to do is why they kicked us out of the other camp.

Tuesday, December 1, 1942 I am on the midnight shift now. I got off work at 8 A.M. this morning. It seems I am going into a slump with this code business. It seems I am getting worse instead of better. Sleeping in the daytime is almost impossible as the temp. reaches over 100°. Our tent is out in the open in sort of a sand pile next to a tin fence. It is almost unbearable in the tent, let alone sleep. Went to the show tonight before work tonight.

Wednesday, December 2, 1942 I slept fairly well today despite the heat. I didn't get up for dinner and went to the Red Cross for supper tonight. I hear they are having riots in Brisbane and have had to abandon the black out in some districts. These Aussies are about as intelligent as a bunch of Indians. Now that the threat of invasion is past, they say they never needed us anyway. I am full of this country to my neck. I went to the show tonight before work. It rained for the first time in a month tonight.

Thursday, December 3, 1942 I put my shelter half over the part of the tent above my cot so as to shade it and make it a little cooler. Went up to the Red Cross for a bite to eat tonight then came back to the tent for some more sleep before work. The war picture looks bright for the allies on all fronts now. Nearly the whole German Army in the Caucauses is in danger of being trapped. The American and British Armies are closing in on Rommel at Tunis. There is talk that Italy may crack any time. It rained hard again tonight.

Friday, December 4, 1942 The rain cools things off for a short time but in a short time it is as hot and dry as ever. I dident (didn't) sleep hardly at all today. I tried to get a little extra sleep this evening before work. Some of the fellows may be shipped to Sidney or Port Moresby, one of the two. They can't decide which one.

Saturday, December 5, 1942 Things are going along in the same routine now. There was a little difficulty at work today in regard to some messages. I in a way was implicated but was not to blame. As it looks at the present I may be stationed in Townsville for a while, but since you can't judge anything by the present and the war game is moving farther north we all may be shipped to New Guinea before long.

Sunday, December 6, 1942 I came back from work ate breakfast and then went back to the station to sign the supplementary pay role. I will probably be paid around the thirteenth. I slept a couple of hours this morning then took a shower and ate dinner. A friend and I went to the show, this afternoon. It has been cloudy, so the weather is a little cooler today. I am staying in tonight to get some sleep as I go on "days" tomorrow. The U.S. has been at war with Japan a year today. Rather Japan bombed Pearl Harbor a year ago today.

Monday, December 7, 1942 Well today out of a clear blue sky I received my first mail. I received three letters from the folks. They were post marked October 10, 20 and Sept. 24. I was disappointed that one of them was not from Marian, but the folks informed me everything is o.k. with her so it made me feel better. I wrote the folks a letter this afternoon. For the past week or so I have been very down hearted and disgusted with the mail service. I sure feel a lot better today since receiving the folk's letters.

Tuesday, December 8, 1942 I haven't been getting along so hot lately on the radio net, but I hope to be better in a short time. I looked forward to receiving some more mail today, but there was none for me. I think now that I have received some mail should receive a lot of it in a short time. I went to the show tonight. The rainy season has started and it has been raining most of the last couple of days.

Wednesday, December 9, 1942 Today the mail man was good to me again. I received a box of candy from Marian and a letter from the folks. The candy had been on its way since August. Leo Hessler and I went to the show tonight. It was just pouring down rain when we got out. I didn't have my rain coat and did I ever get soaked. There was a big riot in Brisbane, the other night. The Australians tore up the American P.X. One Aussie was killed and several injured. Things have been rather quiet around here lately, but you sure have to watch your step when you are alone.

Thursday, December 10, 1942 Things went pretty smooth today, my circuit was off the air all day, which didn't make it very enjoyable, but otherwise I got along pretty well. It has been raining nearly all day. The river overflowed and the water just came up to our tent, but didn't go inside. The candy Marian sent from home sure goes good as the Australian candy isn't much good. I ate dinner in town this noon and spent 4.6 or seventy cents. I received my pay yesterday.

Friday, December 11, 1942 Everything went as usual today. I was rather busy on the net with Portland Roads. They came in good all day after the bawling out the trick chief gave them. It poured down rain this evening and even though I had my rain coat on I got pretty wet. Leo Kessler didn't go to Moresby today after all so we went to the show tonight. I took off my shoes while I was there, as my feet were sopping wet after the rain.

Saturday, December 12, 1942 Everything about the same today. Portland Roads transmitter went blue-e so I didn't have anything to do but try and get through every half hour. The "QRM" ("static") is worse and reception is not so good since the rainy season has set in. Leo didn't leave again today so he and I may go to the dance tonight for the change of entertainment. It may and probably will be a flop. I don't have to go to work until four tomorrow.

Sunday, December 13, 1942 I slept rather late this morning as I didn't have to go to work until the second shift. When I did get to work there were enough operators so I got the night off. I went to the show at the Olympia which is an open air theater. A lot of the theaters have canvas seats very similar to our deck chairs. As I thought the dance last night was not much good. I don't think I will go again. I haven't received any more mail from home. I know there is a lot more that should be here.

Monday, December 14, 1942 I worked Mt. Isa and Canines on the radio tonight. I was quite busy most of the time. I received a letter from the folks as well as one from David Hughes in Texas. I wrote a letter to Marian. It seems the news papers here are a couple or more days behind the news. We have heard by radio that Burma in New Guinea has fallen. The papers still say we are closing in.

Tuesday, December 15, 1942 Well today is our wedding anniversary of 1 year, seven months. The war so far has kept me away from Marian ten months of this time. It is not good to think about but with the job I have I will be in the last troops to go back home after the war, which will be six months after the armistice and I think the war will run another eighteen months. Of course the question always arises - If I get back. You stand a bigger chance of getting knocked off by the Aussies than the Japs: I signed the pay role today.

Wednesday, December 16, 1942 The radio business is getting easier now I handled quite a bit of traffic tonight. We can always tell when there is an air raid at Port Moresby, as they send us the air raid signal and then go off the air. I went to the show this afternoon before work. I spent quite a bit of time sharpening my knife, this evening. Almost all Americans carry one to cut down the odds of ten Aussies to one American. No soldiers are given furloughs to Brisbane now since the riot there.

Thursday, December 17, 1942 Today I received a radio gram from Marian. When the Sgt. dropped it on my table I was busy sending a message so all I could do was wonder what was in it and send at the same time. It was a Christmas greeting. I intend to send some radio grams this Saturday. A friend and I went to a show before work. I guess Leo is in New Guinea now.

Friday, December 18, 1942 The post man was sure good to me today. I received thirteen letters. They were from Sally and Dick, Marian, Jack, the folks, and Vince. They were mostly dated September 14th. Receiving letters from home is as big a morale builder as anything. It sure makes you feel that maybe there is something in the future after all. I had contact with Portland Roads but we didn't have any traffic. There hasn't been any change to speak of in the war in the past few days.

Saturday, December 19, 1942 Today was about the same as any other day, except I sent four radio grams home. They should arrive before Christmas. A friend and I went to the show this afternoon before work. I wrote letters to Vince, Mr. T., Mrs. Plattes, and started one to Aunt Effie tonight. When the messages started to come in tonight I was really busy for a while. It was kind of a pain in the neck. I have been working the same operator for the past few days. I guess he isn't much better at it than I.

Sunday, December 20, 1942 Didn't do much this morning. I took a shower and shaved and then went to early chow, so as to relieve the other operators for chow. The food here is pretty good, in fact, as good as you can get in town, as a rule. When you by buy a meal in town it consists of steak and eggs or ham and eggs. You get no vegetable at all usually, except maybe a small portion of lettuce. It is like pulling teeth to have them bring you a glass of water. They never do that over here. I heard today, maybe I will be transferred to Sydney. I hope it goes through.

Monday, December 21, 1942 It is sure "h" trying to sleep in the daytime, with our tent pitched out in the open and the sun beating down at 100 degrees, you can hardly stand to be in the tent, not alone sleep. It looks as if the Captain up at the hotel has finally succeeded in landing us some dirt. He went over our lieutenant's head, to the Major's, and now on our day off we have to do K.P. I sure hope I get sent to Sydney or anywhere. This place is getting worse every day.

Tuesday, December 22, 1942 I borrowed a friend's head net today. By using this to keep the flies and mosquitoes off I managed to sleep a little bit today. It is now full moon and with a high overcast of clouds, the conditions are ideal for an air raid at night. I received three letters from Marian and one from the folks today. They were post marked the first of September.

Wednesday, December 23, 1942 Tried to sleep today but no use. The only sleep I get is from about 6:30 pm till 11:30. About 1:30 AM the air raid siren started to blow. All we operators sent "222" meaning air raid, turned out the lights and walked down stairs. It was sure a funny feeling walking down to the street. It was an ideal night for an air raid with a full moon and high clouds. We sat outside our shelter waiting, but nothing happened. I heard later the Japs were turned back up the coast a ways.

Thursday, December 24, 1942 It rained a little while this morning, so I was able to get a little rest. I didn't get back from the station though until kinda late as I had to sign some forms, for the allotment, Marian as yet, has not received. I don't think I ever thought as little of anyone as I do these Aussies. More than one night coming back to camp, I have carried my knife in my hand. They are as yellow as they come. They always jump you with the odds ten to one. None of these officers or M.P.s seem to care.

Friday, December 25, 1942 Today is Christmas. I must admit, I have felt rather gloomy all day. It has rained almost all day, and I spent most of it sleeping. We had chicken and beer for dinner. I don't care for either one so it was not much of an event. I am now on the Darwin (WVLZ) circuit. It sure is slow. I haven't sent or received a message for two days. I haven't heard any more about moving to Sydney. I hope it hasn't fallen through.

Saturday, December 26, 1942 Today is my day off so I don't have to go to work again till tomorrow afternoon. It has rained off and on all day. Our Co. O. came down to inspect our tent area. I guess we are going to move back to the "tay" angle camp. Even he agrees, we may get washed away, or eaten up by mosquitoes here in this hole. The water started to come up inside our tent yesterday. The war is sure looking good for us now. Rommel is being pushed back to Tripoli and the Russians are trapping the Germans in the Caucasus.

Sunday, December 27, 1942 Slept late this morning as I don't have to go to work today. I went up to the radio station this noon to see the schedule. I went to the show this afternoon and then up to the Red Cross. We are to move to another tent area tomorrow. I will have to take care of things myself as the other fellows have to go to work. I heard today I am to go to Port Moresby. I was afraid the Sydney deal was too good to be true. It looks like Rommel is in for a "Dunkirk" at Tripoli.

Monday, December 28, 1942 Today has sure been a tough one. It poured down all night and our tent was just like a river. Two of us had the job of moving our tent back to triangle this morning. Loading all our equipment on the truck as well as our wet tent was some job, and then of course the job of putting it back up again. The down pour took all our communication lines down between here and the receiver, so all the operators took their equipment and went out to the receiver station. I was lucky and stayed at the station, I didn't get back to our tent till 2:00 AM though. Boy was I tired.

Tuesday, December 29, 1942 I didn't wake up till ten A.M. I sure slept good last night. This camp area (the same one we were at before) is about ten degrees cooler than the place we just left. The old place was in a vacant lot between two houses where I think the neighborhood had been dumping all their junk. The grass was high and our tent (one of five) was in a spot about two feet lower than the rest of the ground around with the river about two blocks away, which would be nearly bank full when the tide is in.

Wednesday, December 30, 1942 I hung around camp all morning. The tent we are in has no floor, but I think we will get one. Joe Day and myself played a few games of checkers. "Boy is he good". We are still transmitting from the receiver station which is about ten miles out. This time of year is not so good for radios as there is usually a thunder storm which causes a lot of interference. The war is about the same only it looks worse for the Germans every day. Rommel is still on the run and quite a few dev. (divisions) of Germans are near to being trapped in the Ukraine. Burma is being steadily closed in, in New Guinea.

Thursday, December 31, 1942 One thing that is an advantage is we have no reveille, and we can sleep late in the morning. I worked WVLR (Portland Roads) and had a pretty busy night. We are still working out at the receiver. We are cramped in a little room and after dark the bugs are so bad you can hardly work. At twelve midnight we all wished the operators on the other stations a Happy New Year. Well I hope 1943 holds more happiness than did 42. It looks much better for us now, than it did a year ago.

Five Year Diary

1943, Triangle Camp, Townsville, Australia

Friday, January 1, 1943 Since I didn't start this diary until April fifteenth 42 and all pages are blank up to that date I will continue. Didn't do much of anything today. Joe Day and I played a few games of checkers this morning, ate dinner and then went to town. We have been up at the station early as we have to ride out in the country about ten miles. I worked Portland Roads circuit tonight. This radio job is getting easier all the time. I'm trying to learn to send on a "bug". I should be able to gain some speed by doing this.

Saturday, January 2, 1943 Went to town this morning. I tried to get the check cashed I received from Major Caldwell in Tyler, as the bank closed at noon and my C.O. was gone I was unable to do so. I bought a bill fold which cost me a pound & thirteen shillings ($5.40.) It is quite a good wallet but you could do better in the states for the same money. I also bought a money belt and some stamps for a collection. Was quite busy at work tonight. We moved the station back in town after work. I dident get back to camp till one thirty. I received a letter from Marian today. It rained most of the day as usual.

Sunday, January 3, 1943 Didn't do much of anything today. I thought today was my day off so I went to a show this afternoon. Something wrong with the machine so everyone had to leave before the picture was over. I went up to the station, which was then around five p.m. They said I had to work and I didn't think so, so I left. I met the M. Sgt. and he said I had to work so that was that. I am quite sure now I am going to Port Moresby in New Guinea.

Monday, January 4, 1943 Today started off the same as any other. The Sgt. gave me today off. I spent a great deal of time trying to get my check from Tyler, Texas cashed but still no soap. I went to a show tonight, even though I was pretty tired from turning out a big washing today. I received a letter from Marian today, the first one for quite a while. A fellow slept in our tent tonight. From what he said he has seen a lot of action in New Guinea. I think I will see some before long.

Tuesday, January 5, 1943 Today I got the surprise of my life. I walked into the mess hall and who should I see but Ray Flechman, Phill Evans, and Sydney Gates. When I left there I saw my old buddy and pal Ted Fredricks. We sure did have a lot to talk about. We walked down to the beach and then came back and got our swimming suits and went swimming. I was given a three day pass and told today myself and two sgt. were to go to Moresby as soon as they could get passage for us.

Wednesday, January 6, 1943 I was sure tired last night so I went to bed kinda early. Ted and I went swimming this morning and stayed in till nearly noon. There is a fenced in enclosure where you must swim as there are sharks in the water here. Ted had to relieve an operator for chow after which we went to the show. I received 2 letters from Marian today. It gives me a lot of hope to read them. I don't worry about our future, as it wouldn't help and you have to take whatever comes, just the same.

Thursday, January 7, 1943 Things are happening to me fast. It looks like this thing they call the front is going to see me by noon. I got a look at my shipping orders today and it states "advance base" and we all know what that is. The fellows look at me with that funny look that soldiers sometimes have. No one is fooling me because I know what the score is. I know this is the toughest thing that has ever faced me. I will take Marian's advice and keep my chin up. We three fellows to be shipped were moved out to Garber field today

Friday, January 8, 1943 One of my shipping mates and I went to town today. I saw Ted and Ray. Both of them say they wish they were going in my place. I bought a couple of little Australian souvenirs as I still hope to get home. We are to be shipped to Port Moresby by air. I think we are to ride in a bomber. They say it takes about 3 ½ hours to make the trip. I got my check from Tyler cashed today after spending about three days unwinding red tape. I also picked up my wrist watch. We were told to be ready to leave by 4:30 A.M. tomorrow.

New Guinea: "A Hitch in Hell"

Saturday, January 9, 1943 We were awakened at 4:30 A.M. we ate some breakfast and then loaded our barracks bags on a truck, that took us to the airport. After about an hour's wait we loaded our barracks bags into a B.17 (Flying Fortress). There were about thirty five of us. I never thought so many of us could get in, but it seemed to carry us O.K. We all had to get up in the front of the ship while taking off and landing. It was a very enjoyable trip. We traveled the distance from Townsville to Port Moresby (550 miles) in about three and a half hours. I go to work at midnight tonight, and I am pretty tired.

Sunday, January 10, 1943 I worked the busiest circuit there is at the station. I didn't have a minutes rest all night. I handled better than twenty messages. Our camp is near the beach and going swimming is a simple matter. You can sure tell everything is "all out" here. The air is full of planes. The air drone we came into had two runways better then (than) a mile a mile long. Every foot of it was required for us to land. On taking off and landing, all of us had to go forward in the ship so as to put the load in the center. With the load we must have landed around a hundred miles per hour.

Monday, January 11, 1943 Work didn't go so good tonight. I worked Brisbane and boy was that operator ever rotten. I wrote to Marian and the folks tonight. I wonder what they will think about this New Guinea business. We had an alert tonight but Tojo didn't show up. Being actually in a war zone may seem pretty bad to the folks at home, but as the value of human life is at a low ebb, and you get use to expecting to be bombed you carry on as ever without much thought of being a causality. If it comes it comes.

Tuesday, January 12, 1943 Had kind of a tough night, working Brisbane. Damn the operators who think you are no good unless you are fast. Our camp is only about a half block from the ocean and the water is as clear as drinking water. You don't dare go out very far as there are a few sharks around. Our tent has no floor in it and in case of a hard rain is likely to fill with water. I am in the same tent with some friends of mine from Tyler, who arrived here before I did. There is an old ship off shore about five miles that ran on the reefs during the last war. It is just a shell now. It has been there about 25 years.

Wednesday, January 13, 1943 We clear a lot more traffic than we did at Townsville. Taking and sending messages is a lot easier than when I first arrived here. I hear some more operators are to leave here. When they do it will sure leave us short-handed. This island (New Guinea) is quite secure now. The Japs are still holding out at Lae but they are being mopped up. A large Jap convoy tried to land reinforcements, but were repelled with heavy losses from our air craft. This island sure swarms with allied air craft.

Thursday, January 14, 1943 There were just two of us operators working last night. We sure kept busy all the time. Some of the fellows who have been here a little time were made PFC.s. It seems I should get some kind of a rating in a short time. I have been kind of sick all day. I have a bad headache and my chest is awful sore. I have no cold and I can't tell what it might be. I have been in my bunk all day unable to sleep. I ate some peaches this evening and after taking a couple of aspirins I feel a little better tonight. Just had warning of another raid 8:35 P.M.

Friday, January 15, 1943 Well I experienced my first air raid last night about 11:30 P.M. the alert sounded. I put my clothes on and waited. After about half an hour we thought nothing was going to happen, and I lay down and went to sleep. All at once I came to–when all the "ack ack" (antiaircraft guns) opened up. Between bursts you could hear the faint hum of I think one Jap bomber. He dropped one bomb which landed in the bay. He was so high up our ack ack couldn't reach him. I haven't heard from Marian or anyone up here yet. We have been married a year and seven m. today.

Saturday, January 16, 1943 The alert last night lasted about half an hour and then the all clear sounded. About ten p.m. the alert sounded again and at the same time the search lights and "ack ack" went up. You could hear some bombs falling near one of the air ports. A little later the Jap bomber was spotted in the lights. He was too high for our "ack ack" and it was disgusting how far our anti aircraft came from him. Now that it is moonlight we can expect "Tojo" nearly every night for a while. Had an alert tonight but Tojo didn't show up.

Sunday, January 17, 1943 I went to work at 5:30 last night and worked till midnight, we had an "alert" for about an hour, but no Japs. Planes came over. We do not operate during an air raid as the enemy can locate us by our signal. The Colonel came in last night and asked about us transmitting during a raid. We told him it was the General's orders that we do not, so that was that. I received fifteen letters from home today. They were post marked from September till Dec. Had an alert the middle of the night. I was asleep and didn't wake up.

Monday, January 18, 1943 Nothing much doing today. I wrote Marian a letter. I couldn't finish filling this page today as it started to rain and we all were busy trying to keep the water out of our tent of which we were unable to do. So our tent has been like a swamp. I sure had a lot of trouble with Townsville last night. I sat and argued with them for an hour. I finally wore out but it is no fun to try and operate with such a wise guy.

Tuesday, January 19, 1943 Jack's birthday today. I wrote him a letter. I hope he never has to come to a hell hole like this. I think New Guinea is rated the worst there is on earth. Some of we fellows started building a floor out of some scrap lumber this afternoon. We ran out of wood and heck knows where or when we can get any. We haven't had any raids the past few nights as it has been raining. A fellow I knew in Townsville came here from Milne Bay. Boy was he glad to get out of there.[25]

Wednesday, January 20, 1943 Didn't do much of anything all day. I was rather tired all day so I slept this afternoon. I worked Brisbane last night and got along OK with J.J. Rolings worked Townsville and boy did he ever have a time.

---

[25] Jack is my dad's brother. Milne Bay is located E Papua Japanese landing – Allied base – Japanese air attacks.

L.G. down there thinks he is good, but he isn't worth a damn. The food here is sure lousy. The only solid food we get is dark bread. Bread and apple butter is considered dessert. Once in a while we have pan cakes for breakfast which is the best meal of the day. It rained quite a lot today and tonight.

Thursday, January 21, 1943 Nothing new today. The sun has been shining and things are drying up a little. The mosquitoes are sure bad here, and they sure cause a lot of dingy and malaria fever. We are required to take quinine tablets every day as a preventive. These tablets are sure hard on you. They dull your hearing etc. I only take one about every other day. I worked Z.G. on Townsville and what a time I had. The other times I worked him he made me sore. Now I can't wait to get my hands on him.

Friday, January 22, 1943 It wouldn't be so bad here in New Guinea if the food wasn't so rotten. We had four alerts last night from midnight till morning. I was at the station for the first one. Our "ack ack" threw up a barrage, but didn't bring down any planes. There was a low overcast of clouds, which enabled the Japs to fly quite low. I had been back to camp a short time when the alert sounded again. It lasted about an hour, when we all had to grab our tin lids again.

Saturday, January 23, 1943 Everything about normal. The chow is terrible. You eat not because you want to, but because you know you have to. Usually on Friday we have sardines and beans, and bread and jelly is considered dessert. We had an alert but nothing happened. I guess it was just a Jap reconnaissance plane. We all have the feeling that the Japs are getting ready to really plaster where he is by now.

Sunday, January 24, 1943 L.G. from Townsville may try and cause me some trouble, or some of the operators. If he is crazy enough to try anything he will sure find himself in trouble. I have now been in the Army eleven months. We had an alert while I was at work, but nothing happened. After I got back from the station and had just got to bed the alert sounded again, but no soap. I had been in bed but a little longer when the "ack ack" started, but I was tired so I slept on through it.

Monday, January 25, 1943 The chow was pretty good. We had some good beef for a change. Our present Master Sgt. is to go to Sydney. I hope our new one is as good as he. We had an air raid last night that was really interesting for a little while. I was asleep and all at once the "ack ack" started in. The shrapnel started whistling over our tent, and I rolled out of my cot and lay flat on the tent floor. After a short time I grabbed my helmet and went outside. The search lights were focused on two Jap bombers. Our A.A. came close to them but no luck.

Tuesday, January 26, 1943 The same routine today. Another tent mate and myself tried moving the floor into our tent. We couldn't budge it. It will take a lot of help to move that. I have been working the Fall River Net. It is the busiest one here. It is rather tough as the other three circuits in the net all want to clear traffic at the same time. We had another air raid in the night. They spotted three Jap bombers in the lights. There was no "ack ack" used as they sent up some night fitters. I heard one of the bombers was brought down, but don't know for sure.

Wednesday, January 27, 1943 Wrote letters to Sally and Dick and Jack. It rained quite a bit today. A special news bulletin told all operators to stand by for an important announcement. It was a meeting by all high allied leaders. Roosevelt, Churchill etc. asking the axis powers for an unconditional surrender. Japan and Russia are now at war. There has been no declaration of war, but I guess that is out of date anyway: Had a rather hard night on the radio. In fact it seems I have a hard time most of the time. I dislike this operating more and more.

Thursday, January 28, 1943 Sally's birthday is today and I received a couple of letters from her including about seven more from the folks, Aunt Effie and Jack. I received two rather up to date letters from Marian. She spoke of sending me a couple of recordings- recorded that she made. I will have to figure some way to make a phonograph to play them on when they arrive. No raid tonight, however I might mention, Jap bombs destroyed one of our transports and killed five soldiers at a airport near- by. One of our [fighters], brought down one of the Japs. I worked Townsville and Ted Fredricks was on there.

Friday, January 29, 1943 Went to work at midnight tonight. We didn't have a lot to do. I played a few games of checkers with the Sgt. Russia is going to town still mopping up the Germans before Stalingrad. They have a large number of Germans trapped in the Caucasus. We are expecting the Japs to pull something pretty soon. Their air power is growing and they have a large fleet at Rabaul. We don't think New Guinea is so solid yet.

Saturday, January 30, 1943 After working all night Miller got the bright idea of putting the floor in our tent this morning, and we were to be ready for inspection. We worked liked dogs, and were just in the middle of the job, when the lieutenant and first Sgt. came in. They were dumb founded to find our cots barracks bags etc. outside the tent. It looked so bad for us they both couldn't help but laugh, so they let us go. Never let it be said that I take part in a deal like that again.

Sunday, January 31, 1943 Not much doing today. Laid around most of the time. The chow (food) here is not only no good, it is filthy. The bread has bugs baked into it, and it is not uncommon to find worms in the oat meal. It is a matter of not eating until you get so hungry you just go at it anyway. General MacArthur called our radio station by phone last night asking for some messages. (We were not able to give him the information he wanted.)

Monday, February 1, 1943 We had an alert at about 6:30 this morning. No Jap planes showed up so the all clear sounded in about half an hour. I wrote Marian and the folks today. I received a letter from David Hughes and a card from Aunt Effie and Uncle Will. The Russians are still pushing the Germans back and it is looking worse for Hitler every day. Things are rather quiet here in the southwest Pacific and also N. Africa. We are expecting the Japs to try something before long.

Tuesday, February 2, 1943 One day is very much the same as another. You sleep late in the morning on this 5 to 12 shift. You eat early chow to relieve the fellows, write some letters and then go to work. I took my watch over to the photo supply where a former watch repairman said he would see what he could do with it. They sure pulled a fast one on me at Townsville, after leaving my watch five days to be cleaned, after going in swimming with it on, they just took my fifteen shillings and gave it back to me. Now it is all rusty.

Wednesday, February 3, 1943 I spent most of my time writing letters today. I am not as hopeful of an early arrival home as I was a few months ago. When you stop to think the New Guinea and Solomon's campaigns as at a standstill, and these are only on the outer most ring of Jap captured territory, and at the most, fifty thousand on each side, it is hardly the size of an all out campaign- and time marches on.

Thursday, February 4, 1943 We spent most of the morning finishing up the floor in our tent. We were able to do so as we swiped some lumber near the radio station. There has been a lot more activity in the past couple of days. Lots of ships have been coming into the harbor and the sky is full of airplanes. A large sea battle has been going on in the Solomon Islands. No particulars have been given out on its outcome. We had an alert tonight but nothing happened.

Friday, February 5, 1943 Got up early for breakfast. It was a surprise when they had cinnamon rolls and what was more surprising they had pie for dinner. Most of the rest of the day I spent laying around. No mail again today.

Saturday, February 6, 1943 There doesn't seem to be as much traffic on the circuits in the day time. There are four of we operators working the day shift. In the past few days we have combined the Townsville and Brisbane circuits so that makes but two positions to work. Since I am the only pvt. working this shift, I haven't had much to do this shift so far. They are reviewing the station so I have been helping with that job. I am learning something of radio there and my code speed is going up all the time.

Sunday, February 7, 1943 Not much doing at work today. One can notice easily how much cut throat competition there is in army life. Everyone to some extent or other tries to get the most advantageous position. In most cases it is to get a spot that gives the best chance to get home with a whole hide. I went up to the station tonight and helped put up a new antenna. There was a show in our area tonight. This is the first show I have seen since leaving Townsville.

Monday, February 8, 1943 Not much for me to do today. I helped string some wire inside the station. The one thing that makes one more restless than ever is when you are seemingly at a standstill. Here in the Southwest Pacific it appears we are only going to hold our ground until Germany is crushed. Hell knows when we will ever get home. It looks awfully good for us on the Russian front as well as N. Africa. Four of we fellows caught a ride over to another camp area to a show tonight. While we were waiting for the show there was the most beautiful sunset I have ever seen.

Tuesday, February 9, 1943 I helped a radio maintenance Sgt. this morning with some more wiring. He explained a lot about radio. I worked the Fall River circuit this afternoon. I received my first Christmas package this afternoon from the folks. It was postmarked November 16th . Whenever a fellow gets a package from home everyone knows about it, and they all stop in hoping for a bite to eat from the U.S. The folks were smart to enclose razor blades and also a bottle of aspirin because this war is sure a headache. I turned my rifle in this evening for inspection.

Wednesday, February 10, 1943 Everything the same routine today. I am still not working much, on a circuit this week. This war business as it seems to me is not progressing to speak of here in the Southwest Pacific. It is true we have pushed the Japs out of New Guinea, but still we only have regained New Guinea and a small portion of the Solomons. In other words if the Jap conquest would be compared to a checker board we have taken back one square.

Thursday, February 11, 1943 Worked W.V.L.T. most all day but didn't handle so much traffic. We have started to insulate the radio station. Rolins, Miller and myself went up to the P.X. this evening to a show. The woman in the show- she was far from much to look at with a few teeth missing and long straggly hair, her whole personality about the same. But she was white and she was a woman, so even with no talent she went over pretty big.

Friday, February 12, 1943 The same old grind today. I worked W.V.L.T. I took the fastest speed today than I ever have. Think around eighteen words a minute. We had an air raid alert tonight but "Tojo" didn't come over. Now that the moon is coming full we can expect "Tojo" nearly every night. Boy I think we may really be plastered this time. We are preparing the radio station gas tight equipped with an air purifying device, to enable us to operate during a gas attack.

Saturday, February 13, 1943 We worked all day and being we are changing shifts to the midnight we worked also from midnight till seven. It was cloudy tonight so Tojo didn't come over. Our air force has sure been pounding Panball. We might get a heavy raid as a reprisal act. Pres. Roosevelt announced that the war in the Pacific would not be an island to island campaign. This sure gives us a lift as we all know what that would be like and how long it would take.

Sunday, February 14, 1943 The wind has been blowing hard for the past couple of days. I went to sleep on my bunk without my blanket over me and caught a bad cold. I received my first Christmas package from the folks. One of the items enclosed was a bottle of aspirin. They came in handy with my cold. Slept today and went to work tonight. I was feeling pretty punk so I came back to the tent and went to bed.

Monday, February 15, 1943 I received two more packages from home. One from the folks, one from Sally and Dick. My cold is better today but I still feel kind of punk. I laid in bed most all day and only got up for chow. The chow is improving right along. We now get pie and rolls, quite often, and beef roast. The biggest surprise was fresh eggs for breakfast. I received ten "V" mail letters of Oct. and Sept. today. Marian and I have been married a year and eight months. I need not say I wish I were home to celebrate.

Tuesday, February 16, 1943 The same old routine today. Slept all day except for getting up for meals. We had mutton for dinner. I would starve if I had that stuff every day. We had a regular cloud burst after dinner today. The water run over the dike around our tent and our floor was mostly under water. Received my first letters to this address today. Bill Brandt is in Guadalcanal only about an hour and a half by air. I may meet him yet.

Wednesday, February 17, 1943 I wrote five letters today but didn't receive any. It started to rain around noon. I waited up at the mess shack until it slackened up a bit. When I got back to the tent I had to wade in the front door. Most of our floor was under water and the dike we had around our tent was covered out of sight below the water. We were told today we are to move our tent. It will be much better in the new spot but boy what a job it will be to move our floor.

Thursday, February 18, 1943 We tackled our big job today. After getting off work at 7am we started to move our tent. We first had to make our new location level, which was no easy matter. To move our floor we had to saw it in half. The six fellows in our tent cooperate pretty well within the different steps it takes with us crowded in such close quarters. I suppose out of the six there should be one fellow not satisfactory – of which we have. While he is a soldier he is only a boy and don't understand about our tent being a small community.

Joe is second from the right

Friday, February 19, 1943 It rained quite a little bit today. It was lucky we got our tent moved. Everything else is quite normal. I handled quite a bit of traffic tonight on Fall River. The American Army is taking quite a beating in Tunisia. The Germans have driven them back some thirty miles. The Germans are still in a pocket and can't get much of any place. The Russians have recaptured Kharkov, (NE Ukraine) and Rostov, Russia, and it is looking worse for the Germans every day. There are hints even by the Germans now that they are in a grave position.

Saturday, February 20, 1943 All the way from the radio station to our camp area, they are getting precisely more military every day. They are really clamping down on sending plain language over the air. Gandhi, political leader of India, since being confined has been on a hunger strike for some time. His death, which seems at hand will no doubt cause a difficult position for the Allies in India. The news of the large production at home sometimes is disgusting. We are at a standstill here in the SW Pacific because of a small force and our army in Africa s getting shoved around. Where is all this power they talk about?

Sunday, February 21, 1943 I went up and worked around the x miter [short for transmitter] awhile this morning. Messing around there I might learn something of radio yet. As rumors go we now hear that a possible parachute attack might be made here on Moresby. Every person tries to act more calm than his frustrations, but never the less everyone is kinda jumpy. While it was too cloudy to see any of the Jap planes, from the bomb explosions there must have been half dozen.

Monday, February 22, 1943 We had quite a time at work tonight. I was working Fall River circuit and our signal captain came in. They are really enforcing the rule against plain language. I had a smart operator on the other end at WVLN and he started to shoot a lot of plain language over. I started to break him, but the Capt. Told me to let him go. The Sig. Cap, sat down and started sending to him. The fellow asked the cap. "what the Hell he thought he was doing?" The Cap. didn't tell him who he was. That guy better not have any stripes, because he will lose them. Had a short alert tonight.

Tuesday, February 23, 1943 The same routine today. I wrote the folks today. I was quite busy on Fall River circuit tonight. The situations in Africa don't look so good. If the Germans succeed in gaining enough power it may mean another trip across Libya. The rumor of parachute troops has kinda died down. I think the story is that we rather expect the Japs to pull something but don't know when or what.

Wednesday, February 24, 1943 Worked Fall River again tonight, we had quite a lot of traffic. It seems all the traffic falls on the second shift. Our Sgt. stopped me today and told me I might receive a rating in a short time. The Germans are sure giving us "H" in Tunisia. They have succeeded in taking a vital pass that is the gate way to our main supply base. The Russians are still advancing on all fronts.

Thursday, February 25, 1943 I had a record breaking night on Fall River tonight with the clearance of forty messages. Everything else normal: Port Moresby here I don't think would be much of a place even in peace time. At present it is only a military camp. Many of the buildings have been destroyed by bombs and all civilians left here long ago. As far as stores here handling merchandise there are none except our Army port exchange that handles such articles as stationery soup and candy (out of this 25 days a month).

Friday, February 26, 1943 Today was a gala day in our tent. Three fellows received a total of nine packages containing mostly cookies, candy etc. The stuff was rather stale but we all ate as much as could hold. Our chow is not so "hot" now days. It might be alright if you like mutton, there's a lot of us that can't stand the stuff. I sure had a rough time in "Fall River" tonight. That J.A. [Jack Ass] down there is sure no good.

Saturday, February 27, 1943 We all had the day off today and decided to go out to one of the airports. We caught a ride in a truck which traveled many miles along the coast. There is a lot of natural beauty to New Guinea, at least in this part. New Guinea in peace time is mainly a resort country containing a number of plantations. Most traveling is done by boat, as the mountains and dense jungle make other travel impossible: We saw many different types of bombers and transmit ships: We caught a ride to Hoki Mission to see a show tonight.

Sunday, February 28, 1943 Went to work at seven a.m. We are not so busy on the day shift, but reception is quite bad. There was a show in our area tonight. A rather old show but one I had never seen it. The Allies are doing better in Tunisia. They are shoving the Germans back to their original position. The Russian offensive is now nearly at a standstill due to early thaws: Here in the Southwest Pacific everything seems to be more of a reconnaissance nature. Our Air force bomb Rabaul, New Guinea and Lae, New Guinea quite frequently.

February 29 – This is no day as this is not a leap year

Monday, March 1, 1943 Up early and ate breakfast the same old stuff, fried powder eggs, cereal with powdered milk and bread you have to pick the bugs out of, with a substitute of peanut butter for regular butter. Dinner isn't much better as we are getting a lot of goat meat which I cannot bear. About all I eat for dinner is canned peas and carrots and soup with the usual style bread. For supper we had rice with some kind of sauce over it.

Tuesday, March 2, 1943 It has been raining most of the day. The paper and the news doesn't look so good for us here. MacArthur states that the Japs are getting to be more of a menace every day. Communiqué today of a Jap convoy headed for New Guinea. I feel a lot farther from home tonight. In case of an invasion we have no way out, and probably wouldn't leave if we did. We would probably pound the brass at the station until the last dog was hung.

Wednesday, March 3, 1943 Our aircraft found the Jap convoy a short distance from Rabaul on the island of New Britain. Due to bad weather it was almost impossible for our aircraft to intercept them. The latest report is that two out of the eighteen have been sunk. Things have been pretty quiet around Port Moresby here for some time. In fact too quiet, we rather expect a surprise blasting one of these times.

Thursday, March 4, 1943 We now have the radio shack fired up pretty well. We have the walls covered with insulation board, and our work desk covered with composition. We are having the radio fixed with six more stations. They say maybe Honolulu and Frisco may be two of them. Our station is now the most important in the S.W. Pacific. Boy, are they ever getting strict. When you operate you hold a court Marshal in one hand and the key in the other: It was reported that all of the Jap convoy, but one destroyer was sunk, a loss to them of 1,500 men. It is believed they were headed for Lae [New Guinea].

Friday, March 5, 1943 I received four letters today which makes six in the past two days, plus two snap shots of Marian. It is true when they say that letters from home is the next most important thing to food We will all be glad when the baker gets back from his furlough so we can have rolls again. The food today was pretty good. Rolins, one of my tent mates and I went for a swim this evening. We didn't stay in long as at sundown is the worst time to swim as far as sharks are concerned.

Saturday, March 6, 1943 Today we change shifts. We work today and then go to work at midnight. The battle of the Bismarck Sea is over with a loss to the Japs of a convoy of twenty two ships, only one Jap ship escaped and 15,000 Japs were drowned. During the time of the battle the sky was black with our aircraft all the way from heavy bombers to pursuit ships.

Sunday, March 7, 1943 After getting off work this morning Rolins and myself went for a swim. Our Master Sgt. has a small native type boat, called a Factory. It is barely large enough for one person. I paddled it out in the bay a ways. When I was turning around to come back the waves washed it over and down we went. Swimming back pushing the half sunken boat and with the possibility of sharks around it was quite a[n] experience.

Monday, March 8, 1943 We decided to build a raft. Another fellow and I (we'll call it found) found some empty gas drums. We have a lot of scrap lumber at the station so it didn't take us long to throw our raft together. I have gotten a little sun burned, mostly all over my body. Since you only see a woman once a week wearing a swimming suit is not necessary. We had a show at our mess hall tonight.

Tuesday, March 9, 1943 After getting off work this morning three of we fellows got a couple of long poles and pulled our raft out in the bay. We went out about three quarters of a mile a little distance beyond the reef. The water is very clear and you can see the bottom to quite a depth. The coral ocean bed is very beautiful, consisting of all colors of coral and patches of sponge now and then. We found a number of blue star fish and dove in and got a number. I was sure tired tonight when it came time to go to work.

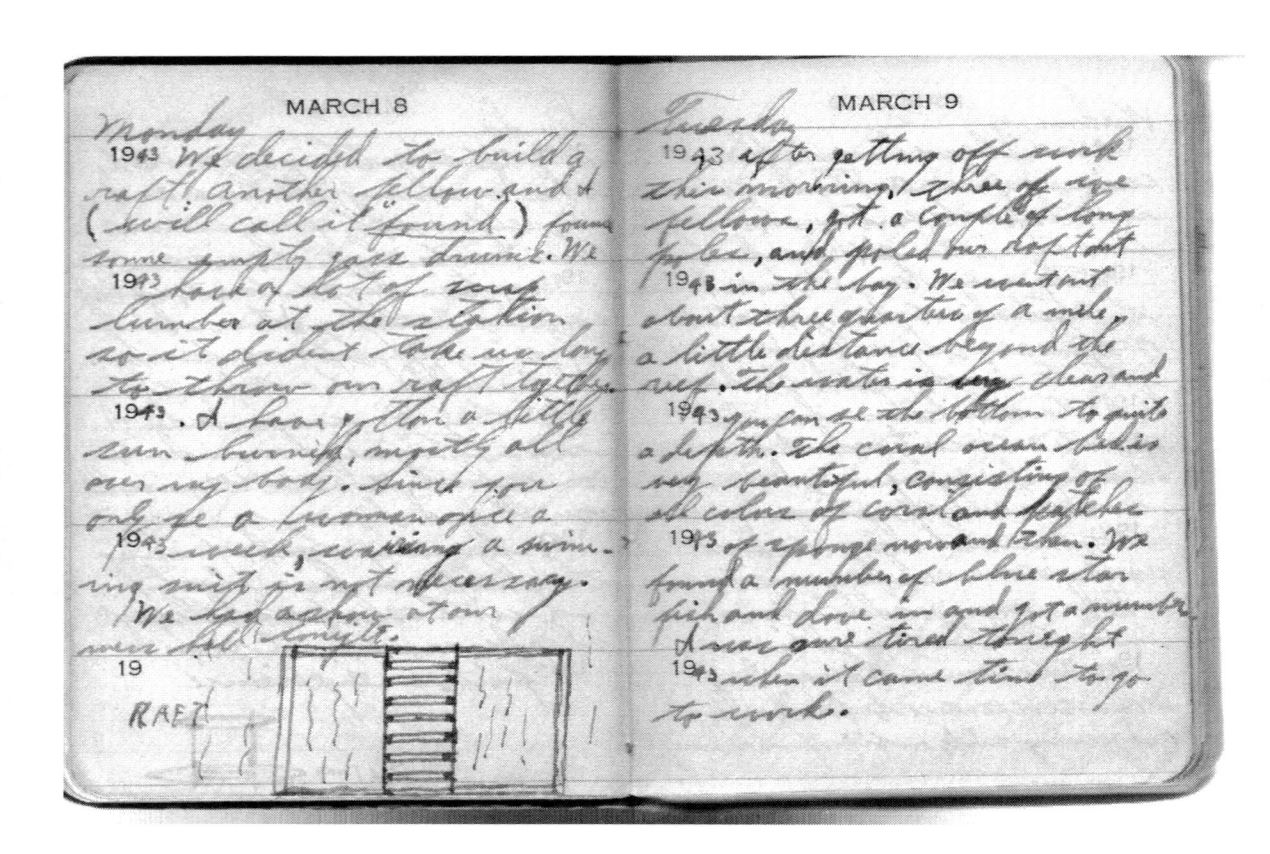

Wednesday, March 10, 1943 A bunch of fellows came up from Australia as radio operators. They have only been overseas six weeks. They were brought from Frisco to Australia by air. Most of them are Corporals. It sure gets under my hide to have to show them how to operate a circuit when I've been up here going on three months' and when I have been operating more than that long and no rating or much sign of one. There was a show at our mess hall tonight. The Germans are making a counter offensive before Kharkov [Ukraine] and gaining quite a bit of headway.

Thursday, March 11, 1943 I slept this morning and wrote letters this afternoon. Went swimming for a little while. I was told today that I just about got put on a small boat as operator. For once luck was with me and they took some other fellow. There is only one boat I ever want to see, and that is the one that takes me home. Mostly small boats are used around the coast here, as their loss is not as damaging as a large one: The German offensive seems to have been stopped for the time being at Kharkov. The Russians are driving towards Smolensk and it looks like it may fall to them. Smolensk is the German's main Russian base.

Friday, March 12, 1943 The chow was exceptional today as we had turkey of which was supposed to have been served for Christmas. This is the best meal I have had since arriving in New Guinea. I slept nearly all day and spent a little time up at the day room reading magazines. I haven't received any mail for the past few days. Just when I started to think it was coming through, it stopped: a friend and myself went down to the beach today looking for a boat some of the fellows once had. An Aussie guard yelled at us from high up on a hill to come up there. After climbing the hill he informed us we were not supposed to be there.

Saturday, March 13, 1943 Our radio shack is like a convention in a telephone booth now that the new fellows have arrived. Something is cooking. I don't think it possible but maybe some of us may get to go back to Australia. I think in my case it might be over near Burma or down at Orion Bay. We had an alert tonight. Nothing happened. It was interesting to watch these fellows fresh over from the States. I am a Pvt. but still I have to train these corporals how to operate.

Sunday, March 14, 1943 Another fellow and I went to church this morning. It was an Australian Lutheran Church. The service was very much different than what I am accustomed to. It consisted mostly of a series of prayers, and resembled quite a lot to the Catholic Church. I received some letters and photos from Marian and wrote some letters. The radio station is sure a mad house. Watching these new fellows try to take messages brings back memories of how it was with me a few months back. It is with them as it was with me. "So simple if you know how".

Monday, March 15, 1943 My mail is starting to come in again. Today I received seven letters and a box of caramels from Marian. Today we have been married a year and nine months. Everything else about the same. Headquarter Co. here is located about two blocks from the business district. That is what is left of it. Many of the buildings have been bombed out. All the other buildings are used as military offices etc. Nothing whatever in a civilian line, may be bought here. You may buy a meal at the P.X. but since their supply is limited, you might as well eat at your regular place. Nearly every meal here brings back memories of the home cooking you once had.

Tuesday, March 16, 1943 We are working the second shift now. The new fellows are beginning to handle the circuits O.K. About all I do is sit around and help out when need be. There are to be some changes made, but don't know just yet what: I received my camera and fourteen roles of film today. "Boy" I should get some good pictures with it:: The Germans are driving hard on Kharkov and it appears as if they would retake it. The Russians however are driving through Smolensk. The Americans and British in Tunisia are making some progress.

Wednesday, March 17, 1943 We have been taking instruction on the sub-machine gun the past few days: as yet Tojo hasn't come over during these moon light nights. None of us trust him though as we expect him to pull a fast one. As soon as we get the Fall River X miter working we will have four positions at the station: We received a communiqué that the American Army in Tunisia had taken Gafsa, one of the main supply bases behind the German Mareth line.

Thursday, March 18, 1943 I received some letters from Marian today. It has been reported that the Germans have taken Kharkov: It makes one feel that the war is far from being won and victory is in the balance. Our Sgt. told us today that our machine gun instruction wasn't all "hip". He said that five fellows were to be picked to go to forward base X. It looks like my number is up as I am sure in line to be moved, and just when I thought I had a chance to get back home.

Friday, March 19, 1943 I received a box of caramels today from Marian. Candy from home sure goes good here, although it is very sticky and runny on arrival. The flavor is all that counts though. It looks like maybe I may get a promotion. Our Sgt. told me today that even though I was a Pvt. I was to become a trick chief. I in this case will be boss over four corporal operators. Perhaps I will miss that special mission after all – up to X.

Saturday, March 20, 1943 Today we change shifts and therefore after relieving the fellows for chow we don't go to work till tomorrow morning. I received two more packages today from Marian - a swell fountain pen, billfold, picture holder, records and best of all a picture of Marian. Some of we fellows went out to fourteen mile air borne this afternoon. We saw many P.38s and a couple of bombers that had crashed. I got a couple of pieces as souvenirs from a crashed B26.

Sunday, March 21, 1943 I was rather late to work this morning as no one woke me up. We had a little excitement in our tent area last night. An Australian officer in a jeep run off the road and through one tent. The jeep stopped just in time as he struck a cot and rolled the fellow to the ground. One cot was ground to pieces under the jeep, but it so happened the fellow was not sleeping in it at the time: Went to the show that was in our area tonight.

Monday, March 22, 1943 I haven't been operating much lately as I have been learning the job of trick chief. The fellow who is trick chief is staff Sgt. who came with me up from Townsville. With me a Pvt. and he a Sgt. and with my chance of an equal job with him, he is doing his best to hold me back. I as yet haven't done anything but take his B.S. Conditions for Allies are looking quite bright. But it's becoming more obvious that the war is going to last a long time.

Tuesday, March 23, 1943 Well today I took all I could from that Sgt. He tried to pull a fast one on me, in regard to some plain language over the circuit. After telling him where to put his stripes I saw our chief operator and asked him to put me on another shift. Tonight I went on as trick chief on the third shift. I got along O.K. It looks like now I will miss this special assignment to station X.

Wednesday, March 24, 1943 I slept rather late this morning. This afternoon two fellows and myself went hitchhiking. One of the fellows from Fort Dodge, Iowa was trying to get information about transferring as a gunner in the air core:

We saw a fellow that one of we three knew. He said if we would come out again we could get a ride in a B25 bomber. We are sure going to take him up on that deal. We went for a little stroll down a by road near this air port: This country is very wild with dense jungle and undergrowth all over.

Thursday, March 25, 1943
I spent most of my time sleeping today. Some of the fellows are getting ready to go back to Australia and are to leave early tomorrow morning. Our tent (Ye Boars Nest) is fast changing. Two of our, bunch of six, have left and soon perhaps I will move up to the trick chief's tent. It gives me a rather sad feeling to see our bunch break up, but after all I guess you are mostly alone in this war as far as staying in one place.

Friday, March 26, 1943
Slept most of the morning. A friend and myself went swimming this afternoon. It is beginning to look like I may get a corporals rating now that I have become trick chief. This trick chief's job is quite a thing. You are the boss of the station during the shift. Naturally anything that goes wrong is your fault, and in the Army no excuses asked. The war looks pretty good at present. Even though Rommel drove the British back to some extent, the American Army is closing in above. The Russians are holding below and around Kharkov, and are closing in on Smolensk: as for us we are waiting till the Germans are whipped.

Saturday, March 27, 1943 Today was quite an eventful day. To start with when getting off work this morning I went to bed. At noon my tent mates went to chow and when getting back they woke me and I went to eat. I was down the road a little way when I missed my billfold. I came back to the tent and found my wallet on top of my mosquito net but twenty pounds, all the money I had, was gone. In U.S. money about $65.00. Our Lieutenant gave me my papers today making me a corporal. This rather helped to smooth over being robbed of my money.

Sunday, March 28, 1943 This afternoon I moved out of "The Bore's Nest" (tent) up to the chief operators tent. All of the trick chiefs, our Master Sgt. and assistant Chief operator are in the same tent. All of the old bunch has been moved and only a handful of the original bunch remain. I know my $65.00 is gone for good and it makes me sick to think of it. The war is still favoring the Allies. It looks like only a matter of time till the Germans are out of Africa. The Russians are holding the Germans in the south and are closing in on the north around Smolensk.

Monday, March 29, 1943 Everything seems to be going pretty pretty well at the station. This afternoon I and the Sgt. took a jeep and went out to the seven mile air drome. We saw a B17 come in with one motor stopped. We talked to a pursuit pilot, who had flown in combat against the Japs. A swarm of soldiers just arrived here from the U.S. You can tell they haven't been in the tropics very long as they all are white as lilies.

Tuesday, March 30, 1943 Slept late this morning. At noon, I went with our Sgt., out to the airport to pick up a fellow who came up from Fall River. Going from place to place here in New Guinea is mostly by air. We stopped at another airport on the way back and had an interesting talk with a pursuit pilot. We watched a squadron of Air Cobras come in and also a Fortress that had one motor stopped. In talking to some of the crew, they said they had been up nine hours.

Wednesday, March 31, 1943 Mother's birthday today and I wrote some letters home. A bunch of us went out to the X miter station this afternoon and fired a few rounds with a Tommy Gun. The country in this district is very beautiful, being covered with tall palm trees and grassy hills overlooking the bay. The only thing to mar its beauty is a half sunken ship that had been struck with Jap bombs.

Thursday, April 1, 1943 Nothing doing today but the same routine. I received a letter from the folks and one from Marian today. I was sorry to hear that Aunt Ella is so bad. The battle of Tunisia is in full swing. The British Eighth Army now has taken the Mareth Line and are pursuing Rommel as he retreats north. The American and French forces at and around Gabes are pushing towards the sea attempting to cut off Rommel's retreat. We are still setting tight, waiting for something to happen.

Friday, April 2, 1943 Nothing new today. I sewed my corporal stripes on my shirt. One of our fellows is rather antagonistic toward me. I think it is because I was made corporal and he only got Pvt First Class. He has been up here a lot longer than I, but has spent most of his time sitting around while I was sweating out a circuit.

Saturday, April 3, 1943 Everything as usual. Being trick chief is not such a cinch, lots of matters come up that make it complicated. It is rather interesting to hear tell about the days when it looked as if the Japs would take Port Moresby. Everyone had their packs rolled and ready to take to the hills: The Japs were coming through the pass, about thirty miles from Moresby. Many of the fellows go out there now to take pictures. The road stops within a few miles of there.

Sunday, April 4, 1943 I received some letters from Marian and the folks today, I answered some of them and will write some of them tomorrow. In Tunisia as well as well as the other fronts operative are at rather a stand still. It looks like Rommel may make another stand. His position though seems to be hopeless, although it is believed he still has a lot of striking power. The Russians are going ahead around Smolensk but rather slowly now: We still sit here in New Guinea.

Monday, April 5, 1943 No mail for me today. Our chow was pretty good today. Maybe because a fight that occurred by the mess hall yesterday between a smart K.P and another soldier. I am getting so I can copy some press, at least I can get nearly enough to tell what is coming over. Nothing new today the same old grind.

Tuesday, April 6, 1943 Not much doing today. The same old monotony. We had an air raid alert tonight. Everyone is much more jumpy now whenever there is an alert . . . everyone rather feels that when the Japs do come again we are really in for a frosting. Received a nice snap shot from Marian today. Even though I have been away from home a year now, I feel quite home sick at times.

Wednesday, April 7, 1943 Everything seemed to go wrong at work today. For a little while all our X miters were out of commission. With the job I have something like this really makes you gray-headed. We took code speed tests today. I had gained four words per min. this week, or in other words I made 22 words per minute which puts me in the upper bracket in our contest, which I am making a try to win.

Thursday, April 8, 1943 Nothing new today. Work did not go so smooth as we were off the air quite a bit with transmitter trouble. I received a letter from Marian today. She mentioned all the nice things she received for her birthday, and I didn't remember when it was. She mentioned about Jack getting a furlough. That is one thing I will probably never experience in this Army: The Germans are in head long retreat in Tunisia. It looks as if the end of the Germans in Africa is near at hand.

Friday, April 9, 1943 Received a letter from Marian today. The way her letter read about Aunt Ella's condition; she must not be alive now. I must admit I feel rather down hearted tonight. I rather imagine Marian is a little hurt because I didn't remember her birthday, even though we are giving the Germans a bad time in Africa. I feel more every day it will be a very long time until I see home again. I have the feeling things will be very much different and changed when I return home.

Saturday, April 10, 1943 Worked all day today, and as today is Sat. we change shifts and worked from midnight till morning. As there was a show in the area tonight instead of sleeping I went to the show: The tent I am now living in

95

is about a block and a half from the docks, up the hill in the center of town. My tent is in the center of an old foundation, formerly a building that received one of Tojo's remodeling jobs.

Sunday, April 11, 1943 Slept a while this morning and was up all afternoon. We had a yellow alert for about a half an hour but as usual a dry run. We have been having a number of yellow alerts (yellow is unidentified air craft). Everyone is jumpy as we are all expecting a plastering from Tojo one of these times. Rommel is in full retreat in Tunisia and his end in Africa is only seemly a matter of time. He is being pressed from all sides.

Monday, April 12, 1943 The war became very much a reality today. I slept a little while this morning and then went to dinner. On the way back, the air raid horn blew which is only a ship's horn and can easily be over looked. We nonchalantly walked up town to find a "red alert" on ("red alert" is positive enemy air craft.) In about half an hour the all clear sounded and I went to bed. I had slept a short time when one of the fellows woke me up and said the red alert was on again. This fellow and I put on our helmets and stood around and talked a little while. All in a matter of minutes our "ack ack" started bursting and high in the sky from twenty or more thousand feet we could see a large formation of Jap bomber surrounded by a swarm of zeros.

In this formation there were 26 bombers and about the same number of fighters. This formation turned and picked out our airports for a target. Our fighters in the mean time engaged and caused their formation to scatter. At the same time of this engagement a formation of new bombers came directly over our heads, at this time a bunch of fellows with myself included, were in a small muddy air raid shelter.

When the bombers had passed by we emerged to see what had taken place. A few miles away, large quantities of smoke was billowing thousands of feet into the sky from one of our oil dumps, that had been hit. This has been the first daylight raid over Moresby for eight months, and the largest raid yet to take place. The raid lasted about twenty-five minutes and a total of nearly a hundred Jap planes took part. About sixty planes were all that came into my view as some of the other formations came in another direction. For the number of planes the Japs used they caused little damage, but we did a poor job of interception as well. As it stands now this raid was not so successful for the Japs but there is no reason why they shouldn't try again. And I am sure they will.

Tuesday, April 13, 1943 Everything quiet today. Rumors of yesterday's air attack are going thick and fast. After the raid our Sgt. two lieutenants and myself took a jeep and went out to where the damage had been done. After getting a first- hand report from some of the pilots and then reading the news in the paper, the Japs are not the only liars in the world. From what we could learn, we definitely did not blunt our enemy's air strength, and they will be back and no fooling about that. At no time did I have any fear, but a person gets, without realizing it, very keyed up, and it has been hard for me to sleep very well since.

Wednesday, April 14, 1943 This finishes this diary. As the next page is where I started a year ago. Most of the record of my Army life from Feb. 24, 1942, (my day of enlistment) up until the following page of April 15 is in my other service book, "My life in the Service". I will also continue my diary in that book as it is all I have at the present.

Today looked as though we were in for another air blitz. We had two red alerts at dinner time (one of Tojo's favorite tricks) but nothing happened. I was quite sure though I saw a Jap reconnaissance plane. An Australian nearby thought likewise.[26]

Thursday, April 15, 1943 Marian has sent me a new diary but as yet it has not arrived, so I will continue in this book. Today Marian and I have been married a year and ten months. I sent her a bracelet made out of a piece of aluminum and some native photographs: Nipon [also Nippon meaning Japan] has not been back since the last big raid. But he is still pounding Oro Bay and Milne Bay. General MacArthur, Minister [John] Curtin of Australia and all high ranking officials are asking for more war materials for this part of the war. It looks if we don't get aid: we will end up in Tokyo (if we are lucky) with a Jap escort.

Friday, April 16, 1943 Everything is quite back to normal, only any illusion anyone had of us taking Rabaul from the Japs is gone. We only have hopes of holding on to what we have already taken. We feel that the Japs before long will be capable of putting an offensive equal to that of Singapore, with a possible same result unless we are reinforced very quickly.

---

[26] My father's diaries are in the form of five badly weathered small hard-backed notebooks. From here he takes up in what he is calling "My Stretch in the Service" which opens up with his entries of February 24, 1942. I have now completed entries from one book.

Saturday, April 17, 1943 Everything about the same routine now. At work tonight a Jap radio station attempted to block our signal on one of our circuits. We had a time for awhile but the Japs finally gave up. The dry season is at hand, but even though it has been raining every day. We catch the water that runs off our tent in a couple of tubs, which is very handy to wash in: Acquiring fresh water is quite a problem. Our drinking water is supplied with iodine which makes it almost unbearable to drink.

Sunday, April 18, 1943 Three of we fellows in our tent got busy today and turned out a big washing. We built a fire and boiled our clothes for a time then rinsed them and put them up to dry. We don't seem to do such a good job, but if you get them to sort of smell clean that is all that is necessary: Our Sgt. came in today with about five dozen hand grenades. He is going to show us how to use them. Who knows we may be throwing them before we know it.

Monday, April 19, 1943 Nothing much doing today so I caught up on some sleep. The war in Tunisia is at a lull as the as the Allied Armies prepare for a knockout blow. The Allies have pushed the Germans back into what they call a "coffin corner". The Germans now hold only Bizerta and Tunis as their sea ports which are constantly bombed by the Allies. In Russia there seems to be the lull before the storm. No one knows what might take place in Russia: Here in New Guinea we sit and wait.

Tuesday, April 20, 1943

Same routine today. There are many ships in the harbor now. Since the last time the Japs were over, they have stopped the practice of being a bunch of them together, but scatter them out around the harbor. For the ships to get into the harbor they come through a small channel in the reef. Port

Moresby is located on a peninsula with the harbor on one side and the ocean on the other such as:

Wednesday, April 21, 1943 Took a ride with the lieutenant and our Sgt. We had a couple of typewriters and a radio that needed repairing and left them at the Signal Repair. We also ate dinner there, which was a decided improvement over our mess. Here of late our mess has been more lousy than ever. The mess Sgt. will have to stop cooking canned dried eggs, pretty soon as he always has them to throw out. Our mess is included in two other officers mess so what we get is what they particularly don't want.

Thursday, April 22, 1943 Nothing new today the usual routine. We did though have an unusual occurrence at the radio shack today. A strange station reported into our Fall Rivers net. Saying he was testing his X miter. Our chief operator messed up this Jap's game as he sent him some procedure in the Jap "Kana code". Before the Jap thought he replied back and then seeing he had made the mistake left the air. We had a regular cloud burst tonight. Some of the sand bags around the station became soaked and fell over: Plans are being made for a new station, which will be much larger and nicer.

Friday, April 23, 1943 Nothing new today work as usual. The final Battle of North Africa is now on. Rommel's German Army has been backed up into what has been termed as "Coffin Corner", near Bizerta and Tunis. The Russians are pressing the Germans north in the Caucasus The R.A. F. [Royal Air Force] has bombed German industrial centers for over a hundred days.

Saturday, April 24, 1943 Everything about the same today at the station. Since I am changing shift I had a little spare time so an Australian friend and myself went out to the falls. This is but a short distance from the farthest advance by the Japs. Rouna Falls are very beautiful. I believe they will carry about two thirds as much water as Niagara Falls in the U.S. but they say these falls are two hundred feet high. Taking pictures at the base of the falls was very difficult, as the spray was like standing out in a cloud burst. I don't think I will ever have as rough a ride anywhere as the approximate fifty miles there and back from Moresby. Out some fifteen miles is an improved road, very rough and badly in need of smoothing off, but for this country a good road. There is twenty mile speed limit but no one ever exceeds this, as at fifteen it will jar your teeth out. Where the improved road stops is a two track stone path that winds up through the mountains. Naturally our truck takes up both tracks and many places your hair stands on end as you look thousands of feet down into valleys where humans have never been and by this route would never return. We arrived back in Moresby that evening wondering if the scenery we had seen was worth the beating we had to take. I guess it was?

Sunday, April 25, 1943 Today is Easter Sunday. As my duties require I work today. I guess I will not be able to attend services. Everything went as usual at the station. I like my job fine, but naturally it has a few draw backs. Mainly I am N.C.O. in charge of many of the fellows that started out from Tyler, Texas together. I reached Moresby a few months after some of them. I have received my rating as well as trick chief or head operator of our shift in charge of the station, since I have been here. "So".

Monday, April 26, 1943 Everything went according to schedule except Tojos, schedule yesterday. Madame Tojo made the statement that the streets of Moresby would run in blood on Easter. We all expected a heavy raid, as Tojo usually keeps such promises, but surprisingly he didn't show up. Today the same routine. Chow lousy as usual, and rained like the devil.

Tuesday, April 27, 1943 Everything as usual. My work at the station for the most part is quite interesting, but rather disgusting sometimes: My duties consist of my being in charge of the five operators as we rotate from one of three shifts each week. One of the fellows acts as clerk, the other four handle the circuits. My job is to see that contact is maintained and everything runs smoothly and efficiently: They are building a new mess hall. I hope this will mean a new food supply.

Wednesday, April 28, 1943 We had a yellow alert today. We never pay any attention to these. The red alerts are what raise "H": A friend who came up from Townsville with me, but who has been over on the other side of the island, came into the station. Conditions over there were plainly written on this fellow. He was all burned out with Malaria and with a spirit that had been crushed long ago. He is alive and that is about all you can say. A fellow, to get out of the war in this part of the world as healthy as when he came in, will certainly be lucky.

```
                    " A  HITCH IN HELL"
       I AM SITTING HERE THINKING OF THE THINGS I LEFT BEHIND
AND I WOULD HATE TO PUT ON PAPER WHAT IS RUNNING THROUGH MY MIND,
WE HAVE DUG SO MANY DITCHES CLEANED A HUNDRED MILES OF GROUND,
A NEATER PLACE THIS SIDE OF HELL I'M SURE CANNOT BE FOUND,
THERE'S A CERTAIN CONSOLATION THOUGH, SO LISTEN AS I TELL,
WHEN WE DIE WE'LL GO TO HEAVEN, "CAUSE WE'VE DONE OUR HITCH IN HELL".

       WE HAVE BUILT SO MANY KITCHENS WHERE THE COOKS CAN STEW THE BEANS,
WE HAVE STOOD A MILLION GUARD MOUNTS AND WE'VE CLEANED THE CAMP LATRINE
WE HAVE WASHED A MILLION POTS AND PEALED A MILLION SPUDS,
WE HAVE ROLLED UP MANY A BLANKET PACK AND WASHED OUR DIRTY DUDS
THE ACTUAL COUNT OF REVELLIES WE'VE STOOD IS HARD TO TELL,
IN THE HEAVEN THERE WILL BE NO REVELLIES WHEN WE'VE DONE OUR HITCH IN HELL.

       WE HAVE KILLED A MILLION ANTS AND BUGS THAT CRY OUT FOR OUR EATS,
AND SHOCKED A MILLION CENTIPEDES AND SNAKES FROM OUR DIRTY SHEETS,
WE HAVE WALKED A THOUSAND MILES AND PITCHED A MILLION CAMPS,
WE HAVE PICKED THE RODOE CACTUS FROM THE SEATS OF KHAKI PANTS,
WHEN OUR WORK ON EARTH IS FINISHED OUR FRIENDS BEHIND WILL TELL,
THOSE MEN ALL WENT TO HEAVEN, "CAUSE THEY'VE SPENT THEIR HITCH IN HELL".
                TAKEN
       WE HAVE TAKES ATABRIN DAILY THAT BITTER LITTLE PILL,
TO ELEVATE OUR SYSTEMS AGAINST THE FEVER AND THE CHILL
WE HAVE SEEN A MILLION ACK-ACK BURSTS ABOVE US IN THE SKY
AND WE RUN FOR SLIT TRENCHES WHEN THE DAISY CUTTERS FLY
"PUT OUT THOSE LIGHTS AND CIGARETTES" WE HEAR THE SERGEANT YELL
 THIS ISN'T ANY PICNIC, IT'S ANOTHER HITCH IN HELL".

       WHEN THE FINAL TAPS ARE SOUNDED AND WE SHED OUR EARTHLY CARES,
WE'LL PUT THE BEST PARADE OF ALL UPON THE GOLDEN STAIRS
THE ANGELS WILL BE THERE TO GREET US THEIR HARPS WILL GLADLY PLAY
WE'LL HEAR GABRIEL BLOW HIS HORN, AND ST. PETER PROUDLY YELL,
"FRONT SEATS YOU GUYS FROM NEW GUINEA, YOU'VE DONE YOUR HITCH IN HELL".
                    PHILIPPINES
```

Thursday, April 29, 1943 Our Master Sgt. is a very likable fellow, and if I could stick with him I am sure I could go places. His temper is quick to act, and even though he may approve of your ability one day, it will be changed the next. He has no favorites and is just one of the boys around the gang. He spent much time in the Philippines and was one of the last to leave Battan before its fall. It is interesting to listen to his experiences but are a little on the exaggerated side. I hit the jack pot on mail today.

Friday, April 30, 1943 Everything as usual: After you have been here for six months you are supposed to be relieved and sent back south. I have spent four months here. Up to now I have been above average in health and have held my weight. In the past couple of weeks I have felt like I am starting to slip. My feet are starting to give me a lot of trouble, of which most fellows are bothered. Even walking to chow is tiring and painful.

Saturday, May 1, 1943 We change shifts today. Everything is quiet here in New Guinea. (Too damn quiet.) While everyone is rejoicing about the success in

Tunisia, Tojo is all set to give us a pasting. Boy we are in a hot spot here. If they wait until the Japs strike to send us supplies, well then they might as well forget about New Guinea, the Solomon's and a good chance Australia – not to speak of all Australians and Americans that had hopes of getting home some day.

Sunday, May 2, 1943 I slept till noon today after working last night. This afternoon I helped our Sgt. put in some electric wiring in the Papupan Hotel. Boy how they do build the buildings in this country. No two pieces of lumber are the same size and no one seems to care how they are put together. Any buildings in the country are built quite light and flimsy. The windows are built something on the order of shutters. You can count on one hand the number of first class buildings left in Moresby. I Stood out in the rain tonight to see a show. Something went wrong so they called it off after I was soaked.

Monday, May 3, 1943 Nothing much new today. Reception on our shift is certainly poor. Almost all our stations fade out. Well today was the last day of our code improvement contest. Another fellow and I are tied for first place. He put up a squawk though so we are to take our test over again tomorrow. The prize is ten pounds or $32.70. The battle of Tunisia is progressing in favor of the Allies. The American, French, and British forces are steadily but slowly pushing the Germans back to Tunis and Bizerta and the sea.

Tuesday, May 4 1943 Nothing much doing today. Had a bad night at the station with all but one station fading out: Went up to the station today to finish the test. The fellow who was not satisfied didn't do as good today as yesterday. I didn't either for that matter. There are still three fellows left to take the test and if everything goes O.K. I will tie for first. I am feeling O.K. but I am starting to look forward to going back south in two months.

Wednesday, May 5, 1943 The same routine today. Slept this morning and wrote some letters this afternoon. There was a show in our tent area tonight. It was a double feature. One of them was "Star Spangled Rhythm." The show we were to see the other night that got rained out of. The other feature was a swell picture with Greer Garson. Well I can't remember the name now. When we have shows some of the fellows bring chairs, but mostly you sit on whatever you can find.

Thursday, May 6, 1943 Nothing new today. It seems I am busy as the devil now days. I went to a new frequency tonight that I hadn't tried before. It didn't seem to help matters much: The battle of Tunisia and North Africa is now in full fury. The American and French forces are closing in on the naval base of Bizerta and the British are but a short distance from Tunis. The end of Germany in Africa is near at hand: Russians have started an offensive in the Caucasus and are making good headway.

Friday, May 7, 1943 The weather is starting to clear a little. For the past weeks it has been raining most of the time. I feel as though something big is about to take place here in the Southwest Pacific. Now would be the ideal time for the Japs to strike, while most of the attention is centered in N. Africa. We are expecting a gas attack on a large scale from the Japs at any time. It is a fact that they have made extensive plans for chemical warfare and with us unprepared as usual, would be, no doubt, very effective.

Saturday, May 8, 1943 The news that Bezerta and Tunis in Tunisia have fallen to the Allies, came through today. We have expected their downfall but we didn't expect the Germans to lose their cities so quickly. This means the end of the Axis in North Africa. All that is left for the Allies to accomplish in Tunisia is mopping up operations. The Germans are trying to evacuate their forces, but with the Allied air superiority, and the British fleet in the Mediterranean it is hopeless for them.

Sunday, May 9, 1943 Everything quiet as usual around here today. Today is Mother's Day, but all I can do is remember it this year. My mail has sure hit a blind spot. I have received hardly any in the past two weeks. I laid around most all day and went to work as usual at five thirty. Took some pictures this afternoon and left them with an Australian friend to be developed.

Monday, May 10, 1943 Up early this morning and went down to the Papa Hotel to do some extra work. I painted a table and then came back to the tent as I sure feel punk today. We had a red alert this noon. Everyone thought we were in for another bad raid. I got my tin lid, gas mask and camera. We all feel that in a short time the Japs may try and gas us out of here. I might get some interesting pictures. The red alert went off in a short time. I guess there was a Jap reconnaissance plane over.

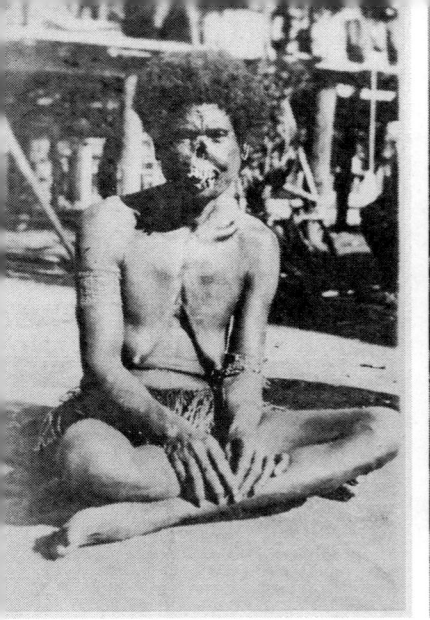

Tuesday, May 11, 1943 Went down to the Pawpaw Hotel this morning and put another coat of paint on the table I painted yesterday. Our Commanding Officer is back and he raised holy heck with our Sgt. Our Sgt. raised holy heck with we trick chiefs (one resigned) and as for the "hell" I caught I dished it out to the operators on my shift. I guess the operators dislike me to quite an extent now. I know I have been right in making my decisions and the fact that the operators hate our Sgt. I will still carry out his orders. The operators on the other shift practically run the Trick Chief off the job, and I think it is clear to my bunch where we stand. The operators only have one point in mind. That is not how much good they can do while here in New Guinea but how soon they can get back to Australia: I received a letter and a package from Marian. Also a bunch of newspaper clippings from the folks of the surprising news that Steamboat Rock High School won the state B.B. Tournament.

Wednesday, May 12, 1943 We had a red alert today. Tojo didn't show up. All clear in about thirty minutes. Had quite a rhow* with one of the operators at work tonight. It was a case of [him] just not giving a damn. Things don't go too smoothly as the operators don't like the orders our Sgt. puts out, and has it in for a trick chief that tries to enforce them: Our chow has improved somewhat of late. I hope when the new mess hall is finished the chow will be an improvement also.[27]

Thursday, May 13, 1943 After our Sgt. having a talk with the boys we all know more where we stand. I guess I rode the fellows pretty hard sometimes, but if they didn't wish to work on their own well the Army has ways to deal with them. Every-

---

[27] Rhow A.K.A. row is another word for heated argument – my dad used this word a lot when I was growing up.

thing went fine at work tonight. We had two red alerts. On the first one there were Jap planes over fourteen-mile airdrome. On the second one no Japs were around that I know of: Operations have ceased in Tunisia with victory for the Allies.

Friday, May 14, 1943 Same routine. Wrote some letters, didn't received any. I felt sure we would have a raid tonight as it is moonlight and quite clear. I took my gas mask and helmet to the station with me tonight, but Tojo didn't show up. We did have a yellow alert for a short time but that is all: A friend of mine just back from Porlock Harbor [A.K.A. Porlock Bay in the ORO Province] told me that about thirty Japs were killed around there after the Bismarck Sea battle. They held three Jap prisoners at the station for a time.

Saturday, May 15, 1943 Today Marian and I have been married a year and eleven months. I don't have to work today, as I change shifts and go to work tomorrow morning. Went to the show tonight in the Hq. tent area tonight. The show you might say was a double feature as we would have to stop our show while the Japs put on a side attraction: The Jap planes were practically over us before anyone knew they were around. The first flight dropped flares over the American docks and released some red flares of which no one seemed to know the purpose. It is bright moonlight and a perfect night for them to raid; with high floating clouds for them to hide in. The flares they dropped looked like a large electric light as it floated down attached to a parachute, lighting up more than ever the whole countryside. Everyone watching the show felt pretty safe by just staying in their place sitting on the chairs or boxes that they had brought along to watch the show. Suddenly a large explosion a short distance away and five hundred or more soldiers fell to the ground like a bunch of dominoes. I ran across the road and lay down on the edge of a sand pile that had been placed there for the purpose of making cement for the new mess hall. High over head we could see two Jap planes circling back over to the harbor, as our search lights followed them. Since the show I had come to see wasn't running anyway, I went back up town, got my tin lid, gas mask and went up to the radio station, behind the comparative safety of the sand bags.

Sunday, May 16, 1943 Nothing unusual today. I heard today that one of the flares that we thought did not work properly when the Japs were over was a Jap bomber that was shot down in flames. It is a full moon now and we can expect to see a lot of Tojo. He is pretty tricky. He tries to throw you off the track by showing up when you least expect it. We are expecting him anytime though.

Monday, May 17, 1943 We had a red alert today. It lasted for about an hour and a half. We thought sure we were in for another heavy daylight raid. Our air force though turned them back before they got here. We also had a red alert tonight but Tojo didn't come over. Just one of his tricks knowing that on such a swell night for him it was a surprise when he didn't come.

Tuesday, May 18, 1943 Everything quiet tonight. The moon shown bright as day but the Japs didn't show up, so we all got a good night's sleep: Reports came through today that the hospital ship "Centaur" was sunk about thirty miles from Brisbane. Two hundred ninety nine lives were lost. The Japs have started a submarine offensive off of the Australian Coast, and have so far sunk about four or five ships.[28]

Wednesday, May 19, 1943 There are radio operators arriving up here every day. Conditions are certainly going to change. We are making large preparations for something but it is hard to tell what: It rained almost all night so Tojo didn't come over. The unrest in Italy since the battle of Tunisia is growing. There are rumors of Italy signing a separate piece. At any rate, the Italians are expecting to be invaded at any time, we the Allied Air Force are bombing Italian targets.[29]

Thursday, May 20, 1943 The building of an entire new station is now in progress. From reports I have heard, when finished it will be the hub of communications in the Southwest Pacific and Far East. It will be net control for Chungking, China, India, Australia, Hawaiian, Islands, etc. This will be one of the largest stations the U.S. Army has. We will have an area of two hundred men. Our layout will cost millions of dollars, and will be a small town within itself having our own mess hall, barracks generating plants, transmitter, receiving stations and service shops.

Friday, May 21, 1943 Last night was very clear and we had every reason to expect a visit from the Japs. We turned our receivers to an air raid warning station and sure enough in a short time there was a yellow alert and a short time later it turned red meaning a raid in progress. We told our station to expect a red

---

[28] The Centaur Hospital Ship was torpedoed by the Japs on May 14 Off of North Stradbroke Island, Queensland. It is fascinating to find facts about the events my dad writes about in his journals.

[29] My father may be speaking of the Attu and Kiska Campaigns.

alert signal in a very short time before they received the warning through regular channels. Did the fellows at the station ever ask us a lot of questions? Of course we acted wise and didn't tell them. We received the warning about ten minutes before the town was warned. Well the red alert lasted about an hour, and perfect as the night was the Japs did not come. I went to bed about midnight and woke up about 2:30 A.M. when our emergency power unit was started, which usually means a raid. We called the station and the trick chief on duty – said there was a fire at the power house. Over in that direction the sky was red. The chief operator and I went down to the power house to see the fire. When we arrived there the whole place was in flames. One of the most impressive things of the fire was the poor firefighting equipment there. What I had formally thought was just secondary equipment turned out to be the sum total of the whole thing – nothing more or less than large steel tubs mounted between two wheels to enable them to be moved from place to place. One of these units being pulled behind a truck lost a wheel so from there on to the fire it was drug. Maybe the Aussies know what they are doing, but we Americans ask the question "Why not a fire truck equipped with rotary pumps, for such purpose, with the ocean so near- by? But since we are in Aussie territory, they do the thinking and we get the pushing around.

To save the power plant was of vital importance, but more important was to put out the fire so the Japs would not have it to use as a target. Everyone worked like fury to put the fire out. The power house was totally destroyed. How the fire really started no one knows. One rumor says one thing another something else. Seems very peculiar that last week an oil drum should catch fire mysteriously, and now the power house.[30]

---

[30] Where this diary is bound together my mother has written a note; "Been away one year four

107

Saturday, May 22, 1943 Change shifts tonight. In other words work all day and then go to work at midnight. There was a show in the area tonight but the machine broke down and so no show. It looks like perhaps with a little luck I may get a good spot out at our new station. If this should pan out, I would probably get a Staff Sgt. rating. Here is hoping. When I think of the responsibility of trick chief of the most important and elaborate radio station in the South West Pacific – "WOW" Someone has to have the job and if they think I should be one of them, O.K. by me.

Sunday, May 23, 1943 Since I have tonight off. my first full-fledged day off in five months. I decided to do my washing. A month's supply. This took me nearly all day: Tonight we had somewhat of an uneventful air raid. At about 2:30 a.m. we woke up when the air raid horn blew. We put on our clothes, got our gas masks and helmets, then went to the station. By the time we had dressed one of our night fighters took off and was climbing as much altitude as he could get. As I understand the type of aircraft being used for this purpose is a Douglas Boston bomber or A20A. It was only a matter of minutes until the hum of its' motors could no longer be heard. In a short time our ack ack started firing and two Jap bombers could be seen in the search lights. They were about as low as I have ever seen them. No more than eight or nine thousand feet. Our ack ack fired at them wide. I think acting as a decoy. While our night fighter got in position to dive on them. When our night fighter made the first pass the Japs dumped their bombs in the bay a short distance away and beat it out to sea.

Monday, May 24, 1943 Nothing out of the ordinary today. At this time of year the winter months are at hand there is very little change of temperature and the only difference in the weather is very dry and windy. Most of the mosquitoes disappear: Something is about ready to take place in the South West Pacific. I some times wonder if the second front they talk about won't take place here. An all out drive against the Japs would certainly catch them off balance, as they think we haven't a chance, and for them the war is over and done.

Tuesday, May 25, 1943 After working last night I slept this morning. It was a swell moonlight night but no Japs came over. This afternoon a Sgt., a friend and myself took a ride out in the country to see a Liberator or B 24 that had

---

months and one day. Still going strong Honey. Honey, I'll always love you."

crashed. All of a crew of ten was killed. The pilot had evidently lost his bearings and thought he was on the approach to the field but instead came in low down the wrong valley. As the ship came near the ground it struck on top of a hill and bouncing over and down the opposite side. It passed through a tent killing two soldiers asleep there.

On the first impact the ship must have caught fire. After going down the hill and on reaching the bottom it crashed a solid blow into the ground, which scattered the airplane in pieces not much larger than a saucer in an area hundreds of yards. All, at this point, that was recognizable was part of one wing, part of the tail and the crumpled fuselage. One of the engines flew off its mountings about fifty yards. The fuselage came to rest in the road where other wreckage was strung. To clear the road it required a number of trucks with a crew of men with shovels and brooms. All in, parts of the plane were strung out over a distance of half a mile. I took a parachute ring I found back to town that had a number of burnt shroud lines attached. Too bad this chute was never used: On the way back we stopped at the hospital to see one of our fellows who had a cancer taken off his face. On his ward were fellows with broken legs and arms. Some of them had been shot up.

Wednesday, May 26, 1943 Just another routine day today. From what I hear our new station is going to be a super affair. I have a good chance of becoming one of the trick chiefs, when the station is ready to go into service. While I am glad for the job in one way, I will have two strikes against me at the start. As I know a lot of tech and Master Sergeants will be against me. Our Master Sgt. may leave Moresby in the near future and take some of we fellows with him. I rather hope to be one of them.

Thursday, May 27, 1943 Nothing unusual today, worked last night and slept most of the morning. When on this shift I sleep mornings- up till after supper and then sleep till midnight: There is five of us in our tent. If we had a few rations and sandbags we could hold off an army. We each have a rifle also access to a sub machine gun. Our Sgt. has two pistols, some trench mortars and about fifty hand grenades.

Friday, May 28, 1943 Have been very busy lately. Seems I hardly have time to write letters home. My job is going O.K. One thing, and that is with the way our Sgt. runs things you will have a good job one day and busted the next. I figure I have done quite well. I have held this job now for two months or longer. Tomorrow I may be nothing, for a reason that no one but our Sgt. could figure out.

Saturday, May 29, 1943 Today I packed up my bunk clothes etc. to spend a week at the transmitting station, to get some experience on transmitters. I had no sooner arrived there than our Sgt. called up and told me I would have to come back to town as some fellows were to be shipped out. I stayed there tonight, but I will have to take over my shift tomorrow.

Sunday, May 30, 1943 I didn't work my 5 P.M. shift, but worked the day shift as trick chief today. Tonight, at around eight o'clock the commercial power went off. We thought at first an air raid was on but when we went outside the tent, the sky was red and a large fire had started across the bay. As it started to become larger we could tell the fire was at the native village. This village is quite near one of the oil dumps and it seemed for a time the fire would sweep through this oil supply. This native village has somewhere around seventy five huts all being built of grass and poles. The entire village was a pile of cinders in not more than an hour. From our view which was a couple of miles from the village but in a direct line across the harbor we could see the flames shoot hundreds of feet into the air. As we were watching the fire a flare was shot skyward a short distance down the beach. In a week more damage has been done by Tojo's ground staff than by his air force in the past six months.

Monday, May 31, 1943 Things are certainly taking a big change around here. We are going to start using another set of procedure signals, which will be a headache all over again. We were just getting to the place where we had the others down pretty well. At present some of the stations are using one thing and we another, which really mixes things up. Nothing else new. No more fires (yet). The native village was burned to a crisp.

Tuesday, June 1, 1943 Everything is more or less normal except the natives are now living in G.I.

tents. Perhaps the native village burning down wasn't so bad after all. There wasn't a filthier place in the world and it seemed you could smell the place for a mile. Everything is at more or less a standstill in all war theaters except for the terrific bombing the British and Americans are giving the Germans from England and Tunisia. There is much talk about an invasion and the Germans and the Italians seem quite worried.

Wednesday, June 2, 1943 They say in two weeks we will move out to our new location. I rather think it will be longer than that though. My name was put in for Staff Sergeant rating for a possible trick chief job at the new station. However, the rating hasn't gone through as at the present no vacancies. I for myself am not building my hopes for anything as the Army has so many ways of changing its' plans.

Thursday, June 3, 1943 Nothing unusual going on. More or less we sit and wait. I got a look at the new 832 radio lay out. Moresby will be the main hub and be by far the largest station in the S.W. Pacific. There were also some possible stations marked out such as Rabaul. It seems the coal miners back in the states or at least Lewis* thinks they are having a tough time. He is too old to act like a kid so he must be a NR 5 member. At any rate Lewis has ordered a strike against Roosevelt's wishes and the government. Had a red alert today, but not Japs.[31]

Friday, June 4, 1943 This week has been very much routine. I have written more letters than usual and have also received a good many. We have had to use our emergency power unit to quite an extent since the power house burned, which causes very much interference in our radio reception. Had a yellow alert today. I heard that a Jap reconnaissance plane was shot down near- by yesterday.

Saturday, June 5, 1943 Today has been a long day as I worked the first shift from 7 A.M. to 5 P.M. and then started the new shift on third shift from 11:30 P.M. till 7 A.M. We have been handling more traffic than usual in the past two weeks. Being that all effort is concentrated on the new station, maintenance on this one is going downhill, with this and that going wrong which results in many service messages regarding keeping contact, which is impossible.

---

[31] My dad is referring to John L. Lewis, who was President and thoroughly in control of the Coal Miner's Union in from 1920 to 1960.

Sunday, June 6, 1943 Slept up until noon then went down to the post office and to chow. I went with our Sgt. out to the new radio site. It is going to be quite a large place, and has a swell location. It is about five miles from Moresby, but if I never get into town. I won't mind as this is but an army camp or reservation anyway. The new station is only about two hundred yards from the bay and a few miles away are the mountains where hunting should be quite good.

Monday, June 7, 1943 It is the dark of the moon now so we shouldn't expect Tojo to fly over until another week. Everything is the same routine; except we are handling about twice as much traffic as before. The Allied forces in North Africa and England are keeping up continuous bombing of Italy and Germany. The Eder Dam in the Ruhr Valley Germany has been blasted away by air and the flood waters from it have caused much damage.[32]

Tuesday, June 8, 1943 Another routine day. I heard that one of our fellows who has been here in New Guinea over six months asked to be shipped back south, which has been the usual practice after six months service up here. They gave him no reason but told him there wasn't a chance. Anyone can guess that with the personnel needed for the new station, no one will be moved from here.

Wednesday, June 9, 1943 Our Signal Officer is trying to get we trick chiefs ratings that will entitle us to the same job at the new station. He has asked for Staff Sergeant's ratings for us but I heard that he was informed that there are no ratings as this to be had. Perhaps, and it is a good possibility, I will be just an operator. If I do go back to operating after a time, I will have a good chance to go back south.

Thursday, June 10, 1943 As far as we are concerned everything is about the same except we are handling more traffic. It is easy to see that much enforcement is being brought in. It is beginning to look like an invasion on Europe will take place at any time. Germany as well as Italy is taking an awful beating from the Allied Air Force. Since German's defeat in Africa they have turned to the defensive.

---

[32] About this raid conducted by the RAF May 16 & 17, 1943. The missions were tagged "Operation Chastise" which bombed German Dams. The one my father is referring to is the Eder Dam, one of three in the Ruhr Valley. In total 1,294 people drowned and 53 airmen were killed with 3 taken prisoner. These men were later called the "Dambusters." The Eder Dam was and is the largest dam in Europe.

Friday, June 11, 1943 Worked as usual last night. Traffic is becoming heavier and heavier on all circuits. Something is no doubt cooking here in the S.W. Pacific. Today I had quite a surprise. Our Signal Officer came into our tent with the news that four fellows were to be Sergeants, of which I am one. This will mean quite an increase in pay. I went to the show tonight before work and there for I only received about two hours of sleep today.

Saturday, June 12, 1943 Well today is my birthday. For my birthday dinner we had B&B (Bully beef and beans) as usual. The chow in our mess has been pretty bad for the last month. This morning I packed up my clothes, bunk, & etc. and came out to the transmitter station. The intention is that I am to be here a week, unless they call up for me to come back with the purpose of learning something about transmitters. There is very little to do out here and so it will be kind of a rest in which I am in need of.

Sunday, June 13, 1943 There is not so much to do out here. All that has to be done is change frequency on the transmitter a couple times a day which takes about ten minutes. This job I am learning to do, which is not so complicated as long as you have a chart to go by. The chow out here is decidedly better than at our place in town. Out here they make an effort to prepare the food so you can halfway enjoy eating it, where as in town they are only as good as their best can opener, and I think more of the food there is thrown away than eaten.

Tonight Tojo paid us a little visit. About 8:30 P.M. the red alert sounded. We turned out the lights. The sky was very cloudy and it was apparent that the Nips would have to wait until the clouds broke up to be able to see their target. In about half an hour the sky cleared and our search lights started searching the sky. In a short time two Jap planes could be seen in the search lights. By this time our ack ack was putting a barrage up around the Jap planes. Their objective apparently was the American docks across the bay, but their bombs missed by a mile and landed in the native village that had burned down. Had the nips flown over the docks in this direction, dropping their bombs in the same way, where they would have landed would have been close to our back yard. As the Japs came over our area a "ack ack" gun about a hundred or more yards away started blazing away, which shook the ground on every explosion. With the danger of falling shrapnel offers, we went down the road to one of the transmitter shacks which is surrounded by sandbags. The Japs always try to pull the unexpected. Very seldom, even with conditions in their favor, will they come over two nights in a row. We should have a number of visits from them now that it is a full moon.

Monday, June 14, 1943 Today is dad's birthday. It is at times such as this that I wish more than ever to be home. There isn't much to do here at the transmitters. We lay around most of the time and change frequencies on the transmitters twice a day, which I am learning how to do. We got in the jeep tonight and went over to a show. This show, as are all of them, was in the open with a sheet for a screen and the machine on some boxes or in the back of a truck.

Tuesday, June 15 ,1943 Today is our second wedding anniversary. Marian and I so far have been apart for our first and second anniversaries. The two years we have been married I have spent twice the length of time in the Army, that we have been together and had our home. I wrote a long letter to Marian today and spent most of the time on my bunk. We had a red alert this morning for about an hour. From where we are you can see many anti-aircraft batteries. No nip planes came over.

Wednesday, June 16, 1943 Three of us climbed on a truck this morning and went after sixteen drums of gas. There are many gas dumps around here, however, the one we received our gas (Australians call gasoline "petrol") at was quite a distance: Since I haven't been through this area for a couple of months the change that this area has taken is appalling. New roads going through the hill here and there. Many new supply dumps, and units. Moresby and area is as much changed in the past six months as night and day: Three of us climbed into the jeep tonight and went up to "death valley" (called by this name as, due to the position of the anti-aircraft guns and when in action shrapnel falls like rain) to a show. I, in my own mind had a nice place picked for cover in case Tojo should come over. However we watched the show without incident, as the sky was covered by a heavy overcast and no good for Tojo.

Thursday June 17, 1943 Didn't do much all day. Received some letters from Marian and the folks and also wrote some: Sgt. Papenburg and myself went to town tonight to attend a meeting in regard to forming a joint Australian and American Sergeant's club as it should give the members a good advantage in acquiring a few luxuries in food that is impossible to get at the present. The amending of reselections the election of officers, etc. took a long time and was very boring and only came to a close when the air raid horn blew and the lights went out. We however finished the election of officers by flash light. When we got outside we could see two Jap planes in the intersection of the search light beams, with the "ack ack" bursting around them. We could hear the thud and flash of bombs over the hills. The Japs soon faded from view. In a matter of minutes the search lights were focused on two more Jap planes coming in from the ocean on the south. They looked to be a few thousand feet lower than the first and our "ack ack" was seemingly bursting very close to them. They made a wide circle over one of our air drones and then started back in our direction. I quickly went to the radio station that is protected by a wall of sand bags. Only a very near miss or direct hit would _ _ _ _ _ _ _ : The Japs however turned and started in the direction of the American docks. All of this time our "ack ack" was putting up a terrific barrage and it was hard to see how the Japs could go through. As the Jap planes went over head, we could notice that one of them was losing altitude and farther over the bay. Some said smoke could be seen streaming from the Jap plane. Whether or not the Jap plane crashed we do not know, but in all probability it never reached its' base: Our Commanding officer in the mean time called me from the small ship section at the American docks and said he was unable to get away from the docks as his jeep had a flat tire. Even though the air raid had not been sounded all clear, we started out in the jeep for the American docks, driving without lights. However it was bright moon light and we could see fairly well. The road is far from being improved and some places the driving is very hazardous. Driving across the causeway that joins the mainland with the island on which the American docks are located was the worst of all, as a heavy sea had made the road very muddy and driving without lights didn't help. We found our lieutenant and brought him out to the transmitter station. I was very tired and went to bed.

Friday, June 18, 1943 Got up early this morning and changed the frequency on the transmitters. Didn't do much all day. The moon was out very bright tonight, but we could hear our night fighters flying around nearly all night waiting for the Japs to show up. The Japs however didn't decide to come over.

Saturday, June 19, 1943 Our Sergeant came out today, and the Sergeant here, he and myself went out to the new receiver location. Quite a number of buildings are ready but there is an awful lot to do as yet. It looks as though it will be another month before it is ready so we can move. We went up to the Signal Repair Station to a show tonight. To show that almost anything can happen, a fellow came into our tent tonight that came in A.W.O.L. from Sidney. One way I can see why he wouldn't like Sidney, but on the other hand why would he think this "hell" hole is any better?

Sunday, June 20, 1943 I got my stuff together and moved back to town today. Naturally a fellow can't learn much about transmitters in a week, but the rest certainly has made me feel better. Sometimes you feel you won't Sometimes you feel you be able to make the route. It was bright moon light tonight but Tojo didn't come over.

Monday, June 21, 1943 Went to work this morning on first shift. I am going to operate until the new station opens. I am getting quite rusty on code. My code speed hasn't dropped but I am not as accurate as I have been. Went to bed as usual tonight but had to get up again around midnight as the air raid horn blew. We stayed up for about an hour until the all clear sounded and then went back to bed.

Monday, June 22, 1943 From the number of messages I took yesterday, my code is about back to normal in fact I think I am some faster than I was. With good sending on a bug I can do nearly twenty five words per min. In order to gain more speed I will have to copy some press station at around thirty words per min. as the speed our circuits work at are slower than twenty words per min: The Allied Armies in N. Africa are now starting an air blitz and offensive against Sicily and Sardinia. The Allies have warned the Italian people to move away from military objectives in Italy.

Tuesday, June 23, 1943 Put a bunch of my clothes to soak today. Being it gets dark shortly after getting off work, while on the first shift, it is hard to guess when I will be able to finish the large washing I have: I heard today that one of our reconnaissance planes by chance discovered a formation of seventeen Jap bombers headed this way. After calling for help our P38, it was reported, shot down the bunch.

Thursday, June 24, 1943 Nothing new the same old grind. I am getting pretty well fed up with everything. Even the thought of the new station doesn't arouse my enthusiasm. At one time my ambition was at a high pitch. All my hard work did bring lasting results to a good advantage, without thanks. I became a corporal whose main task is to carry out orders, handed down from a senior non-com even if they are good or bad. In my case when I carried out the orders but when the time came for the support I had been promised our chief operator never came through. A double cross is a common occurrence in the Army;

however you never give it much thought. From the chief operator's stand point he wanted the good will of the bunch involved and so I took it on the chin and never said anything as he holds the cards. By keeping still I did get another stripe to Sergeant.

Friday, June 25, 1943 Nothing new today. We still sit here in New Guinea while they bomb Germany. Perhaps the slogan "Golden Gate in 48" isn't so far wrong. Went to the show tonight before finishing the last line we fellows had a half hours bull session on our hellish boat ride from the states, and how bad we hate the Army.

Saturday, June 26, 1943 Today has been our long day. We worked all day and then changed shifts to the midnight shift tonight. I received a letter today from Marian with a newspaper clipping with her picture along with an article written all about a hunting knife I had asked Marian to send me. According to the article all there is to hunt in this country is Japs. It looks like I will have to make a trip over to Wau [in NE New Guinea] to get a Jap scalp before I can go home. I received news the other day that an Australian friend of mine was killed over at Wau while on patrol.

Sunday, June 27, 1943 Our regular chief operator Master Sgt. Meszer is going to move out to the new location to do some wiring on the new station. A tech Sergeant will be in charge here while he is gone. This fellow just arrived here from the states a short time ago. With our regular sergeant gone we will get a rest from the "Battle of Bataan" that we have been hearing the past five months.

Monday, June 28, 1943 Now that our Sgt. is gone we have our tent cleaned up for a change. We have exterminated most of the ants that were about ready to walk off with the place. I am getting more fed up with the war, Port Moresby and everything in general. I hope when the new station gets started we will be relieved and sent back to Australia. Moresby is like being stuck in without a pass.

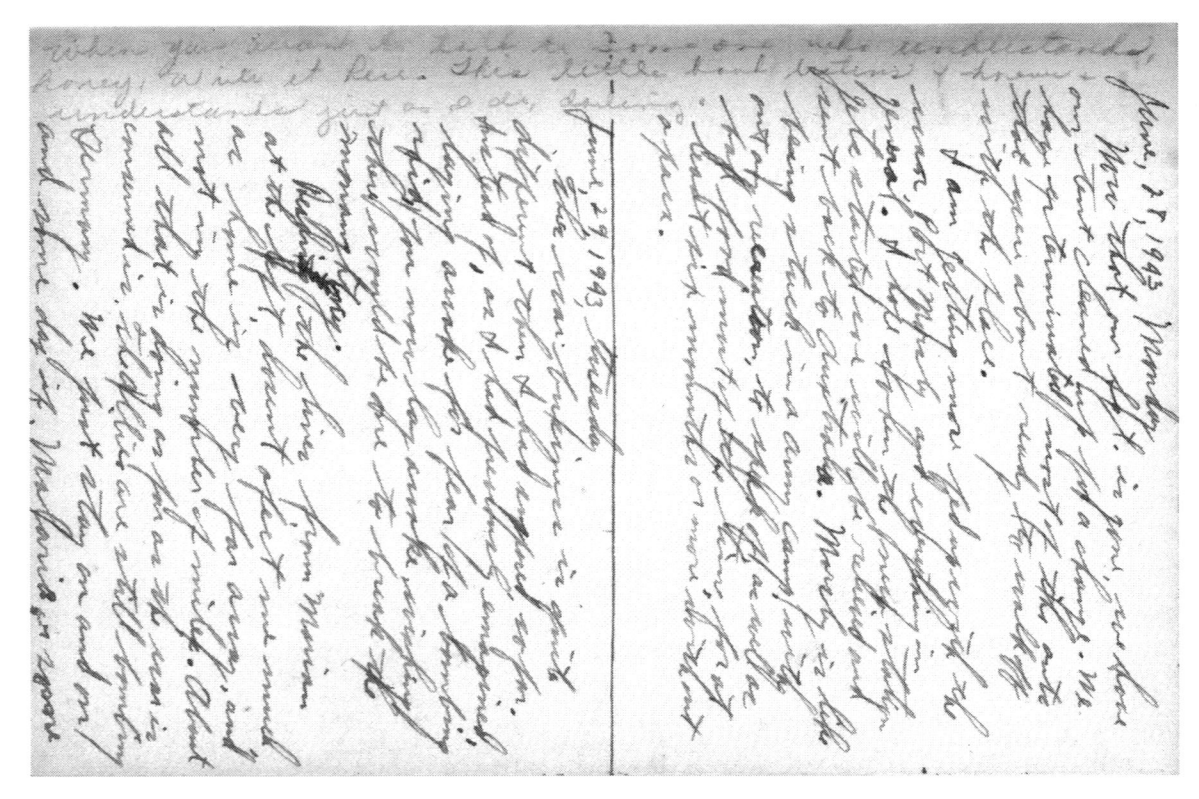

My mother has written in the fold of this diary the following: "Saturday, January 9, 1943 who understands, Honey, write it here. This little book listens and knows and understands just as I do, darling."

Tuesday, June 29, 1943 This war business is quite different than I had supposed so far. Instead of as I had previously imagined, laying awake for fear of a bombing raid, you now lay awake wishing there would be one just to break the monotony. Reading the lines from Marian at the left doesn't affect me much as home is very far away, and not in the number of miles. About all that is doing as far as the war is concerned is, the Allies are still bombing Germany. We just stay on and on and some day if Malaria or some tropical disease doesn't get you and your nerves don't crack, we can go home.

Wednesday, June 30, 1943 Same grind today as ever. We ate dinner down at the Australian/American club this noon. I think like everything else, it will be all Aussie and very little American. Quite a number of transports have been pulling in the harbor, from the States in the past week. There is a slight chance that Jack [Hightower] may show up here one of these days.

118

Thursday, July 1, 1943 Did a little washing this morning. This afternoon I went down and received my monthly pay. A bunch of new fellows came up from Brisbane the other day and will start working at the station tonight. With two extra operators on our shift we should have a day off.

Friday, July 2, 1943 Another offensive was started here in the S.W. Pacific. United States forces have invaded five small islands the main one being nearby Rabaul in the in the New Georgia in the Solomon Islands group. We have now cut Jap supply lines from the Solomons. We have also cut Jap supply lines at Lae here on New Guinea. It looks like the day of Moresby air raids are over. The Japs in two days have lost 121 planes unless the Japs pull a fast one which they are still capable of doing.

Saturday, July 3, 1943 Today I have off as we have two extra operators. I laid around most of the day and wrote a few letters. Now that our Sgt. is out at the new location and not spreading his bull around here, things are a little peaceful for a change. Boy what a line he does throw. We listen to the Philippines campaign every night and his exploits in show business before the war. He asked us to believe that had he saved one eighth of his earnings in show business he would have $500,000. He was also Pacific Coast ice skating champ for four years???

Sunday, July 4, 1943 All the celebrating as far as fireworks are concerned was done by three Flying Fortresses who spent most of the afternoon bombing the old ship that lays on the reef about seven miles from shore. The bombs they were dropping must have been quite large as the explosions shook the ground here at our tent. It looked as if these planes were dropping their bombs from about 15,000 feet. Most of the bombs hit the target. Went to work on the second shift tonight. A large number of operators have come up from Sydney and Brisbane.

Saturday, July 5, 1943 The same old grind goes on and on. With most radio operators being replaced by women down in Australia. It looks as if prospects of getting away from this island are becoming nill. Another six months, like the last especially working for this screwball sergeant and they will have to issue me a straight jacket.

Sunday, July 6, 1943 Didn't do much all day except laid round and wrote letters. One of our fellows wasn't feeling well so he went up to the dispensary to see what was the trouble. After checking him over they took him to the hospital with a case of Malaria. We are given atebrin tablets to take about two or three times a week. I believe that these pills are hard on you but I guess far better than Malaria or dingy fever: Didn't have to work tonight so I went to a show given for the opening of the new Red Cross Club. The entertainers were a bunch of Negroes which were strictly on the amateur side but not bad for this country.

Wednesday, July 7, 1943 Well the Germans have now opened their summer offensive in Russia. Their attack has opened up along a 250 mile front. The first objective, apparently, is Kursk. The Germans have thrown in thousands of tanks, Infantry and artillery. The Germans so far have made no substantial gains and these at tremendous cost. So far it is reported the Germans have lost hundreds of thousands of tanks, ten thousand men and hundreds of planes: In our end of the war here in the S.W. Pacific it is reported that a naval engagement is in progress between the Americans and Japs. The Japs in raiding the resent occupied islands of the New Georgia group have lost over a hundred planes in a week.

Thursday, July 8, 1943 Reports from the Russian front are quite favorable. The Germans without making any substantial gains have lost a large amount of equipment: This seem to be a last ditch stand for the Germans. By attacking Russia in this summer offensive the Russians will now expect the long talked of invasion by the Allies on the continent and it seems logical that they will have to come through ready or not.

Friday, July 9, 1943 The news today reports that the Germans have made slight gains but nothing serious: A naval engagement has taken place here in the S.W. Pacific with four Jap destroyers and a cruiser being sunk. We lost one cruiser. Our forces are in the process of closing in on the airdrome at Munda Pt. [New Georgia] meeting very stiff resistance. Radio (propaganda) Tokyo reports that the Allies have lost 2000 aircraft in the S.W. Pacific so far in the war, almost, according to them most of our Navy and over a 150 aircraft last week.

Saturday, July 10, 1943 The startling news came out today that today at 3 A.M. Allied forces comprising of American, French, English and Canadian forces are proceeding according to plan. The invasion was first started off by the Navy who shelled shore positions then squadrons of aircraft in large waves bombed enemy airfields and communication lines. The Allied invasion force is opposed by an estimated 300,000 Italians and a hundred thousand Germans.

Sunday, July 11, 1943 I am now on the day shift. I copied some press from Berlin, who tries to belittle the Sicilian campaign, and terms it unimportant, that our only objective is to safeguard ships through the Mediterranean. Not much news has been given out only that the progress is satisfactory: My mail has sure hit a slump again. Hardly any letters at all.

Monday, July 12, 1943 Reports from Sicily are that our forces have established a hundred mile beachhead and are steadily moving inland at many points: it is reported that a naval battle is in progress here in the South West Pacific. The outcome has not been reported: Our forces here in the S.W. Pacific are making good progress. Sooner or later the Japs lose Munda Airfield which they are attempting to hold with stubborn resistance. The Air Force here in New Guinea is being greatly strengthened, especially here in the Port Moresby area. Large forces of our B.25s raid Wewak, Lae, and Madang located northwest of here over on the other side of the coast. The nearest point by air is Lae, being about 150 miles Salamaua was our closest objective but our forces now have taken this base: Now that it is coming full moon again, Tojo may try some more bombing missions. However Tojo has had many recent losses and his missions over Moresby may be history. Until, recently Moresby may now be history. Tojo has the habit of striking a time like this.

Tuesday, July 13, 1943 Reports from Sicily state that our forces have captured some important air fields and the drive is moving steadily on: The Russian front is regarded as a show down between the Germans and the Russians. The Germans are throwing in everything they have without regard to loss of men or material. Up to the present the Russians have held on all sectors inflicting heavy losses on the Germans: It is reported that a Jap convoy has been turned back with the purpose of trying to get reinforcements to their battered troops in Munda.

Leaving this war and going into another is something we must do every night. Having to get up in the night and shake the ants from your blankets and sweeping them from your cot is not uncommon. Last night I woke up to the realization that something was crawling across me. I started thrashing my blankets and a large rat jumped on the floor. Today is my day off but being they needed an operator at the small ship's station, I had to work tonight.

Wednesday, July 14, 1943 Yesterday I was to have the day off. However, the small ship's stations needed an operator tonight so I came on shift. The small ship station is located here temporarily in the Pawpaw Hotel. There isn't much work connected with an operator's job, and all I would have to do for a steady job here is to say the word. However, I have a chance, even though slim of being trick chief at the new station. This I would prefer to operate here at the small ships station, BUT if our old Sgt. and chief operator stays out there and is in charge I will do anything in the world to get away from him. Everything I have ever learned about fair play, telling the truth, ideals, and value of friends, he will sit and argue against them by the hour. Among many things he brags about the fact of having not having spoken to his family for years and years. He tells us many times about his wife and child being killed in the Philippines and in the same breath states all American women are no good. He in a way is the most interesting personality I have met in the Army so far. God help the rest if they could possibly be any worse. I have been told that the fellows at the new location dislike him all already. Today the small ships station was moved down to the post office which is just across the street from the docks. There is not much work connected with operating here at this station, only to contact v2, v3, v4 and v6 once an hour. It rained very hard nearly all night. The first rain we have had in many months.

Thursday, July 15, 1943 It has been raining all day. The dry spell seems to have broken all at once. The rain is more like a mist and blows into our tent quite badly. My blankets are nearly soaked, but since there is no way of drying them while it is raining I have to use them as is. I put on a wool underwear shirt that I had, but I got pretty cold last night and didn't get much sleep. I received four packages from Marian today, containing envelopes, small flash light, gum and a Schaffer Eversharp pencil that was for my birthday. I watched an Infantry division embark on a ship today that had been up front. I was told that hardly any of them had escaped having malaria. Getting malaria once is bad enough but more than twice, you will be a wreck the rest of your life.

Friday, July 16, 1943 Nothing unusual today, rained quite a lot at intervals today. During the dry season the hills have became very brown. These rains should turn everything green again. Some of us went to the show tonight, which was pretty good. I suspected it would rain so I took my raincoat, which did come in handy. The war in Russia sure has changed from the German offensive, which gained them practically nothing and at a tremendous cost to the Russian Army

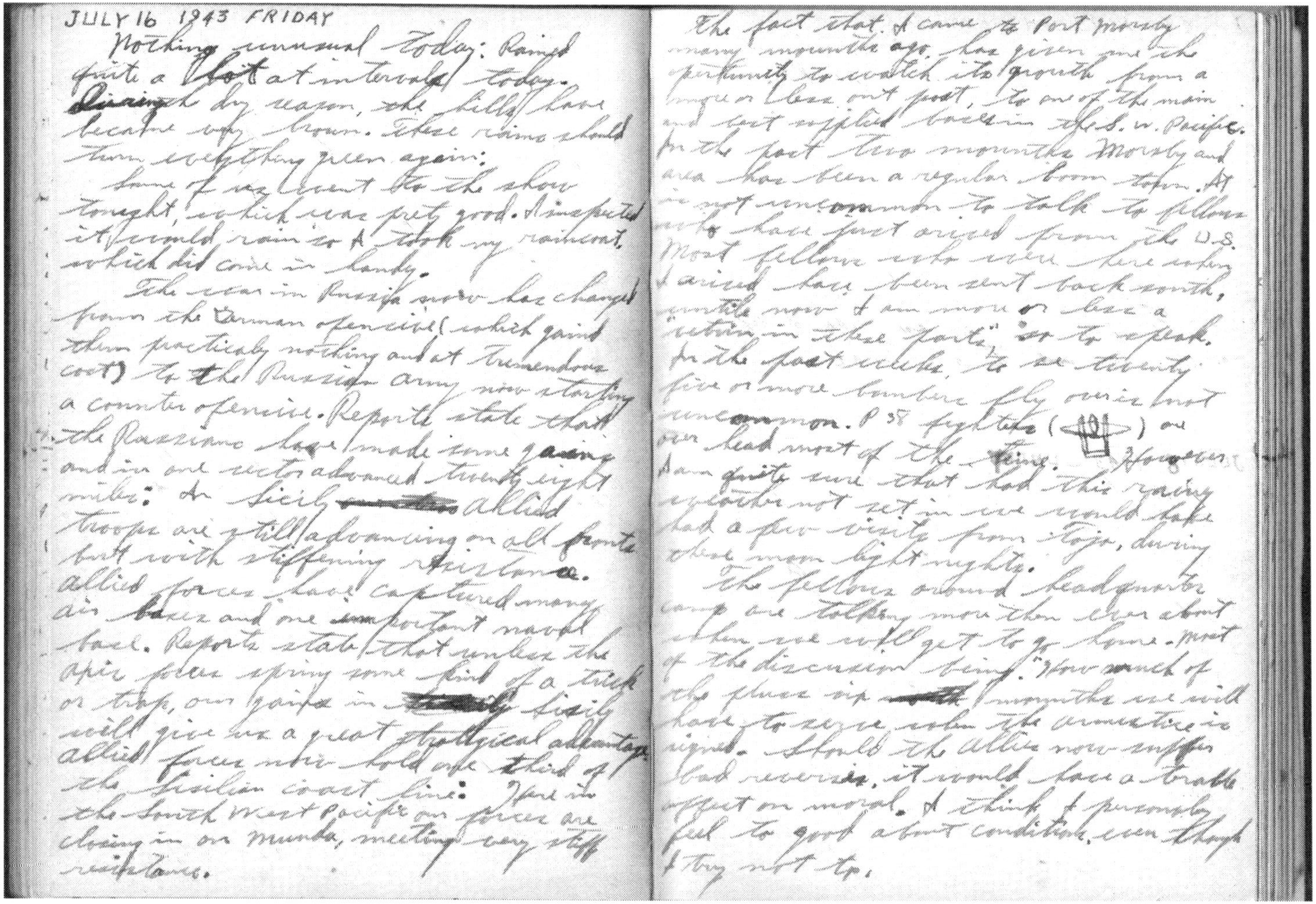

now starting a counter offensive. Reports state that the Russians have made some gains and in one sector advanced twenty-eight miles: In Sicily Allied troops are advancing on all fronts but with stiffening resistance. Allied forces have captured many air bases and one important naval base. Reports state that unless the axis forces spring some kind of a trick or trap our gains in Sicily will give us a great strategically advantage. Allied forces now hold one third of the Sicilian coastline: Here in the South West Pacific our forces are closing in on Munda meeting very stiff resistance.

The fact that I came to Port Moresby many months ago has given me the opportunity to watch its growth from a more or less out post to one of the main and best supplied bases in the S.W. Pacific. In the past two months Moresby and the area has been a regular boom town. It is not uncommon to talk to fellows who have just arrived from the U.S. Most fellows who were here when I arrived have been sent back south, until now I am more or less a "veteran in these parts", so to speak. In the past weeks to see twenty-five or more bombers fly over is not uncommon. P.38 fighters are overhead most of the time, however, I am quite sure had this rainy weather not set in we would have had a few visits from Tojo, during these moon light nights.

The fellows around headquarters camp are talking more than ever about when we will get to go home. Most of the discussion being "How much of the plus six months we will have to serve when the Armistice is signed. Should the Allies now suffer reverse progress it would have a terrible affect on moral. I think I personally feel too good about conditions, even though I try not to.

Saturday, July 17, 1943 The weather was fairly dry today, and things dried up a bit. No mail came for me today. The job here at "small ships" is sure a snap. However I think I will go back up to "Base Radio" as I get no code practice whatever here. There was boxing matches at the stadium tonight, so another fellow and I went to them. A couple of three fights were fairly good, but the others were strictly amateur. A year ago today I left radio school at Tyler, Texas.

Sunday, July 18, 1943 Worked at "small ships" today as usual. I intend [on] going back to base in a day or so. This net doesn't run ten words a min[ute] in speed. I got the surprise of my life this afternoon, as I looked out the window I saw some pursuit ships go over and at first I thought them to be Jap Zeros' but on closer observation and remembering pictures I had seen, I came to the conclusion they were P47 "Thunderbolts." This type of aircraft has on been used in Europe and is rated the fastest aircraft in the world: It is powered by a two thousand H.P. motor.

Monday, July 19, 1943 Same old grind today: I am checking up on the procedure of taking an overtime furlough. A soldier is only authorized seven days after reaching destination and that length of time is absolutely not long enough. If you work it right you can get a couple of extra weeks: All personel realizes that a longer furlough is necessary than is authorized, so nothing much is ever done about over staying your leave. Everything is still progressing as well for the Allies as ever. We now have control of one fifth of Sicily. However our forces are starting to meet much stiffer resistance: On the Russian front, the Russian are still moving toward Orel, a German strong hold, held by them since 1941. The Germans are rushing up reinforcements to try and stem the Russian summer offensive: In China the Chinese are in many cases gaining the initiative and the Japs seem to be making no headway. Here in the S.W. Pacific it is only a matter of time until our forces take Munda Air Field. The Japs are putting up very stiff resistance to hold it.

Tuesday, July 20, 1943 Nothing much going on today. I worked at Small Ships. The lieutenant in charge is one of these "90 day wonders" and thinks the sun rises and sets on his gold bars. He gave me a direct order to keep contact with WVVF at all times with a good readability. After giving this order he stood and waited for the customary "yes sir". It was plain to anyone how impossible his order was so I just replied, I would do all possible to do what he requested. He seemed to puff up and he made the same order again, and I gave him the same answer. After going back and forth in this manner a few more times he kinda dropped it. This same lieutenant has now signed some up as an operator at "small ship". I am just about ready to make a big jump on my own hook, but one of the Signal Officers of signal communications of base radio will back me up in.

Wednesday, July 21, 1943 Went to work at "small ships" as usual today. If the fellows who can, do not replace me with someone else, it will mean they will be short one operator tomorrow because I won't be there. A couple of fellows left today to go on furlough. I think in a short time I will request a furlough. My mail service from home has sure been lacking lately. Hardly any mail from the folks and very little from Marian.

Thursday, July 22, 1943 Well this morning I really upset the apple cart. The first one to suffer was the fellow on the midnight shift, when I didn't show up at work this morning. Before long two lieutenants from small ships, our chief operators and signal officers from base radio were on the carpet before the lieutenant who I was counting on to back me up. In the meantime I went on a little tour out to the air drones. When I got back from the air drones, things had come out as I had hoped and I went to work at base radio on second shift tonight. There are a couple of lieutenants at "Small Ships radio" that are decidedly not in love with me. My tour out to the air drones proved quite interesting. I saw one of the new type P47 ("Thunderbolts" made by Republic) fighter planes. They are rated as the last word in combat planes, carrying eight fifty caliber machine guns.

Friday, July 23, 1943 Started to work at base on second shift. However I wasn't particularly needed so I took the night off. The trick chief on this shift and myself intend to take every other night. With operators coming and going so fast our station is sure in a turmoil. No one seems to mind as most of the attention is given to the new station. Conditions have been quite agreeable around town and in our work as our old chief operator is not in charge. I have heard that he is to be transferred to Milne Bay. We are hoping it is not a rumor.

Saturday, July 24, 1943 Today we change shifts, and on this change go from second to first in which case we only relieve for dinner and go to work first shift tomorrow. I did some washing and lay around most of the rest of the day and wrote some letters. Mail service seems to be getting worse all the time. Headquarter Co. is increasing everyday and yet they are delivering less mail than they ever have.

On the fighting fronts here in the S.W. Pacific our forces here in New Guinea are driving towards Salamaua and are within five miles of this Jap base. However five miles of New Guinea country is a fortress within its self. Our forces are still closing in on Munda in the New Georgia Islands. The war against the Japs in China to the most part has been a stalemate. The Chinese with the help of American Aircraft have gained the offensive in some sectors. Not much news comes out of Burma. The British just seem to be holding a line to keep the Japs out of India. American bombers have for the second time in the war bombed Japanese homeland territory. This long range attack was evidently made from Kiska. Alaskan base recently taken by the U.S., Jap territory bombed was in the extreme northern tip of Japan.

On the Russian front; The Russians in their offensive are making a three prong drive on Orel and seem to be making some headway, under stiffening resistance by the Germans. In Sicily allied forces have now captured four fifths of this island. The U.S. and Canadian forces have been most outstanding. The British eighth army has been hammering at the approaches of Catania an important naval base. The Italian and German defense line at the moment stretches from Messina to Catania. It is reported that Hitler has asked Mussolini to give up the southern toe of Italy and form a defense line south of Rome.

Sunday, July 25, 1943 Today is my day off. Another fellow and I went out to the air drone for a while this afternoon. We saw many P47 fighter planes. There are many arguments arising as to which ships will be superior the P47 or the very successful P38. The P38 has made a fine record against the Japs and will be a hard one to beat. This evening three of us fellows went out to the hospital to the show. It was sort of a special affair put on by "Special Service." They had comedians. The main attraction was a first run picture that has not been released in the States as yet.

Monday, July 26, 1943 I went to work this morning as usual. One thing about radio operating, and that is any important operations or developments affects us first. We can nearly always tell if anything big is taking place, or is being planned as our traffic increases to a large extent. This morning an officer from fifth air force called our station to see if we could take care of emergency transmissions for them on one of our circuits. He asked if it would be possible for us to contact a reconnaissance plane that was out on patrol to be on the lookout for a Jap sub and to act as protection for one of our ships in the same area. However a case of this sort involves a lot of red tape and the message could not be sent in plain language unless an extreme emergency.

Some extremely favorable news for the allies broke today. It was announced from Rome that Mussolini has resigned as dictator. King Victor Emmanuel lll, has taken full command of Italian forces. This is regarded as the beginning of the end of Italy: Allied forces are still advancing in Sicily.[33]

Tuesday, July 27, 1943 Everything is about the same. I have been working every other day at the station and on the days off I help a friend at the Small

---

[33] In the corner of this page my mother has written "I love you darling, don't forget."

Ships station, string some antennas: The Allied leaders have given Italy ten days to decide whether they will continue to fight for the Axis or take the consequences of aerial bombardment and invasion.

Wednesday, July 28, 1943 I worked at the station today and everything is about the same as usual. I haven't received any mail to speak of at all for the past two weeks. I hear now that advance base is at Milne Bay all our mail from the states stops there first and therefore causes quite a delay. We heard they are to move out to the new location soon.

Thursday, July 29, 1943 My mail finally came through. Eight letters all in a bunch: I helped the Sgt. at small ships put up some more antennas today. We had to use a "blow torch" that every time you heat it up you take your life in your hands: It is reported that rioting and fighting between German and Italian soldiers is taking place in Italy.

Friday, July 30, 1943 Worked at base radio today. We had a yellow alert around noon. This is the first alert of any kind we have had for quite a while. During the moonlight period this month it was very cloudy and rainy so no Japs came over. We are giving them a rough time up around Salamaua and Munda Pt. Solomon so most of the Jap air force is being used there.

Saturday, July 31, 1943 Today has been kinda tough. Got up early this morning and started getting packed to move out to the new station. We had the job of taking our tent down and taking the floor, up which was quite a job as well as this we had to move all the radio operators and station equipment. My job was driving the ten-wheel G.I. truck which turned out to be quite an experience. I have never driven a truck and hardly any other vehicle since I have been in the Army. By the end of the day I was kinda getting the art of double clutching and shifting gears forward and backward. We moved our equipment into a vacant tent and just set up our cots for tonight. We are going to put in our floor and put up our tent as soon as we can find time. Even though I had done more than a day's work, a bunch of us had to work from midnight till seven.

Sunday, August 1, 1943 I was certainly tired this morning when I got off work. I slept till noon and then another fellow undertook the job of getting ready to put our floor down. We had to find a certain Lieutenant first for his O.K. on our location. Not being able to find him we didn't accomplish much today: Our camp is located about six miles from Port Moresby around on the other side of the bay. There is a main rode going from here to Moresby but it is so rough it is an ordeal to ride over it. No maintenance is done on it. Typical of the manner the Aussies do almost everything. The tent site here is located on a sloping hill side covered with tall coconut trees with the bay only about two hundred yards away. The radio receiver building is on a flat piece of ground surrounded mostly by high grass about two blocks from the tent area. There are power plants, maintenance shops and other buildings in the area. A new mess hall has been erected and the food out here is fairly good, much better than the joint in town where we have been. The country out here is quite wild. This morning one of the fellows found a lizard about three feet long twenty feet from the tent. Yesterday on one of the field trips I had to make with the truck was out beyond here about five miles. Some of the route you have to travel out across some open country covered with tall grass and scrub trees, the road being just a path where just a few trucks had gone. I don't think white man had ever been here before the war. A whole army could be back in the mountains and you would never know it.

Monday, August 2, 1943 I am working the midnight shift, working as relief trick chief. I understand as soon as things get running here at the new station we are to work four shifts and in that way have a day off. The station at present is far from being ready for efficient operation. Our old chief operator is still throwing the bull and seems to be assuming a lot of authority he hasn't got. Our new chief operator is the same fellow we had in town. He certainly hates our old chief operator.

Tuesday, August 3, 1943 We are trying to construct a floor in between jumps. In a short time they should break in some new operators, which will take some of the load off of us. This evening some of the fellows went to the show in the truck, but I stayed in camp and got some sleep. The moon is coming full again and time for the monthly visits of Tojo: Nearly all the personnel out here have never been through a raid.

Wednesday, August 4, 1943 Took a walk today along the beach. The shoreline along the bay is far different than the sandy beach in town. The shoreline here is covered with thick undergrowth that is mostly under water when the tide is in. Along the shoreline in this particular vicinity a great amount of wreckage, such as lumber boxes etc. floats in. A great share of the lumber used for building floors here in the camp has come from the beach.

Thursday, August 5, 1943 The floor to our tent is progressing very slowly. Every one is a straw boss and each has his ideas how it should be done. I drove the truck down to the beach and gathered some lumber. I worked the day shift part of the day today. Tomorrow starts on the third shift. I haven't received a single letter this week. The mail service seems to be getting worse and worse.

Friday, August 6, 1943 Today was full of good news. News reports came through that the British Eighth Army has finally captured Catania. One of the main naval bases in Sicily. The Allied forces along the line from Catania to Messina have driven into the main axis defense line. These forces were made up of American and Canadian troops: More good news was on the Russian front where Russian Troops have taken Orel. This city was held by the Germans since 1941. The loss of this German strong point is guarded next in importance to that of Stalingrad. Here in the S.W. Pacific our forces are closing in on Munda airfields and its fall is near at hand: Our forces here in New Guinea are now nearly within artillery range of Salamaua. All seems to be more or less quiet in China. As far as this world conflict, China has stayed in the background. No mail again today.

Saturday, August 7, 1943 More good news today. Reports came through that our forces have taken Munda Airfield and base. This will be an ideal base for operations against the strong Jap base of Rabaul. Another fellow and I went after some lumber today. We didn't get any lumber but we did go by three of our air drones, where we saw a flight of Liberators taking off. Worked third shift tonight, I was pretty tired by morning. Still no mail.

Sunday, August 8, 1943 Well, all of we construction engineers decided to remove the foundation that we have fairly built for our tent. One fellow (a singer) thinks he is a carpenter. Another fellow who has never seen a hammer, or a saw, can use one perfectly. Another fellow is always dissatisfied but has no ideas. Our chief operator knows only radio, of course I am no different than the rest and think I know the business also. One big catch is we have no lumber up from the bay, and now and then we get the use of a saw and hammer.

Monday, August 9, 1943 We finally have the foundation to our tent floor in place and are starting to nail it in place here and there. The mail situation is certainly punk out here. I haven't received a single piece of mail yet. Our air force here at Moresby is sure active now. Each morning about thirty "Liberator" and "B17" bombers fly in formation over head, including large numbers of fighters.

Tuesday, August 10, 1943 I worked on the floor a while this morning. This afternoon I got the use of a truck and went out looking for lumber. I drove into Moresby and checked up on my mail and also picked up a couple of boards. I also talked an Australian out of a couple of boards. On my way back to camp I saw a box of anti-aircraft shells lying beside the road, I just had them loaded up when the fellow who lost them came by and unloaded them. They would have made some nice ash trays though.

Wednesday, August 11, 1943 Most of us are still working to get the floor to our tent finished. We are now putting the frame around the edge of the floor. The only wood in this country that is soft is the wood that comes from the U.S., palm trees are comparatively soft but more like pulp. Nearly every nail we drive into the floor has to have a hole drilled for it first. We have already broken three drills. Everything is going quite well at the station. The trick chief's job is sure a heavy one here. So far we have nine circuits and many more will be put in, in the future.

Thursday, August 12, 1943 Well it is coming full moon now and nearly the full completion of the station and the whole camp has never been through an air raid. The Japs are having a hard go of it around Salamana and Lae, so perhaps they won't show up this month. I gave my shift instructions as to the procedure during a raid. Trick chief job is pretty hard at present, as there are many frequencies to change, of which they are all new. I have only two or three operators that have had any experience at all, and it is sure a problem to keep the traffic moving.

Friday, August 13, 1943 The same routine today at the station. When I got back to the tent tonight the fellows had moved it over our new floor. We have a lot of work to do as yet, but at least we will be up off the ground. Received a bunch of newspapers today, but no letters. Some of these newspapers were nearly three months old. The chow is starting to get kinda lousy for some reason. Went to the show out to the hospital) tonight. It was pretty) good.

Saturday, August 14, 1943 News came through today that the Germans are evacuating Sicily. They are succeeding in removing much of their equipment across the two mile straight to Italy. Reports state that the Germans have over 400 anti-aircraft guns protecting the withdrawal of their forces. The Germans are having a rough time in Russia as the Russians make farther gains toward Kharkov. It is reported that the Russians are starting an offensive toward Smolensk.

Sunday, August 15, 1943 Today Marian and I have been married two years and two months. It is not a very pleasant thought, that of that length of time I have spent a year and a half of our married life in the Army. It is beginning to become more real every day that we probably will never have a family. Today I really came through at the post office. I received eighteen letters. Most of them were from Marian, others were from the folks and Jack. I laid off working on the floor and spent the afternoon reading letters.

Monday, August 16, 1943 Our Sgt. told me today that unless we are supplied with more operators my shift will be broken up, which may mean I will do some operating again. Operating is by far an easier job and as trick chief you get no thanks for what you do, but only "H" for what goes wrong. Since my shift is an entirely all student units, it is sure a job. If I should start operating again I am quite sure there would be no hitch as to getting a furlough. Today my hunting knife finally arrived. It had been on the way over two months. It was a good night for a raid but no Japs. Don't look like he will pay us a visit this month.

Tuesday, August 17, 1943 Just another routine day. I guess my shift will stay in operation, at least for awhile. Some new operators came in yesterday which should make the work lighter. Things are sure messed up. Everything is new, and more or less "hay-wired" together. It seems to take forever to change frequency, and in the morning you have them all to change at the same time. You have to tune receivers for some of them that don't know how as well as take messages that the others can't copy. Thank God the Army only has to be used once every twenty years.

Wednesday, August 18, 1943 Well reports have it that we are to move up to G.H.Q. which is the road towards town about three miles. We are to have the keying positions there and the receivers here. I have never heard anyone state that radio reception works worth a damn this way, but bet on the Army if there is any way to screw things up they will find it. A Jap reconnaissance plane was over today. I don't think the plan [is] to leave this place alone, as some may think.

Thursday, August 19, 1943 Well for sure we are to move to G.H.Q. Three positions have been moved already including the operators for these circuits. We fellows in our tent have spent nearly a month and most of our spare time in building our tent for a maximum convenience, and now we have to move. Boy things are sure getting screwier every day. A screwy little second lieutenant who I had the run in with at the small ships station is now our signal officer. Boy how I would like to shove his face in.

Friday, August 20, 1943 More circuits moved to G.H.Q. today. It won't be long now. This trick chief job sure runs you ragged. There are a total of five telephones to answer. You have to keep close tabs on all circuits and make all frequency changes, keep up the master log which must cover all circuits in general, tune the receivers that have been connected with G.H.Q, and also help this clerk with his job.

Saturday, August 21, 1943 I didn't have to go to work until this afternoon so a friend and I climbed a hill near our camp that overlooks the bay. From this point we could see most of the bay, including Port Moresby etc. We took a number of pictures, but we didn't take any of the harbor for military reasons. Went to work at 5 PM, all circuits have now been moved but three.

Sunday, August 22, 1943 Today is a day I will remember for some time. To get the general picture straight the radio personnel is made up of the 232nd, 52nd and our bunch 832. We have been here in Moresby as operators for the past eight months. For my part I have been a trick chief for six months. I have worked very hard during this time and feel I have become quite efficient at this work. The place is loaded down with fellows just up from down south formerly known in these parts as "Per diem Commandos". Our new chief operator is also fresh up here from down south. He has been chief operator for most of this new bunch just recently. Without giving us old trick chiefs any reason of any kind he put us back to operations and gave some of his old bunch the job. With two - - - - - -as this chief operator and our smart second lieuie. We could only expect the kind of a raw deal as the Army can dish out. The job that I once held and carried out in a routine, daily – Now is being done by Tech Sergeants and Master Sergeants. Even a first lieutenant is holding down a job that I once assigned a P.F.C. to do. While we have been roughing it up here and doing a hard job, the bunch down south gets the ratings, and now come up here and grabs the gravy.

Monday, August 23, 1943 Operating is a pretty good job and a heck of a lot easier than the one I had. A fellow can't help but get burned up at some of the things they pull. The one thing that helps you get by is the thought that someday we can go home: Thank God the Army is only needed once every twenty five years. I am going to try and stay out here at the receiver station. My chances are pretty slim though.

Tuesday, August 24, 1943 Well between that D- - - - little Lieutenant and the new chief Op. I am having kind of a tough road. At present I am paying for the bull that was handed in against this Chief Operator by our old Chief Operator. This Chief Operator has no love for anyone connected with W.V.L.P. This second lieutenant is one of those know it alls that is so satisfied with himself he can't act natural. I am getting more fed up with this country every day. A furlough is looking more doubtful.

Wednesday, August 25, 1943 We are really in for a siege of "G.I." It probably won't be long before we start saluting and shinning our shoes. At one time today there was every rank in the station up to a Brigadier General. The general was General Spencer B. Akin in charge of communications in the South West Pacific. It has been raining off and on for the past few days. The rainy season is now near at hand. My mail from home has been pretty good lately. I have been receiving letters nearly every day.

Thursday, August 26, 1943 Today I asked the chief operator if I could stay out here at the receiver station. The Sergeant in charge asked him if I could stay, but it was no use. I guess he doesn't intend to give me any breaks at all: The chow has sure been punker than usual lately. The stuff we have been getting has made me half sick. We get bully beef, canned string beans and dehydrated potatoes, with tomatoes mostly used as gravy. What is made for coffee doesn't even resemble it: I wonder what a glass of milk would taste like.

Friday, August 27, 1943 Today was just another day at the station. I am still living out at coconut grove and ride in, in the mornings with the lieutenant in charge. This lieutenant just received a promotion to First Lieutenant. Upon first meeting him you would wonder how he ever made it to rank of a Commissioned Officer at all as he is more like an over grown kid, and not at all G.I. (term we use for something strictly military.) In a conversation with him the other day, he mentioned he was a lawyer, and in the past number of years had been working for the Federal Bureau of Investigation.

Saturday, August 28, 1943 Today was a long day. We worked all day and then came back at midnight and worked till morning: Conditions on the battle fronts are quite calm now except in Russia where the Russian forces have taken Kharkov and are advancing on west. The Russian government presents a lot of mystery to the Allies. The Russian government has recalled her ambassadors from England and the United States. Russia has not given any reason but it is thought they are dissatisfied at the slowness of the Allies to launch a second front in France. Also there are a lot of questions being asked as to why Russia was not represented at the Quebec Conference held between Roosevelt and Churchill. It is said in some circles that the Russians may sign a separate peace with Germany. If this is done it will throw an entirely different outlook on the outcome of the war as the Allies would have the 200 divisions of the German Army to deal with that are now on the Russian front.

Sunday, August 29, 1943 This morning after getting off work another fellow and I got our equipment and moved over here to G.H.Q. as I was quite sure what would happen [if] I am in a tent with a dirt floor. I asked in the orderly room about a furlough. They say they admit I deserve one, but my chances are slim. I think I will put in my application anyway, as this is all I can do to get a furlough.

Monday, August 30, 1943 Our tent is about a hundred yards from the mess hall and the hill we have to climb is no picnic. The radio station is about a quarter of a mile from here and the walk requires going over about three or four steep hills. We have a nice view of the harbor from here though. Port Moresby is around the bay to our left over on the far point about three miles. Across the bay and more inside of it there otherwise is a long point of land which rises in a number of large green hills on small mountains sloping down to the waters' edge. On around the bay to our right and going out of sight around the mountains and hills the bay stretches for possibly ten miles. The American docks are about three miles down the bay a comparatively small island connected by a causeway that was built a number of months ago by the American Army.

Tuesday, August 31, 1943 Well last night was an ordinary night. This job certainly keeps you busy. On our shift of nearly twenty fellows I am the oldest fellow for number of months spent in New Guinea. A good many just arrived from the states a short time ago. This place is sure G.I. We can write no letters. The General sneaks around trying to catch someone asleep. He dropped in twice on the midnight shift this week so far at 3 and four A.M.

Wednesday, September 1, 1943 Everything is going along about the same. Being trick chief is sure a job. Whenever a lot goes out, there is all the brass in the place swarming around as if there had been an automobile accident. We have to change frequencies, so all circuits will be changed by the time the day shift comes to work. The fact a station is OK makes no difference. We must be changed if it needs to be or not.

Thursday, September 2, 1943 Well today is my first anniversary overseas. This past year has been pretty tough, and perhaps I am a little older than I had lived otherwise. Conditions could have turned out a hundred percent worse though. For the first number of months it was hard for me to do my job for thinking of home. You realize after leaving the U.S. that it is a pretty good place after all. My mail has been arriving quite regularly lately. I have been receiving many letters and parcels from Marian.

Friday, September 3, 1943 In our present tent location, it is nearly impossible to sleep in the daytime because of the heat. This tent location is also occupied by a small number of fellows from 6th Army. They seem to think that because they were here first they can push us around. We understand that we will live in barracks as soon as they are built. Today is our last night on this shift. We will then go to the second shift.

Saturday, September 4, 1943 Today was a day of big news. Reports came in that the allied forces have attack Italy and also invaded Greece. No details have been made public: More good news from our end of the war states that our forces have landed tanks in Lae and the fall of both positions is eminent. Full moon is but a few days away and ever one is wondering if they will see the first Jap plane. Reports from Russia are favorable also. The Russians are advancing on nearly all fronts and are now within 45 miles of Smolensk, the main German operations base.

Sunday, September 5, 1943 This morning in a matter of minutes nineteen medium bombers, eighteen P47 Thunderbolts and 28 transports flew over. I later heard that the transports were loaded with paratroopers which landed up at Lae. Still there is hardly any news from Italy and Greece. We had today off and then go to work second shift tomorrow.

Monday, September 6, 1943 Events have been taking place in rapid order. Italy has made an unconditional surrender to the Allies. Fighting is taking place between Italian and German troops in some parts of Italy. At this end of the war, the paratroops that landed near Lae were unapproved. We were supposed to fall out for fatigue detail, but I didn't show up this morning.

Tuesday, September 7, 1943 I received some good news today. My furlough has been approved. However, one of our smart little lieutenants (mostly Little) has put his thumb on it. He says they can't spare me just now. I would have liked to ask him if I were so valuable why then no rating. One of our Lieutenants told this smart Lieuie that he might put off my furlough, but he couldn't cancel it.

Wednesday, September 8, 1943 Things are in an uproar at the station. A trick chief's job has turned into more of a foot race than anything else. Trying to answer a million and one questions to Lieuies, Captains, Majors, answering the telephones, changing frequencies, finding out about why a station lost contact, what time, giving a reason whether there is one or not (you can't see if the operator at Milne Bay or Brisbane, etc. are asleep or not) When I first started the job of trick chief, I had four fellows working under me. Now not counting the clerks there are seventeen with three circuits compared to twelve now. It is now quite moonlight. I would rather like to see Tojo make a little trip over here, so I could watch the new fellows scatter.

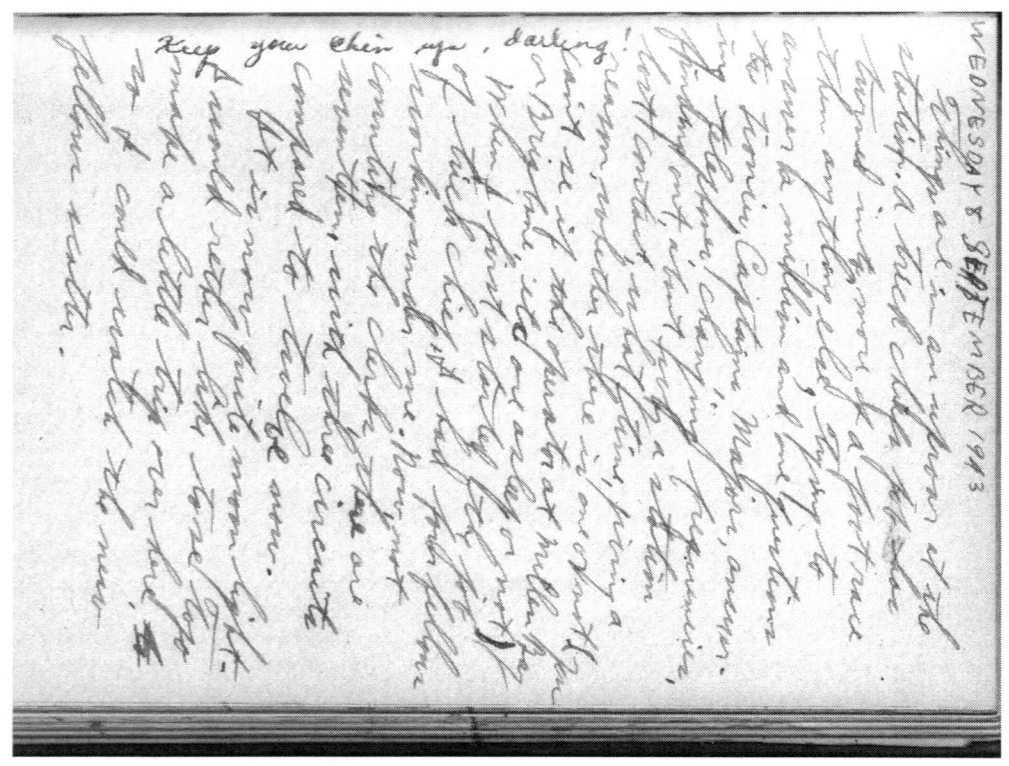

In the corner of this page my mother has appropriately written – "Keep your chin up darling.

Thursday, September 9, 1943 It seems that whenever I miss that detail that the G.I.s have hatched up for us they have role call and I get caught. This makes the second time this week. The top Sgt. rather likes me so, so far he has let me go. The food seems to be improving lately. For the past months my stomach has been off and I have been about sick, but I am beginning to feel better now.

Friday, September 10, 1943 Six of we fellow's furloughs are being held up until some more operators arrive up here from down south. The job I now have is about the hardest job I've had in my life. It takes a lot out of you physically, and the mental strain is more than you can sometimes think you can stand.

Saturday, September 11, 1943 The screwball ideas that one of the Lieutenants get[s], and insist[s] you carry out is enough to fill a large book. One in particular, in fact two, is just when you get in contact with a station with swell signals both ways, then you have to change freq. because his schedule says he should. Of course you catch "H" for losing them. No. 2 Being that things are kind of in a rush around the station in the morning, and a lot of brass is floating around, the fellows on the night shift must change to all day frequencies before the day shifts starts to work. You usually catch "H" because about five stations are out and they won't believe that it is too damn early for some of the high freq. to work on. Enough of this.

Sunday, September 12, 1943 Reports came in today that the Italian Navy has left Italy and are headed for Allied ports. The Germans tried to stop them by bombing attacks, but only succeeded in sinking one battleship. Reports state that nearly 100 Italian ships have reached Allied bases. Germany is getting in a worse way every day. The Russians are still advancing on all fronts. Here in our end of the war, our forces have taken Salamaua Air Field and have Lae completely surrounded. As we change shifts today, I worked from five till midnight and then from 7 am till five this afternoon.

Monday, September 13, 1943 Things went quite smooth yesterday and today for a change. I wish my furlough would come through. I am much in need of a rest. Calling the past eight months strenuous is hardly the word. It is easy to understand why the "section 8" casualty list is so high in New Guinea. The fellows here always joke about how long it will be before they will get theirs. The fellows have a lot of slogans about when we will get home such as "Golden Gate in 48". They also add, "Don't be surprised if we're a little late." Another one that has a little better tone is, "Rosie for me in 43" or "Rosie's door in 44." The way we radio operators have it doped out is "Middle West after all the Rest."

Tuesday, September 14, 1943 It has been reported that Allied forces of the U.S. fifth Army have landed forces south of Naples and by now have established a firm beach head. The rumor that Greece had been invaded was a rumor. Just goes to show what gets around. Salamaua here in New Guinea is now completely in our hands. Our forces have Lae surrounded and are closing in. The Japs have stopped the practice of fighting to the last ditch and evacuated Salamaua. The same as they did in Kiska in the Aleutian Islands off Alaska.

Wednesday, September 15, 1943 Today Marian and I have been married two years and three months. Of that time we have only enjoyed the happiness of married life for eight months. My furlough is still being held up as there is no one to relieve me. Boy how different it actually is in comparison to the way the rules say it should be. Specifications state we get a furlough every four month, and go back south at the end of six. I have been here going on nine months. No furlough no nothin.

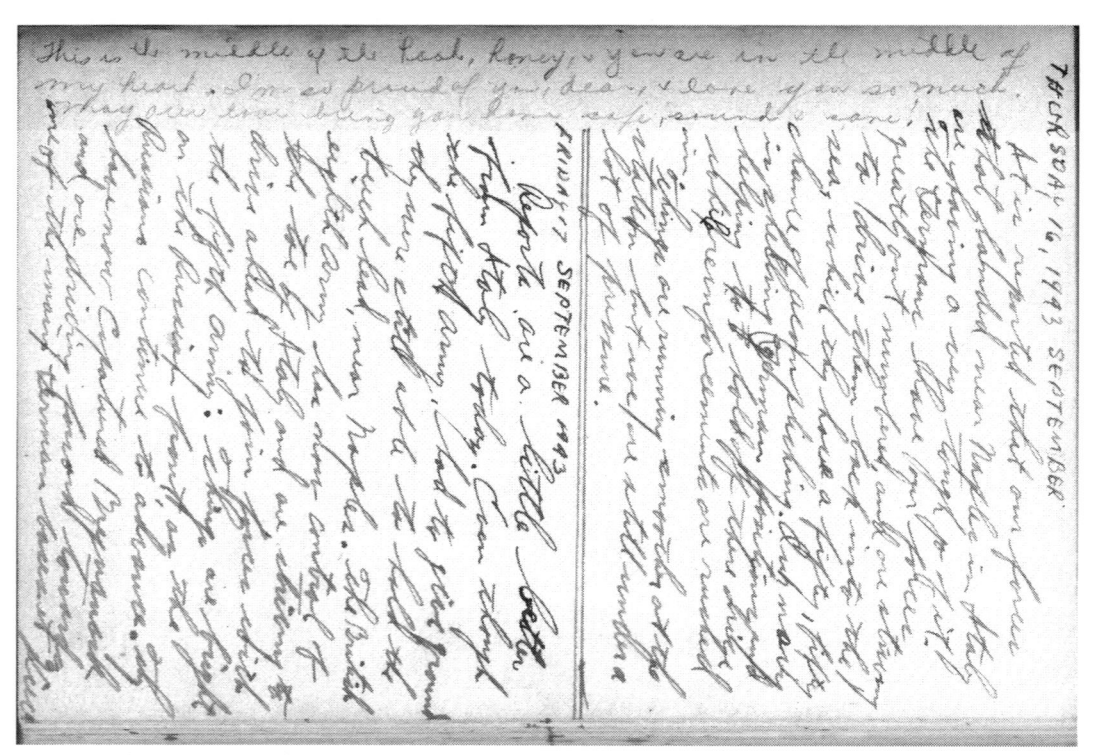

In the binding of this page my mother wrote: "This is the middle of the book honey, and you are in the middle of my head. I'm so proud of you, dear, and love you so much. May our love bring you home safe and sound, and soon!"

140

Thursday, September 16, 1943 It is reported that our forces that landed near Naples in Italy are having a very tough go of it. The Germans have our forces greatly out-numbered and are striving to drive them back into the sea which they have a fifty/ fifty chance of accomplishing. Our navy is shelling German positions and helping to hold their drive while reinforcements are rushed in. Things are running smoother at the station, but we are still under a lot of pressure.

Friday, September 17, 1943 Reports are a little better from Italy today. Even though the Fifth Army had to give ground they were still able to hold the beach head near Naples. The British Eighth Army has now control of the toe of Italy and are striving to drive ahead to join forces with the Fifth Army. Things are bright on the Russian front as the Russians continue to advance. They have now captured Briansk [N USSR], also spelled Bryansk, and are driving forward towards one of the main German bases at Kieice [SW Poland].

Saturday, September 18, 1943 Today we got paid, I now have plenty of cash on hand for a furlough so I will send home fifty dollars this month. My furlough is still hanging fire. I have been trying to arrange things so that perhaps I can get away. However I have been told that two new circuits are going to be put in. I suppose these will be Lae and Salamaua.

Sunday, September 19, 1943 Today is our long day to work. We worked from seven A.M. till 5 PM. then had to come back and work midnight till seven A.M. This trick chief job has sure been a hard one, mainly because nearly half the operators are entirely new. They don't know how to keep a station in and once they have it, the situation is dumped in my lap. Some of them can hardly copy a message (I feel for them as I remember what a time I had) and only until the operator on the other end is so mad that no one can copy them, is the circuit turned over to me.

Monday, September 20, 1943 Tonight we had the first "red" alert here we have had in a long time, the first one for the entire station. When the report came over the telephone we put down the "black out" shutters on the outside. Some of the operators got up and started for the door, but I yelled at them and they sat down again. The black-out curtains didn't help much so we turned out the lights and then went outside. What a punk night for a raid. It was rainy and foggy, even the birds would have to walk. No search lights went on, a couple of "ack ack" guns were fired a couple of shots just for the heck of it. No Jap planes were seen or heard. The alert lasted about half an hour. We all went back into the station and resumed the same routine. All circuits stayed in pretty well tonight.

Tuesday, September 21, 1943 Today we had a "red" alert. I thought that we were in for another surprise attack that the Japs pulled on April 14. However the alert only lasted about half an hour. I heard later that six Jap planes were out over the ocean headed this way. Our fighters intercepted and chased them off. Tonight we had another red alert. It only lasted about half an hour. No Jap planes showed up. Received quite a surprise letter from Marian today. She drove to Huston, Texas and came back on the train.

Wednesday, September 22, 1943 It looks as if I am out of luck for a furlough for quite a while. We have two new circuits and now just enough operators to take care of our shift, that is if none of them get sick. Our chow is pretty good now. We get fresh butter once in a while and also fresh meat quite often. The only kind of milk we get is powdered which you can only use in coffee. I try it on breakfast food once in a while.

Thursday, September 23, 1943 Since the campaign for Lae and Salamaua has ended G.H.Q. has moved back to Brisbane. Our radio station is not handling so much traffic now. I can see that in a short time I am going to have a little trouble with a couple of operators. Out of a bunch of 18 you can expect something to go wrong. Reports from Italy state that the combined American Fifth and British Eight Armies are now getting in position for the capture of Naples: The Allies have also landed troops on Sardinia and are driving the Germans back.

Friday, September 24, 1943 Another week is nearing a close. Still nothing has come through as when I may take my furlough. Two fellows, who have been here in New Guinea the same length of time as I, have applied for relief to go back to Brisbane, and has been approved. One of the fellows just got back from a furlough. Boy if they ship him back south before I leave on furlough, they are really going to hear from me. New Guinea is really starting to get under my skin.

Saturday, September 25, 1943 This is the weekend that we get a little time off. We worked from midnight till seven this morning and now we don't have to go to work till five tomorrow afternoon. However we have to relieve the fellows for chow. Some of us went to the show tonight. A couple of soldiers got into a fight so that made it a double feature.

Sunday, September 26, 1943 This climate sure keeps a fellow run down. It seems you can't get enough sleep. Today I finally clamped down on a couple of fellows who thought I would let them get away with anything they wanted to pull and our Signal Officer gave them a going over: One thing about this job that is different from the one I had over at base, my officers will give me all the backing I need.

Monday, September 27, 1943 Nothing unusual today, just the same routine. The Major told me today that perhaps in a few more weeks I could take my furlough. I am beginning to feel that I don't care if I get a furlough or not. Reports from the fighting fronts state the Russians have now captured Smolensk, main German supple base in the north central part of Russia: It is reported that Germany is to make an important broadcast in the near future, which is to affect the whole world. It is thought that this is some stunt of Germany to make a separate peace with Russia in order to be more able to protect herself from the American and British threat of invasion. In Italy the Allied forces are getting in position for the capture of Naples. Here in New Guinea our forces are consolidating their positions at Lae and Salamaua. Many operators from our station have gone over there.

Tuesday, September 28, 1943 Each morning of this shift for an hour we are supposed to fall out for detail. I miss this detail quite often. That is just as often as I can get away with it. Tonight an unidentified air craft came over. It was very high, but was still flying with its' lights on. It turned out to be one of our planes that had gotten lost. Things are running smoother at the station. Many of the new operators are learning more about working a circuit which goes a long way in making my work easier. I landed in Australia a year ago today.

Wednesday, September 29, 1943 The same old grind. New Guinea certainly is not a white man's country. So far I have stood up to these conditions I think better than average. I don't know how much they expect a fellow to stand. I was supposed to be sent back south after a six month stretch, but I have now finished nearly nine months. My feet are in bad shape. I get around and feel like I am about eighty years old.

Thursday, September 30, 1943 Today I was called into the office because of a mix up in a message that was sent. The message had been transmitted to Darwin giving away information that should have never have gone over the air. The catch was that the message was signed with my initials, I told the Lieutenant it was my personal sign on the message but I didn't send the message. He told me he would believe me if I could prove otherwise. Since this message had been sent nearly a month ago I had to spend nearly the entire shift looking through records before I found the proper dope that would clear me. It seems that another fellow who had been shipped out had the same personal sign as I.

Friday, October 1, 1943 I am quite sure if I could stick it out here in New Guinea, before long I would get another stripe. I think though if I could get out of here now I would be lucky as hardly anyone spends a year up here without getting malaria or at least "dengue fever". Same routing today, food not so bad.

Saturday, October 2, 1943 Marian is telling me in her letters that it is starting to get cold back home. Sally tells me how Bud and Bob are growing up. Mom and Dad are in Searsboro, Iowa and I know will be very lonely this winter. As for me the only thing that keeps me going is the thought perhaps I may someday get back to Marian and home. Today was a long day, five PM till midnight, then back at 7 AM till 5 PM Sunday.

Sunday, October 3, 1943 I worked today and went to bed early this evening, as I was about dead: I guess the six operators that were to come up here from Australia was just someone's dream. I don't expect to get a furlough anymore. I guess all I can look forward to is the end of the war and our forces have to march half way around the world yet and the going is pretty rough.

Monday, October 4, 1943 Today the same as ever. I went in and talked to our Lieutenant today and asked him how he would trade my furlough for a order of relief, so I could go down south. I didn't get much satisfaction from him. I realize he should be quite narrow in opinion of this country now, as there is as much difference as night and day. He never lived on bully beef and rice for months. He hasn't gone nearly a year without such supposed un-necessary things as fresh milk and ice cream and honest to goodness butter. A person can get along fine with the food, we have had, but you work, work, work day in and day out in a climate where not even the natives worked in the middle of the day before. Yes I would very much like to be around and see some of these "per diem commandos" a few months from now.

Tuesday, October 5, 1943 Today they took a fellow off my shift and are sending him to Lae. On my shift I now lack one fellow of having enough to fill all the circuits. The other two shifts lack two men each of having enough. Two fellows are in the hospital with malaria. One of them is a friend of mine. He is pretty well shot. If they don't send him south pretty soon, well there is one answer.

Wednesday, October 6, 1943 Today we went on daylight saving time. This will be an advantage as it will give me more time in the evening to write letters. Reports came in today that our forces have now taken Naples. It is reported the Germans intend holding a line near Rome: The Russians are still pushing ahead into White Russia, inflecting heavy losses on the Germans, everything more or less quiet in Burma, China, Kiska, and here.

Thursday, October 7, 1943 The World Series is now being played back in the States. Here and there a little enthusiasm is shown but generally no one is much interested. The moon is starting to get bright again. We are still within range of Tojo's bombers, but he has to fly quite a long way to reach us. Another fellow and I walked a short distance over to a show tonight. It was a double feature and lasted quite long. This show is run by the Australians. A show is shown here once a week. The theater consists of a hillside with the screen at the bottom stretched between two telephone poles for this purpose. The picture machines are installed in a truck that has a circuit around the country each week. Work went fairly well today. There are quite a number of young fellows on my shift. They all seem to like me quite well. My shift runs quite well but I find you have to be blind to many things that go on.

Friday, October 8, 1943 We had a yellow alert today (unidentified aircraft) it lasted about half an hour and then went off. It did break the monotony and give the fellows something to wonder and talk about. Some of us went down to go to the show tonight at the Navy camp. No reason was given but there was no show. I am sitting here now on the edge of my cot at the door, of my tent writing this with the aid of my flashlight. The moon is very bright tonight. I can easily see the lights of Moresby across the bay from here. I am here alone as the other two fellows in this tent are working at the station. We are building a floor for our tent. As yet I haven't had time. I will be able to work on it as soon as I change shifts.

Saturday, October 9, 1943 Today has been a long busy day. Worked all day then went to work at midnight. Instead of sleeping after supper, some of us went to the show. We were sure a tired bunch tonight. This trick chief job is sure a pain in the neck. I think if I should ever leave here I wouldn't take another such job for love or money. One thing that makes it so tough is the fact that we 832nd fellows are attached to the 52nd and when we moved over here to G.H.Q. from the 232nd camp the 52nd camp was kinda running things. On my shift are three 52nd fellows who are fine operators and probably had a right to expect a trick chief job. One of them was assistant trick chief. From the first day I was made trick chief two of these fellows have done everything possible to undermine me. They have already taken one trip in before the Co. and it looks as if they are in line for another one.

Saturday, October 10, 1943 The other two fellows told me today that they are going to start building a floor in our tent. I am not so hot on the idea but since they want to build one it is OK. So far I haven't had such good luck with building floors. The first one we built we had to tear it to pieces and move it to another location. We only had it re-built for a short time when I had to move. Out at the 232nd I worked like a dog for two weeks helping to build a decent place to live and then away I went. I swore when I came here again I wouldn't have anything to do with building another floor. However being I am on the day shift I won't have time to do any work until I get on the other shift. My chances of going on a furlough are getting slimmer all the time. I guess the operators that were to come up here went somewhere else.

Monday, October 11, 1943 Traffic in our station now is almost nil since the Lae and Salamaua campaign. Boy it was sure a nightmare then. New operators, new equipment that no one knew much about – an entirely new set up. A bunch of officers bucking for advancement with their simple ideas that could never possibly work. Things ran quite smooth today.

Tuesday, October 12, 1943 Now that I am on the midnight shift I am getting caught up on my letter writing to some extent. The station is running much smoother now. During the Lae campaign, even with all the brass around, facing traffic was one big job. One occasion the General had a message that was to go to Milne Bay. It so happened that he had to make a rush trip to this same place. When he got back a few hours later his message was still laying on the table. Boy did he raise "H".

Wednesday, October 13, 1943 It is getting harder to sleep in the daytime as the summer weather starts closing it. We have an occasional rain, that usually comes at night. Reports from the fighting fronts state that Italy has now declared war against Germany. It is obvious why Italy started this action, and so far no other reason than to swing over to the side of the Allies, so to speak, to gain whatever reward that any other victorious power might gain out of the victory that is sure to go to the Allies: The Allied Armies in Italy are steadily pushing towards Rome: On the Russian front Fall rains have slowed operations to some extent, but the Russians are still forcing the Germans back. If the Russians continue to advance that will cut off any German retreat from the Crimea Peninsula (Ukraine / Black Sea). About all the action that is taking place in the Aleutian Islands is small air activity: In China and Burma there are clashes between Allied and Jap units quite often but not of major importance. These activities favor the Allies. They have succeeded in capturing small sections of the Burma Road: Here in the S.W. Pacific Australian and American forces are advancing toward Madang. Important Jap base about halfway from Lae to Wewak. It is believed that there are sixty thousand Japs at Wewak. This base and Rabaul are considered the strongest Jap bases in the SW. Pacific.

Thursday, October 14, 1943 A bunch of we fellows went to the show tonight down at the Navy. It is but a short distance from here and we can walk in a few minutes. The show was quite punk and only made us miss some sleep that I for one needed before going to work at midnight. It looks like my chances of a furlough are less possible every day. Another fellow was taken off my shift to be sent over the hump today.

Friday, October 15, 1943 Today I have been married two years four months. I didn't do much today but sleep this morning and wrote a long letter to Marian this afternoon. My mail has hit a slump again. I have received only three letters so far this week.

Saturday, October 16, 1943 Today is the change of shift for us when we get 30 hours off. We got off shift this morning and don't have to go back to work until tomorrow noon when we relieve the fellows for chow and then we go on the five to midnight shift at five PM. I had intended going out to the air drome today but some of us had to go into town for shots. My arm started getting stiff this afternoon and the serum gave me a headache.

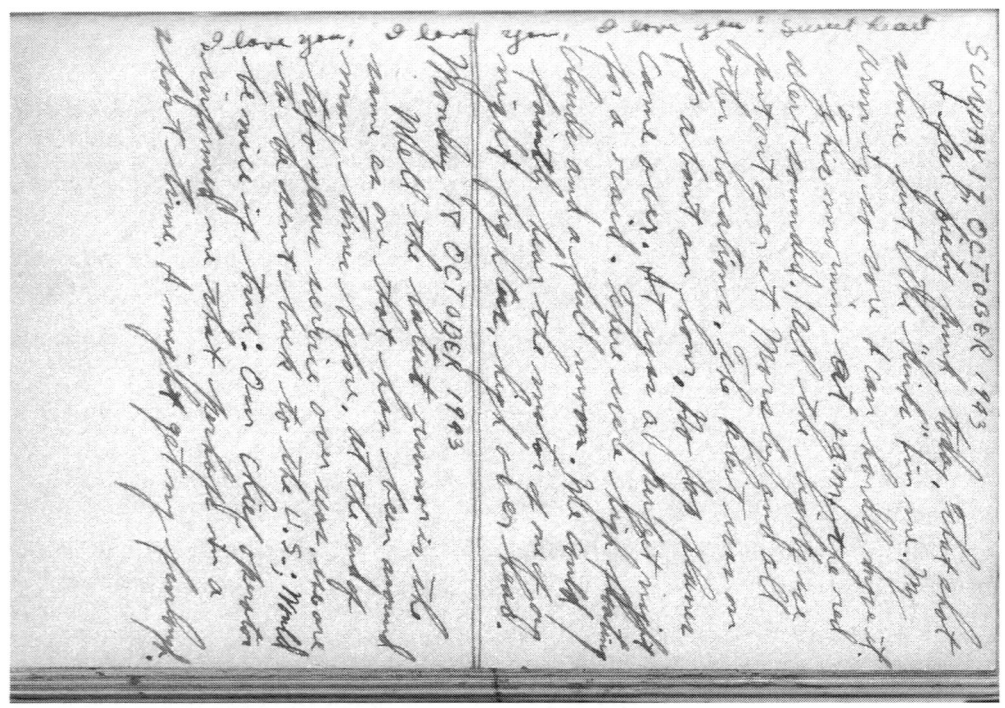

In the binding of this page my mother wrote: "I love you, I love you, I love you! Sweetheart."

Sunday, October 17, 1943 I feel pretty punk today. That shot sure put the kinks in me. My arm is so sore I can hardly move it. This morning at 2 AM the red alert sounded. All the lights were put out over at Moresby and all other locations. The alert was on for about an hour. No Jap planes came over. It was a perfect night for a raid. There were high floating clouds and a full moon. We could faintly hear the motor of one of our night fighters high overhead.

Monday, October 18, 1943 Well the latest rumor is the same as one that has been around many times before. At the end of two years' service overseas we are to be sent back to the U.S., would be nice if true: Our chief operator informed me that perhaps in a short time I might get my furlough.

Tuesday, 19 October, 1943 Today went the same as any other day, except I am now showing a Master Sgt. how my job goes, so I can soon go on my furlough. It might be that by my going on furlough I may lose the job of trick chief. However I don't mind so much as there seems nothing in it for me but a lot of hard work and knocks. Always before, this job has been taken with no less rating than Staff Sgt. It seems in the 832 there are no more ratings to be given out. Each time my name has been submitted for "staff" it always has the same answer, "No openings".

Wednesday, 20 October 1943 Today the Lieutenant told me that tomorrow I may go on my furlough. He also told me he wanted me back in twenty one days. There wasn't much I could say about that but I think he is quite sure it will take me much longer than that. He told me if I get stuck on the way back at some staging camp (and I will), unable to get transportation to send him a wire and he will arrange travel for me. Another fellow (Bill Pendalfi from N.Y.C. N.Y.) is to go with me. He is working the midnight shift so we won't be able to leave tomorrow. Besides both of us have a lot of getting ready to do. I am going into town tomorrow to arrange transportation at the air corps transportation service.

Thursday, 21 October, 1943 This morning I caught a ride over to the marine docks, near Moresby, to arrange for transportation for us to Townsville Aust. They informed me that we could catch a plane tomorrow morning. I came back to camp and spent the rest of the day getting ready to leave. This evening I wrote two letters one to Marian and another to the folks.

Friday, 22 October, 1943 This morning I ate breakfast and then took my baggage over to the orderly room, where we are to get a ride out to the air drone. We arrived out at the airport about seven AM and signed for our transportation. After this we were in for a long wait. Finally at 2:30 our names were called and we started off across the runway and up the road to the plane assigned to us. This plane is the same type that is used for regular airline service back in the U.S. It is commonly known as a Douglas D.C.3. All the aircraft are painted a dull brown with blotches of green here and there: The only means we had of knowing what ship we were to take was the last two letters on the tail being "J.P.". About twenty five of us were assigned to this ship. Ordinarily it should not carry so large a load, but it had no seats, only being equipped with a long bench on each side, each fellow resting his back against the side of the plane. All our baggage was placed in the isle in front of us. After we were all aboard the engines were warmed up and we taxied down to the far end of the runway. This wasn't the end of our long wait, however as about the time we were to take off a flight of planes (B.26, P39s) came back from a mission and we had to wait until they had landed before we could leave. This took about half an hour. Finally we headed down the runway and took off, passing out over the bay toward the ocean. Townsville is about 620 miles and this distance is entirely over water. We flew at an altitude around eight thousand feet. The ocean below was hidden from view to a great extent as we flew above a layer of clouds. I took a picture of the ocean and clouds with the role of color film I have it should be a good picture if it turns out. We arrived in Townsville four hours and fifteen minutes after leaving New Guinea. By boat it would have taken nearly two days. We checked in at the Red Cross and then went out to get an "honest to goodness" meal for a change. However, every place was closed as it was quite late, but a hamburger joint. This was good enough for us. The taste of an American style hamburger and milk and ice cream, boy what a meal. The first of this we have had for nearly ten months. Lots of things you forget, but something like this you never do. I guess everyone in the place knew we had just dropped in.

Saturday, 23, October 1943 This morning we stopped at the air transport station to arrange for transportation to Brisbane. They told us to go to the Red Cross and they would call us there. Well we waited all day. Finally at about four PM they called us and we went up to the transportation office. We are to be out at the field at five AM in the morning. We went to the Red Cross and made arrangements for another night's lodging. There was a dance at the Red Cross tonight. We decided to go but the place looked more like a stag party with so many soldiers there. There must have been fifteen soldiers for each girl. It was very easy to get a partner. All you had to do was to tap the fellow on the shoulder. I "tapped" three times and got tapped three times and had gone a distance of some fifteen feet. My friend and I went up to the radio station where I once worked. Only about two or three fellows are still there that I know. I gave the fellows at Moresby my initials so they know I arrived in Townsville.

Sunday, 24, October 1943 We got up at 4 AM. At 4:30 AM a truck came and took us out to Garber Field. There must have been over a hundred persons waiting to catch a plane. We ate some breakfast at the canteen and then sat down to wait. At about 6 AM our names were called and we loaded our baggage back in a truck which took us down to the end of the field, where a plane was waiting. This plane was the same type as the one we came from Port Moresby in. The engines were warmed up and we taxied down the run way and took off for Brisbane. Being very early we were in the air just at day light. Our ship climbed to around ten thousand feet and we proceeded on our way flying above the clouds, completely blotting out all view of the ground. At sunrise it was the most beautiful sight I have ever seen. The clouds seemed like an ocean and the sun coming up over the edge turned them into a light orange color. Our flying time to Brisbane was around four hours. We followed the ocean to a great extent and most of the country we flew over was mountainous, wooded and desolate. You very seldom see any roads or highways of any improvements. The last thirty minutes of our flight proved to be more an ordeal than a pleasure. As our ship came down to a lower altitude to land the air was very rough and nearly all the fellows started to acquire a light purple complexion. After landing it was Bill and my task to get to Brisbane without the customary military escort that meets all planes that contain soldiers on leave, the purpose being, to take them to report in for further transportation south. Our purpose was to gain perhaps another week before proceeding on to Sydney, as neither of us care if we ever see New Guinea again. Well we left the crowd and casually walked down the road with our barracks bags over our shoulder. We thought we had made it OK when at the outside gate there was an M.P. (military police) station. It was impossible for us to avoid this and we stopped up the road a ways to think the situation over. There was only one thing to do and that was to get by the gate. We walked down until we were a short distance of the gate and stopped to look the situation over. While we were standing there some trucks stopped going out through the gate. We tossed our bags in one of them and road on through. When we got down near town we got out and took a train the rest of the way. We had decided to go to the railroad station and catch a train to IPSWICH, a medium sized town about 25 miles from Brisbane. Here we would be out of the way of the M.P.s and we could spend a few days before continuing on the Sydney. Luckily no M.P.s stopped us as we walked the two blocks from the train line to the railroad station. We arrived in Ipswich about 7 A.M. and got a room at a hotel. We had a big steak supper that evening and went to the show. The civilian shoes I borrowed are really giving my feet a rough time.

Monday, October 25, 1943 This morning we were awakened early and asked if we wanted tea? I told them no, that it was too early. I did not know it was an Australian habit to have a cup of tea just after waking before breakfast. We didn't do much today but rest and fill up on steak and eggs, milk and ice cream. We haven't had such luxuries for nearly a year. We went to the show tonight. The theater we went to was quite new and modern with a remarkable lighting affect.

Tuesday, October 26, 1943 We got up about nine AM and had breakfast. The girl waitress talked very fast, and neither Bill nor I could understand what was on the menu. We settled for eggs and tea. We are rather looking for Mac and Fritz, two of our friends from our bunch to come down, and perhaps try and make it to this same spot. We had steak again for dinner and attended another show this afternoon. Tonight we went to the dance held in the city hall. It was kind of a punk affair and we left early.

Wednesday, October 27, 1943 This town of Ipswich is, I should judge, about five or six thousand. The business district is on one main street. There are many modern cafes which we have taken full advantage of. There are two motion picture shows of which are quite modern. Dances are held in the city hall. Bill and I went to the show this afternoon and decided to take in the dance again tonight, as before the dance was kinda punk.

Thursday, October 28, 1943 We have been waiting for our two friends to drop in all week, but I guess they were unable to get away. Bill and I arose early this morning and decided to catch the train into Brisbane. We kept clear of the Red Cross as the place is full of M.P.s. This afternoon we went to a show and this evening we attended the dance at the town hall. This dance was some better than the one at Ipswich but still the same Australian style. We caught the late train back to Ipswich.

Friday 29, October, 1943 Today Bill and I decided to go into Brisbane and make arrangements for further transportation to Sydney. Since we were each given five copies of our orders we plan to use but one copy at a time, throwing away the one we had stamped at Townsville on our date of departure there. We caught the train and when we reached Brisbane we went to the Red Cross to check in. We handed the M.P. our blank orders and told him we had flown down by bombers in which case our orders had not been stamped. Being we were not assigned to the regular manifest, the M.P. stamped our orders and told us if we wanted to stay a couple of days to try for plane transportation, it would be OK. We were given a bed to sleep in there at the Red Cross and a place to check our luggage. We went down to the air transport command to try for a plane ride on to Sydney. However our chances seem hopeless so I think we will take the train. We went to the city hall tonight to the dance.

Saturday, 30 October 1943, This morning we arose early and went back to the air transport office to see if we can catch a plane to Sydney. There was no chance so we decided to catch the eleven A.M. train. We went back to the Red Cross and got our bags and went to the station. We were required to buy a round trip ticket which was dated and with a week's furlough time in Sydney we were required to be back in Brisbane in nine days. At eleven A.M. we were on our way to Sydney. This type of train is the same gage as our U.S. trains. However they are much lighter and bounce around to a great extent. The coaches are built in compartments such as:

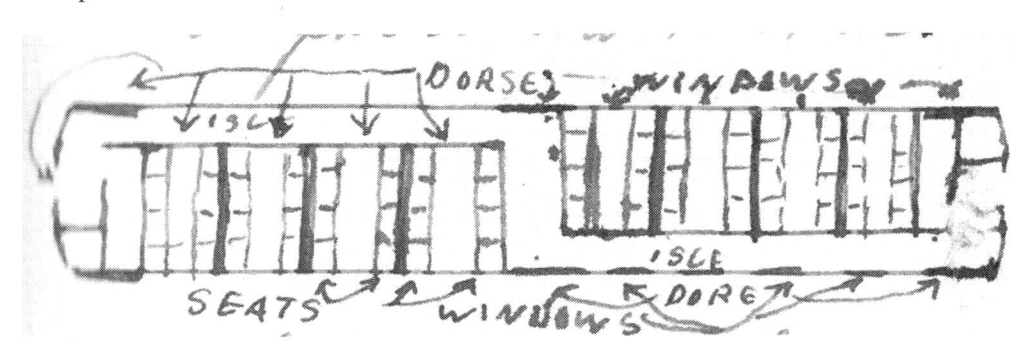

We traveled until around 2:30 P.M. and then the train stopped at a railroad café where we had dinner. Our train is due to arrive in Sydney around 6 A.M. in the morning. The distance we have to travel being something like 550 miles. There were eight of us in our compartment and the outlook for a nights rest was pretty slim. Nearly all the other compartments in our coach were empty. The conductor came into our compartment and said if we would each tip him five shillings he would scatter us out. All of us knew he was pulling a racket but the price wasn't too high so we paid him. All but my friend and an Australian civilian were taken out of our compartment. Most of the country we traveled through was mountainous. We passed through many tunnels and after emerging from each one we could notice we were each getting a little blacker. Our Australian companion offered to give Bill and I seats and he slept on the floor. We were able to stretch full length and got a fairly good night's sleep.

Sunday, 31, October 1943 Under the circumstances we slept pretty well but all of us were awake before daylight. Bill and I plan to get off the train outside Sydney a number of miles and take the electric train on in. By doing this we won't arrive at the main terminal and therefore avoid having our papers stamped and in this way manage a few extra days in Sydney before turning in. We reached the outskirts of Sydney and got off the train at about seven AM. We had about a thirty minute wait until the electric train arrived. It was about a thirty minute ride to Wynyard Station where we got off. We checked our barracks bags and started looking for a place to eat. No M.P.s around and with no stamp on our papers, if picked up we were on our way to turn in. I got the greatest surprise of my life when we walked from the station up to the street. There we were in the middle of Sydney, a city of some two million people but up the street as far as you could see there were no people, no automobiles, or trams. Everything was closed. We walked a couple of blocks before we met a person and this was a U.S. soldier. He informed us that it was like this on Sundays and the only place he knew of where we could get a meal was a very long way, up to some Red Cross. As for finding a room we had one chance in a million. We walked for nearly two hours before we finally found a place to eat. This was at a hotel dining room where, with no luck had inquired for a room. After eating we felt a little better. By noon we were still looking for a room. By the middle of the afternoon we were still out of luck, tired as heck, and no room. After a little rest we resumed our hunt. We passed by a hotel and we saw a couple of soldiers come out. We asked them if they had any idea where we could find a room. They said they were just checking out. We grabbed them by the arm, went back made arrangements for us to take their room. The bed wasn't made and the room was a mess, no one to clean it up, but it looked pretty good to us. We took a taxi and went back to the station to get our bags.

After a short rest we went over to the Red Cross where we had something to eat. While we were there a lady came up to us and asked if we would like to go out to a house party that evening. We declined the invitation but after thinking it over we decided to go. Shortly after five we caught a tram and with comparative little trouble we found our destination. This house party was given by a very wealthy lady who made it a practice to invite service men to her house each

Sunday. This home resembled any large American home and seemed to have all the refinements one would expect.

There was a crowd of around twenty-five. Of service men there were American and Australian soldiers and sailors plus a number of Australian girls. The crowd stood around and talked a while after which we had lunch. The crowd spent the rest of the evening dancing. Bill and I had a pretty good time but we were so dead tired we left comparatively early.

Monday, November 1, 1943 We were in bed till noon. We got up and went to the Red Cross for dinner and then wrote a couple of letters and sent some radio grams home. This afternoon we walked around to see what we might be able to pick up for Christmas. Surprising what a small selection of articles there are to pick from. Australia is pretty well drained of any luxuries. Bill and I went to the Trocadero Dance Hall tonight. This was a fairly good dance. The stage was a revolving platform, a men's orchestra would play for a while and then the stage would turn and a women's orchestras would play. Both orchestras were pretty good. At the end of the dance, since Bill had met a girl, he left and I started back to the hotel alone. At one time I was but two blocks from our hotel but didn't know it. I was in for about a three mile walk trying to find it. I finally found our hotel and it was then 2:30 AM. Bill was there and got quite a kick out of my getting lost. Here in Sydney nearly all transportation stops after 12:30 AM and if you haven't reached your hotel by then, you are in for a lot of walking.

Tuesday, November 2, 1943 We arose about ten AM and went to a restaurant. We each had a big steak which cost us each about three shillings (.50 cents). I guess the same meal back home would cost at least $1.50 or $2.00 each. We then scouted around town looking for a few Christmas gifts. One condition that exists here, we learned in a hurry, almost all soldiers in Sydney are on furlough and more or less throwing their money away. Almost everywhere you go someone tries to hook you. Every once in a while you have to remind a taxi driver that you know your way around, when he tries to charge you ten times as much as the trip is worth. The fact you call their game doesn't squelch them in the least. They just figure they didn't get a sucker that time. It is advisable to buy only at the larger stores as at the smaller ones you are sure to get hooked. Whatever luxuries you may buy are very high, don't amount to much, and are scarce. In the larger department stores there would be show cases in long rows without a piece of merchandise in them. The stores appeared to have only one tenth the stocks, of normal times. It seems they were only more or less a location for a store. Bill and I spent the afternoon taking pictures in Hyde Park. This park stretches nearly the full length of the business district, which is nearly two miles long. At the lower end of the park and skirting the harbor is Botanical gardens. In here there are plants and trees from all parts of the world. There are many statues, pools, and flower gardens. This evening Bill and I went to the dance. There is a dance at the Trocadero every night but Sunday.

Wednesday, November 3, 1943 We slept rather late as usual. We ate breakfast and walked around town. As yet we haven't purchased anything. Tomorrow I intend to have my picture taken so I can send them to Marian, the folks and Sally & Dick. I intend buying Jack something of more use. Tonight we went to the State Theater. Most of the shows here have single feature bills with many short subjects and news reels. The main feature is usually always an American production, as well as the short subjects. The news reels are British, Australian or American. Popularity of shows is definitely in favor of the U.S. During intermission a few numbers of popular music are played by an orchestra. A pipe organ takes a leading part in this short intermission program: We ate some ice cream and then went back to our hotel.

Thursday, November 4, 1943 Bill has an engagement with a girl he met at the dance the other night for this afternoon, so I spent the day by myself. This morning I had some pictures taken at a studio. After eating dinner I went to a show that had only short subjects and news reels. I ate another steak supper and went back to the hotel. Bill and I haven't got around to paying our room rent yet or to check in. We had better get around to doing so tomorrow or we may find ourselves in the street.

Friday, November 5, 1943 We are still avoiding being stopped by the M.P.s as we officially haven't started our furlough yet. However M.P.s are scarce and don't bother much. We have been walking around under their nose for nearly a week now. Bill and I ate at the Red Cross today. We stop in here quite often as we can get Coca Cola and American style ice cream dishes. We went to the show this afternoon and went to the dance again tonight.

Saturday, November 6, 1943 I went today to get the proofs of the pictures I had taken. They are to be sent home for me, but won't reach the folks until around the last of January. The only bad thing about this furlough is the fact that there is no possible way of getting any mail from Marian or the rest of the folks. There is an ever present loneliness as now that I am on a vacation I wish Marian could be here. I spent the afternoon at the museum where I saw many interesting Australian displays. I went to the show tonight.

Sunday November 7, 1943 This morning we finally contacted the hotel manager. We had decided to try to make arrangements at another hotel for a room, as we are not satisfied here. As to what is customary we were charged two more pounds than we originally planned to pay. Tomorrow we intend to move so this is our last night here. Our furlough so far is costing us quite a little sum. Since we both came with ample funds and with the thought in mind of no financial worries our money has been flowing at quite a rapid rate. Being today is Sunday everything is closed. Bill and I walked around through the park and spent part of the afternoon at the Red Cross. This evening we went to the only show open to soldiers. All others are closed.

Monday, November 8, 1943 Bill and I went down to the other hotel this morning to see about our other reservation. We were disappointed to learn that we can't get the room until tomorrow. Since we haven't handed in the keys to our regular room we will stay another night. Bill has a large blister on his foot so he decided to go to the dispensary. We both hope he is not asked for his pass, as he or I haven't any, being we haven't signed in yet, so far so good in this respect. I bought a few trinkets this morning and then Bill and I had dinner. This afternoon I left Bill as he had a date with this girlfriend, he met last week at the dance. I went to the Trocadero tonight. My feet are raising cane so I left early. Theses concrete sidewalks and civilian shoes are sure a contrast to what I am accustomed to walking on.

Tuesday, November 9,1943 This morning we checked out of our hotel. We got a night's lodging free, but in another sense of the word we paid enough for two weeks rather than one. For one week it cost both of us seven lbs .a week or $23.00 for both of us. At this other hotel we will only pay 3 lbs. or around ten dollars: We caught a taxi and it was but a short ride to the other hotel. The room we have here is small but plenty good enough. This evening I took a ride across the harbor on a ferry.

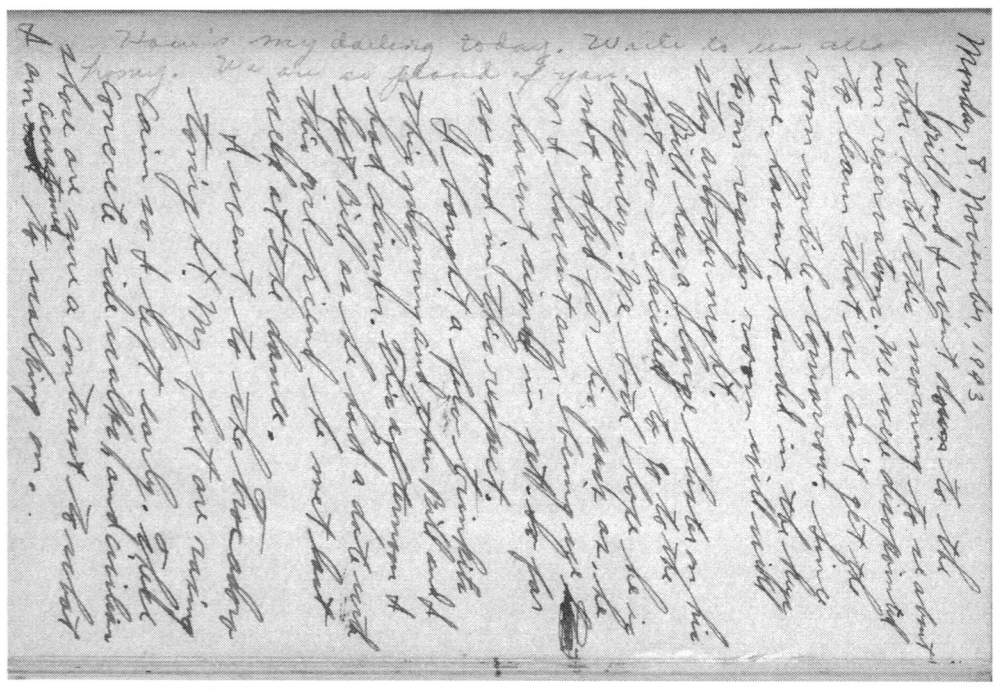

In the fold of this diary my mother has written: "How's my darling today? Write to us all honey. We are so proud of you"

Wednesday, November 10, 1943 This morning Bill and I awoke when someone knocked on the door. After going to the door we were surprised to see Fritz and Mac (two fellows from our bunch in Moresby) walk in. We sat around and talked a while and then started out with the task of trying to find them a room. Our hotel was full. They were finally able to get into a rather ritzy place, about three blocks from ours. As soon as there is a room available they are coming up here to the York. We all had dinner at a café with the usual order (steak, a glass of milk to drink while waiting and coffee and ice cream. Bill and I decided since Mac caught up with us perhaps we had better turn in and start our furlough officially. They haven't turned in as yet and intend to follow our same example. Bill and I walked down to the Red Cross service. We walked in and asked at what place we were to sign in. The lady at the information desk pointed to a counter across the room, where a lot of G.I.s was standing. We waited a little while and didn't get waited on. We looked at each other and were both thinking the same thing, so we turned around and walked out. Any extra day or two shouldn't make any difference. Since Fitz has a badly infected ankle, and can hardly walk, we all stayed around the hotel this evening.

Thursday, November 11, 1943 Fitz decided taking a chance on them not asking for his pass and went to the dispensary this morning. The doctor wants Fitz to go to the hospital but for the time being he has talked him out of it. He was not asked for his pass. This afternoon Fitz and Mac decided to go out some place to some friends that they knew. Bill went with them but I decided to stay around town. I took my camera and went down to the botanical gardens. There I snapped some pictures, finishing up the rest of the roll of color film I have. I hope they come out O.K. but I am a little doubtful. Tonight I went to a show.

Friday, November 12, 1943 Today Bill and I finally decided to terminate our unofficial stay in Sydney. As much as we hate to do so we feel we must turn in. We went down to the Red Cross and this time got signed up. It required a little tricky business. We gave them our blank furlough papers and told them we had arrived by a bomber. There were no questions asked, only that we were given instructions to buy a railroad ticket to Brisbane. This fell in with our plans as we had planned not to use the dated return ticket we had bought in Brisbane. The extra ticket cost around two and a half pounds but the extra two weeks was worth it. Tonight Bill and I went to the dance.

Saturday, November 13, 1943 This morning I got aboard a tram and started towards the direction of the zoo. By asking a number of persons the proper means of getting there, I finally made it. The zoo is on the opposite side of the main part of Sydney across the harbor. The ride of about three or four miles took us across the Sydney Bridge of which is one of the main attractions. All Australians are very proud of this bridge and if you want to raise ones temper just mention that it doesn't amount to much. This bridge is a duplicate of Hellgate Bridge that links Manhattan, New York with Brooklyn, Coney Island. The zoo is located on a large hillside. The main entrance is at the top of the hill where the tram line runs. Your route through the zoo stretches from the top of the hill about a half a mile down to the bay where you may catch a ferry boat back to the main part of Sydney. This zoo contains about all types of animals you would find in any American zoo except probably here they have a larger collection of birds of paradise and a [bigger] kangaroo exhibit. Tonight after getting back to town I decided to go to an opera. This was held at the city civic center. I think I was the only G.I. there. With the aid of a program I was able to follow the performance quite well. The name of the opera was "Orpheus in the Underworld".

Sunday, November 14, 1943 I ate lunch at the American Red Cross after which I sent a radio gram to Marian. Tomorrow we will have been married two years and five months. This afternoon I got aboard a ferry and went across the harbor to Manly Beach. It was kinda cool so I didn't go swimming. Manly Beach is located on a narrow point. On the one side is a calm swimming pool for ordinary swimming. On the other side it is suitable for surf bathing. I caught the bus that I thought would bring me back to town. Instead it wound up far from my destination. Luckily there was a tram line where I caught a tram back to town. It started raining shortly after I got back to the hotel. Since Sunday night in Sydney is absolutely nil as far as entertainment is concerned, I stayed in tonight and went to bed early.

Monday, November 15, 1943 This morning when I went to the washroom the door was locked. I knocked and asked the fellow inside if I could get a glass of water. When he opened the door, who should it be but one of my old radio friends from New Guinea. This makes five of our bunch down here now. All of us went out to eat dinner together. This afternoon Bill and I went to the Censor's Office to mail a few things home. Bill has a large blister on his foot that has become infected so he went to the infirmary. Fitz's leg is in awful bad shape and he may have to go to the hospital. Both of my feet a[re] patched with adhesive tape and are in fair shape now considering I bought me a pair of oxfords this afternoon. Australian shoes are cut much different than American shoes. There is little difference between the shape of the left shoe to the right. The toes are square such as:

Tonight the bunch of us went to a night club. It turned out to be more of a clip joint than anything else. You were charged about ten times as much for everything as it was normally worth. Our dinner cost us on the such as average of about $2.00 a plate.

Tuesday, November 16, 9143 Fitz and Mac are now here at the same hotel. They have the room just down the hall. William Davy our other friend is sharing a room with an air corps fellow. This makes five of our bunch on one floor. The bunch of us messed around the park this afternoon and decided to go to a show tonight. It is still raining to a great extent.

Wednesday, November 17 Bill and I made a last stab at trying to find something to send home. We each bought a couple of trinkets and went up to the censor office to mail them. We hung around the Red Cross this afternoon and went to the dance tonight.

Thursday, November 18, 1943 Well our stay in Sydney is nearing a close. We are due to leave tomorrow night. Bill and I spent the day taking some more pictures. Each of us had three steaks this afternoon, and a pile of ice cream. Once we start back hard to tell when we will get ice cream or milk again. Tonight Bill and I went to a show.

Friday, November 19, 1943 Bill and I spent the day doing our last minute looking around and getting our things ready so we can leave tonight. We reported in at the Red Cross and our train is scheduled to leave at 7:40 P.M. Bill and I both feel the same about leaving Sydney to go back. It isn't a pleasant thought to have to return to New Guinea. We arrived at the station around 7-P.M. We reported at the R.T.O. (railroad transportation office). They stamped our papers and then informed us that we would not be able to leave till tomorrow. Boy did we feel good even for one more day. For the rest of the evening Bill and I went out to his friend's house. Mac and Fitz were there and we played cards the rest of the evening. Since our room rent was paid up till Sunday we turned our room over to Mac and Fitz. Luckily we did this, as this gave us a place to spend an extra night.

Saturday, November 20, 1943 This morning I did some shopping around. I bought Marian an opal. The only way you can purchase any kind of jewelry is to buy the stones in the raw. All jewelry firms here in Australia have gone to war and the Americans have long exhausted the supply on hand. This afternoon I decided to go to the races. I boarded the tram that took me directly to Winrick race course. Being absolutely new at the game I more or less followed the crowd. I bought a program and a news paper as the probable winners of each race was written on the sports page. I didn't intend to bet much per race and since I knew absolutely nothing as to the ability of certain horses to run, I decided to bet only on the favorites. I was standing around wondering what the procedure was to bet. A party of girls saw my predicament and gave me a few instructions as well as a few leads. I stuck with them the rest of the afternoon. At the end of the first four races I was a couple pounds ahead. The last two races took me for three pounds. Results – lost one pound. Oh well not so bad for an afternoon entertainment. The race was over at about five P.M. Luckily I got aboard the first tram to town in spite of the thousands of people waiting for transportation. It was about a 45 minute ride back to Sydney and by the time I ate supper it was nearing the hour of departure. I was to meet Bill at the station around 7 P.M. I got our baggage out of the station, checked the room and proceeded to wait for Bill. 7:15 rolled by and no Bill, 7:25 and still he hadn't showed up. At 7:30 I felt I would have to check in by myself as the first train left at 7:40. I was just ready to get my passage when Bill walked up. We walked in the office and signed up. To our disappointment Bill was to take the first train and I the second. I told Bill I would meet him at the Red Cross in Brisbane. He then only had 3 minutes to catch his train. Bill's train pulled out and it was not a pleasant feeling to have to make the trip back alone. Perhaps clear to New Guinea, a distance of around 2000 miles. I was assigned to a seat in a compartment with six other sailors which lacked but one seat of filling the compartment to capacity. We all knew what our chances were of any sleep that night. Our train pulled out of Sydney station at eight P.M. and as it wound its way through the mirage of tracks in the yards I couldn't help but feel down hearted at the prospect of my return to New Guinea and to resume my duties at the same spot for who knew how long.

Sunday, November 21, 1943 Last night we spent as all in our compartment supposed, without a wink of sleep, and only able to sit upright in our seats. This ride proved to be a very slow and boring one. Our train was running hours behind schedule and not until 6 P.M. did we arrive in Brisbane. Twenty two hours to travel aprox. 550 miles. Boy these Australians trains.

Bill's train had arrived around 3:30 P.M. and he was in nearly as much hot water about my arrival as I was his in Sydney. Both of us were stuck and there was no way of avoiding getting our papers stamped in Brisbane. This furlough form we had to use as it had our departure time from Sydney on it and that stamp has to be present on your papers.

I met Bill at the Red Cross and we had to decide on what our further course would be. We were in a way stuck. We had two days limit to turn in at Camp

Ascot after which time we would be listed as A.W.O.L. since your papers had your arrival date stamped on them. By sticking our neck out and take chances on a plane ride north, we could avoid Camp Ascot. Ascot is known to all soldiers as a sort of a concentration camp, a place where you get punished for having a furlough. After a stay there of a month or six weeks they load the bunch on a ship (freighters) and head for New Guinea. A voyage of eleven days with nothing to eat but cold canned bully beef and field rations C.

In the fold of this page my mother has written: "Hugs, darling. See? I'm right beside you. Always."

Monday, November 22, 1943 Bill and I decided to turn in at the Red Cross. By doing this we were able to get a nights lodging. We have planned to spend the next two days checking up on air transportation. And after this time if we have no luck, I guess we are stuck for Camp Ascot. (This is the same camp I arrived at when I first landed in Australia.)

Bill and I heard of an air corps trenchant camp, that if we by some means or other could check in and eventually they would get air transportation for us back to New Guinea. We decided to take a chance on checking in at this camp, with the hope the clerk wouldn't look our furlough papers over to closely.

Bill and I took a tram and started out to Archer Field. It was quite a long ride and the last two miles we had to thumb a ride. We went to the air transport office and asked what our chances were of going north. The fellow at the desk said there was no chance whatsoever, but he informed us he thought perhaps a bomber would be going north the next day and as far as he knew it would be empty. He gave us the pilot's name (Lt. Turner) and told us where the ship was parked. We walked over to where the ship was parked so as to know exactly where it was. Our spirits now were starting to rise. The camp we were going to try and check into was about a mile from this field. I was wearing my new shoes and each step I took became more painful as the old blisters I had suffered in Sydney once more made themselves known.

Bill and I found the orderly room and after taking a deep breath made our entrance. I handed the clerk my furlough papers as Bill stood peering over my shoulder. We stood in death silence as the clerk inserted a card in the typewriter. He then picked up my papers and asked where my name was listed. I told him at this point it was obvious that he was examining my papers far too closely. When he asked what unit I was attached to I knew we were out of luck. I told him we were in the Signal Corps, but detached to the air corps. He stated that as much as he regretted it, it was the rule that only actual air corps men could be stationed there for possible air transportation. He said it was too bad we were sent clear out here to the wrong camp. We were more than glad to get out of there. Well things were still OK for us, only we had to find a place to stay. We were unable to go back to the Red Cross as we had spent our one allotted night there. Tonight we are supposed to go to a rest camp station when in the morning we would be hauled out to Camp Ascot.

We decided our best bet was to report in to our signal outfit here in Brisbane. I worked for Major Wilkins for a time in Moresby and he should be obliging and let us stay at our unit head quarters for one night.

Major Wilkins was glad to see us and was more than willing to offer to help us. We were given a couple of cots and a truck is to take us out to Archer Field early in the morning. Major Wilkins advised that if we were unable to leave by air tomorrow for our own good we had better turn in at Camp Ascot. We went to a show tonight.

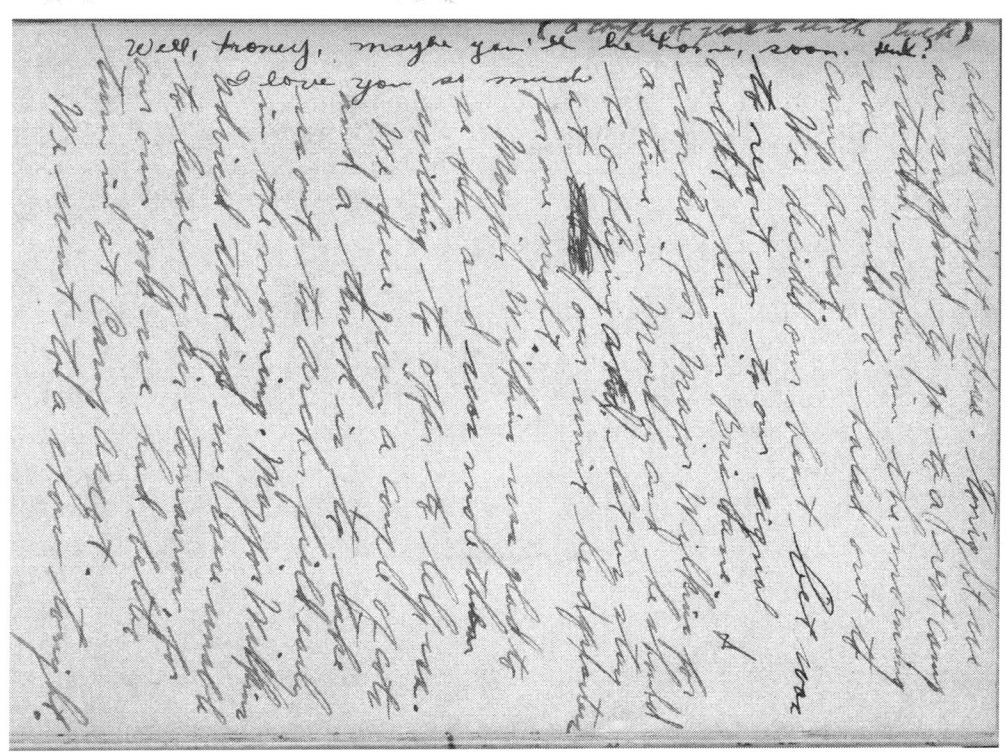

In the fold of this page my mother wrote; "Well, honey, maybe you'll be home soon. Heck? I love you so much. My dad wrote, "A couple of years with luck."

Tuesday, November 23, 1943 We were awakened at 4:30 A.M. We had some coffee in the mess hall and then we loaded our baggage in a command car and started for Archer Field. We arrived there a little past five and it was still dark. We thanked the soldier for bringing us out and then we started out across the field over toward where the plane was parked. This plane is a B-29 or more commonly known as a Liberator. This ship has a gross weight of around 47,000 pounds and is powered by four 1100 horse power motors. It will carry a bomb load of around seven tons.

When we reached the ship there wasn't a person there only the night watchman. He, thank goodness was friendly. After all it was quite early. We sat down to wait. The night watchman wasn't very encouraging. He told us that he doubted if that ship would leave this morning, as a day or so before it had became stuck in the mud and they intended to test hop this ship before taking it on north.

Eight A.M. came and still no one had showed up, the same story at 9:30 A.M. We inquired at a small office nearby, if they knew when Lt. Turner would

165

arrive. They told us the ship would not fly that day as the field was too muddy (this field is nothing more or less than a large flat pasture. No runways, and hardly suitable for a ship as large as a B 24) but that Lt. Turner should be out sometime this morning or perhaps this afternoon. Noon came and still no Lt. Turner. Every officer I saw enter this office I asked if he were Turner. Finally at 3:30 P.M. a car drove up with two officers. I asked if he were Lt. Turner. He said no but the other fellow was. The climax that we had waited for since 5A.M. had finally come. Just one little three letter word meant the difference between Ascot or getting back to our unit. I walked up to Lt. Turner and in rather faltering words asked if we could ride north? The moment between my question and his answer seemed like an hour. Lt. Turner is a young fellow not more than 23 or 24 and by general appearance not filled with the important air that many officers I have met, have. Without any hesitation he said his ship would be empty and we could ride along. However, he said he was going to test hop the ship this afternoon and he would leave from Amberly Field in the morning and we were to meet him there at 7:30 A.M. This was the last lucky break that Bill and I needed. The reason for taking off from Amberly Field rather than Archer was because Archer field only had a grass field to take off from. Since it has been raining it would be better to take off from Amberly Field that has hard surface runways after being loaded.

Bill and I by this time felt pretty good even though our faces had become sunburned from standing in the sun and we had been without anything to eat all day. We picked up our barracks bags and started to town. An airport bus was just leaving so we didn't have to even thumb as we supposed. This bus, however didn't travel clear into the middle of the business district, but stopped about five or six blocks from the railroad station, where we were to catch a train to Ipswich which is but a short distance from Amberly field. We didn't like the idea of having to carry our barracks bags clear to the station, but it was the only means after about half an hour of hailing cabs. After walking and resting we finally reached the station. We bought our tickets and since we had about a two hour wait we walked a short distance to a café for our first meal of the day.

We caught the train and arrived in Ipswich about 6:30 P.M. We acquired a room at the Metrapol Hotel after which, even though we were dead tired walked back to the main part of town and had another round of steak and eggs. We took in a show, in which I fell asleep for nearly the complete program. It didn't take us long to fall asleep. "What a day."

Wednesday, November 24, 1943 We were awakened at 6 A.M. and by 6:30 we were on the street waiting for the bus to take us to Amberly Field. We arrived at the field at 7 A.M. and proceeded to find the location where the ship would take off from. After much walking and inquiring we finally found the spot, but our ship, to our disappointment, was not there. We sat down to wait. 8 A.M. passed nine o'clock and no ship had showed up. Finally I walked into the office and asked if they could find out and details about the B24 we were to catch a ride in. The clerk was very obliging and called the Archer Field. They informed him that the ship would leave there in a few minutes. In about ten minutes we saw our ship approaching the air port to land. Bill and I were ready to jump in as soon as the ship touched the ground. The ship circled, but instead of coming in on the regular runway, landed on the emergency strip, which was just a dirt runway. The ship landed ok but when it started to turn around one wheel sunk hub deep in the soft ground.

Bill and I sat and waited for over an hour. Finally I told Bill to watch our bags, and I would take a walk out across the field to the plane. When I got there, by all appearances, the ship looked as if it would be there for some time. I helped dig and place running striping out in front of the wheels. Three ten wheeler trucks were pulling on one wheel, two more on the other and a caterpillar in

167

the center and still the ship would not budge. Finally by a lot more digging the trucks managed to get the ship out. Even then care had to be taken to keep the wheels on the stripping so it wouldn't sink. At noon the crew left for chow.

I [rode] back to where Bill was waiting. It looked as if we would be out of luck for dinner again. We decided to try and find a P.X. and maybe we could buy some cookies and pop or something. After a little walk up the road, we came passed a mess hall, we decided to wait and see if it were an enlisted man's mess and if so we would try and bum them for a meal, (what did we have to lose ?) We walked inside and spoke to the mess sgt. and told him we were passing through. We had spaghetti and meatballs and I think this rates among one of my best G.I. meals. After eating we went back to wait, for how long, we did not know. We were beginning to feel that the chances of leaving that day were becoming slim.

At 2:00 P.M. they finally got the ship out. The pilot decided we could go to Townsville before dark. At about 3 P.M. we all got aboard. Ten of us besides the crew, and took off. We flew at about 8000 feet, the air was smooth and the trip was quite enjoyable. This ship was built for combat and not for comfort as far as any easy chairs are concerned. I sat on a step towards the rear of the ship, with my legs across a glassed in trap door, used for an emergency exit and an aerial camera position. From here you could see the ground straight below as well as off towards the side through other small windows that run up the side.

We reached Townsville around 7 P.M. and got aboard a bus that took us into town. We intended staying at the red cross that night but they said "no" due to the fact that we were coming back from furlough rather than going. We were supposed to check in at Armstrong Camp, which meant a similar deal as Camp Ascot in Brisbane. We finally got a bed at the Australian YMCA. Bill and I ate supper and then went to a show. We were in bed at 11PM, tired as heck as this day was nearly as rugged as the day before.

In the fold of this page my mother has written; "These little notes to cheer you, honey. I love you."

Thursday, November 25, 1943 We were up at 7 A.M. We took a shower and then went out and got breakfast. We did not have to rush so much this morning as we do not have to be out to Garbart Field until 9 A.M. We left our luggage in the ship last night. So, we do not have the task of carrying it around.

We met some of the crew members and we "thumbed" a ride out to the field. We met Lt. Turner and then walked over to the ship. By the time the ship was gassed up and checked it was 9:30 A.M. I was one of the first ones aboard and got a choice seat in the pilot's compartment. I had a long conversation with the navigator who showed me something of the procedure used in the navigation of the ship and the instruments used. A radio operators' job would be a "cinch." They only work around fifteen words per min. Of course in a pinch they have to act as gunner.

After taking off the trip was the same as the others. We were out of sight of land until reaching New Guinea. The trip was uneventful. The air was smooth with scattered clouds. On one occasion we climbed to 12,500 ft. to go above a cloud bank. We reached New Guinea approximately 100 miles down the coast and followed it along until we reached Port Moresby.

We landed at Wards Drome, the same place from which we departed. Our flying time was 3 ½ hours. After unloading our barracks bags Bill and I proceeded to try and catch a ride into town. We finally caught a ride in the back of a G.I. truck which took us into Moresby. From there we hitched another ride out to GHQ and our headquarters.

It certainly is not a pleasant feeling to know our vacation is all over and we are once more stuck for a long grind. As I suspected might happen, all my belongings have been taken to the supply room and my former tent occupied by a new bunch, and I am back in a tent with no floor again. "Never let it be said I ever again help build another floor for the Army."

I hear they had a pretty good Thanksgiving dinner today. We missed out on this as at that time we were a few hundred miles from here. The only good thing about getting back is to read our mail that has collected while we have been gone.

The fellows tell me that the trick chiefs are now all master sergeants. I don't consider this a loss as I was doing a lot of hard work, taking a big responsibility and working with the handicap of a low rating without any credit or promotion. In the station there are now five master sergeants, three tech sgts. and numerous numbers of staff sergeants. Most of these fellows have just arrived over from the states and were given their ratings before leaving. This is the chief reason for the impossibility to get a rating. The rating quota is always filled up due to the new men all already having them. The fact that I have had to sweat it out for nearly a year here in New Guinea with this result. Needless to say how many of us feel who are all in the same boat.

Friday, November 26, 1943 I slept rather late this morning as I feel now I need a rest from my vacation. Bill and I waited till this afternoon to turn in to Lt. Neilson our commanding officer. When we walked into the office Lt. Neilson gave us kind of a sly grin and asked how long we were in Sydney? He knew as well as we that we had spent more than the allotted week there. I told him our orders read a period of one week. Since our orders were in order all the way to Sydney and back as far as Brisbane, and we were listed as passengers on this bomber we apparently were only victims of difficult transportation to Sydney (thanks to the fact we had six sets of orders). Bill is to go to work at 5 PM and I at midnight. I will take up my old-time duties operating.

In the fold of this page my mother has written: "You better be homeward bound or else write to me for a new book, honey. I'll always love you, dear."

Saturday, November 27, 1943 Everyone has kept me busy the past couple of days, answering questions about my furlough. This noon I got the surprise of my life. I was standing near the mess hall talking to some fellows when I heard a familiar voice behind me, call my name. I turned around and who should it be but Laverne Simpson, an old friend from Des Moines. Boy what a treat to talk to someone you really know and can sit down and have a face to face talk. I borrowed a mess kit and we and we had chow at our mess hall. After eating we talked a while and Laverne suggested that I come out and spend the night with him, and we would try and get transportation for a air ride over the hump (Owen Stanley Mountains) to Nadzab Airport tomorrow. Luckily I get tomorrow off, so I went with Laverne out to the airport where he is stationed. He is attached to an air transport unit. Laverne made arrangements for our ride tomorrow and then we got in a jeep and went to a show.

Sunday, November 28, 1943 Laverne and I arose at 5 A.M. this morning. We went to the mess hall where we had some breakfast. Then a bunch of us got into a truck that took us over where the transports were lined up. Little after daylight we took off. After all transports were in the air, the fighter escorts took to the air. Transports flying across the range are given fighter cover. Especially to Nadzab Air Drome, as this is one of the forward air drones, located in the

Markham Valley, the area taken by a force of paratroopers about two and a half months ago. This air field is constantly bombed and attack by the Japs whenever they can manage to break through our fighter force. Nadzab is located about a ten minute flight west of Lae. The ride we took this morning is rated as a mission since out destination is so close to enemy territory. Today was a nice day and you could plainly see the surrounding country for miles. Our ship climbed to around eight thousand feet, a height required to go through the pass. The Owen Stanley Mountains are quite rugged and covered by dense jungle. Only a very small percent of flyers forced down in these mountains even if landing safely, ever live to overcome such an entanglement. Few fliers who were lucky in cutting their way through the jungle and rescued by friendly natives have ever returned. The mountains on either side of the pass reach an elevation of better than 10,000 feet, leaving a space of quite a number of miles as an area for our transport to fly through. The distance from Moresby to Nadzeb being but an hour flight did not give the required length of time to fly over above the highest peaks. Our first landmark was Wau, a small settlement before the war and now a secondary post with an air strip. Many months ago the Japs made a drive in an effort to capture Wau. However the Allies were successful in driving them back. From here our plane changed course and we flew in a north westerly direction. We were now over the range and the country was becoming more level as we neared the Markham Valley. Our ship had left the others as we were the only ship going to Nadzeb. As we approached Nadzeb Air Drone, swarms of fighters were flying everywhere. Unless our forces keep an "air umbrella" over head all the time the Japs would fly in bomb and strafe* and are gone before our ships can get into the air. Nadzeb is bombed and strafed constantly day and night. However our forces have air superiority so are able to hold them off pretty well. Our ship landed on the somewhat crude and underdeveloped runway and then taxied over to the unloading location. While the ship was being unloaded Laverne and I stood out of the way in the only shady spot available, under the wing of the ship. A little look around might have been in order, but everything to be seen was easy from our shady spot. After about an hour the ship was unloaded and we got aboard again to take off for Moresby. A bunch of Australian infantry soldiers road back to Moresby with us. They have seen a lot of action and going to Moresby for a little rest. To these fellows Moresby is quite a civilized place. We arrived back in Moresby our trip lasting a little over three hours. I ate dinner at Laverne's mess hall after which he brought me back to camp since I have to go to work this evening at 5 P.M. Work went as usual tonight. I am very rusty at operating since I have done very little of it in the past seven months.[34]

Monday, November 29, 1943 Today is just a routine day. I spent most of my time writing letters and reading over some more of my mail. I was surprised to find after returning from my furlough that many of the old Tyler Texas bunch, the fellows I went to radio school and came across with, are now here. It seems good to have a chat with them.

Tuesday, November 30, 1943 Today is just another day. I am still writing letters in an attempt to catch up with my neglected letter schedule. We are on the edge of summer now and it rains every once in a while. Before long, it will be raining everyday and then the mosquitoes will become more of a menace again. Today is the last day of November as well as the last page of this book. This is book number two.

Wednesday, December 1, 1943 I was given today off so had some extra time to write letters and read over some of my old ones. I have been thinking lately that perhaps I might take a try at officer's training school. A fellow's chances are very slim of getting through even if you are admitted. They usually wash out about two thirds of the class. I went to the show down at the navy camp tonight.

Saturday, December 4, 1943 Today is our long day to work as we have to come to work tomorrow morning at 7 AM. I wrote some letters today and fixed up around my bunk. We found a nest of four black widow spiders and didn't waste any time getting rid of them. Black widow spiders are very common around here and we are always on the lookout for them.

Sunday, December 5, 1943 Worked all day. This evening when I returned from the station I shook a centipede out of my shelter half that was about five inches long. I also found another black widow spider. The carpenter brought some lumber up to our tent today and made a side wall wrapping around our tent. The fellows also raised our tent up two feet higher.

Monday, December 6, 1943 Worked as usual today. I have now spent eleven months here in New Guinea. No one seems to care how long you have been

---

[34] strafe; to attack with machine gun fire.

sweating it out up here. Since it doesn't directly concern them they don't care. Nine soldiers out of ten who are around this area haven't been here in New Guinea as long as I have. Some of the fellows who were relieved to Brisbane and spent five months there are now back but no effort is being made to relieve us.

Tuesday, December 7, 1943 The fellows in my tent today dug the floor out level and covered it with gravel. Since I was on the day shift I didn't help the fellows. The U.S. has been at war with Japan three years now.

Wednesday, December 8, 1943 December A number of the pictures I have taken didn't turn out very well. Some of the film I have saved have become damp and are nearly useless. It is impossible to get any film in the states now. In Australia if you want film you have to stand in a long line and if you are lucky may get one roll. Work as usual at the station. When I started working a circuit again I was sure rusty, but I am picking up now. This is the first operating I have done for seven months.

Thursday, December 9, 1943 Work as usual today. At noon I saw our Co. Commander and told him my intention to try for Officer's Candidate School. He told me where I could get my forms to fill out. I went to the orderly room, but was informed that it was too late to put in application for this school period. I will have to wait two or three months.

Friday, December 10, 1943 I saw a second lieutenant friend of mine today that came over from the states as a private with the bunch of fellows I was with. He just finished Officer's School. He has informed me of a number of things I should study up on. Tonight we had a red alert. It was rather foggy and to any Jap flying up there he could only know where he was at by his instruments. The alert lasted without any fire works for about an hour.

Saturday, December 11, 1943 I got today off so I caught a ride out to see Laverne. He was busy today so we didn't catch a ride by air any place. We sat and talked most of the afternoon and in the evening we went to a show. After which he brought me back to camp.

Sunday, December 12, 1943 It is always a pleasure to get away from the day shift. You work ten hours, three hours longer than the other shifts and there are always big shots around. There are a number of high army generals and admirals here at G.H.Q. now: George Marshal, Gen. MacArthur a lieutenant general who is a personal representative of Churchill and a couple top notch admirals.

Monday, December 13, 1943 My mail from home has sure hit a slump. I guess letters are being held up for Christmas packages. The mail service on Christmas packages is a hundred percent better than last year and they arrive in much better condition. Work the same as ever.

Tuesday, December 14, 1943 Nothing unusual today. The same old routine. My furlough is fast becoming a memory. When the day comes that letters will no longer be censored I will be able to tell Marian a more accurate account of my furlough, As it was I could mention but one week since our commanding officer censors a good share of the mail. Went to the show tonight.

Wednesday, December 15, 1943 Today Marian and I have been married two years and a half, of that time we had eight months of happiness together. A bunch of us went down to the Navy to the show tonight. The show was quite long and therefore we got no rest before going to work. We were sure a tired bunch.

Thursday 16, December 1943 I felt rather low today. I received a letter from Marian at last and it informed me due to her displeasure over a certain matter had not written to me for a week. Every day I get more fed up with this place. I have almost decided to ask to be sent up to our forward most station which is with the infantry about seven miles behind the front lines.

Friday, December 17, 1943 We were all taken into town today and given shots for cholera. My arm is rather sore tonight and has made me a little ill. I get tomorrow off as it is the change of shift where we have gained thirty hours. I intend to go out and see Laverne: I didn't feel much like working tonight, but I got on a slow circuit and made it OK.

Saturday, December 18, 1943 I slept this morning. This afternoon I wrote some letters. One of them to Laverne's wife and then caught a ride out to see Laverne. I got there just in time for chow. After supper we took a few pictures and sat around and talked. There is another fellow in Laverne's tent who is from Madrid Iowa. After talking to him I learned that he once collected cream on a route near New Virginia, IA and knew a lot of people I know. Laverne had a sty on one of his eyes so we decided to skip a show for tonight. The fellows in the tent rigged up a bunk for me and I stayed with them all night.

Sunday, December 19, 1943 Since Laverne was going to be busy today I caught a ride back to my camp. I arrived there just in time for dinner, after which I wrote a number of letters. Went to work on the second shift tonight.

Monday, December 20, 1943 I received three packages today, two from Marian and one from Don Walker, & family. I am keeping one of Marian's packages to open on Christmas. Work as usual today. A bunch of my old buddies are being moved. There are still a bunch of the fellows on furlough. Mac and Fitz were lucky and got air transport. The rest of the fellows who came behind them are stuck in Camp Ascot in Brisbane. The new ruling for fellows who go on furlough is that every six months (more like twelve months) you are given 15 days furlough and furnished transportation by boat which amounts to two weeks round trip.

Tuesday, December 21, 1943 Received a Christmas card from Aunt Effie and Uncle Will today. No other mail arrived. Nothing unusual today, work as usual. I worked Townsville tonight and had a good operator. I am stuck for police detail this week, since I am on the second shift. Another fellow in my tent is in the same boat so we each go turn about and call the others name.

Wednesday, December 22, 1943 I spent the busiest night at the station I ever have. The operator at Brisbane sent at a speed you could barely keep up with for message after message. I worked constantly for four hours receiving messages. After receiving 27 messages, the trick chief sat down and took a few. Received another package today of which I am saving to open on Christmas. I will have to wait till I open it to find out who it is from as there is no address on the outside.

Thursday, December 23, 1943 The same routine today. My friends who were transferred to the air corps have sure gotten a bad deal. They are stationed out in the bush. The station [is] no good. One simplex circuit has eight stations in it. The chow is bad, and no wash water. I worked Townsville tonight was rather busy. Not as much so, as last night though. That was really something. No mail today.

Friday, December 24, 1943 Nothing happened out of the way today. Tonight at work we greeted the ops on the other end of our circuit MERRY CHRISTMAS. Received a couple of Christmas cards today and wrote some letters

Saturday, December 25, 1943 Today is Christmas. That is it is in name only, with the surroundings such as they are. Such as everything you see is Army G.I. trucks on the ground and fighter planes in the air and all this at 100 degrees in the shade. So this is far from the old fashion Christmas most of us are use to. I opened my two remaining presents in the presence of the fellows in my tent a little past midnight. One of the packages contained candy of which all of us had somewhat of a feast. We really had a swell dinner today; turkey, dressing, sweet & mashed potatoes, scalloped corn, radishes & olives, fruit cocktail, cake & ice cream. This is a far cry from what the fellows had up here last year. I was lucky and had not arrived here at that time. The fellows who were here for Christmas had a Christmas dinner of sardines & bean and coffee.

Sunday, December 26, 1943 I have had a headache for the past two days. Today I told the trick chief I was going to take the day off, after going to work this morning. I came back to my tent and spent the rest of the day in my bunk. I went to sleep and didn't wake up until evening. I wrote a couple of letters and went to bed early. Two of the fellows who went on furlough succeeded in getting relieved from up here. Neither one of them have been up here as long as I have. However I don't mind as by my coming back up here to New Guinea gives me a better chance at O.C.S.

Monday, December 27, 1943 I feel a little better today. I always hate the day shift as you have little time for anything but work. There is little more than an hour and a half of daylight to write letters in. I thought sure I would get some letters from Marian today, but no luck.

Tuesday, December 28, 1943 The same old thing today. Worked ten hours, wrote a couple of letters this evening and then went to the show. The Allied forces are making slight gains on all fronts. The Russian forces have made marked gains in the North Central front. American forces have now made a landing on New Britain Island near the Jap base of Gasmata. The Japs are striving to reinforce Rabaul, as its loss would mean a vital blow.

Wednesday, December 29, 1943 Things have started popping around here. Major General Aiken, Signal Officer of South Pacific was waiting for air transportation of which was requested via an urgent message through one of our circuits. It seems the message became messed up and so did the General's plans: The General strode into the station this afternoon and asked every circuit how long they had been in contact, luckily all circuits were in. Still no mail from home. I heard, and I guess it has become official that 15,000 bags of mail went down with a ship. No doubt some of my mail is in the bottom of the ocean.

Thursday, December 30, 1943 The General sure does get around. He was in the stations from one till 3:30 AM this morning. The operator working the LX circuit sure had a tough night with the General standing over him and asking questions every few minutes. Tonight all operators had to report to the radio station at 6:30 pm: as we all suspected we were in for a bawling out which lasted about 34 minutes. I received a Christmas card from Simpsons today. Still no mail from home. I wrote a letter to Marian tonight.

Friday, December 31, 1943 This brings to a close 1943. A year packed with history that will last till the end of time: 1943 was not a pleasant year for me, nor for anyone else in the same environment. However, I am able to say, "Things could have been a lot worse." Many Americans are lying in the jungle over across the range, who will never return home. The fact that I have nearly gone "nuts" the past few months from boredom, leaves no fear in me what so ever of the chance, sometime, I may go up to the front. If it were not for the fact that I am planning on O.C.S. I would volunteer. Yesterday a lieutenant informed me that the fellows who spent the past year here in New Guinea and handled messages during the Papua campaign, will get some sort of decoration. At midnight a bunch of fellows took their machine guns, and hailed in the New Year. I was a little worried for fear they might turn on the wrong direction and spray the hill.

This is the end of this book. To be continued in Green 1944 diary, or book three.

Desk Secretary

APPOINTMENTS   MEMORANDA

1944

Saturday, January 1, 1944 Well here we go again, the starting of a new year. It makes me wonder what I will write on the last page of this book a year from now. However, since we are at war, a fellow forms the habit of not thinking in terms of what might happen next week, next month, or a year from now. Most of us only think in terms of the end of the war. There is nothing to look forward to from today to that end. Today was just another day. I worked at the station and went to the show down at the navy tonight.

Sunday, January 2, 1944 I worked the day shift again today and go on the midnight shift tonight. No mail what so ever again today. It's an awful feeling when day after day not a single letter from home.

Monday, January 3, 1944 I slept this morning to a small extent. Being our tent is right out in the open, to sleep is impossible after about 11 AM. This afternoon I went with a lieutenant friend of mine out to one of the airplane junk yards. All sorts of ships were piled up. All sizes and shapes from fortresses down to permit ships. Most of them showed signs of battle, having shrapnel, cannon and machine gun holes in the fuselage. Slept after supper and went to work at midnight.

Tuesday, January 4, 1944 I slept till noon today, and this afternoon I caught a ride into town. I went to the Sergeant's Club and picked up my membership card. I am a charter member and one of the oldest members of the club. Originally there were only about 75 Australians and American members combined. Now the membership is in the hundreds and has over $2000 cash fund on hand. The club is now in the Moresby Hotel and it is out classed by no other officers club of any kind in New Guinea: I went to the post office and got a money order to send to Jack as a wedding present. If his plans worked out, he is probably married by now. It was planned that I was to be his best man, but war causes many disappointments. Still no letters from home.

Wednesday, January 5, 1944 Spent this morning in my bunk trying to get a little sleep. It is getting hotter everyday: The food at our mess hall now is sure getting punk. For awhile we were getting fresh vegetables and meat but the past couple of weeks we have been getting hardly anything but field rations and dehydrated vegetables such as potatoes and cabbage: There is still no mail from home. It is an empty business writing letters home with no reply: Seventy soldiers of the

832 Sig. Co .which I am one, received citations for the active part we played in the "Pagat Point Campaign (Guam, Mariana Is.) The fact the 832nd must have some 1,500 members causes me to be a little proud that I receive this award. War news continues to be as encouraging as ever. The Russian forces in a large-scale onslaught have advanced farther on west of Kieice. It is reported that they have now crossed the old Polish border. Berlin is reported to be two thirds in shambles. The American and British air forces are continually increasing their onslaught on German cities. It is hard to see how a country can take such a pounding. German propagandists keep the flame of a secret weapon alive and continually say that England and the other Allies forces will meet terrible retaliation. The only new weapon the Germans have come forward with is a type of rocket gun used by their permit ships. This seems to be quite effective, but the Allied air force has effectively devised a means of counteracting this weapon. It is reported that the Germans are constructing huge rocket gun emplacements along the French coast. Reports state the Allied forces in Burma are making slight gains.

The Chinese theatre is rather quiet. Operations in Italy are going very slow due to the mountainous country and bad weather conditions. We are making substantial gains here in New Guinea. Our forces have made landings at Cape Gloucester in New Britain and have, after weeks fighting, captured the Jap air stripes. Our forces have also made a landing just forty miles from Madang and have cut off the Jap retreat from the Huon Peninsula.

Thursday, January 6, 1944 Nothing new today, the same routine. The fellows in the 52nd around here have the rumor started that they are to be sent home. They say the reason being that their outfit has been over here for so long. It is true the 52nd was in Australia first, in Melbourne and Sydney. But when they tell me they have caught so much hell in this country that is a lot of bull. I personally know what the score is – Never at any time did the 52nd have many more than a dozen men in New Guinea at a time, and they operated only two circuits one to Townsville and Brisbane. They were under the supervision of our 832nd officers at base radio.

Friday, January 7, 1944 Boy the 52nd guys are going wild. All you hear from one end of the camp to the other is "We are going home". Someone saw the orders "We will be home in two months." I wouldn't be surprised if some of them were not packing their clothes: All they can think, and with not a bit of reason is "going home." To ask them who will take their place and how a war can be won by sending everyone home, goes in one ear and out the other. It has even spread around now that all personal of all units overseas eighteen months and in the tropics one year will be sent home. Two months and I will be in line, "whoop pee". This has been the top notch rumor for as long as I can remember.

Saturday, January 8, 1944 Today I had planned to go out and see Laverne Simpson, but being I worked last night, I decided to sleep till noon. I felt rather tired this afternoon, so I decided to wait until tomorrow since I don't go to work till 5 PM: Boy the affects of that walk up into the hills has sure left its' mark. I have been tired ever since: This "song and dance" about going home has sure reached an all time high. They have me believing it. The fellows don't talk about just going home now, but argue who is eligible to go first. For my past I have the required length of duty in the tropics and only have two more months to serve for completion of required 18 months over- seas. I am not going to get excited. Not until see the order on the bulletin board.

Sunday, January 9, 1944 I hitchhiked out to see Laverne this afternoon. We sat around and talked for a while. This Friday Laverne is going to try to go up to Finschhafen. All I have to do is see if I can get Friday off. I finally received a letter from Marian today. Another fellow in my tent is nearly sick because it has been so long since his last letter from his wife. I'm beginning to wonder if there isn't something to have fellows going home. I can't help believe, if going home is true that there is something special for us. Maybe the big show in Europe? The whole thing by all logic just don't add up. As far as I can learn the whole island of New Guinea is all up in the air about going home. A friend of Laverne's gave me a mattress cover.

Monday, January 10, 1944 The same routine today. As far as I can learn the only thing being talked about in New Guinea is about going home. Many of the fellows are writing home about it. For myself I hope none of my folks hear about it. As if this thing blows over, I will be the only one disappointed. I don't intend to mention a word to Marian or the folks until I reach San Francisco.

Tuesday, January 11, 1944 Today is just a routine day, except the fact I have a bad cold and feel like I was getting the flu. It rained a little bit today but didn't amount to much. It has been comparatively dry this summer. Last year at this time our tent was swamped most of the time. I hear there is a chance we fellows may get to go back to Brisbane. Now that this going home deal requires six months in the tropics, all the boys down south are crying to come up here.

Wednesday, January 12, 1944 I feel a little better today, however, I still feel quite washed out. I received a package from mom today. It had been mailed Oct. 15. It was in quite good condition, however, some of them are pretty well beat up when they arrive. This brings my average to two letters and a package in the past month. The quality of chow has sure dropped off lately. We get mostly dehydrated foods such as potatoes, cabbage, canned string beans (they never miss) for a meat dish we are given canned field rations which is a cross between soup and stew. The coffee is more like battery acid.

Thursday, January 13, 1944 I get today off it rained most of the morning and I spent my time writing letters. Early this morning we had to go over to the station and see some motion pictures on "security." The reason for these films was because our outfit was blamed for the news of "our going home" (getting out.) I wonder how they expect to keep anything like that a secret. The news has spread all over the Southwest Pacific and I suppose by now it has reached the U.S. In a short time I expect to receive a gob of enthusiastic letters from home. I intend to throw cold water on the whole thing. Something like this can blow up entirely too easy to have anyone plan on it. I went out to Laverne's camp this afternoon.

Friday, January 14, 1944 I stayed out with Laverne last night since I didn't have to work until 5 this afternoon. The plane ride we planned to go on over the hump this morning didn't plan out as it has been raining continuously. Both ward and seven mile air drones are now practically empty. All bombers have been moved over the range. About all that is here now are a few fighter planes and a couple transport squadrons. In a short time Moresby will become a back number as far as this war is concerned. About the only purpose Moresby has for now is advanced G.H.Q. and a hospital evacuation area. Lavern brought me back in time to go to work tonight.

Saturday, January 15, 1944 I go to work tomorrow on the 7 to five shift. This is a long grind working from five tonight till midnight: I guess this going home news is pretty authentic. Two friends of mine were called into the orderly room to check up on their length of service overseas. As far as rumors go a fellow's priority on going home is done by the point system. For each month in N.

Guinea you get two points for each month down south you receive one point. Each soldier must have 18months overseas and the ones with the higher number of points leave first. I still have a couple of months to go to complete my eighteen months. At the present time as far as points go I have 29. Twenty-four points is eligible and twelve of these must be here in N. Guinea.

Sunday, January 16, 1944 I worked as trick chief last night as the regular fellow had the night off. We had to come to work on the first shift this morning. Still no mail from home. There was no show tonight so I stayed in my tent and wrote a few letters.

Monday, January 17, 1944 Work as usual today. And finally I received a "V" letter from Marian. This is the first word I have heard from her since before Christmas. I could have had today off but I plan to go out and see Laverne on Thursday. I wrote some letters and then went to the show tonight.

Tuesday, January 18, 1944 Two more letters from Marian today. One of them contained news of a circumstance that I was very sorry to hear. Hard for me to understand. I worked at the station as usual, the same old routine. The operator at Townsville tries to snow me under on nearly every message. I am able to sweat him out, but he gives me a pretty rugged go. I went to the show tonight. Boy did it stink. It was a western and a punk one at that.

Wednesday, January, 19, 1944 Went to work as usual today. I have been working WVLT (Townsville) lately and business has been rather slow. The only time there is much to do is whenever the high speed breaks down on the WVLB (Brisbane) circuits and we route traffic through WVLT. I expected Laverne Simpson to come over tonight. I waited until nearly time for the show to start but he dident (didn't) come. I went down to the show by myself. Today is Jack's birthday.[35]

Thursday, January, 20, 1944 Since I was given today off and had planned to go out to Laverne's camp, I caught a ride after breakfast and went over. You can make nearly as good time hitch hiking as if you drove yourself. Laverne and I had planned to take a plane ride over the hump, but Lavern was busy this morning

---

[35] There is a note at the bottom of this entry stating: "Turn on over three leaves, past inserted sheets then come back." I am not sure of the significance regarding this.

and couldn't go along. He fixed it with the pilot so that I could make the trip by myself. About 10:30 AM they finished loading the ship, the cargo consisting of two large two wheeled fire extinguishers (the kind they used the night the power house burned down) and a cement mixer. We took off and headed up the coast flying over swamp country for around fifty miles. Then we turned inland and headed over the mountains. By this time we were around eight thousand feet high. After about thirty minutes we were in the pass and going over the Owen Stanley Mountains. Mountains rose thousands of feet above us on either side, even though we were now more than eight thousand feet up. You would get a fantastic sensation as one minute we would cross the top of a peak and perhaps be but a couple thousand feet from the ground. As we flew on the ground would drop away into the valleys and we would be thousands of feet above the earth again. The windows of the plane had small holes in the center for the purpose of shooting a machine gun out of if attacked by Jap planes. However I used these openings to take pictures out of with my camera. All told – I took two roles. I certainly hope they turn out ok and the censor does not hold them. We passed over the mountains and reached the coast near Salamaua (E. New Guinea.) From there we flew on up the coast to Lae, our destination. Lae from the air looked like quite a nice place, but it was plain to see it had taken an awful beating from the air by our bombers before we captured it from the Japs. Bomb creators all over and the tops of the trees gone. The air strip stretches from the water's edge of the beach inland, and is about three thousand feet long. The terrain beyond the end of the runway is quite level and the trees have been cleared so as to allow planes to take off in that direction. Nearly directly in front of the runway on the seaward side is a Jap ship that our planes sank. Off to one side at the other end of the airstrip is a junk yard that contains mostly wrecked Jap planes. Since our plane didn't require much time for unloading I didn't have time to get a couple of pieces of the Jap ships. We were only in Lae about forty five minutes and then we took off for Moresby again. We flew over the same route we had come. Again crossing a couple of hundred miles of mountainous jungle and swamp country,. About half way back the pilot just to see if he could scare heck out of me, and the two Aussies that also were aboard shut off one of the motors. Had the other motor stopped we would have been 100 percent out of luck. When we reached this side of the range and proceeded on the last leg of the trip across the stretch of swamp country. The pilot brought the ship down and we flew for a number of miles, about twenty five feet above the treetops. It was about 2:30 PM when we arrived back at "seven mile" air strip. It is also called "Jackson Drone." I walked part of the way back to Laverne's camp, and caught a ride the rest of the way. I spent the rest of the afternoon making a bracelet out of some Australian coins. This evening we watched a show that was in Laverne's camp area, after which Laverne brought me back to camp.

Friday, January 21, 1944 To work as usual today and the same old grind. On the Russian front – the Russians are in the midst of a full scale offensive in the Leningrad sectors. They have driven a wedge some thirty miles through the German defense system, which consisted of concrete pill boxes and permanent fortifications of which the Germans have been building for the past two years.

Saturday, January 22, 1944 I worked all day and now go in again at midnight, being this is the day of change. I work as trick chief tonight, since the other fellow is taking the night off. It was reported today that an American force has made a landing back of the German lines about thirty miles from Rome. There are no reports as yet as to the success of this operation.

Sunday, January 23, 1944 I worked WVLT tonight, and being the high speed is out to WVLB (Brisbane) I was busy most of the time. Still not much specific news as to the landing made by the American 5th Army near Rome. It is reported progress has been made but little resistance was offered by the Germans.

Monday, January 24, 1944 Slept most of the day. This evening Pat, one of my tent mates and myself ripped up some blankets for a dark room and tried our hand at developing pictures. A bunch of the other fellows came in and what knowledge all of us could dig up on the development of films, we were finally successful in getting a few prints. I didn't have to go to work tonight. Had the night off.

Tuesday, January 25, 1944 The same old routine. A few letters are starting to trickle through to me. I still haven't heard from my folks. It is going on two months now. The new beach head established near Rome by the Fifth Army is gaining some ground. As yet our forces have not met serious ground opposition. The Germans however did some damage in a large scale raid on our shipping. They put everything in the air that they could spare in an effort to cripple our recent gains. Our forces near Rome are advancing toward one of the German's main air drones and a highway leading to Rome: The Russians are still driving ahead in the Leningrad sector: All other fronts are mostly quiet.

Wednesday, January 26, 1944 The same routine today. I have been spending some of my spare time making a frame for the purpose of developing pictures. It is kind of a tough job as all I have to work with is my hunting knife and a worn out piece of sandpaper. It has been raining quite a bit lately. We have two five gallon cans in which we catch rain water off our tent. We also have a drinking water can which we keep filled with rain water.

Thursday, January 27, 1944 The talk about going home has kinda died down, although you can notice a big boost in moral. It is now just a process of putting in your time. The difference being that a fellow gets to return home after a given length of time, whereas before all we could look forward to was staying here till after the war: and the war hasn't even started over here yet. Our forces are just getting in position so we can take a crack at Japan's outer defense ring. Worked as usual tonight. Although I cut one of my fingers yesterday and I am unable to take any messages for the time being.

Friday, January 28, 1944 We had to go over to the station after chow tonight and take a "Q" signal test, which is a pain in the neck. This is the base signal officer's idea. There are a total of some seven hundred "Q" signals. Not more than twelve of these do we ever use and most of these perhaps once a week or less. Our chief operator knows himself what a bunch of hooey this is, but he has his orders so that is that. Naturally should we fellows fail their test of which we have one a week it would reflect on the signal officers of our station, the chief operators, and the station in general. So no notice is taken when we help each other along. Next week's test has already been seen by most of us. Today is Sally's birthday. *(Sally is my dad's sister)*

Saturday, January 29, 1944 I worked as trick chief last night as the regular fellow had the night off. I was very tired tonight since I went to the show before work. It rained nearly all day and was a swell day to sleep. I didn't get up until 3:30 PM. A few minutes ago as I sat here writing I thought I heard the air raid horn blow over at Moresby. It blew again in a few minutes and Moresby was blacked out. However no one was aware of the warning in this camp as hardly anyone around here knows what the air raid horn sounds like anyway. I walked down around some of the tents and told them of the alert. It wasn't long before the whole camp was dark. The alert lasted about half an hour and as usual no Japs.

Sunday, January 30, 1944 It rained again nearly all day. I spent my time writing and sleeping. Tonight Pat and myself rigged up some blankets for a dark room and tried to developing some pictures. We didn't have much luck. No mail again today. It has been about two months since I last heard from the folks.

Monday, January 31, 1944 I slept late this morning. I haven't felt so good lately. I wonder if my eyes are causing my headaches. It has been raining now for the past three days and it looks like the rainy season has broke at last. Still no word from the folks today. I am a little worried as in Aunt Effie's last letter she mentioned that dad might go to Rochester or Iowa City to the hospital for a checkup. I have never told them I knew about it, as I think I am not supposed to worry.

Tuesday, February 1, 1944 We received a bunch of new magazines in the day room today so I spent a little time reading them. I worked WVLT tonight. I had such a headache I couldn't hardly stand the sound of the signal: The war is moving along about the same plane. Gains are being made on all fronts. Russia in the Leningrad sector is now but eight miles from the Estonian and Latvian border. Only a gap of 27 miles is left as an escape route for the Germans. The Allied air forces are still hammering the European fortress. It seems the intention is to wipe out Berlin. The main topic is still the second front, but it has been delayed so long it seems time might work for the Germans: Small advances are being made in China and Burma: Our forces in Italy are making some gains and the new beach head near Rome is gaining ground: Slight progress is being made towards Madang. Japs in the S.W.P.A.

Wednesday, February 2, 1944 I feel a little better today. I worked WVLT tonight and boy what a speed demon on the other end. I only wished I could have dished it out like he was handing it to me. My sending with a bug is rather rugged. While every other station in the S.W. Pacific was learning to use a bug, we fellows back at base radio station had to use a hand key. I received two letters from Marian today. Still no word from the folks. I am getting kind of fed up with this letter writing business. Not counting Marian, in the past five weeks I have written fifteen letters home and only received three, two from Sally & Dick, one from Jack.

Thursday, February 3, 1944 I was given the day off and spent most of the day lying around. This afternoon I built a box for the purpose of sending a model boat and [an] alligator model home. These gadgets were made by the natives. The intercept station is being closed down so we will have forty five more operators. Tomorrow we are going to start working six hours on and twenty four off. Plus a couple of days off a week. This is sure a break. The first one I have had since coming to New Guinea. A fellow doesn't notice the difference in complexion until you see a fellow just over from the states. All of us have been fed a steady diet of [Atabrine], a medicine to counteract malaria, and [it has] made us a yellow color.

Friday, February 4, 1944 It has been raining steady for the past four days. I guess the rainy season has broken at last. Since I don't have to go to work until midnight tonight, I decided to go out and see Laverne today. As usual I had no trouble catching a ride and I was out there in thirty minutes. I talked to Laverne for quite a while and spent the afternoon making a bracelet out of Australian coins. Laverne brought me back in time for work tonight: It is reported that the Americans have invaded the Marshall Islands and are meeting with great success. This puts our forces in line to strike at Truk, the Jap's main naval base, and Rabaul, the Jap's strong base in New Britain. I finally received a letter from the folks. Everything seems to be ok. They have heard about the plan of we fellows getting sent home. In my letters home I am leading them to believe I will not be one of the lucky ones.

Saturday, February 5, 1944 Boy I am sure tired today after working last night and no sleep before hand. I now don't have to go to work until 7 AM Sunday morning and then work only till noon. This new shift set up is sure the thing: An airplane crash took the lives of two of our fellows in our company yesterday. They went out to the air drone where they caught a ride in a B25 bomber to do some practice bombing out in the bay by the old boat. At the moment the bombs were released the ship went into a spin and disappeared in the ocean. No trace of them has been found. One of the fellows I [knew] very well. He was my tent mate for a short time and used to run the laundry at which time he did me many favors. The saddest part of the whole thing is that he was to be sent back to the states in another month: We had a dance in our mess hall tonight. The 52nd has a four piece orchestra who furnished the music. They managed to scrape up six girls who are Red Cross workers. This brought the odds to about fifty fellows to one girl. It was a tag dance, and if you were lucky to get the first slap on a fellow's, back you had the pleasure of making a turn (should say a twirl) then you were beat almost to the floor by forty-nine other guys. Some fun.

Sunday, February 6, 1944 Worked from 7 AM until noon. Tomorrow it will be noon to 5 PM. Boy this is more like it now: I didn't stay at the dance so long last night. Laverne and a couple of friends came down and we went into town to the Sergeant's Club. Laverne and the other fellows got membership cards. I worked W.V.L.B. today for a change. With the hours so short a fellow will have to work a busy circuit to keep up your code speed.

Monday, February 7, 1944 Went into town this morning for dental inspection. My teeth are not in too good shape. Worked from noon until 5 P.M. I sat on Brisbane circuit again and handled quite a bit of traffic. I have received no mail of any kind for the past two days.

Tuesday, February 8, 1944 I had today off and had quite a number of things planned, but didn't carry them out. I wrote a number of letters and laid around the rest of the day. There was no show tonight so I went to bed early. The rainy weather has sure made the mosquitoes thick. They hum around your net all night and if it isn't tucked in well, you will be eaten to a pulp. The German armies are making a big attempt to stop the Allied drive toward Rome. Most of the pressure is being exerted against the new beach head near Rome. An all out counterattack is expected on the new beach head by the German Armies at any moment.

Wednesday, February 9, 1944 I laid around most of the day and wrote letters. The weather is so hot and damp a fellow doesn't feel like stirring around much. Any exertion you put forth more than ordinary, you can feel for days after words. It rained again today, and we once more have our water containers full. Pat, one of my tent mates acquired a couple of empty lard cans. We burned the remaining grease from them and cleaned them up with soap and water. Now we have two more water cans: Went to the show tonight and then to work at midnight. I worked WVLN Finschhafen (E. New Guinea) and boy what a time. The operator there was worse than none at all. Two messages that should have been cleared in fifteen minutes required three hours.

Thursday, February 10, 1944 I slept this morning and got up for chow. Why I don't know as you only go to eat because you have to not because you want to. We are surviving on field rations and dehydrated vegetables. Everyone in the camp knows the moment a boat enters the harbor as it means that maybe we will have fresh meat for a day or two. My mail is sure coming through slow. No letters at all this week. I have been writing Marian every day. No show tonight so I went to bed early.

Friday, February 11, 1944 Went to work at 7 A.M. this morning. About 8 A.M. we got word of a Red alert. The Lieutenant who is the duty officer, answered the phone and wasn't sure what the message had been. He was all up in the air, as he didn't' know who to call back to find out for sure. He received verification from the switch board, who had originally called. The alert only lasted fifteen minutes without event. I went to the show tonight and it poured down practically steady throughout the whole show. I had a rain coat, but even though, I got pretty wet.

Saturday, February 12, 1944 Went to work at noon and worked until 5 p.m. I have been working the busiest and fastest circuit in the station lately. Now that our working hours have been cut down I rather work a long busy circuit and keep my code speed up better. I guess I can copy around twenty seven code groups per minute. The black widow spiders are sure thick in this area. I think in the past month I have killed nearly a dozen of them. I received a letter from Jack today, the only letter this week. I am quite sure now that some of my Christmas mail will never reach me. I think some of it was lost in a boat that was sunk.

Sunday, February 13, 1944 A boat pulled in the other day so we had a pretty good feed today, fresh beef, fresh potatoes, beans and onions, and cold drink. We had ice cream for supper. The ice cream is made from powdered milk so about the only good part of it is that it is cold: I traded a pair of leggings for the plumage of a bird of paradise, this particular bird is only found in New Guinea and are very rare. The natives use them as head dress in their tribal dances.

Valentine Day 14 FEBRUARY Sweethearts

Monday, February 14, 1944 The above item from my thoughtful wife. Valentine's Day just another day here. When I got up this morning the air was filled with dust, and so thick it seemed to fall like snow. Nothing but a volcano could cause such a condition in this country.[36]

---

[36] My mother wrote on this page: "Valentine Day—Sweetheart."

VOLCANO ERUPTS 130 MILES FROM PORT MORESBY

THE volcano on Mt. Goropu, 130 miles east of Moresby and beyond the Owen Stanleys, is in eruption. Preceded by rumblings like the sound of a thunderstorm, the volcano became active on Sunday afternoon. Yesterday the air over Port Moresby was thick with pumice dust. Goropu is the only active volcano in Papua, and one of the few on the entire island of New Guinea. It is located 20 miles SSW of Wanigela, where American troops landed by air in September, 1942, to take up the right flank in the pincers movement on Buna. Goropu erupted twice in October, and again on December 27. In Dec., volcanic dust reached Abau, on the coast, west of Moresby. The present eruption is thought to be of greater intensity.

Tuesday, February 15, 1944 "Our Anniversary" We have been married two years eight months today. I received a letter from Marian today. They have been very few and far between lately, due to the punk mail service. I also received a Christmas gift of a pair of shower shoes from Iva: It was reported today that the dirt condition yesterday was caused by a volcano, about 130 miles from here.

I spent my time this evening writing letters: Had to go to work at midnights: The weather in Italy has cleared and our aircraft are active and giving our ground forces great support. Our beach head near Rome has now become quite secure.

Wednesday, February 16, 1944 I had today off and thought I would go out and see Laverne, but I had kind of a headache so I didn't go. It seems my mail slump has broken. I received five letters from Marian and one from David Hughes of Tyler, Texas, and two folders of snap shots I had sent to Sydney to be developed. One negative and the print they did not return to me. I had taken a picture of a Liberator bomber and the photo gave away the position of the raid hour antennas. Went to the show tonight.

Thursday, February 17, 1944 The latest rumor is that our forces have attacked Truk – (W. Pacific, Caroline Island) Japan's main naval base. Truk is to Japan as Pearl Harbor is to the U.S. – No reports have been issued by forces, but Japan reports we have landed an invasion force. Of course, any reports coming from Japan is B.S. The Allied beach head near Rome, Italy is becoming more secure every day. The Germans are attacking with heavy forces without success. The invasion of "Europe talk" has died down. Everything is said to be ready. However I think most of the talk in regard to the invasion is a part of the way of nerves against the Germans. It is the general opinion that the allies will have an extremely tough time whenever the invasion takes place.

Friday, February 18, 1944 My mail has finally started to come through. In the past few days I have received letters every day from Marian and the other folks. Boy it sure gives you a feeling of relief to once more get mail from home. A report came out today about the Truk Operation. The propaganda the Japs put out about an invasion of Truk was false. However, our forces did raid this base with a naval and air task force causing heavy damage.

Saturday, February 19, 1944 Sometimes I get so fed up with this place it seems I just can't make it another week. My mail from home sometimes fails to accomplish my ease of mind. I have thought some of asking for relief to go south but I would be little more satisfied there as here. This going home plan is swell, but it is a bad thing to have on your mind, as I don't know what would happen to a fellow if he had his heart set on it, and everything fell through. Went to the show and then to work at midnight. Rained nearly all night.

Sunday, February 20, 1944 Off work this morning and slept until noon. My mail is still pouring in. I average about three or four letters per day. One letter I received from mom reached me in five days. I received a role of snap shots today. They are one of the two roles I took flying over the Owen Stanley Mountains. I was very disappointed as hardly any of them were any good. The film was old and had gotten damp. I am keeping my fingers crossed on the other role.

Monday, February 21, 1944 Went to work at seven this morning just a routine day. I hear our chief operator is going to be sent down south. While I always got along with him he has always been partial to his Brisbane bunch. Months spent up in this country mean nothing.

Tuesday, February 22, 1944 It has been reported the list has been made out for the first shipment home. Only 52nd men are on this list as they only take care of their own men. The 832nd as usual is left out in the cold. Seemingly no one in this country or anywhere else that gives a damn. Just a bunch of fellows scattered all over the S.W.P.A: One of our fellows who has been overseas more than two years in the tropics— twenty one months and has been through most of the hell of Darwin *(N. Australia)* and New Guinea, is not on any list to return home. There is no one I know of has any more priority to go home than he: It looks like this will be a typical Army deal. The fellow who can pull the hardest and talk loudest will get the breaks.

Wednesday, February 23, 1944 I intended going out to see Laverne today, but didn't get around in time: My mail is still coming through quite well, although I haven't heard from Marian for a number of days. I received another role of film back from Sydney and I really got some swell pictures. These pictures were mostly of our camp area and a group of four different snap shots showing the entire bay. By cutting these pictures to match I really have a swell picture of Moresby and surrounding country. My only hope now is that my next role will be ok. It hasn't arrived yet. This role is of some aerial pictures. I went to the show tonight.

Thursday, February 24, 1944 Yes it's true. Today is my second anniversary in the army. The only thing I am thankful for is these two years are behind me, and I still have my good health, even though my nerves are on the ragged edge. If it wasn't for the thought of getting home: I have to stop and think though how lucky I have really been compared to many other Americans who will never see home again. I received the color pictures from home, that I took and sent back to be developed. I was really pleased with them, and all my friends think I have a prize collection: The other shift forgot to wake me up, so I didn't go to work, but slept right on through.[37]

On Feb. 24, 1941, we stepped from civilian life to Military life, — together.

Friday, February 25, 1944 I thought some of going out to see Laverne today but the weather looked quite threatening so I didn't go. Sure enough, by afternoon it was pouring down. Luckily I spent this morning doing a big washing and by leaving it hang in the rain this afternoon it did a good rinse job. I laid around this afternoon and wrote some letters. Sat through a steady down pour of rain tonight to see a show. Not much news on the war fronts. Slight gains here and there.

Saturday, February 26, 1944 Went to work at seven A.M. and worked until noon. I haven't felt so good lately. Headaches, my shoulder and arms are stiff, and the muscles in my jaws seen stiff. I don't know if it's my eyes, teeth or just nerves. It looks like this going home business is being done in the typical Army fashion. Not how much priority you have, but who you know. The only move the 832nd is making is for the fellows down in Australia. If I get home by next Christmas I will consider myself lucky. I have the required length of time in now, plus an extra nine months in New Guinea. Of course as I mentioned before, priority means nothing, and being on detached service, leaves us without anyone to pull for us.

---

[37] A note on this page written by my mother, "On Feb. 24, 1941 we stepped from Civilian life to Military life, - together."

Sunday, February 27, 1944 Just a routine day today. Received a nice valentine and a letter from Sally. Haven't heard from Jack for a while. Don't know if he is married or not. The folks told me Jack's girl has made a trip to Buffalo on some sort of secret government mission. Went to the show tonight. It was a sound picture without any sound. All the fellows hooted and yelled throughout the show. One part where some soldiers were marching, all the fellows chimed in and counted cadence (hup to three four).

Monday, February 28, 1944 It rained nearly all day today. Since most of our mail is flown up from Townsville, hardly any came in today: It looks as if our work honeymoon is over. We went back to the old routine of working full days: Major General Aiken and the General in charge of the U.S. Army Signal Corps came in the station tonight.

Tuesday, February 29, 1944 I had to inset this extra page, since Feb. this year has an extra day. No letters again today. The rainy weather we have been having kinda slows up delivery. I took an easy circuit at work tonight and wrote a couple of letters. I got paid today. I won't be able to save as much this month, as I have some insurance to take care of. Reports came out today that our forces have invaded the Admiralty Islands. These islands are located nearly straight west of Rabaul and north of Madang. With our control of these islands the blockade of Rabaul is complete. Around 50 to thirty thousand Japs are cut off on New Britain. Our air force has pounded Rabaul so thoroughly that this former Jap fortress is no longer a threat of any kind. The Jap air force has been squelched and what ships haven't been sunk in the harbor, have left.

Still in New Guinea

Wednesday, March 1, 1944 It rained nearly all day and night. Our tent area, even though it is on the side of a hill is a regular swamp. Our tent floor is about the same way. The water seeps up through the floor and it becomes as soggy as if it were not covered by a tent. Our floor is covered gravel but it is going down and out of sight fast. A new station has been opened up at Sydney. Most of the operators for this station have been transferred from Milne Bay. The only reason I do not want a transfer is I can save a large percentage of what I earn and I am hopeful that a fellow's service in New Guinea will give him a little priority on going home. I sure have my doubts about this: One of my friends is going to town today to try and find out what the score is. He should have been in the first bunch to go home.

Thursday, March 2, 1944 It still continues to rain and you almost need a pair of hip boots to get around our tent. Robinson, our chief operator has been sent back to Australia. Our chief operator is a master sergeant, who has been my trick chief since I got back from my furlough. He is a pretty good fellow and I am sure will be an improvement over Robinson. My mail is still coming through OK but not quite as good as it was.

Friday, March 3, 1944 The same routine today. It is reported that the American force that landed on the Admiralty Island —caught the Japs completely by surprise, and made the landing with hardly any opposition: The Japs, however, made a strong counter attack with forces they had on surrounding islands. The

Japs were repelled with heavy losses. It has been raining for nearly a week now. Our tent has gotten in such a state that we are going to have to decide on something. After a discussion today we decided to dig a ditch along the backside of our tent floor.

Saturday, March 4, 1944 Went to work at seven this morning. Today is the change over from the five to twelve P.M. shift. While I was at work today the fellows dug a ditch back of our tent floor extending it out the sides of our tent. A steady stream of water has been running from this ditch all day and our tent floor is showing signs of drying out.

Sunday, March 5, 1944 The fellow who wakes the day shift, passed me up this morning and I didn't get to work until eight A.M. No one asked me for an excuse, so I didn't give any. When I got back to my tent this evening, the water was still draining from our ditch as much as ever, and it had cleared up until it was clear as drinking water. At the end of one side of the ditch I dug a hole and put a five gallon can in it, enough water flows to fill this can once every forty five minutes. If our spring keeps flowing and it looks now as if it might, our water worries will be over. We will have enough for all our washing, etc.

Monday, March 6, 1944 Four of our old bunch who saw about transfer, are going to leave to go to Brisbane in a short time. I have still decided that I will stay here for a while. However one thing I am now reasonably sure of and that is we 832nd fellows here in New Guinea will get a back seat as far as going home is concerned. I am going to town tomorrow with a friend of mine who should have been on the first shipment that went home. He is going to try and find out what the score is.

Tuesday, March 7, 1944 Today was my day off. My friend and I went into town to check up on his going home. We found out for sure that he took a back seat for a lot of guys who mostly were 52nd group. I got a money order at the post office to send to Marian for her birthday.

Wednesday, March 8, 1944 No one woke me up this morning so I was an hour late to work again. No one said anything, but if they had or not it doesn't bother me as to what anyone around here thinks. The way I feel about this 52nd outfit, the whole thing can go to "h". Our spring is running as freely as ever. This evening one of my tent mates placed a five gallon can on the other side of the tent in the same manor. We now have enough water, till we could furnish every tent on this side of the hill. We figure our spring puts out about 250 gallons of water every twenty four hours. Ours is the only tent in this area with running water.

Thursday, March 9, 1944 I have been thinking the whole matter over about getting a transfer down south. If I could believe (& I cannot) that a fellow would get a fair deal in his priority standing as to going home, I wouldn't mind staying on here a while longer, but I now believe if a fellow were in Brisbane at 832nd headquarters, you would have a better chance to holler: Many of our bunch is being transferred and a condition may exist later on where I could not be relieved because of a shortage of operators.

Friday, March 10, 1944 Bill Pandolfi, and I have decided to go into town when we change to the midnight shift to make application to be transferred. Bill is the fellow I went on furlough with. It has dried off to some extent in the past two days. One of our springs has slowed up a little, but we still have all the water we need and give most of it away. Our tent is the main attraction on the hill now, as another water supply has solved a problem for most everyone here. I mailed Marian her birthday present today. It should reach her on or near her birthday.

Saturday, March 11, 1944 The fellow on the midnight shift woke me up this morning for the first time this week. However he looked at the station clock and forgot it was on "zed" time (an hour early) and woke our shift up at 5:30 A.M. rather than 6:30. We thought something was screwy as when we got down to the mess hall, breakfast was not half ready. This is the day for the change of shift and so if we go to the show tonight and then to work at midnight, it will be better than twenty four hours without sleep. It rained again tonight a lot of our equipment etc. is damp and getting covered with mold.

Sunday, March 12, 1944 Luckily didn't have to go to work at midnight last night as I had the night off. I slept rather late this morning. It started raining shortly after dinner and has been pouring down ever since. One of my tent mates moved out today as he has been transferred out to another unit. All the fellows in my tent, (four left including myself) are telephone operators. They get quite a kick out of listening to some of we radio operators talk. Nearly always our conversation is either in code or by "Q" signals etc. I admit it must sound like a fellow blowing his top.

    I had just finished writing the above entry and had gone to bed to get a little rest before going to work at midnight. I was laying there thinking, listening to the rain, beat down on our tent. Hein (one of my tent mates) was starting to get undressed to go to bed. A few minutes later I heard the hum of an airplane. I didn't think much about it, as there are usually planes in the air most of the time, although I was about to mention to my tent mate, "What a heck of a night to be flying." The plane passed over flying very low. A few minutes later we could hear this ship coming back. The plane was seemingly flying at cruising speed, having difficulty locating the field as visibility due to the rain and fog, was "zero zero" as the plane came nearer we suddenly heard the engines roar in a burst of power. Almost at the same instant we heard a dull thud and the sky lit up as light as day in a huge sheet of flame. The ship had crashed just over the hill from our tent. I jumped out of bed and dressed as quickly as possible grabbed my flashlight, rain coat and helmet and started climbing the hill. I don't know if you would call this a hill or a small mountain, it is some six hundred or more feet to the top and seemingly straight up. I partly walked and crawled up the hill. It seemed I had gone but a short distance when my flash light gave out. I was never so tired and out of breath in my life and being soaked, besides a bum knee, I had hit on a rock, I felt pretty miserable. I could see the glow of the flames over the hill and the thought that if someone could reach the plane soon enough, might save some fellows life. I climbed on in the dark until I ran into a barbwire entanglement, cutting the heck out of my shins. Behind me a fellow was coming with a flash light, so I waited and we climbed toward the top. It seemed as if we never would reach the top and we only stopped when we were so exhausted we could climb no more. After about a half an hour we reached the top and started down the ridge. We walked a short distance to a spot overlooking a valley. There before us was a sight neither of us will ever forget. From one end of the valley to the other and high on the opposite hill from where we were standing was strewn with burning wreckage. The pilot apparently thought he was making an approach to land but was not familiar with the country or was turned around. At any rate the pilot gunned the motors to try and clear the ridge. The plane struck one small hill at the entrance to the valley, which caused the ship to start to disintegrate. It is hard to describe how completely wrecked this ship was. Something like a ripe tomato thrown against a building. No particular part of the plane could be found anywhere, and parts of it strewn everywhere. From the first point of contact to the last heap of burning rubbish it must have been a distance of 400 yards. This fellow and I stood on top of the hill for a short time. There was no need to hurry any longer. All the optimism in the world wouldn't let you believe a human being could live through such destruction: By the time we reached the bottom of the hill there were possibly a dozen other soldiers prodding around through the wreckage. The first piece of the ship I saw that was any clue to the type of aircraft it was, was part of one of the landing gear wheels.

The ship was a B24 (Liberator) bomber. This ship I learned from a control operator at Ward's Drone was from Townsville Australia. He had been in contact with the ship up to the time of the crash. Ward's were informed by the plane that they had four hours of gas left. The question arises, Why were they not instructed to stay aloft for a while or why didn't they choose to fly around until the weather would clear, or at least stay up and see if it would clear up? The sad part of the whole thing, an hour after the crash, the weather cleared and the moon came out. The air strip could be seen clear enough until they could have landed without any lights at all.

It was a strange feeling prodding around through the tall grass, looking for something that would be more gruesome than anything you knew you had ever seen, After a short time someone yelled that three of them were up on the hill, I met a fellow coming down the hill who said they were mangled beyond recognition. My friend and I decided not to go up and stopped for a little rest. In the meantime a party of Australians came by us with a powerful spot light. The beam fell on a small tree about eight feet from us. There draped over one of the lower limbs were the remains of a human form, indescribably mangled. Some Australian came up with a lighter. One Australian attempted to remove the body, but it was in such a state that ordinary handling was impossible. At this point I could stand no more and walked away. I trudged on up the hill. I learned from another fellow that there were fourteen crew members aboard. Since there were now droves of soldiers coming, I decided to climb on up the hill and go back to camp. I came upon some other soldiers who had found another body and they asked me to help them. I had to refuse; I couldn't stand to see no more.

After climbing on up the hill I saw a place where they had been piling mail. Since at first I came into the valley I, like everyone else, had picked up whatever mail we came across. Most of it [was] letters a few packages and some valentines. I think only about a fourth of the mail was saved as most of it was either burned, torn to bits or water soaked. I met a couple Australians who were going back the same direction as I, so we started back towards camp together. The air was full of smoke, and the smell of burnt flesh was everywhere. I made my way slowly back to camp, soaking wet, dog tired and sick: How I feel toward those poor fellows, their friends and families at home.

Monday, March 13, 1944 I was supposed to go to work at midnight last night, but I was given the night off as I have never felt so sick in my life: All day today it has been impossible for me to eat. This afternoon Bill Randelfi and I went into town and made application to be relieved. It is raining again tonight.

March 14, Tuesday, 1944 I worked last night. I missed writing to Marian yesterday, the first time in nearly two months. Whenever I go to chow, I take a few bites of food but that is all I can get down. About all I have been eating the past couple of days are apples. This afternoon I extended our spring drainage ditch and made some of the others deeper. No mail today.

Wednesday, March 15, 1944 I worked quite hard last night as I got stuck on a Finschafen circuit. It is beginning to look as if my manual operating days may be nearly to an end. They are installing a bunch of radio teletype and perhaps I may go on that job after a while. My digestion is getting a little better now. I still can hardly eat any meat. I sit down to eat and the memory of the plane crash goes through my mind and I am through. Marian and I have been married two years eight months today. The war has kept us apart just two years so far. It looks like it will be quite a number of months before I can start to think about going home.

Thursday, March 16, 1944 The same routine today. Three of our bunch left today to go to Brisbane. Our orders should come through in a short time. It seems the weather is getting hotter each day, I spent about an hour in the sun with my shirt off the other day and my back is about blistered. The way traffic is piling through the station some move must be near at hand. Most of its destination is Finschafen and Oro Bay.

Friday, March 17, 1944 Today is my day off. I intended going out to see Laverne but I decided I had better do my laundry instead. Things are rapidly being changed in our station. Many of our manual circuits are being changed over to Radio teletype. This, up to the present time, is the last word in radio communication. One of these circuits could handle in four hours what the entire station processes manually in twenty four. There is a chance that I might become a teletype operator. There is no softer job in the Army than this. I constructed a chair from a couple of old boxes, so I could have a seat to sit on at the show.

Saturday, March 18, 1944 Since today is the change of shifts we don't go to work until five P.M. tomorrow night. I reconstructed my mosquito net and fixed up around my bunk. A lot of the fellows have been going over the hill where the plane crashed, picking up odds and ends. As for myself, I saw enough the night of the crash. I am just getting to the place where I can eat again. Tonight Pat and I tried developing some pictures. A few of them turned out O.K

Sunday, March 19, 1944 Nothing new today. I wrote a few letters and laid around. I still feel the effects of the jaunt over the mountain in the rain the other night. My barbwire cut is healing up ok, but my knee is still a little sore. On the Russian front in the Ukraine, the Russians are steadily forcing the Germans to retreat. It looks as if the Russians will be on Rumanian soil before long. It is reported that Rumania has put out peace feelers with Russians on the north of Russia. The Russian forces are forcing the Germans to retreat also. Russia offered Finland peace terms, but Finland rejected them. Seems funny since Russia can write their own ticket. American fortresses are now bombing Berlin by day. The invasion coast is being pounded by medium bombers.

Monday, March 20, 1944 I Hope your birthday present arrived today. Happy Birthday Honey. Work is going the same as ever. The one radio teletype circuit to Brisbane has taken a big load off the other circuits. The "Bowmie" high speed has been taken out.

Tuesday, March 21, 1944 Two fellows from our shift are leaving on furlough tomorrow and this will be the end of our days off. It looks like it will now be a day in and day out schedule. All I can look forward to now is for my transfer to come through. Today is the first day of spring back home. It is only the 21st here.

Wednesday, March 22, 1944 I worked Milne Bay circuit tonight and was quite busy. I didn't mind so much as there was a good operator on the other end. No news has come through about my transfer yet. Things finally came to a head as to we 832 fellows being left out in the cold: Our bunch finally found a warrant officer downtown who has been willing to act in a official capacity. However, the command of the 832 in [Australia] began to wonder why all 832 requests for relief were coming through this warrant officer when the 52nd, the outfit we are attached for administration were doing nothing to this end. The 52nd must have got jumped on hard as a memo has been posted to the affect that disciplinary action will be taken for anyone going down town for any company requests.

Thursday, March 23. 1944 It has been raining continuously for the past two days. I didn't do much work tonight and took a slow circuit, and wrote some letters. A major general and a couple of colonels came through the station tonight. I don't know who they were. One thing about this place, there is usually a lot of rank snooping around. I hear that MacArthur and his staff are coming up here again soon. That usually means a campaign of some sort. We don't expect anything but lousy chow anymore. On rare occasions when we do get fresh meat, it is usually mutton. With most of us it is a matter of taking it in our mess kit and then throwing it in the garbage.

Friday, March 24, 1944 The same routine today. Still no news as to my transfer. It sure takes a long time to unwind the red tape. Warn Rawlins, one of my friends who has been over seas a long time is on the roster to go home next month. He should be given his release and be transferred to Milne Bay in a few days to leave for the states from there. He is sure sweating it out as he should have heard something by now. It is still raining by spells.

Saturday, March 25, 1944 Today is the change of shift. We work from five P.M. until midnight and then back at seven in the morning for a ten hour stretch. At times it is hard to understand this existence of ours. What I have had to go through here in New Guinea and what Marian and I are sacrificing, and yet what events have taken place back home.

Sunday, March 26, 1944 This week we worked the most hours. Being we get no days off, we will work seven, ten hour shifts. There seems to be quite a feeling among some of the fellows who shape T – 5 ratings. Many of them are very good operators and certainly deserve more than they have. There are two tech sgts. (one stripe bellow master) who don't come close to being the operator these fellows are. But that is one outstanding trait in the army, at least in the 832, not what still experience or all around good man you are, but the case being, were you at the right place at the right time. The right place seems to have been 832 head quarters in Brisbane. Nearly everyone who has been stationed there is a Staff Sgt. I was pretty lucky to get sp/4.

Monday, March 27, 1944 I worked a pretty busy circuit today. I had a smart guy on the other end: Boy operating has sure gone to the dogs. There isn't a decent circuit in the place. Either you get an operator that is bad and admits it. (You can get along with one of these, even though you don't get anything done) or one who is punk and tries to bluff his way through by trying to make you think when you send to him there is bad readability.

Tuesday, March 28, 1944 The same routine today. I worked Milne Bay and passed quite a bit of traffic. However, as the rule is on most circuits the fellow was hard as heck to copy. Went to the show here in the area tonight.

Wednesday, March 29, 1944 Well my friend Rawlins is still sweating it out. We got roped on shipment last month and it looks as if history is repeating its self. He should have got his orders to leave nearly a week ago. The boat on which he leaves (if he goes) will leave from Milne Bay. Nothing yet has come through as to my transfer down south. This joint is becoming more unbearable every day.

The 832nd fellows are taking more B.S. than usual. Today at the P.X. they had "Yank" magazines on sale. The supply was not sufficient enough for everyone to have a copy. On the bulletin board was a list of names of men who could buy them. The only catch was that they were all 52nd guys.

Thursday, March 30, 1944 On the average the letters I receive from home are pretty slack. I received a letter from Marian telling me she missed a few days during her trip to Texas, so I will now receive fewer letters than ever for a few days. The chow is nearly at rock bottom. We are living nearly altogether on dehydrated food and field rations. No news as yet about my transfer. Tomorrow is mom's birthday.

Friday, March 31, 1944 To work as usual today. I am sure getting tired of operating. The only gratifying thing of it is that perhaps the inexperienced operators we are working now are the ones who will make it possible for us to go home. The Russian Armies are now at the Romanian border and the Germans are in retreat all along the line. Germany has taken over complete control of Hungary and Romania. Rumors are springing up again about the European invasion. It sure should come off sometime this spring or summer: The Allies in Italy are not doing so well – the Germans seem to have reinforced themselves in Monte Cassino. Operations on the beach head near Rome are at a standstill.[38]

Saturday, April 1, 1944 We make the change to the midnight shift tonight. I am lucky and get the night off. Boy, the food is really getting bad. For super we had coffee (no sugar) a barely beef sandwich and a few potatoes. Moresby is sure a back number now as far as the war is concerned. The fellows up at Finschhafen calls us Moresby Commandoes and Finschhafen is over a hundred miles from the Japs. Nadzab, Dumpu Lae and Finschhafen are no longer in a combat area. When I first came over seas, even Brisbane was classed as a combat area. The city blacked out at night with all windows covered with stripes of tape and sand bagged. Today was pay day. Am sending my money home this month so I won't add to my savings account.

Sunday, April 2, 1944 I went into town this afternoon. Was sure burned up - a guy from the 52nd passed me up without even thinking to pick me up. A few

---

[38] Without realizing it at this time plans are probably in the works for D Day / Normandy Invasion.

minutes and one of their trucks did the same thing. "Boy" what a bunch. I finally got a ride. I stopped at the post office and got a money order then caught a ride out to see Laverne. I was in for a disappointment though, as when I arrived out there I learned that Laverne was on detached service over at Dobodura. I talked to some of the fellows for a while caught a ride back to town. I stopped in at the Red Cross for a short time then came on back to camp. Slept a little while after chow then went to work at midnight.

Monday, April 3, 1944 I worked a pretty busy circuit last night. I got a long pretty well but as is usual the case, anymore, the other fellow was a hot head. I am quite sure something is about ready to take place in this theater, probably a direct attack on Madang. Slight chance it could be Rabaul but I hardly think so yet.

Tuesday, April 4, 1944 I was busy nearly all last night. I am working most of the faster circuits, (What speed a guy can find) as I want to be in good practice when I get down south. However I talked to some fellows who say there is no good operating down there either.

Wednesday, April 5, 1944 It seems I am in the middle of another mail slump. No letters at all. I received some November newspapers. This afternoon I cut some grass around our tent. My hands are sure tender and in five minutes I had a blister on my thumb. I was unable to operate tonight on account of my blistered finger so I worked a slow circuit. Well the Russian Army is now within the Rumanian border. The Russians are calling on the Czechoslovakians to revolt. The Germans are retreating and seem to be leaving Romania to her doom.

Thursday, April 6, 1944 Chow for breakfast took a hundred percent improvement. They got in some fresh eggs and they sure came as a life saver. In the past weeks I have only been going to chow because I have to. It looks as if Rawlins will not be in on the home shipment again this month. His moral is about as low as it can be. He cannot and will not operate anymore. He comes to work early and sits on one of the stand-by circuits. I worked Townsville tonight and had a good operator on for a change. Reports are out that an American task force has bombed a small group of islands 1100 miles west of Tuuk and only 500 miles from the Philippines: I have been in New Guinea 15 months today.

Friday, April 7, 1944 Slept this morning. This afternoon Pat and I dug our spring out deeper and reset the five gallon can. It looks as if before long our spring will go dry. In not too many weeks it will be the start of the dry season and then for a number of months there will be no rain at all. The grass gets brown and the hills bare. Today was one of our "twice weekly" Atabrine pill days. We are required to take four of these pills a week. Atabrine will not stop you from getting malaria but it sort of retards it. A fellow won't know until after he stops taking Atabrine if he has malaria. I am keeping my fingers crossed.

Saturday, April 8, 1944 I spent a little time cleaning and sorting out one of my barracks bags this morning just in case I get a rush order to leave. I haven't heard any news about my transfer yet. Since the other fellow moved out there had been only four of us in our tent (G.I. capacity is six). This gives us quite a bit of room and we are quite comfortable. We always have to keep an eye open for centipedes and black widow spiders. These are the main characters. We have just had to get use to the ants, and small lizards that scamper around the tent. Mice and rats show their faces once in a while. We don't argue with the mosquitoes, we are under the protection of our nets when it gets dark. They are not so bad in the day time. After sleeping this morning I was awakened with a start when I felt something crawl across my face. I made a quick pass at it with my hand. Luckily I missed as there climbing up the side of my net was a large black widow spider. There was no question as to it being a black widow, the black smooth body and legs with a red spot on its underside the shape of an hour glass, makes them easy to identify. The mysterious thing about these spiders is they are supposed to be very poisonous but no one that I know of around this area has been bitten with one, and boy they are really thick. I think I have killed over a dozen since moving in this tent in November. Had a show in the area tonight as has been the case for quite a number of pictures lately, hardly any sound.

Sunday, April 9, 1944 Today I heard some awful disappointing news. It was to the effect that even though my transfer comes through, our signal officer will not let me go. He says shortage of operators, but two fellows came up from Brisbane the other day and on each shift three fellows are given the night off. For the past eight unfortunate months I have been under the command of this guy (I can't call him an "officer" he doesn't qualify in my or anyone else's estimate). I have never liked him and my contempt for him is indescribable now. He wouldn't last two minutes if he were up at the front and I don't mean it would be a Jap bullets that would get him. Fifteen months in this God forsaken country. How damn long does he think a guy should stay here anyway?

Monday, April 10, 1944 Went to work second shift tonight but being there was extra operators and I was due to get tomorrow night off I got tonight off instead. It rained nearly all night and this should refresh our spring which in the past two days has nearly gone dry: There has been springs springing up here and there around the area. One has started flowing down by the mess hall and the water is running out of it like a small river.

Tuesday, April 11, 1944 I received a bunch of mail today, the first in some time. I sat on Darwin circuit tonight so I would have some spare time to write letters. We now have a new circuit to Honolulu. Not much traffic on it just a standby. It looks like something is going to happen around here before long.

Wednesday, April 12, 1944 Just another routine day. I spent most of my time in my bunk. Our spring is flowing quite freely again, as it rained some yesterday and has been raining off and on again today. I took an easy circuit at work tonight with the intention of writing some letters but instead I had to work the noisiest – lousiest – circuit in the house. I sure got disgusted when I changed freq. and couldn't get anyone interested enough (trick chief or teletype operator) to tell my station to call me. I took off my head phones and just sat there for about an hour until the trick chief came by. I asked him if he was ready to do something then.

Thursday, April 13, 1944 Today was a tough day. I had to report for police call and work from 8 A.M. until 11 A.M. eat chow at 11:30 and go to work. The fellow on the day shift had to go and get shots so that meant I had to work until 3 P.M. then I went into town and got a cholera shot. By the time I got back to camp it was nearly time to eat chow. My arm was pretty sore and even though, I worked one of the busiest circuits in the house. It rained again tonight.

Friday, April 14, 1944 Boy this place is really getting worse and worse. They are now moving the tents down off our hill. I guess it was too hard to keep tabs on the fellows up here. There will not be room for all the tents down there and we fellows in this tent are holding our breath. They say the best looking tents will stay up here. In a short time our station is going to undergo a big change. All teletype and radio positions are to be moved into the large building adjoining the present operations building.

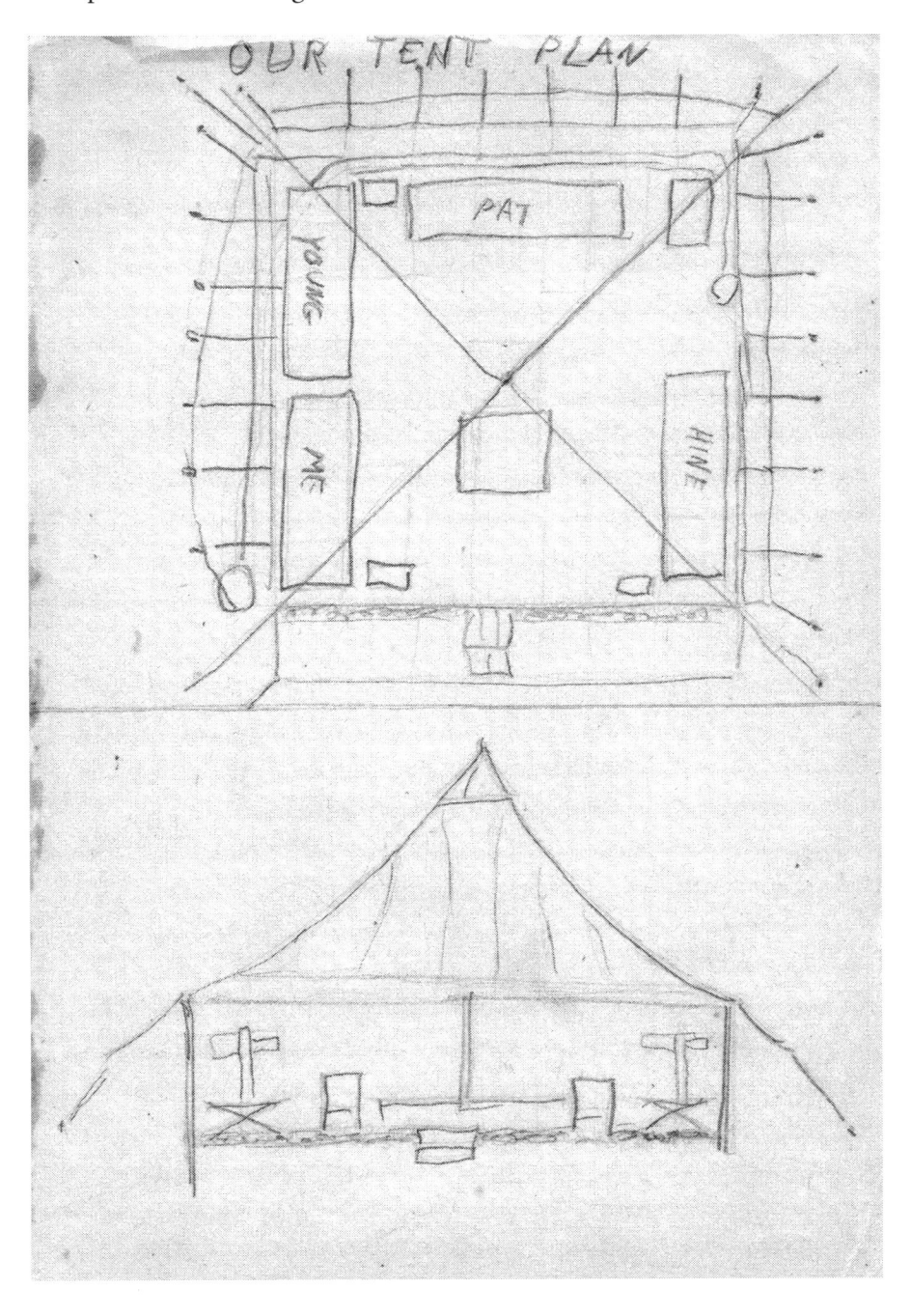

April 15, Saturday, 1944 Today Marian and I have been married just two years ten months. It was far from being a holiday, even if it started out as such. I was to have the day off but all of us had to work on detail digging a ditch until nearly noon chow. This afternoon everyone was called out again and was to go on detail again. I skipped out on this one and came back to my tent and cleaned one of my tent mate's rifles, just to look busy. The last straw came at 5:30 P.M. when Rawlins came up and said I had to come to work. Well, I worked until midnight. We start on the day shift tomorrow working from 7 A.M. until 5 P.M. "O Sh" how I wish my transfer would come through.

Sunday, April 16, 1944 So far we are still up here on the hill. We had a couple of inspections today by the Colonel, who is General Aikens's right hand man. Boy this place is sure tightening up. They sure were not so cocky when the war wasn't going so smooth in this country. One of our operators got broke from Sgt. to private for using plain language on the circuit. He had it coming though. Things are sure building up to a big operation in a short time. It is hardly a secret any longer. Probably Madang or Rabaul, a slight possibility of an action to cut Wewak (NE New Guinea) off, at least it looks like a big jump this time.

Monday, April 17, 1944 The B.S. is really flying, one inspection after another. Some of our fellows whose headquarters is out to another outfit are getting released to move back there and will ride back and forth to work. Worked all day at the station so didn't get in on the work that is going great guns around the rest of the camp.

Tuesday, April 18, 1944 Today the same as yesterday only a fellow can't hardly move it is getting so "G.I." We are no longer allowed to do any washing at our tent. The joke is when the hell would you find time to do it anyway. Rawlins has given up going home this month. I guess being the first one in Australia and 25 months in the tropics is not enough. Any they say after 18 months you are eligible to go home.

Wednesday, April 19, 1944 This morning when we got to work we found that everything had been moved into the other building. Everything was in a turmoil. No telephone, lines crossed up. "O Sh." What a mess. I am so disgusted tonight I don't know what to do. A notice was passed around today that from now on we meet in front of the orderly room and march to work. "My transfer" "My transfer" where can it be. (?)

Thursday, April 20, 1944 Things are sure in a turmoil a fellow is lucky to find a circuit that will work without something burning out or getting out of whack some way or other. I got up too late this morning to go to work by marching. This evening the fellows left work and made a beeline for the mess hall. Out of about twenty five guys only five were left to march back: A big drive is to start anytime now, there are many places they can strike. I wonder if this one would be in the Dutch East Indies. Perhaps Java. If this were done the Allies could control a vast amount of natural resources the Japs now hold.

April 21, Friday, 1944 Up too late to march to work again this morning. If I could make this work every day I would sure be satisfied. I received inside information today that tomorrow is the date for the fireworks: No one knows exactly where our forces will strike. Naturally about all that would have to be secret. Today was an ordeal on a circuit I will long remember. If it wasn't my transmitter that was out of commission, its' warning keying lines or receiver. I would contact one of the stations in the net, get him to send "V'S" and then my transmitter would kick off, and no way to tell the guy to stop. He just sent until he got tired then stopped.

Saturday, April 22, 1944 I heard this morning that the big drive has been started, as I expected. The location is still rather vague but I believe it to be an operation to knock out Wewak (NE New Guinea): I was to have the day off, but which seems to be the practice lately, they came after me. I did manage to duck them until noon. I was in for a little excitement this morning. I was walking up the hill and as I walked I heard the faint hum of an airplane that was so high it could barely be heard. The sound was coming from over my head and I looked up. This ship must have been twenty five or thirty thousand feet as it could not be seen. All at once the sound increased and far above I could see a little feather of white smoke. The plane in a few seconds came into my view, still plummeting in a power dive straight down. At first I thought the plane was testing some smoke device. The ship kept on coming and now it was evident the pilot was trying to pull out. The ship seemed to respond slightly, but it was on fire and out of control. About ten seconds now had passed and the plane could be recognized as a P.38 (see sketch on following page of the diary) at about twelve thousand feet. The pilot bailed out. How at such a terrific speed he ever did so, I will never know, but his shoot opened and he seemed to safely float down. The plane continued its head long dive and went into the bay just on the other side of the point of land on the other side of the bay. The impact must have shot a geyser of water two hundred feet into the air as the hill behind which the plane fell is easily a hundred feet high and I could see the water go high above it. A puff of black smoke rose, and drifted away, and that was all. The pilot was still very high and he was drifting out over the hills toward the ocean on the other side. Three or four planes that were flying nearby now were circling the pilot to direct the crash boats to the spot. I heard later the pilot was rescued and did not suffer bad injury.

Sunday, April 23, 1944 Reports came through today that our forces have made a landing at Hollandi,a (N. New Guinea) which is some two hundred miles north of Wewak (NE New Guinea). The estimate that the Allies now have over a hundred thousand Japs cut off in the South West Pacific. Went to work at midnight. Before long manual operating will come to an end. Nearly all circuits are being replaced by radio teletype.

Monday, April 24, 1944 I am absolutely certain now that anything can happen around here: the fellow who delivers and picks up messages now has to wear roller skate. At one time I rather liked working a circuit but anymore it usually turns out to be an ordeal: In days past a fellow could get along with a slow operator, by working slow, but now most of them try and cover the fact by saying your sending is bad and the unreadable stuff they send is your inability to copy.

Tuesday, April 25, 1944 I received some film from Marian and the folks today. Yesterday two roles arrived from Aunt Effie and Uncle Will. In a day or so I intend to go on top of the hill back of our camp and snap a color picture of the sunset. Went to the show before work tonight.

Wednesday, April 26, 1944 Reports coming into the radio room state that the allied landing at Hollandia – N. New Guinea met with very little resistance. The air strike was captured five hours after the landing and our Air Force moved in. 250 Japs were killed in taking the air strip. Our casualties were light. I heard a rumor today that the reason my transfer hasn't gone through is because of the present operations going on. This month's quota for fellows going home going home was also canceled. When they call this rotation program the eighteen month plan it is like referring to this as the six month war.

Thursday, April 27, 1944 Today is just a routine day. The British and American Air Forces are striving to knock out the German's Air Force. In one operation

Allied bombers bombed German aircraft factories and other military objectives with a force of 2000: Everywhere, the tension of the second front is growing. The Germans in their broadcast leave no doubt as to their concern of future events: In the past number of weeks, fighting on quite a large scale has flared up in Burma. The Jap forces attacking in great force for a time had the Allies on the defensive and many cases caused them to withdraw. However, the position has been improved and the Japs forced back to the Indian border: Everything is more or less quiet on the Italian and Russian fronts. It is thought the Russians are getting in position for a decisive thrust at the Germans.

Friday, April 28, 1944 Three hours sleep a day is about all I get when I am on this shift. I didn't have to go to work last night so I got caught up a bit. Today I spent my time writing a few letters and straightening up our tent. A good many tents have been moved off the hill and now we have no electricity in our tent. This wasn't such a loss though as so many tents were on the line, before that our light would hardly come on at all: This evening I walked up to the top of the hill in back of our camp and took a number of pictures of the sunset. One of my tent mates that works at the telephone exchange proceeded to tell a full fledged colonel off, and now my tent mate has been relieved from duty and is awaiting a court martial. It looks like he will be broke as well as maybe serve time.

Friday, April 29, 1944 After working from midnight until seven this morning all of us in camp had to get ready for inspection. About nine A.M. our tents were inspected. Immediately afterwards we were to have a personal inspection and form in ranks down by the orderly room, which I know would include being marched up and down the road for a while. At the last minute Heaven was on our side and it started to rain, so he called it off: To work at the station at night doing a job to win the war isn't enough, a guy has to sacrifice his sleep besides, for this B.S.

Saturday, April 30, 1944 I haven't received any letters from anyone in the past few days. I guess I shouldn't expect too much after hitting the jack pot on film from Marian, the folks and Aunt Effie and Uncle Will.[39]

In a letter I received from Jack and Myrtel they tell me Jack is to be moved and is now on the alert. I hope he will not have to go overseas, but I am afraid

---

[39] Aunt Effie is my Grandfather's sister on my dad's side and her husband Will. Jack is my dad's younger brother and his wife Myrt.

this is it: Everyone is on edge about the invasion. Everyone is sure it will take place in a very short time. Some think a week or two: The Russian Forces in Rumania are on the march again and are locked with the Germans in some fierce tank battles:

Today was pay day and I will be able to put away twenty more pounds.

Monday, May 1, 1944 I am now on the five to midnight shift. We have to pull two or more hours detail in the morning, relieve the day shift for noon chow. About all the spare time we have is a couple of hours in the afternoon. There isn't much doing on the manual circuits now, nearly all the traffic is passed over R.T.T.

Tuesday, May 2, 1944 I worked receiving intercept trafficker tonight and was busy most of the time. On this shift a fellow is busy practically all day and half the night. We have police call and detail in the morning. Then work through the noon hour to relieve the day shift. We eat early supper and work five to midnight.

Wednesday, May 3, 1944 I don't know what ever happened to my request for relief. It has been around two months now. This outfit does not care in the least what happens to the men. The officers are only concerned about their own personal being. I have had a headache for the past number of days. I am afraid my eyes are giving me trouble. I wear my sun glasses whenever I am out in the open. Due to the Hollandia (N. New Guinea) campaign, the going home quota was cancelled this month. I think this thing will finally fade out like most everything else.

Thursday, May 4, 1944 The latest rumor going around is that the troop rotation plan has been cancelled. I don't believe this as nothing official has come out on it yet. This is the reason I have kept most of the folks at home in the dark on whatever chance I had of getting home. There are quite a bunch of efficiency experts around the station now. They should do some good. At least they can't do any harm, the muddle everything is in now. I worked Darwin tonight. Nothing much doing on the circuit.

Friday, May 5, 1944 I was given permission today to do my laundry rather than go on police call. This was quite a job but we have things quite handy to do washing now. A conversation was over heard by one of our fellows today just about telling the story around here. One of the efficiency experts who have been around the station for the past few days was talking to our sig. officer:

Efficiency Expert – "What do you do for the men in the station who do a good job, do you give them rating?"

SIG. OFF. "NO all the ratings have been given out. There are no more!"

Efficiency Expert – "Do you give the men a day off?"

Sig. Off. "No we don't have enough men to give days off."

Efficiency Exp. "Do you give any furloughs or relief?"

Sig. Off. "We can't give furloughs, we don't have enough men!"

Saturday, May 6, 1944 We had inspection today, and had to go down in front of the mess hall and form in ranks. After we got through we came up to our tent. They blew the whistle for us to fall out for police call and detail. No one budged from their tent as all of us had on clean uniforms and digging a ditch somewhere would be about the last straw. The Sgt. in charge of detail blew his whistle a while and finally gave up, as no one came down. I walked up into the hills this afternoon and took some pictures. Mail service was kind of punk last week. I did receive two letters from Marian today.

Sunday, May 7, 1944 Just a routine day today: It looks as if the usefulness of manual operators here in WVLP is about a thing of the past. There are rumors that perhaps a bunch of operators may be sent up to Hollandia. It wouldn't surprise me if in a short time I would be sent up there: Rumors going around also are to the effect that the going home plan has kinda blown up. I have lost all faith in this rotation program, and only think of getting home whenever the war is over. To think how long that might be gives me an awful empty feeling. "Boy" what a mess. I'm more disgusted every day. I sometimes wonder why I bother to keep this damn diary up. What difference does it make?

Monday, May 8, 1944 I am working first shift now. Traffic is slowing down to a great extent and since most of it is handled on R.T.T. the manual circuits are dead altogether. Only two circuits have any traffic on them at all. I hear that instead of changing shifts once a week, as we have in the past, we are going to change once every four days.

Tuesday, May 9, 1944 Worked as usual today. They gave me a detail job this morning. Making some wood floor pieces. I took advantage of the situation and spent all morning doing a job that could be done in twenty minutes. There was supposed to be a show in the area tonight but it was called off. I went to bed very early tonight.

Wednesday, May 10, 1944 I don't have to go to work until midnight tonight so I have the whole day off. This afternoon some of we fellows went to town. Bill Randolf and I stopped in at the signal office and saw W.O. Henny, the fellow who put in our request for transfer. He showed us the letter he wrote, and the reply. The reply was a typical G.I. turn down. He said that maybe we could try again in a couple of months: I took a few color pictures around town after which we went down to the Red Cross. We came back to camp about 3:30 PM: After chow a friend in the other tent wanted to go up into the hills so we started out. We walked over to where the plane crashed, which was still about the same as the night of the wreck. We then went up on the peak of the tallest hill and watched the sunset. We got back to camp just at dark.

Thursday, May 11, 1944 I was sure tired when I went to work last night, however, the T.C. did me a favor and told me to take off. He was the fellow I walked over the hill with. This afternoon another fellow and I went out riding in his jeep. We messed around town at the Sergeant's Club, and then took a ride out past "Wardesy Air Drone." From there we drove on over to the receivers. On the way back to camp I took a picture of the "Macanic" a ship that was sank by the Japs in the early part of the war: I went to the show tonight. It was typical of the shows we have been having. "Articles of War, Why we fight" and "Dextarity".[40]

Friday, May 12, 1944 This afternoon I moved down into the company area into another tent. I hated to move but in a short time we will all have to move down from the hill anyway. I jumped at the chance of moving into this tent as chances are that they might put me in a barracks. I don't have to go to work now until five PM tomorrow. Our Signal officer chief operator and personal officer of 832 have gone down to Brisbane to a meeting. The personal officer is going to see what they can do to getting some of us relieved.

Saturday, May 13, 1944 We are now on the five to midnight shift. This is the busiest shift, but even so there isn't much to do on the manual circuits. It was reported that the Allied forces have started a drive against defense line in

---

[40] I'm not sure about the Air Drone – the name of the ship or the name of the movies.

Italy. The Allies are meeting with fierce resistance and are if at all making slow progress. Another campaign is in the works here in the South West Pacific: The Chinese in Hunan Province in China are in bitter combat to hold the capital of this province, which is an important communications center. The British and Indian troops in Burma are advancing and taking many Jap prisoners: Things are very quiet on the Russian front.

Sunday, May 14, 1944 I went up to the receiver maintenance shop today and made a couple of bracelets and pins. Another campaign is due to start here in New Guinea in a short time. I suppose it will be on up the coast from Hollandia (N. New Guinea). Allied troops in Italy have succeeded in breeching the Gustav line in Italy. Cassino (C. Italy) is being surrounded. Partisan Communist leader Tito's army in Yugoslavia is now nearly 300,000 strong. His forces are gaining back quite a bit of Yugoslavia territory. Invasion talk is still the main topic: There is a lot of guessing going on as to where the invasion will strike. With the Italian campaign resumed, the Russians getting ready for a new offensive and the invasion forces ready, the all-out blows should start very soon.[41]

Monday, May 15, 1944 Today Marian and I have been married two years eleven months. It has been nearly two years now since I last saw her. Well my friend Rawlins finally left to go home. We were all glad to see him go as we all knew how he felt. I think all of us have kind of a sick feeling as we would give anything to be on our way home also.

Tuesday, May 16, 1944 Coming back from work tonight, we ran across a six foot python in the middle of the road. We managed to kill it, but he was sure a tough customer.

Wednesday, May 17, 1944 We came to work this morning and will work the day shift for the next four days. I worked Townsville on the circuit today and things ran fairly smooth for a change. The Allied forces in Italy have made a large breech in the Gustav Line (C. Italy) and are advancing toward the Hitler Line near Rome. Cassino (C. Italy) is nearly cut off and its capture is only a matter of time: Here in New Guinea, American troops have made a landing on Wakde l. (Dutch New Guinea) This Jap base is about 125 miles up the New Guinea coast from Hollandia (N. New Guinea).

---

[41] Tito – born Josip Broz (1892–1980) later became president of Yugoslavia 1945-1980.

Thursday, May 18, 1944 I worked Townsville again today and past some traffic which is quite unusual of late. The manual circuits are only used as stand-by for R.T.T. there for handle little traffic. I have never worked on radio teletype for the reason that I have been in New Guinea for so long. They figure there is a chance I might be transferred, and they don't want to train anyone who might leave this station. There was a bulletin on the board today stating that personal would be rotated back to Australia after six months here: I read that same bulletin 11 months ago. I wonder who they think they are kidding.

Friday, May 19, 1944 Just a routine day today. I worked W.V.L.T. again. I have pretty good luck working this circuit. The operator on the other end is pretty fair and easy to get along with. Mail service has been pretty punk lately. The fellows are starting to raise a little holler, due to the fact that the fellow in charge of the mail room often plays baseball rather than go after the mail. I don't think he bothers to get it only every other day.

Saturday, May 20, 1944 The July quota for fellows to go home is now up on the bulletin board. Only one percent of personal will be sent home from the S.W.P.A. each month so it is sure a mistake to build hopes to get in on this "one percent". Total time overseas is about all that counts. The latest report is that service in New Guinea doesn't cut any ice. It is the same old story; fellows who are down south are keeping the same old superiority as far as any gravy is concerned. I went to the show tonight. I slept through most of it as it was P.P.

Sunday, May 21, 1944 Today is our last day on the day shift. We do not have to go to work now until tomorrow at midnight. There are many things I would like to do. Take pictures maybe make bracelets, fix up around my bunk. One thing I have to do is go to town to get a money order to send to Virginia for Marian's anniversary present. News today is still good. Allied forces have forged ahead in Italy over running the whole length of the Gustav Line and advanced swiftly to knock out positions on the Hitler Line – C. Italy – German offensive) near Rome. A naval task force has raided a strong Jap base at Surabaya Java (Surabaya Java – E. Java) Japanese landing –Japanese propaganda radio station – Japanese Port & POW camp here in the South West Pacific.

Monday, May 22, 1944 We don't have to go to work until midnight tonight so I spent the day taking a few pictures. Two friends and myself went over in the hills and took some pictures. This afternoon I laid around and wrote some letters. I received four letters from Marian today.

Tuesday, May 23, 1944 Worked as usual last night. I slept this morning. This afternoon I went into town and got a couple of money orders, one for dad's birthday and one to send Marian for our third wedding anniversary. Bill Randolfi, the fellow who went with me to see about being relieved to Australia is being sent over to Oro Bay. (E. Papua). All of us may move somewhere before long.

Wednesday, May 24, 1944 Just a routine day today. I guess my moral is the lowest it has ever been. This camp is plain B.S. All my friends have left here but me, and they say there is no chance to be moved out of here in either direction. There is a drive on to get "stripes." For the slightest reason they will take your rank. From one day to another you don't know if you will have your stripes. One fellow got broke from P.F.C. to Pvt. We get a good meal once in a while, but only on the average of once a week or so. The rest of the time it is field rations, rice (captured from the Japs) cheese, coffee and cold tea.

Thursday, May 25, 1944 Got off work this morning as usual and went to bed. One of my tent mates got hold of a radio and is sure working the most of it, so sleeping is about impossible. I received two letters from Marian today. Mail has been kinda slow lately. The fellows who were to be sent over the hump are back to work again. The Sgt. forgot to wake them up so then missed their plane, so they called the whole thing off. There was a show tonight but I didn't go as I had seen it a couple of times before. All the pictures have gone the rounds two or three times.

Friday, May 26, 1944 Today we have to change shifts. We work five to twelve for four days now. Good reports are still coming in from Italy. The Allies have broken Hitler's Line wide open. Forces on the Anglo Beachhead (Anglo-Egyptian Sudan – n/c Sudan) have linked up with other Allied forces advancing from the Cassino sector. Allied forces are reported to be within twenty miles of Rome. For chow tonight we had a small slice of canned mutton, two biscuits, peanuts, little portion of candy, carrots, and coffee. If it wasn't for the apples we have been getting I think my stomach would cave in all together.

Saturday, May 27, 1944 Chow was about the same today. I can feel my waist line going down. Found out two Staff Sgt. Ratings were given out. One fellow deserved his, but no one understands the other guy getting this rating. He is just an office clerk. He at one time worked for me, and he was pretty poor then. It is the same old story as far as ratings go. Not whether you deserve one, but who you know, and where you are. I am sure I will never get another rating here. The fact I have asked for relief, puts me behind the eight ball. Another operation is going on up the coast. I guess it is above Hollandia somewhere.

Sunday, May 28, 1944 It is reported that our forces have landed on Biak Island (N.W. New Guinea). This island is about 300 miles northwest on up the coast from Hollandia. By taking this base it is considered now that the New Guinea Campaign is over. Jap resistance in New Guinea is now impossible. Starving Japs by the hundreds are being picked up by patrols. Chow was a little better today. We had cured ham for a change. I hear a number of WAAC (WAAC – Women's Auxiliary Army Corps) arrived in Moresby to work in the post office recently. Today was just a routine day. There isn't much doing at work now so it gives me a chance to write a few letters.

Monday, May 29, 1944 Just another routine day. I have had a headache now for the past few days. I am afraid my eyes are causing the trouble. Sometimes I feel like I can't take it here much longer. My nerves seem to be on a wire edge all the time. An officer made the remark that he could talk to a fellow a few minutes and tell how long a fellow has been in this God forsaken country, A fellow here in camp went nuts the other day. He is not the first.

Tuesday, May 30, 1944 My mail came through in pretty good shape today. Letters from the folks, Jack & Myrt, Aunt Effie & Uncle Will, and Marian: Went to the show tonight. It was the usual program. An hour of flag waving and a picture most of us has seen two or three time.

Wednesday, May 31, 1944 I wrote a number of letters today at work. Didn't have much to do as usual. An intelligence officer interviewed me today and asked me a number of questions on some of the fellows I know. I don't know what the score is, just checking up on some of the fellows characters. The Allies are still driving ahead in Italy. Some of our forces are but fifteen miles from Rome. The fall of Rome seems but a short way off: It is reported that the Russians do not recognize the Polish government in London. It seems that it is always necessary to explain what good friends we are of the Russians. It rained today. This is the dry season of the year here.

Thursday, June 1, 1944 The same old routine today. I wrote a few letters today. I worked WVLT today and I think there was a dame on the other end, and code speed about eight words per min. Our forces that landed on Buka without a hard fight. I left twenty more pounds in the orderly room today. This makes a total of sixty lbs. I have there in the safe now.

Friday, June 2, 1944 To work as usual this morning. I worked WVLT again today. Worked the same operator as yesterday. No mail again today. A bunch of packages came in but none for me. I got a headache again this afternoon. Don't know why I have been having these headaches but they sure get me down. I guess I will have to have my eyes checked or something. If I feel OK tomorrow I intend going out to Rouna Falls.[42]

Saturday, June 3, 1944 We do not have to go to work until midnight tonight so M/Sgt. Potts and I decided to go out to the falls. After six or seven rides we still were two miles from our destination and being this far from Moresby it looked as if we were to go the rest of the way on foot. There [were] six natives coming up the road and we were about to snap their pictures when a truck came along and picked us up. We got out of the truck near by the falls and decided going up to the top of them first. We walked up the road a little way when a couple of fellows came along in a jeep and picked us up. They were just riding around so we decided to go with them. After going through the pass the road and country side became comparatively level and the road was quite improved. A far cry from the days when Australian and American forces had to drag artillery and other battle equipment through the mud and underbrush of this country. There are still traces of the battle that started the Japs retreating back toward Buna We drove along the road quite a number of miles until it became only more or less a path through the jungle. We drove through a rubber plantation. This plantation was run by civilians and for New Guinea they had all conveniences of a modern farm. Milk cows, chickens etc. We passed through Papauan Infantry Camp, which is the neatest and best kept came in New Guinea. On our way back our way back to Moresby we stopped at the falls. To get to the bottom we had to walk about half a mile down a narrow path. After reaching the falls we climbed to the top of a large rock where we had a good view. Since it has been raining

---

[42] Rouna Falls Descends from the Sogeri Plateau into the Laloki River.

to quite an extent [lately], the Laloki River was a little higher than usual and Rouna Falls was at its best. After a little while we climbed back down and walked along the river bank watching the rapids. In a distance of some three hundred yards down the river from the base of the falls are three smaller falls with a drop of around forty feet. The water passing through here is a mass of foam and spray. After we had walked a short distance my friend decided to jump from one rock to the other across a small section of the rapids. The distance was greater than he thought and in he went. Luckily the rapids carried him back toward the bank and he was able to catch hold of a rock and pull himself out. Should he have been swept toward the main channel he would have gone over two of the forty foot cataracts. As it was, he was but about twenty yards from the first one when he got out. I guess I was white as a sheet and about as scared as he was. Besides getting a sprained knee and breaking his wrist watch he came out O.K. We walked up to the M.P. station, had his knee bandaged and then caught a ride back to Moresby: Many months back when I made my first trip out to the falls, the roads were more like trails. It was surprising the improvement that has been made in the roads since then. At that time it was nearly impossible to go beyond the falls, but now you can drive for miles over quite improved roads. We stopped in at the Sergeant's to check but [were] informed that it had been closed. For what reason I don't know. We then caught a ride back to camp. I was sure tired and had to go to work at midnight.

Sunday, June 4, 1944 I made the guess that today would be the start of the invasion two months ago. It looks like I missed my guess. A report that the invasion was underway was not accurate, put out today. It took but two months to deny this report but the news spread like wild fire. A ball game was stopped at the polo grounds in New York for a minute of silent prayer.

News came through today that Allied forces are but a few miles from Rome. Here in the S.W.P.A. Americans have landed on two small islands near Buka. Americans are moving ahead toward the air strip on Buka. I got the day off for a change the first for a long time.

At the top of this page my dad has written "INVASION??" this deception was intentional by the Allied commanders;-see printed page of dairy.

Monday, June 5, 1944 Today I went to the dentist. The way he went after me you would think he was drilling for oil. It has been reported that Rome has been taken by Allied forces. The city was overcome so quickly that little resistance was encountered and Rome was spared the ravages of war. One of our operators who is now in Brisbane said over R.T.T. that soon some of us are to be sent back to Australia. I to Sydney!!!

Tuesday, June 6, 1944 It is now 6:10 P.M. The news, all the world of free loving people have been looking for has just come over the air. Allied forces have landed in Northern France. The start of the invasion of Europe is now underway. General Eisenhower just gave a speech directed to the people of France.[43]

Wednesday, June 7, 1944 Everyone is up in the air about the invasion. All the fellows who can stay as near as radio a possible to hear news flashes: Not much detail is being given as to the as to the progress of the invasion. News flashes state only that operations are proceeding according to plan and progress is better than satisfactory. A force of 11, 000 air craft and between 4,000 and 6,000 boats of all types were used. A beach head of 150 miles is being established from Cherbourg near Boulogne. At the same points Allied forces are seven miles inland. Forces here in the S.W.P.A .on Biak Island have captured Manokwari

---

[43] My father is speaking of the deception created about the dates of this invasion which is tagged "Normandy." Even as the landing had been made (on June 6, 1944) for this invasion to take place the Germans were still unsure as to whether this was a major invasion or not.

Airdrome. Everyone here in camp has his mind intently on the invasion, but the fellows don't talk about it so much. Everyone is just anxious as to developments.

Thursday, June 8, 1944 The invasion is still going well. Troops and supplies continue to pour in. Weather conditions in the channel are not very favorable but is not affecting operations. A counter attack by the Germans has not yet been launched, but stiffer opposition is being encountered at some points: All shore batteries were silenced by Allied battleships at point blank range, as well as 10,000 tons of bombs being dropped on the invasion area. All enemy resistance was wiped out here before the landings. It seems that the japs are making an all out effort to conquer China before Allied forces can establish supply lines to defend it as well as set up bases: The Russian Armies are also starting an offensive in the East: Allied forces are 30 miles beyond Rome.

Friday, June 9, 1944 Just a routine day. This afternoon I went up to the transmitter shack and worked on a bracelet for Marian. It rained a little while today. Rather unusual for this time of year. It is usually dry now. The rains don't usually start until around September. Invasion reports are still good. The Germans, as yet, have not staged any major counter attacks. The success of the invasion can be judged there. Allied forces are inland eleven miles at some points. Allied commanders say the beach head will not be stable until our forces have advanced fifty miles inland.

Saturday, June 10, 1944 It has been raining all night and all day today. It was quite cool last night and I got a little cold before morning. I still haven't heard anything as to going down south. The 832nd just doesn't care how a fellow gets along. There are any number of fellows who have been in Brisbane since coming over seas two years ago, and who could just as well spend a little time in New Guinea.

Sunday, June 11, 1944 I got today off and spent most of it working on a bracelet for Marian. It is still rainy and has been raining off and on now for a week. Invasion reports are still good but no major drive has been made against the Allied beach head. The Russian Armies have started a large scale drive against Finland. The Allies in Italy have pursued the Germans forces fifty miles beyond Rome: Allied forces in Burma are making some gains but in Hunan Province, China's rice bowl, the Japs are making gains: Here in the S.W.P.A. our forces have overcome enemy resistance on Biak Island. The Japs have made a stronger bid to hold their base [so none] get captured.

> My mother has written at the top of this entry: "Happy Birthday to my Husband! By this time I pray to have peace on earth! "I love you twice as much today as yesterday, & only half as much as tomorrow."

Monday, June 12, 1944 Another birthday overseas. I celebrated it today by going to the dentist and laying in my bunk the rest of the day. The war is progressing favorably there is far from any peace on earth.

June 13, Tuesday, 1944 Back to work today. The T.C. was kinda sore because I wasn't to work yesterday. I wonder if he ever went to this G.I. dentist down town. My mail has been coming through pretty well lately. I still haven't received the films from down south. These pictures should have arrived over a week ago.

> My mother has written at the top of this entry: "This is your Dad's Birthday.")–(this would be my Grandfather Hightower.

225

June 14, Wednesday, 1944 Yes darling today is dad's birthday. It is our special dates such as this that I realize that time is flying by and I miss being home, more than ever. I wrote some letters home today and also received some. The recreation center the Australians have built downtown is sure a swell place. The only catch is Americans are not allowed. The Aussies say they haven't enough help to accommodate the American troops. However there is only a British and Australian flag flying outside. The Australians sure do have a short memory. The Burma campaign has long been forgotten and what importance the outcome meant to their homeland.

My mother has written at the top of this entry: "Today is our 2nd wedding anniversary. Always know your wife loves you more than anything in all the world! It's the most wonderful thing that ever happened to her! Being married to you! I love you, Honey!"

Thursday, June 15, 1944 Not our 2nd but our third anniversary, Darling. Maybe next year will be our first anniversary together. Of the three years Marian and I have been married, we have only had the enjoyment of our own home eight months. We received an anniversary present today in the form of a news flash, American super bombers, the new B29s, have bombed Japan, flying from bases off Burma or China, no details have been given as to the point in Japan that our bombers struck.

Friday, June 16, 1944 The T.C. was a little sore because I wasn't at work yesterday. I guess he hasn't ever visited a G.I. dentist. I heard today that a bunch of fellows names have been recommended for ratings, and I am included. I don't have much hopes of a rating though. I think the same reply will come back that has been before. No vacancies. This makes the fourth time I have been recommended for a rating. The way I feel lately, I will do good to keep what I have. I know I can't do my work at times like I once did. I blow up sometimes for little reason at all. I know I could never work a circuit like I use to.

Saturday, June 17, 1944 I slept this morning and this afternoon I worked on the necklace I am making for Marian. This evening I went to the show that was here in the area. It rained pick forks, but I had my raincoat with me so I kept pretty dry. The war news is still good. The Allies, after a little set back, are continuing to cut off the Cherbourg Peninsula. The Allies are striving to encircle the city of Cherbourg. This position is strongly fortified by the Germans. The chow here in camp is now on a standard so that a fellow can just keep going and that is all. Only field rations and dehydrated vegetables.

Sunday, June 18, 1944 I slept most of the day today as I had to go to work at 5 P.M. I received some pictures from down south that I took a while back. They were part of a series of shots I took from up on the knob. Our chow improved a little today. We had fresh beef for a change. This is the first fresh meat we have had for a long time, and the first need for the use of a fork or knife in equally as long. What we get you are usually are able to consume with a spoon. I went to the dentist this morning. I still have to go back – five more to be filled.

Monday, June 19, 1944 Today was really a red-letter day. I received ten letters. I worked at small ships station tonight. I received an emergency message on voice to send aid to a sinking boat at Oro Bay. He was very hard to understand and I sure had a tough time getting his message.

Tuesday, June 20, 1944 Laid around most of the day today as I haven't been feeling so good lately. The fellow in charge of our little mess shack over at work went crazy the other day. They say they had to take him away in a straight jacket. He was just about ready to go home. Been overseas two years and having nearly the same length of time here in New Guinea as I. Went to the show tonight, it was pretty good.

Wednesday, June 21, 1944 Received three letters from Marian today. My mouth has been coming through pretty well lately. The chow has hit a big improvement in the past few days. I worked Brisbane tonight. My Sgt. was all crossed up with another, so I was out of contact most of the night. It is reported that a battle engagement is taking place with the Jap fleet somewhere near the Philippine Islands. They must have decided to bring out their fleet due to the recent landing of American forces at Saipan in the Mariana Islands. This landing isolates Truk - the former Jap navy base.

Thursday, June 22, 1944 The same old routine today. Quite a few boats have been coming in lately and consequently our chow has made a big improvement. We even had fresh eggs for breakfast this morning. It was a relief to get away from those powdered eggs for a change. Latest reports state that the Jap fleet got quite a mauling from our carrier based planes. After getting an aircraft carrier sunk, a couple of cruisers, destroyers, in fact 14 ships in all, the Japs fleet fled toward the Philippine Islands. Things still don't look so good in China. The Japs have captured the capitol city of China's rice bowl.

Friday, June 23, 1944 Today we change shifts and now work days for four days. This morning I made another trip to the dentist. I had a little trouble with the T.C. He doesn't like it that I have to go to the dentist. He instructed the time I was to be back to work. I told him I intended having all my teeth fixed before I was through and since the medics didn't work on a time schedule that might suit him most I would be back when I was through. This guy seems to be scared he will lose his stripes or something. He runs around like someone is chasing him most of the time.

Saturday, June 24, 1944 Worked today as usual. Today is our last day on this shift and we get the long breaks between shifts this time. By rights and according to the "days off" schedule I was supposed to have tomorrow night off.

That would have given me practically two days off. However, the T.C. pulled a fast one and shoved the fellow at small ships in ahead of me. Chow is becoming first rate now. We get fresh meat and fresh eggs once in a while now. Quite a number of ships have been coming in lately. It will be the same old field rations when the boats quite coming in again.

Sunday, June 25, 1944 I worked at small ships tonight. I picked up a distress call from a boat that was evidently on a reef down at Oro Bay. My mail is slacking off a little now, it seems the general trend all round. The invasion is still going well. The fall of Cherbourg is near at hand. The Russian forces are driving into Finland with a steady advance. The situation in China is critical. Gains are being made by the Allies in Burma but farther north in China the Japs are continuing to make progress, striving to cut these areas off. It's the opinion that should the Japs succeed in their present champagne it will prolong the war at least a year and might mean the breakup of the Chinese Army.

Monday, June 26, 1944 Today is my day off. I didn't do much today but lay around. I haven't felt so good lately. I wrote a few letters and worked on a necklace I am making for Marian: I signed up to go on a boat trip tomorrow.

Tuesday, June 27, 1944 This morning a bunch of us climbed in a truck that took us over to the American docks. We got aboard a motor launch that took us over to Fisherman's Island. There is a swell beach there and the ocean water is crystal clear. You can see the bottom where it is thirty feet deep. We had a lunch of field rations with cold coca to drink. We ran around the beach and went in the water now and then. I found some pieces of cord that I intend [to send] home. The sun didn't shine so much today and it rained off and on, but we had a good time. We got back around five P.M.

Wednesday, June 28, 1944 Reports came in today that Cherbourg has fallen. Many Germans prisoners have been taken. The Russians have launched a full-scale offensive toward Minsk, former capital of White Russia. They are advancing on a 200 mile front. Our forces on Saipan are making progress against stiff resistance. The Japs are using strong forces of tanks, but most of them have been knocked out. The American Fifth Army in Italy is driving on towards Leghorn, this is a port nearly 100 miles north of Rome. Went to town today. We stopped in at the Red Cross and signed up for the boat ride this coming Friday.

We also stopped at the Australian Recreation. We bought some small pies and cookies that weren't bad. I was supposed to go to the dentist today but missed. I made another appointment.

Thursday, June 29, 1944 Today just a routine day. Slept this morning until noon. Chow has sure taken a big jump for the better lately. We have been getting fresh meat nearly every day. We still have dehydrated cabbage and potatoes, but fresh meat fills in a big space that formally was occupied by field rations. We are getting canned milk rather than powdered milk for our coffee (battery acid) and we get canned fruit more often. Went to the show tonight. Had seen it before, but it was a pretty good show so I sat through it.

Friday, June 30, 1944 This morning three of my tent mates and I went down to the marine docks where we were to get aboard a boat that was to take us over to a small island to spend the day. In the party there were about twenty fellows plus a woman Red Cross worker. The boat was a two master fishing boat formally belonging to the Japs, but ceased when war broke out: It took us quite a while to get out to the island as we had to tack. This was a different island than we went to the other day. This one is called Laloki Island. We swam and laid around in the sand most of the day. We had a lunch of sandwiches and cold drink. At three P.M. we started back, reaching the dock around four. I sure got a nice sun burn today and had an awful headache tonight.[44]

---

[44] Tack: change in direction of the boat in order to get into the direction of the wind: to change the direction of (a sailing ship) when sailing close-hauled by turning the bow to the wind and shifting the sails so as to fall off on the other side at about the same angle as before.

Saturday, July 1, 1944 I got off work today at seven this morning and being today is the day of the change, I had to go back at 5 P.M. Two more manual circuits have been taken out. Manual circuits are just about a thing of the past around the station. The only manual circuits that have any traffic is Hollandia and that is all intercept. We transmit hardly any to them. I believe a big change is going to take place around here in a short time. Darwin seems to be coming into the lime-light lately. It wouldn't surprise me if a bunch of us weren't sent over there. Yesterday was pay day. I left 20 more pounds in the orderly room, which makes a total of 80 lbs. in cash. I have besides that, 95 lbs in solders' savings.

Sunday, July 2, 1944 I wrote letters and laid around nearly all day. It seems that most of the fellows here in camp are Catholic so I am rather negligent about going to church. One of these days I will get one of my friends to start going to church with me. They say since the WACS arrived here in Moresby and a few of them have been seen in church, that the male attendance has increased 150%. The Russians are closing in on Minisk (Minsk NW USSR) which was the former white Russian capitol. The Russians are now but a short distance from the 1939 Polish border.

Monday, July 3, 1944 Work as usual today, I worked Townsville and received quite a bit of traffic for a change. Our chow is still pretty fair. We still get fresh meat quite often. Some more circuits have been taken out. We now should get more days off.

Tuesday, July 4, 1944 I went to town this morning to go to the dentist, but being today was the "fourth" they gave me another appointment for Friday. As I had the day off, I spent this afternoon working on some jewelry. It seemed like whatever I touched I messed up. I got disgusted and came back to my tent. I went to the show tonight. It was pretty good for a change.

Wednesday, July 5, 1944 I worked at small ships station today. There wasn't much doing. I contacted a couple of stations on voice. I also intercepted an emergency message on 500 KCS. It is reported that the Russians have taken Minsk and annulated a large German force. It is said the Russians then captured and killed destroyed 146,000 Germans. Fighting in Normandy is becoming more intense. The Germans have launched heavy counter attacks but without success. Germany is still sending flying bombs into Southern England. They are offering something of a menace, but nothing vital as the Germans propaganda puts out.

Thursday, July 6, 1944 Worked WVLB today without any traffic at all. There are now only six C.W. circuits left and very little traffic on any of them. With so many circuits now gone, we operators get nearly every other day off. This will not last long though. I have a feeling that a bunch of us will be moved, where I don't know. Maybe Hollandia (N. New Guinea), Boganville, (Bogodjm – NE New Guinea), perhaps over to Darwin (N. Australia.) Who knows, who cares. I would welcome going to the Marianas. I get tomorrow off. I have spent a year and a half in New Guinea – today.

Friday, July 7, 1944 I got today off again. There isn't enough work at the station to shake a stick at. There are twelve operators on our shift and six circuits, therefore we get about every other day off. As little work there is on the six circuits two fellows could easily take care of them. This afternoon I worked a while on a broach I am making for mom. I went to the show down to Navy tonight.

Saturday, July 8, 1944 I was to work at small ships station today, but being I had to go to the dentist the fellow at small ships will work for me today and I will give him the day off tomorrow. Today was my last trip to the dentist for I hope a long time. I hear the rotation plan has been revised. Time in New Guinea no longer counts extra. You are classed in three brackets. A. class = up to 18 months overseas, B class = 18 to 25 months overseas, C. class + 25 to 30 months plus. A fellow has to be in C. class to have priority enough to go home. That is if a fellow has enough pull to be put on the quota. Many fellow down south, who never saw New Guinea are going home at twenty or less months. Talk about a crooked set up, this is sure it.

Sunday, July 9, 1944 I wanted one of my tent mates to go to church with me this morning, but he had to work. Since the other fellows in our tent are Catholic I didn't have anyone to go with so I neglected to go. This afternoon I worked on some of my homemade jewelry. I have quite a job on my hands making some sort of gadgets for all the folks at home. I worked at small ships station tonight. There wasn't anything doing there. It is reported that Allied Forces have captured Caen (N. France) an important German communications center. The Russians are plumaging full speed ahead. The Germans are starting to talk about a possible defeat. American super fortresses have again attacked the mainland of Japan.

Monday, July 10, 1944 I slept until noon today. After chow I started making a ring for dad. I borrowed a small hammer and acquired a piece of flat iron on which I shaped a florin *(florin – an old British coin)* into a ring. I signed up to go on a boat trip tomorrow.

Tuesday, July 11, 1944 This morning a bunch of us met up at the orderly room when a truck picked us up to take us out to the American docks. We got aboard the same motor launch as we road in before when we went out to Fisherman's Island. The boat anchored about twice as far out as it did the last time I swam from the boat to shore and boy what a long haul. After swimming all day we started back at 3:30 P.M. There was a stiff breeze blowing from the ocean and even though we were inside the reef the waves sprayed the whole boat: A plane must have crashed over by another island as we saw a crash boat with a bunch of planes circling it.

Wednesday, July 12, 1944 Didn't do much today. I planned on going over to the signal center and ask about a furlough. Bill Pandolfi wanted to wait until tomorrow to apply for furlough so we will go then. Bill is the fellow I went on furlough with before. A friend and I went to town today for a little while. We stopped in at the Australian canteen. The Sergeant's Club is open again. They now have a membership of over 5000 members. Few of them are around here anymore. I am sure tired from the swim I had yesterday. Had to go to work at midnight: I received the surprise of my life today. I received a letter from Meredith informing me of a gift of $420.00 besides a $25 a month until victory. Boy this will sure help out our savings account.

Thursday, July 13, 1944 The same old routine today. C.W. operating is about a thing of the past. We only have four circuits now. Since advance G.H.Q. has moved up to Hollandia we are no longer net control. A fellow would think now that C.W. is practically nil, they wouldn't bother with so much B.S. That isn't the case at this station though they have started another drive on procedure violations. They have a fellow at the receiver station listening in on every circuit. If a fellow makes an extra "dit" or "dah" they call up the signal office and report you. Out of forty operators, only twelve got by without being reported last week. I happened to be one of them.

Friday, July 14, 1944 Today Bill Pandolfi and I went down to U.S.A. S.O.S. head quarters to try and get a furlough. With no relief in sight this is about the only thing there is to do. Our company commander had gone to Brisbane so there was no one to see. I happened to think of W.O. Henry. I didn't know he could do anything but I asked to see him anyway. He told us to make out our furlough papers and he was sure he could put them through for us. He said we should hear from them in four or five days. I have learned not to plan on anything until it comes through.

Saturday, July 15, 1944 It has been a month since our third wedding anniversary. The way the war is progressing maybe Marian and I will be able to celebrate our fourth anniversary together. The war in Germany can end at any time, but the guess I am making is November 11. I think that much of the winter will be about all I can take. Tonight I went over to another area to see Laney Ross. He was to appear with an amateur show. However, Jack Benny and his show came in and Laney Ross had to leave to meet them, so we didn't hear him sing after all.

Sunday, July 16, 1944 I had the day off so this afternoon I went out to see Jack Benny; Harry Statler (rated as the world's best harmonica player). Carol Landis; and Martha Tallon (top notch songstress.) The program was good and I was lucky in getting a spot near the stage. I had my camera along and I snapped a number of pictures. If they turn out I should have some good ones. Tonight some of us went down to the Navy to the show. They had a boxing match before the show tonight. I was sure tired and I slept through most of the show.

Monday, July 17, 1944 I received quite a bunch of letters today for a change. Most of them were from Marian. I have been acting as door guard for the past two days. Tonight a captain came into the station that I had to stop. It looks like C.W. operators will be used only in the fields from now on. This fixed station is a softer life, but a fellow would be better satisfied in the field.

Tuesday, July 18, 1944 I had the day off again today. I spend most of my spare time making homemade jewelry. It is a slow process though as a fellow has to get along with crude tools, and junk that has been thrown away: It is reported that British troops have taken Caen (N. France) on the Normandy front. The Russians have advanced twelve miles a day since they started their offensive and are now only 20 miles from the Prussian boarder.

Wednesday, July 19, 1944 I worked WVLH (Hollandia) today. I handled more traffic than I have in a long time. I also had a good operator on the other end which is unusual for Hollandia. It is a tough circuit to work through as there is a Jap circuit in between, which is more than likely at Wewak (NE New Guinea). One thing about the Japs – they sure have transmitters with a lot of soup. This Jap rode on top of us all afternoon and we could only pass traffic when he would stop keying. We would only go about three groups at a time, when he would start slacking. It is an unofficial report that Tojo has resigned as Premiere of Japan.[45]

Thursday, July 20, 1944 Went up to the radio repair shack this afternoon to work a little while on some jewelry, however, they were building a recording machine so there wasn't room for me to do any work. This afternoon I got into a hot argument with one of my tent mates. Ever since I moved into this tent he has thrown the air that because I was last here, he could shove me around as he wished. I think from now on he will have a different view of things. It is official that Tojo and his cabinet have been forced to resign. It doesn't prove that Japan will give up, but it does prove they are not satisfied with the way things are going for them.

Friday, July 21, 1944 I think my furlough will go through O.K. as yet though I haven't received any news as to how things are going. This afternoon I

---

[45] Tojo Hideki 1884 – 1948 – Military commander & statesman for Japan. Attempted suicide – was arrested by the Allies and tried for war crimes and executed in 1948.

went up to the radio repair shack and finished the ring I am making for dad and Jack. Tomorrow I plan to mail a bunch of gadgets home.

It is reported that American forces have invaded Guam (C. Pacific) little resistance has been encountered so far. The Russian forces are driving towards East Prussia and Warsaw (C. Poland) at about twelve miles a day. As yet the Germans have been unable to stem their advance. Flying bomb raids on Southern England are not as intense lately. The Allied Air Force has destroyed a large percentage of the launching platforms.

Saturday, July 22, 1944 Just a routine day today. I am kinda getting a few of my things together just in case my furlough does come through. The nights have been a little cool lately. This is the coolest time of year now. I mailed some rings, broach, and bracelet to Mom, Dad, Jack, and Myrt today. I have a bracelet under construction as well as a couple of bracelets for Marian. It looks like if I go on furlough I won't have time to finish them. I heard today that our furlough papers had been approved by our operations officer. If they get by one more department we will be all set. I messed around all day. Wrote some letters and sorted some more of my junk. In one of Marian's letters today she said that Jack and Myrt had been home on a furlough ,and all of the relatives and folks had a picnic. Boy I wonder when I will ever get home. Two years and a half since I last saw the place.

Monday, July 24, 1944 After working midnight until seven A.M. a couple of fellows & I went out to a beach to find some special kinds of shells. These shells are quite scarce and classed semi precious. After walking nearly two miles through jungle and swamp we arrived at the beach where these shells were supposed to be. We combed the beach until 3:30 P.M. and then started back to camp. I found about a dozen shells. Most of them had been on the beach quite a while and were not in very good condition.

Tuesday, July 25, 1944 I was sure sore last night. The T.C. called me in to work at midnight. One of the fellows had to take another to the hospital). There wasn't a darn thing to do and all I did was look at the newspaper. This T.C. is a timid soul always afraid. I only had to stay at the station an hour.

Wednesday, July 26, 1944 This morning while I was down at the shower one of the fellows who also applied for furlough said that our C.O. wouldn't approve anyone's furlough who had had one while in New Guinea. Boy that sure took the wind out of my sails. This afternoon I had decided to just forget about a furlough, when my friend came in waving his orders in one hand. Our furloughs came through after all. Boy it didn't take me long to get up to the orderly room to get my orders. They are going to let us stay around camp until Flag Day. We will not have any duties to perform, or have to work over at the station. I am really getting my stuff together in earnest now.

Thursday, July 27, 1944 Ever since getting my orders I have been busy as heck sorting and packing my stuff. I have collected so much junk and a lot of it I don't want to throw away. I am going to carry as much with me as possible in one bag and put the rest in my other bag to be mailed to me in case I am lucky in getting a transfer. This afternoon I turned out a big washing. All the dirty clothes I have now, is what I have on.

Friday, July 28, 1944 I am getting pretty well squared away. The barrack bag I am leaving behind is jammed full and weighs about a ton. Boy they will sure curse if they have to send it to me. I traded a hunting knife a fellow gave me for an O.D. cap. Probably when we get as far south as Brisbane we will have to change to winter uniforms as this is the coldest time of the year there now. This will be the first winter clothing I have worn for nearly two years. After so much time in the tropics I wonder how I will be able to take such cold weather. They gave me a package of Atabrine to take along. I don't think I will take any as I want to find out if I really have malaria.

Saturday, July 29, 1944 I haven't worked over at the station since I got my orders the other day. I have been spending most of my time sorting over my junk so that I can get all my extra junk in the one bag that I have to leave behind. In case I am lucky and get transferred to Brisbane, Sydney, etc. They will send me this bag, in this case. Chances that I will ever see my other barrack bag is practically nil.

Sunday, July 30, 1944 Well we are still laying around camp waiting for pay day. I forgot to sign the payroll this month so I probably will be red lined this month. Luckily I don't have to depend on this pay for my furlough fund. As far as Signal Corps is concerned, we are out of luck as far as the rotation program is concerned. Fellows on May and June quota still haven't left and an order came through the other day that no Signal troops would go home on July quota.

Monday, July 31, 1944 I am kinda anxious to get out of here. Sticking around camp is no good. They could decide that they need you back at work and away goes my furlough. I heard that there is a chance we can get out tomorrow afternoon on a C54 transport to Townsville. I would sure like to get a ride on that plane.

The Mansion Furlough
Aug. 2 - 25, 1944

Tuesday, August 1, 1944 I went to get paid this noon, but as I expected I had been red lined: At 1 P.M. all of we fellows going on furlough loaded our baggage in a jeep and went out to the air drone. The C54 that we hoped to get a ride on was loaded so we were out of luck there. We had our names put on the manifest so that they can call us when transportation is available: We hung around the air drone until 5 P.M. and then came back to camp. We are going out again in the morning.

Wednesday, August 2, 1944 I got up this morning at six o' clock and a few minutes later a fellow from the motor pool came down and said we were to get to the air port as soon as possible. I started out to round the fellows up. I soon got all of them up except one guy and he had slept in a different tent. We all looked for him for 25 minutes without any luck. We stood in the middle of camp and yelled until I thought someone would shoot us. We finally decided that if we were to catch the plane we would have to leave without him. The five of us (Bill, Suiter, Jenson, Signat, and myself) barely got there in time to weigh out luggage. We were just about ready to get on board when here came Fritz, the fellow we left behind. By a little fast talking we got him on the plane. The plane we rode in was a C54 or a Douglas Skymaster. This is the largest plane the Army has in service next to the new super bombers. We took off from Jackson strip at 8 A.M. this was the most enjoyable plane ride I have taken yet. This ship being very large rode exceptionally smooth. I had Bill take a picture of me inside the plane cabin. There was quite a bit of light but I am doubtful if this picture will turn out. As we came into Townsville I took another color shot out the plane window, I also got a picture of our ship after we had landed. It took us just 3 hours and ten minutes to cover the 620 miles from Moresby, flying at 9000 feet.

Thursday, August 3, 1944 A fellow's chances of getting extra time on his own while on furlough is pretty slim now. All the loopholes that there once was have all been clogged up. The M.P.s stamped our papers the minute we got off the plane. There was nothing left to do but turn in at Armstrong Camp. Last night after getting set up here in camp we went into town and had a steak supper. Boy what a meal, fresh milk, and everything. Today what we had heard about this camp sure worked out for Bill and I. They grabbed us for detail and what a job. Cleaning out two mess halls – ass holes. After today I am going to get out of here if I have to go back to Moresby to do it. What a "Hell Hole" this turned out to be. Tonight we ate supper in town, visited some of the fellows at W.V.L.T. We went out to the NCO club for a while then came back to camp.

Friday, August 4, 1944 We got caught on another detail this morning. This one wasn't so bad but it still gets under my hide that a fellow going on furlough has to do all their dirty work around a camp like this. We were informed this afternoon that we are to leave tonight at 8 P.M. by train for Brisbane. I was quite sure this would happen but "oh" how I dread that ride. At 7 P.M. we loaded our junk in a truck and went to the railroad station. The train fare for the 800 mile trip to Brisbane is 38.30 ($110.00). Our coach was a coach behind the baggage cars. The coach ahead of ours was carrying two Jap prisoners. Our coach just behind was a prisoner's car with iron bars over the windows also. The railroad is narrow gauge (36") and the cars are very small. The thirty fellows in our car filled it full with little room to stretch out for the night.

Saturday, August 5, 1944 I spent a miserable night trying to sleep on the floor of the car. It was very cold and with only my raincoat under and my field jacket over me I about froze to death. This morning when we stopped for breakfast we had traveled just 160 miles. The train only runs 25 to 30 miles per hour and stops every fifteen minutes or so: We have our mess kits with us, but the grub at the railroad cafes is pretty punk and the waiting line is long. We usually try and get a bite to eat at some near- by restaurant. We have been living on sandwiches and fruit for most of the trip. We arrived in Rockhampton (NE Australia) for supper tonight. We made better time today than last night.

Sunday, August 6, 1944 Waiting in this prisoner's coach is giving us a lot of amusement. When we go through or stop at a station for a short time everyone looks at us and a number of times we were asked why we were prisoners. Last night I slept on the cushion. That is, I got as much sleep as possible which was hardly any. We finally pulled into Brisbane at 7 P.M. Boy furlough regulations are air tight now. The M.Ps. are right on top of you the minute you get off the train. We intend on staying in Brisbane a few days to see about getting released here. Our chances are slim, but we are going to try. We stayed at an Army dormitory recreation center. There was a dance here tonight, so we stayed around here for that. There was an awful crowd, so I didn't do much dancing.

Monday, August 7, 1944 Today we went out to our unit head quarters. When we got there we met a bunch of our old gang who are stationed here. We went out and had a steak dinner and then went to another place right afterwards and had a spaghetti dinner. For supper, another steak. Today I gained two pounds and I never felt so full in my life: We stopped in at the personal office and inquired about relief. The personal officer took our names but made no promises. He said, should our orders come through we will be notified through the Red Cross in Sydney.

Tuesday, August 8, 1944 We caught the eleven o'clock train for Sydney this morning. This trip will not be as bad as the other from Townsville. The railroad from here on to Sydney is wide gage and this train makes much better time. With six of us in one compartment sleeping was "nill". We still have our summer clothing on and keeping warm is impossible.

Wednesday, August 9, 1944 We arrived here in Sydney at 7 A.M. as usual the M.P.s were all over the place to catch us as we got off the train. We spent most of the day going here and there, after our winter clothes, rations coupons, and inquiring as to a place to stay. At the Red Cross we were informed of an eight room house that we could rent. That sounded like a good idea so at 3 P.M. we caught an electric train out to Homebush, Australia which is about a 30 minute ride. We started walking up the street looking for the house we had been informed of. We walked and walked passing many nice places that we would like. Finally one of the fellows looked across the street and saw an old mansion sitting in the center of a large lawn. We jokingly said that, that was probably it. After looking at the address, by gosh it was it. I never had anything strike me so funny in my life. I thought I would have to get down and roll.

Thursday, August 10, 1944 After looking this place over we decided to take it. We have all the house but a few rooms downstairs that are occupied by the caretakers. Our rent is two pounds a week a piece. Bill and I have a room together downstairs. Our room isn't too clean but it overlooks the town, has two large windows and a fire place. It rained nearly all day today, the same as it did yesterday. The weather is very cold and nearly all the fellows have caught cold. I caught a train into town tonight and went to the Trocadero Dance Hall. The dance was quite nice, still having the same two orchestras as when I was in Sydney the last time. Bill stayed in tonight as he has a bad cold and is about half sick: We have tried our hand at cooking, but the idea isn't so hot. No one wants to do dishes and it is afternoon before we can get away.

Friday, August 11, 1944 Bill and I went into town today. We left our watches at a jeweler's to be fixed. I also left my Army and Cameo rings. We looked around for a few things to send home but to find anything is a pretty hard job. We were given but five clothing coupons and with only this many you can hardly buy anything. It takes twelve coupons for a pair of shoes. Bill and I had steak for dinner. Food rationing is in full effect here in Australia. More often than not you get no butter with our meal. Vegetables are also scarce. Bill and I went to a show this afternoon and to the dance tonight.

Saturday, August 12, 1944 One of our fellows was sent to the hospital today with a bad cold and I guess the flu. Bill isn't at all well either and is afraid he will have to turn in to the dispensary. All the other fellows but me have had colds. It has been raining here nearly every day since we arrived and the change from New Guinea has been terrific. All of we fellows take atabrine regularly as the chance of malaria breaking out is a good possibility. I had stopped taking atabrine for a couple of days and started to feel light headed and dizzy. I went to a show tonight. My feet couldn't stand another dance such as last night.

Sunday, August 13, 1944 There is nothing at all going on here in Sydney on Sunday. I slept until noon today and then went to town. This afternoon I walked through the park and over to the art gallery. I looked around for a while and then went over to the American Center where I met Bill. He had a friend with him who had invited us to their home for supper. We caught the ferry boat that took us across the harbor. For supper we had lamb chops, peas, potatoes, bread and butter. Australians drink no water with their meals, and coffee or tea after the entire meal. For dessert we had apple pie with a sort of cream sauce over it. While Americans use only a fork to eat such dessert, the Australians us a fork and spoon. Australians always use a fork in the left hand and insert it in their mouth upside down. We stood around the piano and sang songs until time to leave.

Monday, August 14, 1944 We fellows have been cooking our own breakfast, but I am not so hot on the idea. A fellow never gets away until noon, and only a few guys realize that the dishes have to be washed. Bill turned into the dispensary today and thought he would be taken to the hospital. They gave him some medicine though and said he would be OK. Switer, the fellow who went to the hospital the other day, is still there. I guess he has a little touch of fever. Looked around this afternoon for things to send home. Went to the dance tonight.

Tuesday, August 15, 1944 Didn't get away from our mansion until around noon. Had a dinner of steak & eggs then went to the show. I wrote Marian a letter at the American Center. This evening I went to the dance again. Sydney is loaded with sailors, as the fleet came in the other day. The dance wasn't much good, awfully crowded.

Wednesday, August 16, 1944 Bill is a little better today but he still has a bad cold. Switer got out of the hospital today and is O.K. now. I am still feeling the best of anyone in our bunch. I make it a point to take atabrine every day. More rain today: I looked around today again for something to send home. I finally decided on some boomerangs, kangaroo skins. "Boy" what a tough job, a fellow could spend his whole furlough shopping and not find anything. Being away from New Guinea is a break, even though for but a short time. I guess my chances of being transferred to Brisbane are nill. We stopped in today to find out if any orders had come through, but no luck. I went to the show tonight.

Thursday, August 17, 1944 I met one of my friends from New Guinea this noon and we decided to go ice skating at the inside ice rink. Not having skated for nearly five or more years, boy I had quite a time. My ankles could only take the beating for an hour so we left. Tonight Bill an Australian friend and I decided to take in a night club. It was rather a small place and very crowded. We had a supper of chicken and then sat around our table and talked. A fellow came around selling chances on a sheep skin rug. Bill and I bought one. Since I didn't have any change. Bill paid for my "chance." The fellow called out the number of the winner an hour or so later. "66" won (my number): I looked kinda screwy carrying a sheep skin mat under my arm at 2 A.M. I stayed here in town at the Red Cross tonight.

Friday, August 18, 1944 I slept rather late this morning. I met Bill at the American Center around noon and we went out to dinner. As usual steak and eggs. This afternoon I had my sheep skin mat packed & censored and sent it to Marian. A fellow in many cases around Sydney runs into an entirely unwelcome atmosphere. The Australians are practically out of the war now, and in many cases their attitude is to endure the presence of the "yanks" and forget our accomplishments in the early days of the war when the Japs were knocking at their backdoor. In this country you have to look a long way to find a person who thinks England should have much to say, as to the drawing up of peace terms. It seems even now England is getting in position to try and make a grab for bases in the Pacific.

Saturday, August 19, 1944 Ate dinner here in Sydney and then went to a show: I met one of our fellows at the American Center and he said our bunch was invited out to a house party tonight. We all met out at the mansion at 7 P.M. and caught a train to these people's house. We stood around the piano and sang songs until the wee hours of the morning. Since we had no way of getting back to our house we stayed all night.

Sunday, August 20, 1944 This morning a friend of one of our bunch who was at the party last night came by with his car to take us for a ride. He is a bookie at one of the race tracks, and a former jockey. He was rated as top Australian steeple chase Jockeys in former races. We drove down the coast over a hundred miles, traveling through the mountains and many small towns. The farmland in this part of the country seems quite fertile. This is the agricultural district of Australia. We visited a farm that had the oldest race horse stable in Australia on it, which is over a hundred years old. Six Melbourne Cup winners came out of these stables. We drove back to Sydney a different route and it was even more scenic than the other. We arrived back around 6 P.M. I was very tired so I went to bed early tonight.

Monday, August 21, 1944 *two years from today's date I was born – Marijo Anne Hightower.* Didn't get downtown until afternoon. Got something to

245

eat then looked through some of the stores. The main department stores here in Sydney are, David Jones, Farmers & Mark Fays. What these stores do have worth having requires coupons and that is what I haven't got. I went to the dance tonight. The town is still over run with sailors and the Trocadoro as usual was loaded full of them.

Tuesday, August 22, 1944 This furlough is doing me a lot of good, but I sure wish I were back home and in civilian clothes. Now that the end of the war seems in sight, I am more lonely than ever. I don't think about when I might get home, but I hope it won't be very long now.[46]

Wednesday, August 23, 1944 I went to town today and picked up my watch. When I got back to our mansion I dropped it and it broke again. Tomorrow I am going to see again if I can get it fixed. Bill and I went to town this evening, ate supper at the Red Cross, then I left him and took in a show. The war is sure going well in Europe now, Americans have broken out of the Normandy Beachhead and are driving towards Paris, as well as tromping most of the German's seventh army near the coast. Maybe, my guess of November eleventh won't be so far wrong after all.

Thursday, August 24, 1944 Well today is the last day of my furlough. As yet we haven't received our orders from Brisbane. So I guess it means we will be sent back to New Guinea. The manner in which the army operates is one military secret that will never get out. Not even God can tell, or what kind of system the Army uses. We went to a night club tonight. We had supper and left rather early.

Friday, August 25, 1944 I went to town early this morning as I have to get my watch and make a last check on our orders from Brisbane. (No luck) My watch still won't run. I am not going to waste any more time or money on it over here. The first chance I get I am sending it to Marian. I arrived back at the mansion about 2 P.M. packed my stuff, then Bill and I caught the train out to Warwick Farm to turn in. After being assigned to a tent and drawing blankets, we got a pass and went back into Sydney.

---

[46] My father still has until November 19, 1945 before he and my mother are reunited in Kansas City.

Saturday, August 26, 1944 Last night I went to the dance and then came back to the Red Cross where I stayed all night. I don't intend staying out at Warwick Farm anymore than I have to, as it is bitter cold sleeping in a tent down here. We got up at 5 A.M. and caught the 6:10 train. It is around twenty miles to Warwick Farm and requires about fifty minutes to make the trip. After roll call we were put on detail, which only lasted an hour or so: A bunch of fellows are being shipped out, so the camp is restricted and no passes are given out. Bill and I left camp a little this afternoon without a pass and went to town: When we got back to camp Bill's camera, my camera & some of the other fellow's things had been stolen. No soldier can stoop lower than this, to steal from his own mates.

Sunday, August 27, 1944 Bill and I went out to the dance last night and then came back here to the Red Cross. Since we had no pass we couldn't book a bed so we had to sleep in a chair here in the lobby all night. We arrived back to camp in time for roll call. We were put on a clothing detail this morning, which kept us busy until noon. More fellows are being shipped out so the camp is still restricted. They say it will be some time before we will be put on a boat to go back to New Guinea. Bill and I went to town anyway. We took a boat ride over to Manila Beach tonight. We went into the aquarium where they have a lot of sharks, sting rays, king fish, etc.

Monday, August 28, 1944 Sat up again last night in the Red Cross lobby and was in camp in time for roll call. Boy I am sure wore out and tired with hardly any sleep in the past two days. Eight fellows had a job of shelling a bushel of peas this morning. In a staging camp such as this, rank means nothing. Our crew consisted of two Staff Sgts. three Sgts. a Corporal and a Master Sgt.

Tuesday, August 29, 1944 The restriction was lifted so we were given a pass to town today. For the first time in the past days I slept in a bed: Most of our bunch feels pretty good now, only it is my turn to have a cold. Bill had a date tonight so I took in a show.

Wednesday, August 30, 1944 Warwick Farm isn't so bad apparently. We have roll call at 8 A.M. after which we have a short detail that might last only half hour or at the most for the morning. In case you are on K.P. or guard duty you get a 24-hour pass. I had to work on the clothing building this morning. This afternoon I took my barracks bag over to the transportation office and asked them if I could leave it there so that I would have some of my stuff left to take back to Moresby. I took my musette bag containing my briefcase, photo album, etc. into town and checked it at the Red Cross. Tonight I went to the track. I only stayed a short time as I was very tired. I came back to the Red Cross and went to bed.

Thursday, August 31, 1944 Boy my bank account is sure running low. I put in for partial pay today and should get it Saturday. The most we can draw is $5. Nearly all of we fellows are broke. I hear it will be some time before a boat comes in. The longer it takes the better. I have been pretty lucky lately in keeping out of details. By moving from one place to another while in ranks and dodging the fellow who makes up the list. Bill and I got to town around noon and went to the Red Cross for dinner. They serve pretty good meals. I eat steak most of the time drink lots of milk and eat ice cream. I have gained around ten lbs. so far (161 lbs.)

Friday, September 1, 1944 Stayed again at the Red Cross last night. I won't sleep at Warwick Farm if at all possible, as it is bitter cold out there at night. In order to get to camp at 8 A.M. for roll call we have to get up at 5 A.M. and catch the 6:10 electric train at Town Hall Station. I got stuck on a detail this morning but it only lasted half hour. We only had to clean six rifles and load some boxes on a truck. Went to town again at noon ate dinner, cleaned up here at the Red Cross, wrote some letters and went to the dance tonight.

Saturday, September 2, 1944 I thought for a while we would be in for an "all day" detail. Twenty of us were loaded into a truck and taken down to the docks. We had the job of loading boxes on a truck. Being this is Saturday, this place only works half a day so we got to come back to camp at noon. I went to town, stopped at the Red Cross and cleaned up. I had an invitation out for dinner tonight, and really enjoyed a home cooked meal. We had lamb chops, brown potatoes, peas and milk. Train service has been cut down as the coal strikes here in Australia have caused a shortage. The government doesn't seem to be able to cope with the situations and "John Curtin" the Prime Minister is behind the eight ball. Australian generals seem to look at the war as being behind her now. There is no reason for alarm in this country now: Two years ago today I sailed out of San Francisco.

Sunday, September 3, 1944 I didn't report out to camp this morning for roll call. I ate breakfast and dinner at the Red Cross as usual Sunday it's an awful dead day here in Sydney. This evening I went to the show. I had to get there at

6:30 in order to get a seat for the 7:30 show. The war news is sure good now. It looks like Germany may crack at any moment. Our forces have taken nearly all of France, forcing the German forces to fight. The latest rumor is that we may be shipped out Wednesday. I guess there is no hope for relief to Australia. Boy how I hate to return to New Guinea.

Monday, September 4, 1944 I sat up in the Red Cross lobby last night as I didn't have a pass. I reported for roll call at 8 A.M. this morning. We had a short detail this morning after which I went to town. Boy I am sure in a bad way as far as funds are concerned. Being that the camp is to be moved we can't sign for partial pay.

Tuesday, September 5, 1944 Bill and I tried at the Red Cross today to borrow some money but no soap. Boy it is darn disgusting. The first time I have ever applied for anything from them and I get turned down. Everything you get from the Red Cross you have to pay for. The biggest percentage of soldiers I know thinks they have a racket. The field directors and others on salary are getting more wages than they have ever received.

Wednesday, September 6, 1944 Today the six of us were called over to the transfer office. Orders had come through from General Cluger that we were needed back at our base and we were to have priority air travel. These orders were not correct as to our organization, so they are going to check. We could have let them go as they were, but there was a chance we might get "shanghaied" and besides we don't want to leave yet anyway. I went up to the grace building this evening and borrowed five pounds from one of my friends. I went to the Trocadoro tonight. It is better dancing now since most of the navy has left.

Thursday, September 7, 1944 I heard today that the furlough boat is in and that we may be shipped out Saturday. Boy, the prospect of leaving to go back up North sure is hard to take. When you look around and see so many fellows who have gotten good breaks, it can't help but make you feel a little bitter. Fellows down here are going home on the rotation plan with equal or better priority that fellows in New Guinea. The regular manifest is posted and we are not on it as yet. I am sure holding my breath. If I can only miss this shipment then it might be two weeks until another boat arrives again. I stayed at the Red Cross tonight. Luckily I had a pass at about 2 A.M. everyone was awakened by the M.P.s who checked passes.

September 8, Friday, 1944 – at the top of this page my mother has written – "ARE YOU NOW IN THE U.S.?"

"Hell no! @%^*& — is the war over!?" Today an alternate roister was posted and all of we fellows are on this one. Fellows on the regular roister are taken first and those absent are filled in with fellows on the alternate. There is a chance, but a very slim one, that we won't go. The camp was restricted today but I left camp around 4 P.M. and came to town. Bill spent the evening out at Burwood, I went to a show. I came back and slept in camp tonight as the M.P.s would probably be watching the Red Cross for guys without passes.

Saturday, September 9, 1944 Roll call at 8 A.M. after which we handed in our blankets, cots, & clothes. Everyone on the regular and alternate roister went over to the grand stand to await roll call for shipment. My spirits hit rock bottom when my name was called. All of we fellows met the same fate. After a lunch of sandwiches and coffee we were loaded on a troop train that took us to Sydney directly to the docks. We went on board at around 3:30 P.M. assigned bunks, given instructions. We pulled out around 4P.M. As we went down the harbor, past the docks, one fellow dove over board and started to shore. The M.P.s following in a small launch picked him up and put him aboard again: They say five jumped overboard on the last trip.

Sunday, September 10, 1944 I went to bed early last night. The thought of going back to New Guinea is sure hard to take. I seem to be taking this voyage pretty well as so far I am not the least bit sea sick. We are still insight of the coast as we travel north, I guess we stay fairly close most of the route. Our boat is a fairly fast ship with a capacity of not over 800 persons. We eat three times a day and the food is quite good. We have to wash and shave in salt water. They say the voyage to Oro Bay takes five days. I think I will wait until then to shave.

Monday, September 11, 1944 I slept a little better last night but it is still rather cold. Not having any blanket with me, and only a rain coat to throw over me. My bunk is far from comfortable, and is made of a frame with a canvass laced in between with rope. There are six bunks to each rack such as: (see diagram on diary page)

I am still feeling pretty well and think I will make this voyage without getting seasick: The ocean was smooth and the sky clear today.

Tuesday, September 12, 1944 The weather is getting much warmer now. They say we should land at Oro Bay sometime Thursday. We fellows from Moresby will have to get air transport back across the range: Our co. here aboard ship has but one detail and that is scrubbing down the deck three times a day. Our Co. is divided into four crews so this job only comes around once in a while: Our boat is not such a large vessel being some 150 yard long by 50 feet wide. Her name is H.M.S. British Columbia Express, with a speed of about 20 knots.

Wednesday, September 13, 1944 It is very hot on deck today. The ocean is slightly rough and the boat is rocking around quite a lot, but so far my stomach is staying put pretty well, and I haven't missed eating yet. Going back to Moresby is sure a dark picture. As soon as I arrive there I am going to see why I can't get out of there for a while. I hear also that more ratings have been given out, but the clerks in the office are the only ones getting them. Boy it was a sad day when I hooked up with the 832 Sig. I have been connected with the radio station W.V.L.P longer than anyone in the 832nd. As long as anyone in the U.S. army, as far as that is concerned. After dark regulations are enforced on deck. No smoking, no lights of any kind. Hard to figure out why they have the two most lights on all night. Oh well that is typical of the way the army operates.

Thursday, September 14, 1944 It is very hot below decks now as we get nearer the equator. Even though my bunk is next to a ventilator it was impossible to sleep much last night. For comfort these bunks are not much better than laying on the steel deck. We sighted the coast of New Guinea at 8 A.M. and spent most of the morning going among small islands as we rounded the southern tip of New Guinea on our way to Oro Bay. They say we will reach Oro Bay late tonight. Those of us who get off will get into landing barges or ducks. I hope we are able to get a plane over to Moresby in a short time. It has been very hot on deck today. I spent quite a bit of time below writing letters, which I intend mailing at Oro Bay. I went below at 9 P.M. to take a nap before we get to port.

Friday, September 15, 1944 We finally reached Oro Bay at 3:00 A.M. I was in the first landing barge to go ashore. After which we were loaded into trucks and taken to the staging camp which was on up the coast about 8 miles. It was 5 A.M. before we were finally given cots and assigned to a tent. Since they started serving breakfast at six, I didn't go to bed. This camp sure doesn't look very promising. It has all the ear marks of a "Hell hole." After breakfast I slept until noon when we were called into formation for roll call. As I expected we are in for some tough details. Some of the fellows had to work this afternoon. Luckily I wasn't elected. I guess our chances of air transportation out of here are pretty slim. Oro Bay is a back number the same as Moresby. The fellows went over to the signal center this afternoon and sent a message to our C.O. to try and get us air transportation. Bill and I went to the show here in the area tonight.

Saturday, September 16, 1944 Up at 5:30 this morning. It seems to take forever to move through the chow line. This mess hall doesn't seem to run in any particular manor or any set schedule. After breakfast we had roll call and then assigned to details. I caught kind of a tough one. Three of us had to go on a truck over a road that went through the jungle. We had to load up a bunch of poles that the natives had cut. While we were having a rest I wondered over through a bunch of vines and found a bunch of banana trees. On one there was a large stalk of bananas just right to be picked. After slipping and sliding I finally climbed the tree and cut off the bananas. This stalk was very heavy and I had a tough time carrying them to the road. A lieutenant was driving by and stopped and said it was against regulations to get bananas, so I had to leave them. He probably went back and picked them up.

Sunday, September 17, 1944 Well today I caught the detail of all details. I was put on K.P. This is the first time I have caught this job for over two years. The job I had wasn't so bad, but it lasted from 5:30 A.M. until 6 P.M. Went to the show here in the area tonight. Bill and Sine got air transportation to Moresby this morning. Some of we other fellows should leave tomorrow morning. "Boy" I can't get out of this place quick enough. The dust is so thick you can hardly see through it. Even though this camp has been here two years you would think they had just moved in. There is no place to shave and wash, only of make shift shower. There isn't a wood tent floor in camp, and the ground in and around camp is just like the bush. You can't walk anywhere without getting your shoes full of sand.

Monday, September 18, 1944 I was disappointed when no orders came through this morning for our transportation to Moresby. They told us to report up to the orderly room — that we were to go to Milne (E. Papua) Bay by boat. We got out of this however as we have good priority on air travel. If we were to go to Milne Bay we would probably be there a week trying to get to Moresby.

Tuesday, September 19, 1944 All the other fellows left this morning who had air transportation to Moresby. I thought something was screwed up, and I started to check. I made the guys in the orderly room half sore at me, but we were on the top of the list for air priority. Luckily this afternoon Warrant Officer Henry who was to be at Moresby and in charge of transportation drove into our camp. We told him our predicament. He went to the orderly room and raised heck. Come to find out they had "screwed up" and taken us off the manifest. Two of our fellows went over to base HQ. and got us put back on for air travel. We should leave in the morning.

The Last Leg of The Journey, Back from Furlough

Wednesday, September 20, 1944 They had a U.S.O. stage show here in camp last night. It was pretty good. Had five girls and three G.I.s. They woke us up at 5:30 A.M. this morning as we are to be shipped out. We ate breakfast at 6 A.M. turned in our blankets, etc. at 7 A.M. we were on the way to Dobodura (E. Papua) to catch a plane. This plane (C. 47) wasn't to take off until 9 A.M. but this bunch here at the orderly room are kinda worried, as if they made a slip again there would probably be some changes made. The plane was loaded with mail, barracks bags and about 20 fellows, which was quite a load. We were a little late in taking off as they had to wait on a weather report from Moresby. After taking off and flying a number of miles the clouds closed in. We flew high enough to clear the Owen Stanley Range, but we were flying blind through the clouds most of the time. We arrived in Moresby 45 minutes after take-off. We had to wait for transportation out to our camp, and it was late afternoon when we reached there.

Thursday, September 21, 1944 We moved into a hut. It is a pretty good place, but it sure needs cleaning up. Boy this camp has sure changed. There is only a comparatively small number of fellows left here, all of which are 832nd. Nearly all of the tents are gone, with only the barracks left. The station is the same way. There are no C.W. circuits at all and only three R.T.T. positions, which do not handle any traffic at all. This station and camp is to be completely eliminated by the last of October. Then that will be the end of W.V.L.P. Being the C.W. is dead that means I have to learn some other job now. I asked Captain M.C. Kinny if I could go into "sigabaw" or in other words coding and encoding messages. I start on this job at 5 P.M. tomorrow. In the office today one of the personal told me I could expect to be part of the quota to go home before long. All the new fellows have been put on teams. We old guys are just standing by: boy I had a stack of mail, 72 letters, 52 from Marian and five packages. I have spent nearly all day reading them. I intend to start my letter schedule tomorrow.

Friday, September 22, 1944 I spent most of the morning straightening up our tent. This afternoon I turned out a big washing: Since there is no C.W. at all now, I stopped in at the signal center and saw Captain McHenry about being assigned to some other job. He assigned me to the code room. There really isn't much for me to do, but I have to have some kind of a job. I am still listed as a C.W. operator, but I doubt if I ever work a circuit again. Very little C.W. exists anymore. W.V.L.P. is in the process of being closed. At present all there is, is three R.T.T. circuits and a couple of teletype circuits. There is only about 100 fellows left here and most of them will leave in a few days. What is to happen to me, I don't know. I am on no shipping list, the job I am doing is temporary and all Americans are to be out of here by the last of next month: The chow is terrible. We are living on mostly field rations. Everything is now on a temporary basis. Went to work at 5 P.M. I wrote a few letters and didn't do much else.

Saturday, September 23, 1944 Today we had to move out of our tent and into the barracks, as they are going to tear the tents that are left down. I spent most of the day getting situated in the barracks. I went to work at 5 P.M. I did a little work tonight, and learned a few pointers on my new job. I wrote a couple of letters home. Boy I wonder if I will ever get caught up on my letter writing. There is a lot of talk that the rotation program is going into full swing now. All fellows on the three month's back quotas have been sent home; they say fellows with two years overseas service will be sent home by the first of the year. I don't think this will happen, but maybe I will get home by spring. They asked me in the orderly room if I would choose rotation or a furlough. I told them rotation. Who the heck would want to come back over here?

Sunday, September 24, 1944 There is hardly any work to do at all at the signal center. I am learning quite a bit about my new duties, but most of the time there is no work and we sit around and write letters. Luckily I have this extra time as I sure have a lot of letters to answer. The war in Germany is progressing pretty well, but the three divisions of air troops landed in Holland are taking an awful beating. Our main forces are trying to link up with the isolated forces. It looks like whoever planned this air born operation miss judged the German strength. In a matter of weeks the Americans are going to invade the Philippines. This is no secret to the Japs either. Our forces have staged two heavy air attacks on Manila.

Monday, September 25, 1944 I went to work this morning. There wasn't much doing, so I spent most of my time writing letters. There are fellows being shipped out every day, and compared to the number there use to be here, there is only a small group left. There was no show tonight so I sat around the barracks and talked, and then went to bed early.

Tuesday, September 26, 1944 Things were the same at work today. Hardly any work at all. I wrote a few more letters. Didn't receive any mail at all today. A bunch of us rode out to another area tonight to a show. It was the same place that Laverne used to be stationed. Our forces in Germany are meeting stiffer German resistance. The air born divisions are still in great danger of being overcome by the enemy.

Wednesday, September 27, 1944 We were a little busier today. We had our hands full most of the morning. I am catching on to my work a little more each day and don't have to ask so many questions. I came back to the barracks early this afternoon and started making a necklace for Marian. A bunch of us went down to the navy tonight to the show. They are starting to tear the barracks down at the navy. All American troops are to be out of Moresby by the end of next month. I guess I am to be among one of the few to stay here until W.V.L.P. closes.

Thursday, September 28, 1944 Today a bunch of we fellows received orders stating that we are detached to the 997th Sig. Co. who is to take over this station until it closes in another month. There is hardly anything doing over at the signal center at all. Even now Moresby has few American soldiers left. Old Headquarters Company, the first camp I was in when I first came to Moresby, has been completely cleaned out. No sign of the camp is left. All buildings in Moresby have been cleared of all official forces and Army personal. All buildings in Moresby are vacant. It is a ghost town if there ever was one.

Friday, September 29, 1944 My shift has been changed around, so to find out just when I do go to work again I walked over to the signal center this morning and found out. I go to work at midnight tonight: I borrowed a 620 camera from a friend today and snapped up my last roll of film. This is the end of my photography until I can get another camera of my own and some more film. I went up to the radio repair shack this afternoon and worked on a necklace for Marian. This evening Bill and I went to the show at navy. Two years ago today I arrived in Brisbane, Australia.

Saturday, September 30, 1944 This morning seven of we fellows were loaded into a truck and taken out to the Quartermaster's Supply Dump on a detail. We had the job of loading all sorts of equipment into trucks that took it to the docks to be loaded on a ship. There are so few American soldiers here in the Moresby area now that jobs have to be done by whoever they can get, whether it be the Signal Corps, Medics, etc. They don't seem to take much interest in what becomes of the station. The main task is to get all Americans and equipment, out of Moresby.

Sunday, October 1, 1944 I was in hopes that we wouldn't have to go out to the quartermasters today, but no luck and what a job. This morning we loaded 550 bags of Coke. This afternoon we loaded 1,500 cots. "Boy" was I ever tired tonight. This is the first hard work I have done for over two years. It looks like I will be one of the last Americans to leave Moresby. I wrote a couple of letters and went to bed early tonight. About two thousand of the force air borne troops dropped into Holland have been able to withdraw to the allied lines. The rest of the estimated eight thousand were wounded, killed or captured. The advance against the Germans in France seems to be at a standstill now. It looks like the Germans cannot be whipped this year.

Monday, October 2, 1944 We waited until after eight A.M. for the quartermaster truck to come and then another fellow and I went to town. I stopped in at the post office and got a couple of money orders and envelopes. We then went down to the Australian Canteen and got a haircut. We got back to camp at noon and learned that the quartermaster truck had been here at ten A.M. but we were not around so he left without us. I got out of detail for today anyway. I spent this afternoon writing a few letters and working on Marian's necklace.

Tuesday, October 3, 1944 Back on detail again this morning. We worked stacking canned rations which was sure a tiresome job. I hope this is the last day of this business. They say the boat is loaded and ready to leave. Went to the show here in the area tonight. We now have movies in one of the empty barracks. The show area on the hill is no longer used.

Wednesday, October 4, 1944 This morning I took a walk over to the message center before the trucks came to take us out on the detail. My back was so sore, I told the fellows I was taking off today. The quartermaster seems to be working a good thing to death. They will probably keep this detail thing going as long as they can get away with it. I worked a while today on a necklace I am making for Marian.

The coconut trees around here are loaded with coconuts now. Every once in a while one comes loose and falls to the ground. I avoid walking under these trees as much as possible. I have heard of a number of fellows getting killed by being struck on the head by a falling cocoanut.

Thursday, October 5, 1944 I worked over at the signal center today. I am getting on to this job pretty well now. I heard though today that I am to be transferred to a teletype operator. Boy what next? In a few days the 997th Sig. Bn. will move into this camp. The 832nd fellows, of us who are left, will be attached to the 997th for ratings and quarters.

Canadian and British troops in Holland are still punching away and making slight progress. The American Armies are attempting with slow progress to get through the Siegfried Line or the West Wall = (The German Defensive line): Allied Armies in Italy are making slow progress against stiff German resistance: The Russian Armies are driving into Hungary and Yugoslavia: Allied Armies are advancing in Burma, but the Japs are going in the central section of China: Our Air Force here in the S.W. P.A. are still bombing the Philippines.

Friday, October 6 1944 This morning I started learning teletype. I am to take a fellow's place who is going to Brisbane. It is the same old story. He came to New Guinea eight or so months ago, and now is going back. The difference is he is in the 52nd Bn. and I am in the 832nd. Today marks my 21st month here in New Guinea. I have no urge to do anything anymore. My ambition is all used up. One of these days maybe I will finally get out of here by going home. They say "rotation" has stopped due to coming operations in the Philippines.

Saturday, October 7, 1944 This guy who is supposed to show me about this teletype is so wound up about going to Brisbane that all I can learn is what I stumble on to myself. I can see if I get this stuff at all I will have to get on another shift with someone else. I asked Potts, (chief operator) for a change of shift. I hope he fixes it. I didn't try to learn anything about this job today; there is no use with this guy. I spent my time writing a few letters. It was reported that Allied forces have invaded Greece. Only slight resistance was encountered. The Germans are withdrawing from Greece to Avoid being cut off by the Russians and Tito's partisan army.

Sunday, October 8, 1944 I was late getting to work this morning as I thought today was the change of shift. I found out tomorrow is the day of change. It made no difference though as whether I am there or not, makes no difference to this guy, who I am still with. However, another friend of mine was there and he showed me a few pointers. Mail service has sure been punk lately. Not even the mail comes into Moresby anymore. Boy this place is sure dead, past number. I went down to the show tonight. Coming back up the hill from the Navy is always a tough climb. The hill is only about a quarter of a mile long but it is very steep. The 997 signal Bn. moved in today. Maybe we will have better chow now.

Monday, October 9, 1944 Went over to work this morning and found out I am to go on the 5 P.M. shift tomorrow. I will be alone on the job. Back in the states to become a teletype operator you go to school a couple of months. Here after four days you are a teletype operator. Spent this evening writing a few letters. "Boy" mail service has sure been bad lately.

Tuesday, October 10, 1944 Was over at the station a short time this morning. Then I went up to the repair shack and worked on a couple of gadgets I am making. Went to work at five. Things went pretty smooth on teletype tonight. I passed around thirty messages. It is reported that one of our task forces have bombed and shelled an island just sixty miles east of Formosa. Things are about the same on the other war fronts.

Wednesday, October 11, 1944 This morning all of we fellows were in the barracks when one of my friends came in and said Potts (our chief operator) was coming after six fellows to do detail over at the message center. All of us tore out of the barracks and kept out of sight. As soon as possible we made a dash over behind the day room. Pretty soon Potts came by with just one guy that he had found. They went up over the hill towards the signal center. I waited a little bit and then took out in the same direction to go over to the radio repair shack. When I was about half way there, here came Potts back up the road. Why he turned around and came back is more than I would know. I worked on detail this morning.

Thursday, October 12, 1944 Went to work at 5 P.M. today. The teletype operators have been sent to Brisbane, so now I have the job alone. I am sure not much of a teletype operator, but I got along O.K. tonight. The fellows on the other end are a new hand at it too. We get a lot of practice shooting the B.S. back and forth. Reports came through today that a U.S. task force had bombarded Formosa. This island is one of Japan's strongest defenses and but a short distance off the coast of China. Things are still moving rather slow in Germany. Beyond a doubt it will take the rest of the winter to beat Germany.

Friday, October 13, 1944 Today I learned that the teletype operators that went to Brisbane are not working in teletype but have been put on radio teletype. This is the job I am actually supposed to be doing. "C.W." operators became radio teletype operators after "C.W." was replaced by radio teletype. I will never be able to figure this one out. I have to learn to do a job so that these fellows can go to Brisbane and I have been on this island nearly two years, and three times as long as some of these fellows. My morale is at rock bottom. A fellow spends his time in school learning fair play and sportsmanship, and then three years of army life, and the whole thing slaps you back in the face. I guess I just can't get accustomed to being classified as Army material, rather than a human being.

Saturday, October 14, 1944 If I thought my return to civilian life would give me equal treatment as this army life, — WELL what they say we are fighting for is a lot of hooey. The Army can't represent what the U.S. stands for. They say the government is drawing up a demobilization plan that is to the effect the release of a million or two men after the fall of Germany. After seeing the mess that was made out of the rotation plan, I can't believe this would be any different. It looks like our forces will invade the Philippines any time now. MacArthur has gone north again.

Sunday, October 15, 1944 This teletype business is going pretty well. It isn't such a bad job but I don't have any interest in it. I went into the office today and saw our signal officer and got a load off my chest. What I thought about these fellows going to Brisbane. Of course he couldn't do anything. He said there must have been a mistake somewhere. It is the same story, I am still here, and it looks as if I always will be.

Marian and I have been married three years four months today.

Monday, October 16, 1944 Work as usual today. Mail is sure slow in coming though. I haven't heard from Sally & Dick for four months. It is hard to figure out. I have written two or three letters asking them to write, but no go. There was no show tonight so I stayed in the barracks, wrote a few letters and went to bed early.

Tuesday, October 17, 1944 We changed to the midnight shift today so I get kind of a long break and don't have to go to work until midnight. There isn't much to do on the midnight shift so I took a blanket along and caught a little sleep: The Japs are throwing a lot of propaganda about the action we are taking against Formosa and the Philippines. The Japs say they have inflicted severe losses. We say we have.

Wednesday, October 18, 1944 I slept this morning until noon and then got up and ate chow. Our chow is sure poor, we get a lot of canned bully beef, chili, field rations, and bologna. The only fresh meat we get at all is mutton, and I would starve to death if I had to eat this. One lucky break we have fresh potatoes quite often. We are eating a lot of tropical butter now. I didn't do much of anything this afternoon. Took a nap and read part of the first of last year's diary.

Bill and I have decided to go over to "base" tomorrow and remind them that we would still like to go to Brisbane. I guess there is no hope but it doesn't hurt to try.

The Japs say that we have made landings in the Philippines. Washington hasn't confirmed it yet, but I imaging it is true.

Thursday, October 19, 1944 This afternoon Bill and I went over to base to see Captain McHenry about chances of going down to Brisbane. We received the answer we thought we would. No chance. However, it didn't cost us anything to try and maybe if we go and remind them enough we might finally make it. A big bunch of fellows in Brisbane are being moved out so it seems there should be a place for us somewhere down there. The one fellow who arrived in New Guinea before me was relieved south. I guess I hold the record in the 832nd now for time spent in New Guinea. If all branches of the Army were run like this outfit we would have lost the war a long time ago. There is still no official report on the Philippine invasion.

Friday, October 20, 1944 No mail has come in at all in the past few days. Mail service has sure been punk lately. Chow has been rotten lately. This afternoon some other fellows and I went down to the Aussie canteen to eat. They had pork on the menu but it turned out to be mutton. The natives do most of the cooking and they are as filthy as they come. The saucer that my desert was on was black with soot and grease. None of us ate hardly anything. Our chow at camp is lousy but at least it is clean.

It has been officially announced that our forces have invaded the island of Leyte in the central Philippines. About 250,000 men are in this operation with about 600 ships of all types. The Japs have offered little resistance so far. It is thought they have but one division defending this island. The same division that overcame the Americans back.

Saturday, October 21, 1944 I worked on K.P. all day today. The 997th is sure handing us a bad way. These fellows don't do hardly anything around camp and the 832nd fellows have to pull the K.P. when we hardly have enough fellows to run the signal center. I think our signal officer is going to try and do something about this.

I was supposed to go to work at 5 P.M. but I was on K.P. so I didn't go in. One of the fellows in the code room will have to watch the teletype.

Operations in the Philippines are proceeding to schedule. Our losses so far are exceedingly light. General MacArthur and the former president of the Philippines went in with the first troops.

Sunday, October 22, 1944 I received a letter from Marian today, the first one in a week. I still haven't received a letter from Sally & Dick. No letter from them in four weeks??? I didn't do much today, but just loaf around until time to go to work at five P.M. I didn't have much to do and what messages I did send I poked out on tape. This teletype business is getting easier all the time and I can go along pretty good now without making so many errors. In my spare time I wrote a long letter to Marian tonight.

Monday, October 23, 1944 Nothing unusual today. Stayed around the barracks most of the day and listened to one of the fellow's radio. Boy these Aussie news report really get you down. You would think they were winning the war alone. Today is the second anniversary of the battle of El Alamein (NW Egypt) in Egypt. The Aussie news reports state that the Aussies made the big break in the German lines, resulting in victory. They say El Alamein was the turning point of the war, and "SO" I guess they never heard of Stalingrad.

Tuesday, October 24, 1944 Just a routine day today. Mail is quite nill now. I received but one letter last week. Wrote a couple of letters and went to the show tonight. All the fresh potatoes have been used up and we are back to eating dehydrated spuds again. The only fresh food we get is bread: It is reported the Jap fleet is under way and a sea engagement is at hand. *(Referring to The Battle of Leyte Gulf)*

Wednesday, October 25, 1944 I was informed today that I am to start working at "small ships" radio station, and am to move out to the transmitter camp area tomorrow morning. The camp is on over around the bay about eight miles. The country out there is really rugged. They say there is wild boar back in the hills, and the Wallaby are thick as flies.

I worked on teletype this morning and had the afternoon off to get my junk together to move tomorrow. I hope a little later Bill will be able to get out to small ships station, as when the move comes, we would have a better chance to stick together: In a way am glad to move and I will get away from Potts (A stupid guy that I can't get along with). He is a Master Sgt. but just the same I have told him off a few times. Most of the fellows in the barracks have the same opinion of him.

Thursday, October 26, 1944 A truck came in from the transmitter station this morning and moved me to my new camp: I have no regrets on leaving here as my years stay in this camp has not been a happy one. I moved into a tent with two other fellows. However these fellows are in the hospital so I have never seen them and until they get back I am here by myself. This is the best tent I have ever lived in. It has a wood floor, built up off the ground, is all screened in with two screen doors, one to the front, another at the back. The tent covers the roof with a rafter system replacing the center pole. This tent is tight enough so that no mosquitoes can get in and for the first time since coming to New Guinea I am not using my mosquito net. There are also electric lights, as well as a water pipe just outside our tent.

Friday, October 27, 1944 I didn't have much time to get straightened up yesterday as I had to go to work in the afternoon. This station is about five miles from my new camp. It is the same place that W.V.L.P. used to be before moving up to G.H.Q. There isn't much to this job. All transmissions are made in voice and about all I have to do is broadcast the time once an hour. Once in a while if we feel like it we exchange read-abilities with one of the other stations. As far as traffic is concerned a message a month is more than we usually pass. One of the main jobs is to listen in on 500 DCS for distress signals. We get no days off but we work as four shifts; 7 A.M. to noon, noon to five, five to midnight, and midnight until seven A.M. I received two letters from Marian today.

Saturday, October 28, 1944 I am somewhat straightened up in my tent now. I got four new pair of suntan pants from supply today. I was down to about my last pair. Went to work today at noon. Buck, my top sergeant informed me that he had to go over to base to see Captain McHenry. He thought it was about a transfer of some of us to other bases. I asked Buck if he could get me transferred down south. I would welcome that change. Otherwise I would just as soon go to the Philippines. However when Buck got back from seeing McHenry it was only to inform Buck that the Australians are taking over the station in a few days. Where we will go or what we will do I don't have the least idea. Mail is picking up. Letters from mom, Brandts, and Marian. Had a show in one of the old transmitter shacks tonight.

Sunday, October 29, 1944 Today I changed shifts and went to work at 7 A.M. About ten o'clock I received an S.O.S. message from a ship that was hung up on a reef down the coast somewhere. Some Australians came into the station today to get acquainted with the "set up" here. They say they are taking over the station Tuesday. We should be moved anytime now. Chow is even worse out here, as the food we eat is hauled out here from my old camp and it is pretty well messed up by the time it gets here. I took a little walk today over in the hills. One creek bed I had to cross was very tough to get through as the under- brush was almost a solid entanglement If I had had my rifle along I could have shot a wallaby or two as three of them jumped up not far off from me.

Monday, October 30, 1944 For the past three days the biggest and most important sea battle of the war has taken place off the Leyte Island, one of the Philippine [Visayas] group. Everyone has been keeping close tab on developments. Had the Japs been victorious, our supply line to our invasion forces would have been cut and the situation of our 250,000 troops would have been very serious. However the Japs met a decisive defeat and suffered staggering losses. Work as usual today. It looks like in a couple of weeks we will be headed west.

Tuesday, October 31, 1944 To work as usual this morning. I went up to the 997th today to get paid but found out I had been red lined. I signed on the wrong line. It makes little difference as I just leave my money in the orderly room here, and they say that is at your own risk. I have 65 lbs. there at the present time: Got in the truck tonight and went up to the old company area to the show. There were high floating clouds and a full moon tonight.

Wednesday, November 1, 1944 Went to work again this morning. The Australians were in the station again today getting familiar with the set up so they can take over the station. When this will be is still a question. They say we will be moving out of here in two weeks so it has to be before then, that is if we do move. I came back to camp at noon today, ate chow, which is as bad as ever. I was told today that our camp got hold of some bacon, canned peas, jam, etc. from the "Sea Bees." It seems for these supplies some of our trucks helped them move some of their heavy equipment to the docks. I went hunting this afternoon and for the first time since coming into the Army I shot a 30\ 30 Army Spring Field. I didn't see any wallaby today. Maybe if I walk farther next time I will have better luck. Received more letters today. Mail is picking up.

Thursday, November 2, 1944 Went to work as usual this morning. After arriving there I learned that I am on the alert to be moved along with some of the other fellows. No orders have come out yet and as usual there are a lot of rumors as to where we are to be sent. Among some of these supposed places are Biak, (NW New Guinea), Hollandia (N. New Guinea), Oro Bay, Philippines. I hope when our orders come they I will read the Philippines. W.V.L.P. once the largest and the most important radio station in the Southwest Pacific is "no more." All equipment has been moved out in the country to a small little shack which is known as AR2. All they have is a circuit to Hollandia and one to Brisbane. I spent the afternoon doing a big laundry. It rained tonight for the first time in quite a while. Received two letters from Marian today. Sent papers etc. home.

Friday, November 3, 1944 Since the Australians are taking over "small ships" station and moving all equipment out there is nothing now for me to do. I didn't go to work this morning, but decided to go up to headquarters this noon and check up on my shipping orders. After reading them over, it looks like I am headed for the Philippines. I am to go to Hollandia, where I will be put on temporary duty, on high speed radio equipment, after which we will be given full field equipment, and then the Philippines. Since a friend of mine who is also leaving wanted to do his washing this afternoon, I consented to work for him. I guess Bill Pandolfi, my good friend is to stay here. At least he hasn't been told that he is to leave.

Saturday, November 4, 1944 Went over to the station today and finished making a box for my "bug" (speed key.) No word yet as to when we are to leave, probably not until Monday. I have my things all packed and ready to leave. I have managed to pack most of my personal things in one bag, the one I will take with me. My other bag with the rest of my equipment I will have to leave behind and have shipped to me by boat. Got on a truck tonight and went up to my old camp to the show. The show tonight was exceptionally good. The name of it was "Song of Bernadette." I finally after months received a letter from Sally, also three from Marian, and one from Mary Bowers.[47]

Sunday, November 5, 1944 We were awakened early this morning to get ready and be out to the air drone in half an hour. Suitter, one of the fellows I went on furlough with, who has the idea the Army rotates around him hadn't even started to pack his junk. Even with all this "to do" he killed more time by going down to breakfast. Once you are put on the alert you are supposed to be ready to leave when given the word. If he wasn't with an easy going outfit, they could break him and at least throw his stuff on the truck and make him throw it in his barracks bags on the way to the airport: Results were, we missed the plane, the "air transport command" is sore as heck, threatened to send us by boat. All of we fellows have been confined to the immediate area. Received a letter from mom today.

---

[47] Mary Bowers stood up with my parents when they got married.

Monday, November 6, 1944 I was rather disappointed that we didn't leave this morning. I guess we have been shoved on the end of the manifest. I only hope we haven't been taken off altogether and will be sent by boat. I have been staying around camp pretty close and ready to move on a minute's notice. Wrote some letters tonight.

Tuesday, November 7, 1944 AND we still sit and wait. We were not called again this morning: I played a few games of checkers and wrote letters today. This evening I took my rifle and went out to try and get some "wallaby." I got a couple of shots at some, but they are the fastest things I have ever seen and you would have to be more than lucky to hit one.

Wednesday, November 8, 1944 Well today is the 7th of November back home and Election Day. At a little after noon some of the election returns started coming in. It is Roosevelt again. We are still on the alert and didn't move out again today. If a ship comes into the harbor that is bound for Hollandia, before we get air it just means we will go by boat and it would more than likely be a Liberty ship to boot. My tent mate Pettroff (Russian) and I went out after wallaby tonight. I got a good shot at one but aimed to high and missed. Received another letter from Sally today. Wrote letters to Marian and Sally & Dick tonight. We are getting a little rain for a change tonight.

Thursday, November 9, 1944 Still no sign of transportation out of here. It is beginning to look for sure we are stuck with a boat ride. I asked the Sgt. in the orderly room tonight to check with A.T.C. (air traffic control) and find out if we are still on the air manifest, and if not to take us off alert. I intend going to the show tonight "alert or no alert" but it rained so I didn't go. The food at the mess hall is sure awful. Dehydrated cabbage, potatoes, and field rations is all we get. Of the thousands of Americans that used to be in Moresby, there is now only about 300 left.

Friday, November 10, 1944 This morning early we loaded our stuff on a truck and [were] told to be at the air strip in half an hour. Since we live clear down around the bay and have to travel around 15 miles over rough roads, we were really pressed for time. It sure seems good to finally get the word to leave. We got aboard a C.47 air craft which had a load besides six of us, Allison and P47 airplane engines. It took all of the length of the air strip to get off the ground. We flew over the mountains towards Buna (E. Papua) flying within sight of Rouna Falls, which was a beautiful sight from the air. The sky was clear and the hour and thirty five minute trip to Finschhafen (E. New Guinea) was most enjoyable. At Finschhafen the air base is very busy and there are hundreds of fellows waiting for transportation. We will be unable to get out of here for Hollandia today.

November 11, Saturday, 1944 (my dad has written at the top of this page his guess for the war's end)

TODAY IS MY GUESS FOR THE END OF THE WAR WITH GERMANY)

It looks like I guessed wrong...... There are no accommodations at all for fellows passing through here. We went up the road about a mile to a mess hall where we got supper, but otherwise we ate sandwiches and drank coffee at the Red Cross truck. Fellows waiting for transportation slept under the building and on the benches in the A.T.C. office last night. Of Switer, Jenson (Iowa) and myself, I am the only one to leave this morning. I was ready and loaded on the plane at 4:30 A.M. There were 21 of us aboard counting of PVTS, Sgts. Liute, Cap's, a Dutch naval commander, and a colonel. The day was clear and the trip very scenic as we flew up the coast. The country along the coast seemed fairly level and we passed over many plantations. Inland were high mountains much higher that the Owen Stanleys. Near Madang you could see signs of recent engagements with the Japs. We flew within sight of Wewak (NE New Guinea) still held by the Japs but we couldn't see it at the distance we were away. We landed at Hollandia (N. New Guinea) after 3 hours 40 min. of flying time from Finch.

Sunday, November 12, 1944 I waited all morning, probably, for someone from the 997th to come out to the strip to get me. I arrived in camp barely in time for dinner. I have been assigned to a tent in the casual tent area as we are on the alert to move to the Philippines. We are all guessing if we are to go to Leyte (S. Philippines) or are to go with the task force in the coming invasion of Luzon (N. Philippines.) I hear that many of my old friends from Moresby were in the first wave in the invasion of Leyte (S. Philippines.) I guess many of them were killed. It looks like it won't be long until I get a taste of actual war. It rained very hard last night and I had to get up and dig a trench around my barracks bag to keep it dry, as the water was running through our tent. I worked on R.T.T. at the signal center today. Switer and Jenson are both here now.

Monday, November 13, 1944 I am on the midnight shift now. However, no one woke me up to go to work at midnight so I wasn't there last night. There is more help around there than they know what to do with, so I wasn't missed. I am still putting New Guinea on my letters but I think I will gradually stop as I don't want any of the folks to know for sure that I am in the Philippines, when I get there.

Tuesday, November 14, 1944 Messed around all day repacking my barracks bag, and wrote some letters. Didn't go to work again tonight as they didn't wake me up again. Some of we fellows who are to be on team 5 are wondering if operations might try and keep us here, which would mean cancelation of our orders to Leyte. We are going down to U.S.A. S.O.S. tomorrow and try and check up on the situation.

Wednesday, November 15, 1944 Went to work tonight and worked again on R.T.T. On the Leyte circuit the traffic is piled up as we are out of contact with them most of the time due to air raids. An air alert was on up there for five hours yesterday. The Japs are throwing in all the air power they can and have landed 35,000 troops on Leyte. The Japs are trying at all costs to hold Leyte. Sparks, Owen and I went down to USA SOS this afternoon to check up on the status of our orders. We found out that our orders are unchanged and the only thing holding us here is our wait for transportation. I kinda hope we will be here for Thanksgiving as there will be no turkey in Leyte. Marian and I have been married just three years and six months today.

Thursday, November 16, 1944 Nothing new today. I worked at the station for a change tonight and was on the Leyte circuit for a change. From recent reports I guess some of the old radio operators were killed in the Leyte landings. Some of them were fellows who I had worked with at Moresby. We are not sure if these reports are authentic but the radio boat these fellows were on was sunk and all persons lost. Another boat with some of our fellows on it was hit by a bomb and four persons killed and a bunch injured. The fellows over at the motor pool have a Jap truck they are fixing up. It is a Ford truck but seems to be much lighter than the American models.

Friday, November 17, 1944 A fellow sure gets tired standing beside a R.T.T. machine all night. Getting any sleep in the daytime is impossible as the heat in our tent is terrible. In this location we are only a little over 200 miles from the Equator. Hollandia is a bigger base than Moresby ever was. It is stretched out up the valley for more than 35 miles. There is a stream of trucks on the road day and night. It is common knowledge that in a few days there is to be another invasion of the Philippines. Some of us wonder if we won't take part in that one. Rumors have it that our forces are to invade Manila (C. Philippines) but I doubt if this is true.

Saturday, November 18, 1944 It rained steady all day today. I spent most of my time in my tent writing letters and shooting the bull with the fellows. About 8 P.M. six hundred signal corps soldiers came into camp just off the boat from the states. This camp is not such a large one, and with the four hundred soldiers already here it really has given them a problem as to where to put all of them. After filling most of the tents in the area with as many as nine fellows, and moving everything out of the day room, and using that for a barracks. There was still nearly two hundred left. These fellows were given cots and set them up around the area out in the open. Luckily it had stopped raining around seven P.M. Went to the show tonight.

Sunday, November 19, 1944 With all the new fellows in from the states, this camp is sure in a mess. Since there are two complete companies, they are taking up the first three tent rows of our casual camp. Besides that there are many teams of fellows who move into a choice string of tents. Being that a lot of fellows as well as myself are more or less "free lance" we have had to take what was left over. The three of we fellows didn't do so bad in moving though as we moved into a tent on the front of one of the rows of our area. We are a little crowded as there are seven of us in one tent. Still no letters. I didn't have a chance to write Marian today.

Monday, November 20, 1944 Spent most of the day getting things fixed up in our tent. Trying to cut a b[o]ard in two, I cut heck out of my leg. I was put in C.W. tonight at work. This was the first I had worked a circuit in four months. I worked Brisbane, one of the busiest circuits in the station. All C.W. as well as R.T.T. are loaded with traffic. Rained tonight.

Tuesday, November 21, 1944 Didn't do much today. I have kind of a headache from working C.W. last night. This afternoon I walked over the hill to an old wrecked Jap plane, and hacked off a couple of chunks of aluminum to make a bracelet out of. I was sure busy on C.W. tonight. I worked steady the whole shift. Taking so much code all at once after being away from it for so long sure puts your head in a spin. It rained again tonight.

Wednesday, November 22, 1944 Just a routine day. Still working C.W. at the message center. Since not working C.W. for so long my "sending" is pretty lousy, but it is improving. Each day I can receive as fast as ever if not a little faster. Switter is in the hospital. They say he might have stomach ulcers. The rainy season has apparently arrived. It rained hard again tonight. Even though it rains often there is hardly water enough to take a shower. The food here is pretty good for G.I. chow. We have fresh meat quite often and fresh butter once in a while.

Thursday, November 23, 1944 This noon we had our Thanksgiving dinner. This is the only day a G.I. gets some really good chow. We had roast turkey, dressing, mashed potatoes, (fresh) corn, asparagus, apple sauce, hot rolls, and Coca-Cola to drink. I couldn't take so much time to eat as I had to relieve at the station for chow. We weren't so busy at work tonight as usual. Even so there was little time to rest. I have been working Biek (NW New Guinea) most of this week. It rained most all day, and the area around here is a sea of mud. Our mess hall sits on top a steep hill and even when dry is a task to climb, but when muddy, "Boy."

Friday, November 24, 1944 It has dried up a little bit today. I took a walk over back of our camp where at one time the Japs had had positions there. There were many fox holes and camouflage back in the thick underbrush. There were also some old Jap bombs there, which were quite crudely made. They looked like nothing more than a piece of heavy water main pipe about two feet long with a nose and tail section screwed on. These were only about 100 pounders. I had a tough night at the station tonight. I was working a good operator, but the traffic never did stop. I received messages until my head was in a whirl. Rained again tonight. Finally received some mail from Marian. One letter didn't leave me very happy.

November 25, Saturday, 1944 Maybe next year I will spend Thanksgiving at home. Christmas and Thanksgiving hold little meaning. My feelings seem to be deadened to such pleasures. We are to move out in a short time as we were put on the alert today. We drew full field equipment from supply. Carbine rifle, ammunition, shelter half *(a poncho with multiple uses; a tent etc.)* Cartridge belt, machete, bags, shoes, etc. Since we are going by boat I likely can take all my belongings. The voyage to the Philippines takes around five days. I don't know if we are going to Leyte or being in on another invasion. Even the thoughts of an invasion doesn't excite me anymore.

Sunday, November 26, 1944 This morning six of us got all our stuff together and were brought over here to the casual camp. We were supposed to catch a boat to Leyte, but something got screwed up and so now we are stuck here. What a hole this is. They dish us up our chow and then we have to sit on the ground among the ants and bugs and eat it. This camp area is just a place hacked out of the jungle. There is hardly enough water so you can get a bath once in five days, and lucky to keep water in your canteen. In our tent there are eleven guys with all our equipment. We used to think a tent like this crowded with six fellows. Marian has been raising "H" because I told her I took a drink of beer. By gosh a fellow has to drink something: I was able to get a helmet of water this evening, which I took a bath in.

Monday, November 27, 1944 This morning we were called out on detail, and instructed to dig a drainage trench around our tent area. After digging and sweating most of the morning they decided there were too many stumps and roots to complete the job. Any one of us could have told that smart Major that before we started. It looks like we may leave soon. We have been put on the alert, and are to be processed tomorrow.

Tuesday, November 28, 1944 This morning at 7:30 we fell out to get our equipment check. Finally at noon after standing in the sun all morning we were issued a pile of junk. Even without this I have all I can carry. I now have a full pack, carbine, gas mask, pistol, belt and two barracks bags. This afternoon even though I feel pretty much all in from standing in the sun, I had to go over to the quartermaster and help issue clothing. This evening we fell out with all our equipment. At ten P.M. a truck convoy picked us up, took us to the beach, where we were put aboard a LST.

Wednesday, November 29, 1944 We came aboard last night to find our boat already loaded down with trucks, and with 700 soldiers aboard besides. Conditions are indescribable. Our sleeping quarters are whatever space we can find on deck, under trucks, on coils of rope, hatches. It is impossible to get to the latrine in any length of time and with a good many of us sick from eating conditions in the casual camp, the railing is the only solution. We spent all day moored at the beach before pulling out into the harbor and joining the convoy. I dread to think how tough this voyage is going to be after another blistering day in the sun. They say it will take six or seven days to reach Leyte. The nights on the ocean will be very beautiful with the moon full, but it will also be a good light for enemy subs to see by.

Thursday, November 30, 1944 Crossed the equator this afternoon. Very little sleep was had by anyone last night. About midnight it started to rain. I pulled my shelter half up over me but after a short time water running down the deck soaked my blankets from underneath: Today our group caught all ship details. As for me I spent my time on K.P. This proved to be a good break though as the work I had to do was very easy and being able to eat first, this relieved me of having to "sweat out" the chow line which takes a good hour for each meal. Strange as it may seem chow on this boat is fairly decent.

Over the radio tonight a news campaign said that Jap planes had heavily raided the harbor at which we are to land at Leyte. This afternoon a Jap plane raided a position just an hour and a half from here. The last voyage to Leyte, this L.S.T. shot down two Jap planes. Personnel aboard believe they will see action this time.

Friday, December 1, 1944 I slept a little better last night as the weather was clear. A steel deck does not, at best, make a good bed. The soldiers on board are getting more irritable every day, and as is to be expected, the army in its usual "snafu", way make conditions all the tougher. In the different emergency drills we are herded around the deck like cattle. According to regulation all personal but gun crewmen etc. are to go to go below decks at the sound of "general quarters." How it is possible to get 700 soldiers in two narrow passageways? [It] is more than impossible. More than one officer was told off in no uncertain terms this morning. The most stupid person on earth can see that all soldiers would be lost, in case this ship were sunk. To each life raft 51 soldiers are assigned. The raft capacity is 26: The weather was clear and the ocean very calm all day.

Phillippines

Headed to Leyte

Saturday, December 2, 1944 If I ever went through Hell it was last night. As usual crowded conditions prevail, and nearly all soldiers have to find a place to sleep on deck, which maybe under a truck, on a pile of rope, a hatch, or the deck itself. A friend and I had our blankets laid out with my shelter half as a cover. About 9 P.M. it started to rain. In a short time the deck was like a swamp with the water sloshing everywhere. Ours as well as everyone else's blankets was sopping wet. All available space was packed below with fellows laying everywhere. In the companion ways, on the shower room floor, even the latrine stools were used as a sleeping place. The damp hot air, and no circulation, made it almost impossible to breath. My friend and I found a place to stand in a corner, which we occupied for several hours. Finally with our disgust at high pitch we opened the door to the officer's quarters and went in. All the officers were asleep so no one saw us

274

enter. We found a place in a corner where we laid our wet rain coats. Soaking wet with rain and sweat we laid down and soon fell asleep. Early in the morning an officer woke us up and wanted to know what we were doing there? For the next few minutes this officer and all others present got a pretty clear picture from us on the living conditions that we have to put up with on this boat. We were not a very pretty picture for them to look at, being wet, dirty, and unshaven. How could conditions be any better for us devils with accommodations for 200, and 700 aboard? I am still happy to be a[n] enlisted man, because I am with the majority, and after the war the majority will rule, and this war is temporary. We will have a better idea what a democracy should be like.

Sunday, December 3, 1944 Last night was another rugged night, but not so bad as the night before. I took our blankets which are fairly dry by now and found a place to sleep on the floor downstairs. In a bunk across the aisle two fellows are keeping watch over a fellow who went crazy yesterday. He was barely stopped from jumping overboard. We lay down about 8 o'clock and tried to get a little sleep, but as before it was so hot and close in these quarters sleep was impossible. I finally took my shelter half and rain coat and went up on deck. It had not yet started to rain, so I lay down on my shelter half beneath a large anchor hoist on the fan tail of the ship. It did not rain tonight so I got a comparatively good night's sleep. Chow continues to be fairly good. Our mess hall is whatever truck fender we can find to put our mess kits on. More often than not we use the deck as a table. We really caught another dose of Hell this afternoon. About 4:15 P.M. and just fifteen minutes before chow, the general quarters alarm was sounded and all soldiers were herded below. I along with the rest of the gang climbed down through a hatch into one of a bunch of small compartments. In each compartment were around 35 soldiers. The water tight doors between compartments were locked and then the hatch, the only other opening was closed and fastened. This left us without any fresh air what so ever. The compartments were terribly hot to start with, and then being closed off from all air, in a short time everyone was ringing wet with sweat. A half hour passed, 45 minutes and no change. A Few fellows got sick and were laying or sitting on the floor. If ever anyone experienced dying in a submarine, this must be what it is like. Finally after nearly two hours we climbed up through the hatch, back on the deck. This ordeal was for no reason but gun drill. The actual gun practice lasted but ten minutes. All the rest of the time of our confinement was spent while the boat pulled out ahead of the convoy. It was nearly dark when we got on deck and again formed in the chow line. The whole bunch was mad enough for mutiny, and the biggest share of the fellows were yelling at the captain in no uncertain terms (who was standing on the bridge.) I heard that for this bright idea of the captain's, he is going to have to report the fleet command. I managed to get a little supper, and then I found a spot on the deck where I threw my blankets. I never felt so sick and "blurry eyed" in my life. We are in dangerous waters now. Our position is sixty miles from Palau (W. Pacific) Island and I guess something like 500 miles from Leyte. So far our voyage has been through calm seas, and thank God for that. We had church services aboard today.

Monday, December 4, 1944 This morning we had a tough time eating breakfast as it was pouring rain. The deck is the only place to eat and our food was well soaked before we could eat it. I got very little sleep again last night as it rained and made conditions on deck pretty punk: We are now only about 180 miles from Leyte, and but a short distance from Mindanao (S. Philippines) Island. They say we should reach Leyte early Wednesday morning.

Tuesday, December 5, 1944 Last night I slept a little better but at best sleeping conditions are no good. I guess during this voyage I have only had about three nights sleep. I am sure getting on the razor's edge and today was sure no help. This morning we expected enemy action as the sky was full of low broken clouds and we are but 60 miles off Mindanao, which is Jap held. At 9:30 A.M. I was sitting on deck beneath one of the gun turrets cleaning my rifle when we heard a plane diving down through the clouds. We looked up just in time to see a Jap bomber sweep in low over one of the Liberty ships that was back toward the end of the convoy. He dropped two bombs that barely missed, that threw a geyser of water high above the ship. The captain from the bridge of our ship yelled over the loud speaker to crawl under the trucks. It was appalling how 700 fellows disappeared so completely. Not a fellow could be seen. I grabbed my helmet and life jacket and slid under some drums until I found out they were filled with gasoline, and I slid right out again, and hid behind a coil of steel cable. Everyone laid low for around half an hour, and then since nothing more happened we all got out in the open.

Noon came and we went to chow as usual, everything is still quiet. After washing my mess kit I went below deck for a little while. While I was below, the alert sounded. This time a Jap torpedo plane came in low over the water and headed for a Liberty ship two boats behind ours. Different than before, the convoy wasn't caught completely by surprise and the boats of the convoy opened fire. No one seemed to even come close to the Jap and he got away. The Jap's aim was better this time as his torpedo struck the Liberty amid ships. Being below I didn't see this action, but fellows who did said the ship was mortally wounded. When I got on deck the Liberty was dropping out of the convoy and sinking lower in the water. Two destroyers went back to pick up survivors. The Liberty was still a float when we last saw it on the horizon. We heard later that it sank. There were a few causalities but nearly everyone was rescued. All was quiet again for the next couple of hours.

No enemy action, but it seems there are Jap planes above us most of the time trying to get into and advantageous position for attack. About 2:30 P.M. everyone ducked again when a Jap zero started a long sweeping dive toward a Liberty a short distance from us. The zero kept coming and coming. By this time nearly every gun in the convoy was firing at him. Still the zero kept on diving on the Liberty at top speed. The zero (a Jap aircraft) was diving head long for the Liberty firing his guns as he came. I had heard before that the Japs do not fear death, but not until now did I witness one in such an act of suicide. The zero swept just above the bridge of the Liberty and crashed on the bow. There was a terrific explosion and a sheet of flames as the Liberty was enveloped in a plume of smoke. The Liberty dropped out of the convoy and it looked as if she too was lost. About this time another zero was spotted, starting a long sweeping dive on another Liberty nearby. On he came, the same as the other. "Down – Down" he came. How he could survive through such murderous fire is more than anyone could understand, but on the zero plunged. It was plain the Jap was carrying out the same suicidal attack as the other. Closer and closer he came. The breath taking moment was now at hand. A huge spray of water enveloped the Liberty. We could not be sure what had happened. Slowly the mist cleared and we could slowly see the Liberty emerge into view. She was the same ship as ever. The Jap had over shot his mark and plunged into the ocean. One thing sure, he couldn't have come any closer to that ship and missed.

The Liberty ship on which the other Jap plunged, about 3:30 P.M., had the fire under control and re-joined the convoy. The bow of this ship is one twisted mass of metal half way to the water line. I heard that the forward gun crew were all killed. The alert is still on, and we are really praying for darkness to come. The convoy has now picked up speed and we are heading into a rain squaw that is up ahead. There is still a Jap torpedo plane flying close to the water a few miles away from the convoy, waiting for a chance to strike. At about dusk and with the sun low, the Jap came in low over the water toward a Liberty ship near the front of the convoy. A destroyer nearby made things too hot for him, so he launched his torpedo far out. The torpedo went wild missing all ships. The Jap turned clear of the convoy and flew out of sight. It looks like it will rain in a short time. With the darkness and the rain we should make it "O.K." We had supper quite late tonight. The chow line was formed below decks and by this method about two hours was required to get supper. I washed my mess kit out with water from my canteen. I guess I am awfully tired tonight but too "keyed up" to notice it

Wednesday, December 6, 1944 Last night I laid down in a narrow place on deck between two coils of rope to sleep. I rolled up in one blanket, which was still damp, and threw my shelter half over me. It rained a little during the night, but I slept fairly well anyway. The rain with its discomfort was very welcome, as it concealed us from the Japs. This morning at daylight we got our first glimpse of Leyte. We came into the harbor at Palo (C. Philippines), which is full of American ships. As we came into port the air raid alert sounded. No Japs though. The sky was full of American fighter planes, P38, P40 and many corsairs. We could have used a few of them yesterday.

Our boat came directly up to the beach. It took quite a few hours for bull dozers to make a short roadway out to the ramp of our ship. During this time, Filipinos in small boats paddled around our ship begging for blankets and clothing. The G.I.s were very generous and in a short time their boats were loaded with all kinds of clothing and blankets.

Finally at 3:30 P.M. we got our equipment together and disembarked. We carried our stuff over on the beach to wait for further instructions. No one seemed to know we were coming, and cared less. Finally one of our fellows found an officer he knew, who had arranged for transportation for some signal troops off another boat and agreed to take us along to the place we were supposed to go. We waited and waited for the truck to come. During this time we had three air raid alerts. The fact an ammunition dump was just across the road gave us reason for a lot of discomfort.

Suppertime came so one of our bunch of seven went over to one of the L.S.T.s and got some K rations for us to eat. Finally as it was getting dark the truck finally came. We were to go to a camp which was a distance of 25 miles. This proved to be another ordeal that left me completely exhausted. Being that this is the monsoon season the roads are hub deep in mud. Our truck was heavily loaded with about fifteen fellows and all our baggage. We had barely started on our way when the air raid alert sounded. This meant we were to travel with no lights on. After about five miles of barely moving through the mud, the roads became fairly good and we went along a little better.

The anti-aircraft guns opened up with heavy barrage, but being they were firing quite far away we kept on driving. We passed through a number of small villages that had been ravaged by war. After moving slowly along in the darkness for some eighteen miles, and on one occasion driving into the ditch, we came to a sudden stop when the "ack ack" opened up all round us. We all jumped out of the truck and got underneath for protection against falling shrapnel. We could hear the crunch of bombs falling some distance away.

Finally, things quieted down and we resumed our trip. On many occasions when we came up to a turn in the road one of the fellows got out in front of the truck with a half shielded flashlight to guide us around. Finally we reached our destination. This camp was totally blacked out, and getting around in the dark was sure a task. They had some rations warmed up for us and we passed by for our "helping" in the dark. My mess kit was not at all clean, but I was hungry so it made little difference. After chow we lined up at the supply tent to get our cots. My spirits took a drop when the fellow just in front of me got the last cot. My bed was to be a table in the mess tent. Since my barracks bags were still on the truck the clothing I had on was to keep me warm. After laying there for a short time a fellow came in and told me there was a cot out on the truck I could use.

Shortly after arriving in camp we were told to sleep with our rifles and ammunition handy, as reports came through that Jap paratroopers had landed nearby.

Thursday, December 7, 1944 This camp has sure turned out to be a Hell hole from the old school. This is the 3169th sig. company and just over from the states. The fellows in this camp with some exception seem to be pretty square, but the C.O. is a H.A. and one of his men would take a shot at him if given half a chance. The first thing the C.O. told us seven fellows was that since we did not belong in the outfit not to expect any favors. Perhaps in the near future we may have to move out of this squad tent and live in our pup tents. With all this rain we will have quite a time sleeping on the ground. In any other camp I have been in we would be given a day or so to get set up, do our laundry, and a little much needed rest, but not in this outfit, we had to go on detail this afternoon. Our job was putting up a couple of tents for the officers. Last night about 400 Jap airborne troops landed on a airstrip about 18 miles from here. The Japs have succeeded in capturing the strip. The Japs say that in four days they will have every strip in Leyte. This is a usual Jap brag and they will gain nothing by this action. In a few days these Jap troops will be cleaned up. We keep our rifles handy at all time, just in case some of the Japs try and filter through this area to an air strip, a few mile down the road. The front lines are about forty miles from here and you can see the flashes from the artillery at night. The Americans are slowly driving the Japs out of their positions. The Jap air force is still very effective. In fact, we as yet do not have air superiority. There was almost a continuous air raid all night last night. Jap bombers were over head nearly all the time, and our "ack ack" kept up a continuous pounding. The Japs pulled quite a clever trick in landing their airborne troops. One of the Jap type troop transports very much resembles our C47. About the only difference is the landing gear and with this raised it is difficult to tell the difference. The Japs would come in low making a regular approach to land but leave the landing gear retracted and land the plane on its' belly. A number of Jap planes coming in like this, made their surprise effective. One story being told for the truth is about a negro who was in C.Q. duty, when he saw the first Jap transport come sliding in, thought it was one of our planes making a crash landing. He ran out to the plane, opened the door to find it full of Japs. The Japs were not fast enough for that negro. The air raid gave me no alarm last night. I just kept my rifle and helmet handy and slept right through. I was too tired. This was the first time I had had my shoes off in three days, and the first my clothes had been off in over a week.

Friday, December 8, 1944 We got up early this morning to go on an all day's detail. G.H.Q. is just being built and we will be stuck on the bull gang until it is finished. Our jobs are to dig ditches, haul sand, water, and cement to a mixer, and a "hundred one" other jobs. I didn't feel at all well today and it was difficult for me to keep going. I have a cold and feel hot and feverish. Some of the other fellows in our bunch are the same way. If I don't feel better tomorrow I will report for sick call. After working all day, I wrote a letter to Marian, and then a friend and I went down the road a little way and took a bath in a creek. This was my first bath in nearly two weeks, and I was really filthy. They say the Japs are still holding the air strip they took last night.

Saturday, December 9, 1944 Everything was quiet last night. It rained steady all night and I really had a good night's sleep. This morning, without blowing a reveille whistle, the mess Sgt. blew the chow call. Ten minutes later the chow line was closed, and he refused to give us anything to eat. There were about 20 of us and we really raised heck. The mess Sgt. being one of the captain's boys was contrary as heck. All of us went back to our tents and told them "No eat – No work." We stayed in our tents a while and then the chow whistle sounded again. All of us ate chow and went to work. Reports came through that Japs had filtered through within 6 miles of here: It rained most of the day. We had a couple of alerts. Nothing happened.

Sunday, December 10, 1944 It rained again last night so there was not much air activity. However, early in the evening while the sky was comparatively clear, we had two alerts. The Japs succeeded in setting fire, and sinking a tanker, which caused the sky to have a red hue. We worked on detail again today out at the transmitter site. This is only about six miles from the air strip the Japs landed. Our forces have succeeded in driving the japs off the strip, but there are yet many Japs who escaped, still in this area. At intervals we could hear shots fired a short distance from where we were working.

I got acquainted with a Filipino today. He told me in broken English how he and his people had been treated by the Japs. All the rice, potatoes, etc. that were grown, were taken by the Japs and he and his family went hungry. His 8 year old son was taken out of school and put to work on a farm.

Monday, December 11, 1944 We fellows who have been on the construction detail were surprised when we were given the day off. We heard that some of our old bunch is in a camp a short distance from here, so we stopped by the orderly room and got a pass to go see them. The clerk went to see if there was any work to be done. We finally were given a pass, but had to be back at noon. Boy is this camp basic. I wonder if all outfits are like this – just fresh from the states: A friend and I went to a show over at Tolosa tonight. We have to carry our rifles and steel helmets.

Tuesday, December 12, 1944 The rain continues to pour down. It again rained all night, and has continued on through most of the day. Everywhere the mud is over your shoes and in many places it is above your knees. The main roads are covered with slushy mud and water. Underneath they say there is something of a paved road. Near- by is the town of Tolosa. In peace time I suppose it's populations would be around two or three hundred. It hardly resembles a town though, as it is very much run down and beat up by the war. All the buildings, excepting a few, have thatched roofs and are built mostly of bamboo. No improvement has apparently been made since the invasion of the Japs. The streets are dirt, and being there are no sidewalks the road seems to run right up to the buildings. There are no ditches for drainage, and the roads are a sea of mud. There are no modern conveniences, and the people wash and bath[e] in a little stream that runs through town. There are two or three half modern buildings. One of them is the town hall, another formerly a school, and the other a church, while most buildings of the town have no paint on them at all. The town hall and other such buildings show signs of once being painted. Most of the houses and other buildings look as if they might fall down on you, should you enter. Business is all but at a stand- still. The only commodities for sale are reed baskets, wooden sandals, straw hats, etc. that are made by town people. No clothing and very little food may be bought. The Filipinos are now getting a small ration of flour which is being shipped in from the U.S. This is the first flour they have had for a long time. Some of we fellows went to the show again, which is held on the town hall lawn. The screen is fastened to the town hall balcony. There were two alerts during the show, which made it quite late when the show was over. No Japs came over.

Wednesday, December 13, 1944 We fellows had nothing to do again today. It is hard to figure out why they are leaving us alone for a change. It only rained a little bit today, and the weather seems to be clearing a little. This evening at dusk, the red alert sounded. The alert signal is three shots from an anti aircraft battery near-by. As usual we fellows were standing in front of our tent. All at once we heard a swishing sound and three bombs landed not much over 100 yards from us. Not until after the explosion did we make a dive for a fox hole. The bombs dropping in the thick underbrush, and among the panlon [Paulownia] trees stopped the concussion and shrapnel. Had the bombs landed in the open our chances of being hit by flying steel might have been pretty great. These bombs were not heavies, but seemed to be of the "daisy cutter" type.

Thursday, December 14, 1944 The weather seems to be drying up a little. No rain last night and the sky was clear all day. We had nothing to do this morning. This afternoon we helped on a show area they are fixing at the back of the camp. It is hard to figure out the way things have changed for us in the past few days. We have been pulling hardly any detail at all, in fact less than anyone in camp. Everyone seems to be breaking their necks being nice to us.

Tonight Sparks and I had to go on guard duty over at the G.H.Q. area. Even when off duty we could scarcely sleep, as the mosquitoes were terrible. Had a couple of alerts during the night. We heard some bombs drop in the distance. Reports came through that the Americans have invaded Mindoro (C. Philippines) Island. This is but 70 miles from Manila.

Friday, December 15, 1944 Today Marian and I have been married three and a half years. We have been apart nearly three years. Some of the fellows think I will be home before eight more months pass, but I don't think so. For the fellows who do get put on the quota, it usually takes three or four months to finally get transportation home. We were given warning today that a typhoon is approaching. There isn't much we can do but sit tight and hope not to be blown away. It started to rain this afternoon and rained most of the night. One of my teeth started to give me trouble today. I hope there is a dentist around here somewhere.

Saturday, December 16, 1944 The expected typhoon turned out to be only a heavy rain which has been a daily occurrence anyway. This morning we had to move into the other squad tent. We won't have as much room as we did have but we will have enough. This afternoon a bunch of us had to put up a couple of tents. There is very little rank in this outfit so I had to take charge. This detail didn't last long and I spent the rest of the afternoon writing letters and getting straightened up around my bunk. It started raining again shortly after dark. We had three alerts before I fell asleep. The Japs dropped a few bombs quite a distance from here. They were addressed "To whom it may concern" as it was raining and they couldn't see.

Sunday, December 17, 1944 This morning I went to Palo (C. Philippines) to have my tooth x rayed at the hospital there. This didn't take long so I decided to go on in to Tacloban (C. Philippines.) Tacloban is the largest city in Leyte with a normal population of around 20,000 and is the capital of Leyte. There are quite a number of modern type buildings, but these are in bad need of repair. About two thirds of all the buildings and houses are made of bamboo and covered with thatch and these are in even worse shape. The streets at one time were graveled, but with hundreds of G.I. trucks, and with the rain, there has been, the town is a sea of mud. There is hardly any drainage, and the mud from the streets has rolled up over the narrow sidewalks. There are quite a number of little shops. About all they have is a few Japanese trinkets and at a price ten times what it should be. I bought eight post cards which cost me a dollar or two pesos.

Monday, December 18, 1944 Went to the dentist again this morning. The x ray I had taken yesterday was no good, so I had to go into Palo again. Palo is about nine miles from here and has a normal population of around 3,000. There is a large church there which is being used as a hospital at the present time. Most of the buildings in Palo are still standing and are in fair repair. We found out today our team is scheduled to go on the next invasion operation. We are supposed to operate radio from a small coasted freighter. We are replacement for casualties suffered on the invasion of Leyte.

Tuesday, December 19, 1944 Had a tooth pulled today, and the dentist sure had a tough time getting it out. I spent the rest of the day in my bunk not feeling so good.

Wednesday, December 20, 1944 I was sure sick today. I haven't had anything to eat since yesterday morning. My mouth is awful sore, I am weak as a cat with some fever, and I have an awful headache. We had a heavy raid tonight.

Things were sure hot for a little while. The Japs picked a fighter strip down the road a couple of miles as its target. They were dropping their bombs so thick and fast there was one continuous roar. I wasn't very fast getting out of my bunk, so I lay flat on the tent floor. I could hear some stray bombs whistle down and explode a short distance away. As soon as I could I put on my helmet and got in a fox hole. A Jap medium bomber flew directly over our heads and started strafing shortly after going by. He was not over 1200 feet high at the most. All this time our "ack ack" was blazing away for all they were worth.

Thursday, December 21, 1944 I didn't sleep hardly at all last night. My mouth is very sore and I am all round pretty sick. I went on sick call this morning. They confined me to quarters and gave me some pills to take. I spent all day in my bunk. I felt well enough to go to a show tonight, which is in the show area just back of our tent.

We fellows are to be ready to go on board our assigned boat any time after the twenty fifth. We will no doubt lay out in the harbor quite a number of days before moving out. We kinda think this operation will end up in Luzon (N. Philippines) Island. We are also issued ninety more rounds of ammunition for our carbines. I kinda wish now I had an M-1 or a Springfield rifle. A Jap hit with one of these stays, put better. I guess we can have some hand grenades if we want to carry them.

Friday, December 22, 1944 Went on sick call again this morning. They gave me some more pills and confined me to quarters. I am feeling a little better, but I still have a little fever. I sorted out my barracks bags today and put the stuff I want to keep with me in one of them. I sold my picture developing stuff today. Chances are I would not get to use it again, and in the future I won't be able to carry so much junk with me. The Germans are sure raising heck in France to Belgium. They have launched an offensive and are pushing ahead towards Antwerp (N. Belgium) on a 60 mile front. The Germans are making a lot of initial gains and our forces have not yet checked them. We had two alerts tonight but no Japs came over. We can expect some pretty heavy raids now that the moon is getting full.

Saturday, December 23, 1944 Went on sick call again this morning, and got more pills. My fever is gone and I feel much better today. I am still awful weak. The Germans are still driving ahead, and the Americans as yet haven't stemmed their drive. Germans have driven ahead 35 miles in some places. Things are becoming rather serious. A lieutenant in a tent near ours has a pet monkey. We fellows sure get a kick out of it. He is tame as a cat and climbs around your shoulders. We had a long air alert tonight. The Japs bombed a port area quite a number of miles from us. We could see the "ack ack" bursts but it was far enough away so we were out of danger of falling shrapnel I still haven't received any mail and I guess it will be a long time before I do.

Sunday, December 24, 1944 I am feeling much better today. I am still pretty weak, but I should get my strength back in a few days. The small shower enclosure I built is pretty handy for we fellows to bath[e] in. Four helmets of water is enough for a pretty fair bath. By digging a pit in the ground seven or eight feet deep makes a pretty fair well. The soil here is very sandy and with all the rain we have had lately the ground is well soaked. This evening some of we fellows took a walk over to Tobosa (W. Philippines) we walked through town and on down to the beach. We thought some of going to church but none of us were dressed for it so we went back to camp and went to bed. Had a couple of alerts tonight, but nothing happened around our area.

Monday, December 25, 1944 Today is Christmas. We had but two meals today, breakfast as usual and then dinner at 2:30 P.M. We had a good dinner of turkey, dressing, corn, peas, potatoes, pumpkin pie, cake, and fruit salad for dessert, and grape juice to drink. My mouth is not very sore now and I enjoyed my dinner quite a lot. The mess hall was crowded so I used the fender of a jeep for a table. Below – notation from my wife. Maybe we will be together next Christmas.

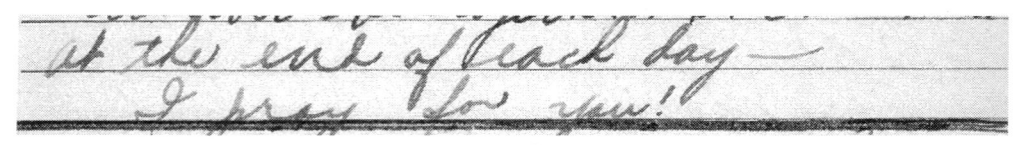

Marian wrote, "At the end of each day I pray for you!"

Tuesday, December 26, 1944 We had a show in the area last night. During the show we had an alert but they decided to continue with the show unless the "ack ack" started burning near-by. It did start bursting quite near, so the projector was shut off. At the same time a truck came down the road. It sounded like a low flying air plane, and the crowd ran in every direction. As soon as we found out it was a truck the crowd came back and we continued the show. We were awakened at 5 A.M. this morning, packed our stuff, ate breakfast, and then got on a truck which brought us into Tacloban (C. Philippines.) We went all over town trying to find out where we were supposed to go. One camp we stopped at we saw some of our old friends. Finally we came over to the Leyte Capital building where we unloaded our baggage. The Leyte capital building is a rather modern type building with long stone steps leading up to the entrance, and a row of stone pillars running across the front. As is most buildings here, the capital is in much need of repair. Many of the windows are out, and it is in bad need of paint. This building is about three stories high and built quite long across the front and rather narrow towards the rear. It would hardly be as large as one wing of our state capitol building. Being there was a signal unit in the capital basement, we stayed for morning chow. We thought we were to stay here all night, but in the afternoon a lieutenant told us to get our stuff together we were going to board a ship. We are to be radio operators. On this boat which is to take part in the invasion of Luzon Island (N. Philippines) which will be coming off soon. This ship just got back from Hollandia today where it has been repaired of damage done to it in the invasion of Leyte. Several men were killed and many injured when a Jap bomb dropped just off the star board bow and sprayed the ship with fragments, which tore small holes in the hull. We put our baggage aboard a small landing barge which took us out to the ship. After a pretty rough ride of about half an hour we got there and drew up alongside. Some of the crew were busy painting the recently wielded shrapnel holes. This ship must have looked like a tin can shot at by a shot gun. The side of the ship is one mass of patches. This ship also went aground during a typhoon and this caused the bottom to get bent pretty badly. All in all though she seems to be a pretty fair ship. The other army fellows on board say this is a good assignment. This is just a small ship. She is only about 200 feet long with a total of 150 soldiers & sailors aboard. This ship was built as a U.S. sub. Patrol boat.

Wednesday, December 27, 1944 After coming aboard last night we were assigned bunks which are very comfortable, as there are mattresses on them. We do not use our mess kits here, but eat chow in the crew's mess and are served our food on large trays. The food was excellent today, fresh meat, potatoes and ice cream for supper. We may come into the mess hall any time during the day and get coffee. Boy what a difference there is from the "no good" camp we just came from.

One lone Jap bomber pulled a sneak raid over at the air strip which is about a mile away from us. I intend [on] going to town tomorrow and make a last stab at collecting my mail. I know after we leave here for the Luzon operation it will be months before I receive any mail. The folks at home are going to suffer a mail slump from me, as it will be a long spell before I write. In a few days all outgoing mail will be held up until after the operation.

Thursday, December 28, 1944 I didn't sleep well last night. It seems my bunk is so comfortable I am not accustomed to such luxuries. We fellows who just came on board received some very disappointing news today. We learned we are to only be on board this ship for transportation. On the day of the invasion, we seven fellows are to go on the beach just behind the first wave of infantry and set up equipment to transmit back to the ship. After what is supposed to be five days we report to our unit. "Report To Our Unit." The 832nd is strong here and they are all the way back to Brisbane Australia. It seems we fellows are "cast outs" and not wanted anywhere.

Didn't go to town today. I helped load a L.C.M. but it was too late to go, when it left for town. More fellows came on board today. We will probably be very crowded.

Friday, December 29, 1944 We fellows of our team received some good news today. Our status has finally been settled. We are rated as ship's personal and not on board just as a landing party. However, nine chances to ten we will be chosen for the landing party. It is going round that the landing is to be made around a hundred miles north of Manila on Luzon. There is no question in our minds, but what this invasion is going to be tough, and calling it "tough" is hardly a correct explanation. If I can just get by this operation I will more than likely be sent home, but home never seemed so far away. I am going to need an awful lot of luck, plus some good sound religion this time.

Saturday, December 30, 1944 The past couple of days I have been working in the radio room helping to get it in shape for the coming operation. Major General Aiken's quarters are being made ready since he is to be on this ship. General Aiken is commander of Army Signal Corps in the S.W. Pacific and Far East. Lieutenant Sparks informed me that there is a letter for me over at one of the boats. I hope he brings it tomorrow. I am sure anxious to get this letter as it has been a long time since my last mail. Had a show in our mess hall tonight.

Also had a red alert. No Japs showed up. News reports were good today. The Americans Armies have halted the German drive in France.

Sunday, December 31, 1944 Well today is the last day of "44." It was just another ordinary day. This morning we pulled up anchor and went over where the biggest bunch of ships are laying to take on water and oil. The other ship that Russell Kerr, Smith and Sparks are on was taking on water and oil, and our ship tied up alongside. Consequently, I got to talk to them for a little while. We had a show in the mess hall tonight. It was a western, but it was a show anyway. After the show I decided to stay up until midnight, so I played a few games of checkers, and drank coffee. That is a privilege that is sure OK. We can get a cup of coffee at any time. I received a letter from Marian today. The last one I will receive for a good long time.

To Uncle Sam's Best Soldier.
from your.
"Military Mrs."

1945

Book 4

Monday, January 1, 1945 The start of another book and another year. I now have over 28 months overseas, and by the end of February I will have three years in the Army. At one time a few months ago I was in a position to believe my going home depended only on putting in the required time overseas. Now the picture has entirely changed. I am glad for some unexplainable reason to be in on the coming operations, what is to be the invasion of Luzon. I am quite sure to be among a party to go ashore in the first wave. The chance I will be a victim of enemy action, is a slim one, but there will be a lot of causalities somewhere along the line. I will think of going home when this job is finished. Just a routine day today. The General's quarters and the wardroom have a new coat of paint. Had a show in the mess hall tonight. My mail is coming through, five letters today.

Tuesday, January 2, 1945 It seems my luck will never work in my favor. I was told today I am to be taken off the ship and to go back to Toboso (W. Philippines). I really felt down in the dumps all day. This evening an officer told me a more complete story, which brightened things up quite a bit. I am still assigned to the ship, but am going on board another ship for transportation being our ship will be very crowded. I am to take along one barracks bag with whatever equipment I will need plus any field pack, etc. I spent the afternoon sorting out my junk and deciding on the personal things I most wish to keep, and to take along. I have put my diaries in a water proof sack as I hope above all else to save them, as well as Marian's picture. I stand a good chance of losing everything I have on this coming trip.

Wednesday, January 3, 1945 I brought the stuff I am taking along up on deck this morning, and then sat down and waited for the L.C.M. We had a pretty heavy air raid this morning early. No ships were hit in the harbor but the air strip took a pretty heavy pounding. Several of our planes were destroyed and a fuel dump set a fire. The L.C.M. came long side our boat at about 11:00 A.M. Myself and four other fellows put our baggage aboard and then went over to the 849. After unloading a bunch of baggage and officers, it was nearly noon so we ate dinner on the 849. We then came into Tacloban and stopped at the Capital building for further instructions. Everything is sure in a muddle. Of the ninety more rounds of ammunition I was supposed to get I only got thirty, and lucky to get this: The five of we fellows (none of them any of my buddies) are to go on board a L.S.T. for the voyage. When we reach our destination a boat containing shore party personnel is to pick us up. This landing boat will be from the 848.

Thursday, January 4, 1945 After stopping for a short time at the Capital yesterday, we were brought on over here to the 230th signal company to stay until we leave. This camp is located in between a bunch of Filipino houses and this district is more like the slums than any place I have been. The Filipinos run around through the tents, and all over the camp in general. The small children run around half naked with but a short undershirt as their only clothing.

Friday, January 5, 1945 The five of we fellows put our gear on a truck this morning and came over to where G.H.Q. personnel were assembling. We reported in here and had our names put on the shipping list, and then went on over near the Capital to the beach where we went aboard a small landing craft. Shortly after shoving off for our ship out in the bay it started to rain. Luckily I had thought to take along my rain coat from my barracks bag. Most of the fellows got soaked. After about twenty five minutes we came long side our L.S.T. (landing ship tank) another landing barge was unloading, so we had to wait a while. This will be my second trip on board a L.S.T. My first was a month ago when I came to Leyte from New Guinea.

Our landing barge finally came up to the ramp and we unloaded. It is the same story as before. We have to make our bed where ever we can find a space. The boat has a full load of trucks and jeeps. I found an empty jeep so I threw part of my luggage in it so I could reserve it as a place to sleep. Just so I could be sure of a spot, I also put some of my junk in a truck cab. Just as I suspected all the vehicles on board have drivers so I lost my priority on a place to sleep. For a while I felt pretty much out of luck as to finding anyplace half dry and large enough to stretch out in. I finally walked up around the front gun turrets. Underneath the forward most gun turret I found a spot fairly dry and while hard to get in and out of it is large enough to sleep in. At the best this steel deck doesn't make a very comfortable bed. There will be about 450 men aboard, which will make the boat less crowded than when I came to Leyte. There is also a mess hall below in which to eat, and the chow isn't so bad. I guess boat 898 has already pulled out as it is no longer in its former place. The biggest share of the boats have gone and about all that is left is a bunch of L.S.T.s and a couple of hospital ships. When we reach our destination a landing barge from the 898 is to come over to this ship and pick us five fellows up and take us ashore as part of the landing party. However, I am very doubtful if it will work out that way. More than likely we may have to look around for days to find our bunch.

Saturday, January 6, 1945 At 9 A.M. this morning we pulled up anchor and got underway. Our convoy is heading south west down the coast of Leyte. Nearly sundown we met another convoy of Liberty ships and LSTs and after our two convoys formed into one, the ocean is full of ships from one horizon to the other. The more ships there are the more secure it makes you feel. We were given instructions in abandon ship, air raids, fire fighting, etc. today. We must have our life jackets and steel helmets with us at all times. Today was quite uneventful. There is no outward tension among the soldiers on board, and everyone is settled for the voyage. Our convoy passed through the straight between Mindanao and Leyte tonight. There is quite a menagerie of pets on board. Four monkeys, two dogs, a rooster, and a duck.

Sunday, January 7, 1945 The voyage so far has been uneventful. We spent most of the day passing Negros Island, which is still Jap held. Our Air Force must have naturalized its air and sea power, as our convoy was not more than ten miles off its shores most of the day. Many planes of our Air Force were overhead during the day. Negros seemed to be quite an inviting island with its long straight shore line, occasionally altered by a large bay, with long rolling green hills blotched by patches of timber here and there gradually rising up into the comparatively rugged mountains inland. We had an excellent dinner today, turkey, dressing, potatoes, peas, cranberry sauce, and lemon pie. The G.I.s are treated quite descent on board this ship. A lot will depend on them the next few days. It rained a little last night, but I kept comparatively dry.

Monday, January 8, 1945 Another dull day aboard ship. Shortly after midnight last night the wind rose and continued to blow throughout the day. The ocean has been quite rough causing our ship to pitch and roll. A few of the fellows are getting sea sick but I am continuing to take the voyage as well as ever. A fellow who has his bed next to mine gave me fifty rounds of ammunition. This makes a hundred and ten rounds I now have. Every fellow on board takes care of his fire arms with the greatest of care. There isn't a weapon on board that isn't checked everyday.

We had air cover from our planes most of the day today. I guess someone stole my fountain pen. It isn't in my writing case where I always keep it, and I can't find it anywhere. Losing it make me feel quite badly as this pen was a Christmas present from Marian two years ago.

Tuesday, January 9, 1945 Everything quiet again today. Our convoy is heading north west and we have been in sight of Mindoro Island all day. The ocean is quiet today and the sky is clear. Our air craft have been overhead nearly all day. Tomorrow we will be too far northwest to have protection of our land based aircraft. Mindoro Island appeared to be very rugged with high mountains and wooded slopes. Reminds me of some of New Guinea country I have seen. Mindoro Island is one of the larger islands of the Philippine group.

Wednesday, January 10, 1945 Around noon today our convoy was over taken by a force of our cruiser battle ships and air craft carriers. Planes from our carriers gave us air cover most of the day. Late in the afternoon this force left us. In the middle of the afternoon a line squall came up and the wind increased into a gale. By night our boat was pitching and rolling, plunging into one swell after another. Nearly everyone was somewhat sea sick. I managed to eat part of my supper and keep away from the railing. I went to bed early tonight, as the only way I can keep feeling half way well is to stay on my back. By laying my shelter half on top of two life jackets, with my blanket on top, makes somewhat of an improved bed.

Thursday, January 11, 1945 This morning early our convoy entered the Lingayen Golf (N. Philippines) which is only about 150 miles northwest of Manila on the west coast of Luzon. At about 10 AM we arrived at the point of attack. There are hundreds of ships of all types here in the bay. We tried to spot boat 847 but as we expected no luck. Our ship anchored off shore a ways as we learned the beach was not secure and the first forces had only gone ashore this morning. Landing barges and amphibious tanks were circling in the bay in preparation to landing. The Japs were seemingly putting up a string of resistance as their mortar and artillery fire was still landing on the beach. Many of our destroyers were firing salvoes *(a concentrated burst of firing or bombing from multiple sources)* at Jap positions and the shore. Occasionally a Jap shell would land near one of the destroyers. Finally late in the afternoon our boat pulled up anchor and went into the beach. Our boat couldn't get in so very close to the shore and a long dirt road way was to be built out to the ramp of our L.S.T. Boy by the time they fooled around deciding what to do it was nearly dark, so they decided to pull back out in the bay and unload in the morning. In the meantime another L.S.T. had pulled in close to us, and when our boat started to back away from the beach we drifted into the other boat and became fastened. To make matters worse the air alert sounded. We felt sure the Japs would bomb the beach and we were practically sitting ducks. Several Jap planes did come over but our intense "ack ack" kept them at a distance. Finally our boat managed to get free and we anchored out in the bay at about 11 Pm. Jap Mortar and artillery opened up on the beach. We were but a short distance offshore and some of the Jap shells landed in the water a short distance away. We pulled up anchor and moved further out in the bay. In the meantime a smoke screen was laid over the beach and the harbor, by destroyers and patrol boats. Only a small portion of the beach is ours at the end of the first day. We hold an area but about 3 miles long by a mile and a half deep.

Friday, January 12, 1945 Having all my stuff packed I laid down on five life jackets to sleep last night, not bothering to undress. However this was no different than the other nights. I have slept on this boat, as I haven't had my clothes off since I came on board. With all the life jackets as a cushion I got more rest than usual. At day break the air raid alarm sounded and a group of ships nearby were throwing up a heavy curtain of "ack ack" high overhead we could see some Jap Zeros darting in and out of the clouds. One Zero dove from a high altitude straight down until going out of sight in the smoke screen near the water. Whether he dove into a ship or just plunged into the water, we couldn't tell. Jap artillery was busy at the same time. We heard one shell whistle past our boat which landed on out in the bay. We spent most of the day again out in the bay. Our L.S.T. having lost its stern anchor has had quite a bit of trouble setting into the beach after four attempts, which took nearly all day. We finally made it. At 4:30 PM we started to unload. By the time all the trucks were unloaded and we got our gear on shore it was dark. After waiting nearly two hours some trucks came. We loaded our stuff, got on, and started heading up the beach. The beach is quite secure now, as during the day our forces have pushed the Japs back a number of miles. Our progress was very slow, as our navel boats had laid a smoke screen over the ships in the harbor, and driving without lights, it's impossible to see more than ten feet ahead. After driving four or five miles along the beach we turned on to a narrow road that took us to a small town. It was hard to tell much about this turn as it was total blackout. From what I could tell it seemed to be quite a clean place, and kept in quite orderly fashion. Appeared much cleaner than any of the Leyte towns I have seen. Evidently the war had passed this village by, as it showed no ill effects of gun fire. Here we were in for a long wait, as some army pontoon bridge had to be repaired, that spanned a large area of swamp land and fish hatcheries. The Japs had destroyed these bridges on their retreat from the city of Dagupan (N. Philippines) two days before. Even though the hour was late the town people turned out and sang over and over "God Bless America." Finally our convoy got underway again.

These pontoon bridges were sure a hazard to cross. Only one truck at a time and after each one the bridges had to be repaired. Pontoons in the form of rubber boats slipped out of place and their roadway plankings cracked and broke. A number of trucks and jeeps went off the side or fell through. Having to cross these bridges with no lights made matters even worse. At this point we were only about four miles from the front. We could hear the rumble and see the flash of artilleries. The countryside over the battle area was continuously illuminated by parachute flares shot in the sky. Our truck made the crossing without incident, however only two trucks made the crossing after ours, as one section of the bridge went completely out and left the other trucks stranded on the other side.

The road from here on was fairly smooth and after a few miles we reached the city limits of Dagupan. Here was destruction if I ever saw it. The shelling of our war ships, the bombs dropped by our bombers, and the burning by the Japs left this city in total ruin. After going slowly through town, we came to a market place where the pavilions were in good shape and undamaged.

We unloaded our stuff and made our beds in some of the surrounding buildings. Those who had jungle hammocks or cots put them up. Not having either one I laid my shelter half and blanket on the floor and went to bed.

Saturday, January 13, 1945 I was up quite early this morning and about as tired as ever, as the cement floor of this market pavilion is no softer than the steel deck of the L.S.T. Not being set up to serve any meals all we had for breakfast was a cup of coffee and a couple of crackers. Evidently three of the other fellows in our group were on one of the trucks that was stranded on the other side of the bridge. I found the other fellows in our group, and we started out to try and find where and if the signal center was, & to get information as to the location of our ship PCE 848. Luckily the signal location was here by the place we had spent the night. From here we learned of a radio set up that had contact with our ship. Luck was with us again and we didn't have far to walk to send a message out to the ship. Our signal officer informed us that a boat would be in this afternoon and pick us up. By the time we finished our running around the town had become very much alive with the civilian population. All of them seemed very happy and in good spirits amid the rubble of their city. It is the same story here as in Leyte. The Japs have drained the Filipinos of everything they have. There are many Catholic nuns, and even though their convent was partially destroyed by our naval guns, they too were very glad the Americans have come. After dinner we loaded our gear on a truck and drove down by the boat landing area along the river. Fairly large launches and barges come up the river a distance of a couple of miles from the ocean. While waiting for our boat from the PCE 848, General MacArthur and General Henry came in, in a Navy launch. After waiting around a while, our boat arrived after loading our gear in the boat. Being that General Aiken had come in from the 847 we had to wait around a while longer. Finally we were given permission to shove off, so we left. This turned out to be a boat ride I will never forget. The river was very smooth, but at its mouth, and out in the gulf, about half a mile, the ground swells caused terrific surf. Going head long into the breakers we continued on our way to our ship. The surf came in, in mountainous waves and the spray was getting us soaking wet. Our boat road them pretty well, but every wave got bigger and I thought sure we would swamp. Our boat would stand on its stern and then drop with a jolting thud. It was sure a relief to get finally to the ship. We unloaded our stuff, were assigned bunks and sat down to a good supper. I had to stand watch on a voice radio circuit on the bridge until midnight. I was sure dead tired when I finally got to bed.

Sunday, January 14, 1945 Didn't have much to do today. Spent most of my time getting my equipment put away. Found someone had stolen my G.I. trench knife. One of these days I am going to catch one of those guys. I guess our mail is going out now so I wrote some letters home. I worked a little while up on the bridge this morning, operating the voice circuit. General Aiken was there and I had quite a number of messages to pass for him. Our forces are steadily pushing the Japs back and we have advanced twenty five miles towards Manila. We now hold about a 30 miles beachhead and are extending it daily. About three miles off to our left and on the inland side of the gulf is the left flank of our beach head. The Japs seem to be in strong force as we can see arterially fire continuously. The Jap air force must be nearly completely out of action as no air attacks have been made in the past few days. Every day at dawn and at dusk a smoke screen is laid over the harbor. The Russians have launched a large scale offensive and are driving the Germans back in southern Poland. American forces are compelling the Germans to withdraw in some section of their bulge in Belgium. *(At this point in time "The Battle of the Bulge" is on going")*

Monday, January 15, 1945 This boat seems to have served its purpose as far as we Army fellows are concerned. General Aiken has gone ashore, the voice circuit on the bridge has been closed and we are keeping watch on but one C.W. circuit. Didn't do much all day but lay around. This good food, soft bed, and the cold water sure is a treat after the rugged week I spent on the L.S.T. Marian and I have been married three years, seven months today.[48]

Tuesday, January 16, 1945 Today was as uneventful as ever. There is still a lot of artillery fire over on the beach on the left flank of our lines. They say the Japs have a 12-inch naval gun concealed over there. I doubt that, as if there were the ships out here would really be catching a lot of shells.

---

[48] Actually my dad has lost a year – they were married June 15, 1941.

Wednesday, January 17, 1945 I was on K.P. all day today. I managed to write a letter to Marian this afternoon. The latest rumor is that this ship is to act as a patrol ship for an invasion to take place near Bataan Peninsula (C. Philippines). If this is true, we Army fellows will probably not go along but be stationed on shore here. Our ship pulled long side a tanker this afternoon to refuel.

Thursday, January 18, 1945 Since the loss of my good pen this is the only one I have to use. I bought this one in San Francisco just before coming overseas, for the sum of .27 cents. It works and that is about all, and after using, your hands need a wash job. There is no more talk as to when we are leaving. A third of the ship's crew is getting shore leave each day. We had a movie in the mess hall this afternoon. We Army fellows haven't hardly anything to do now as all circuits have been closed down. It seems they just won't let us sit out here, but will likely send us ashore to work. News reports continue to be good. The Russian Armies have taken Warsaw, Poland. Our forces here in Luzon continue to drive toward Manila.

Friday, January 19, 1945 Nothing doing today. Spent most of my time in the mess hall, up on top side, and on the fan tail. I really hit the jack pot on mail today. Two letters from Marian [Dec. 19 & 26] a letter from Mom & Dad [Dec. 2] a letter from Sally & Dick [Oct. 24] a letter from Mrs. Platts [Oct. 21] and a New Virginia news paper [October]. Today is Jack's birthday. I wonder where he might be. I guess overseas somewhere. I guess the Japs are really dug in, in the hills across the bay from here. I guess they actually do have some 12 inch navy guns. So far they haven't opened up on any of the ships here in the harbor. I suppose they don't want to give away their position. Artillery fire is constantly exchanged. I guess we now have an air strip near here now, as some P38s and transports came in today.

Saturday, January 20, 1945 Each day is the same routine. We Army fellows are just putting in our time as our work has been concluded here. Our day is spent by first getting up around six A.M. We eat breakfast at 6:15 after which we make up our bunks, and sweep, and mop out our quarters, and radio room. For the rest of the day we mostly loaf around. We write our letters in the radio room, and use the mess hall for card games, and reading room. There is coffee to be had 24 hours a day. As for the Japs all remain quiet. Not a Jap plane has been over this area since the first days of the invasion, I don't know if you would call these Japs mysterious or just plain stupid. It is hard to believe all the aircraft the Japs have are in Japan.

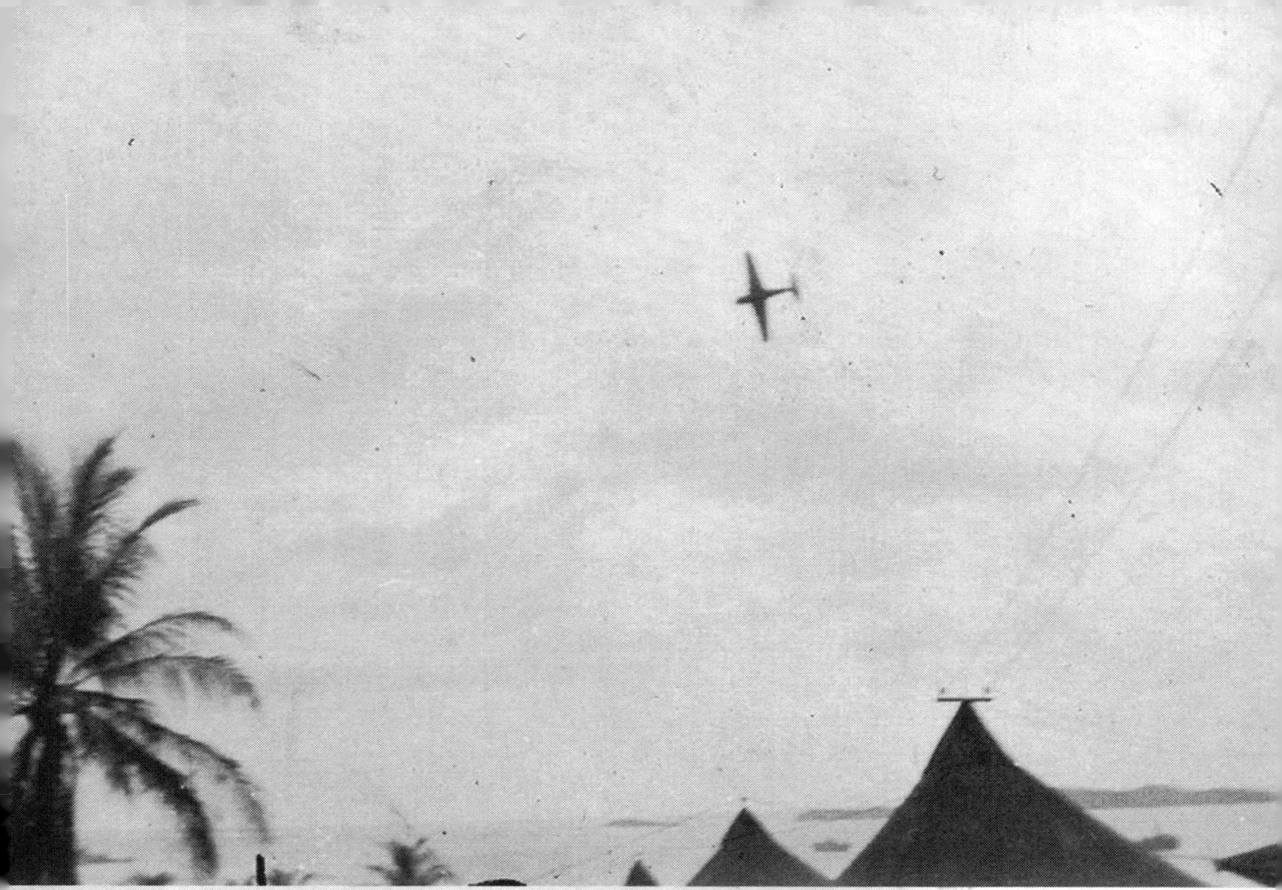
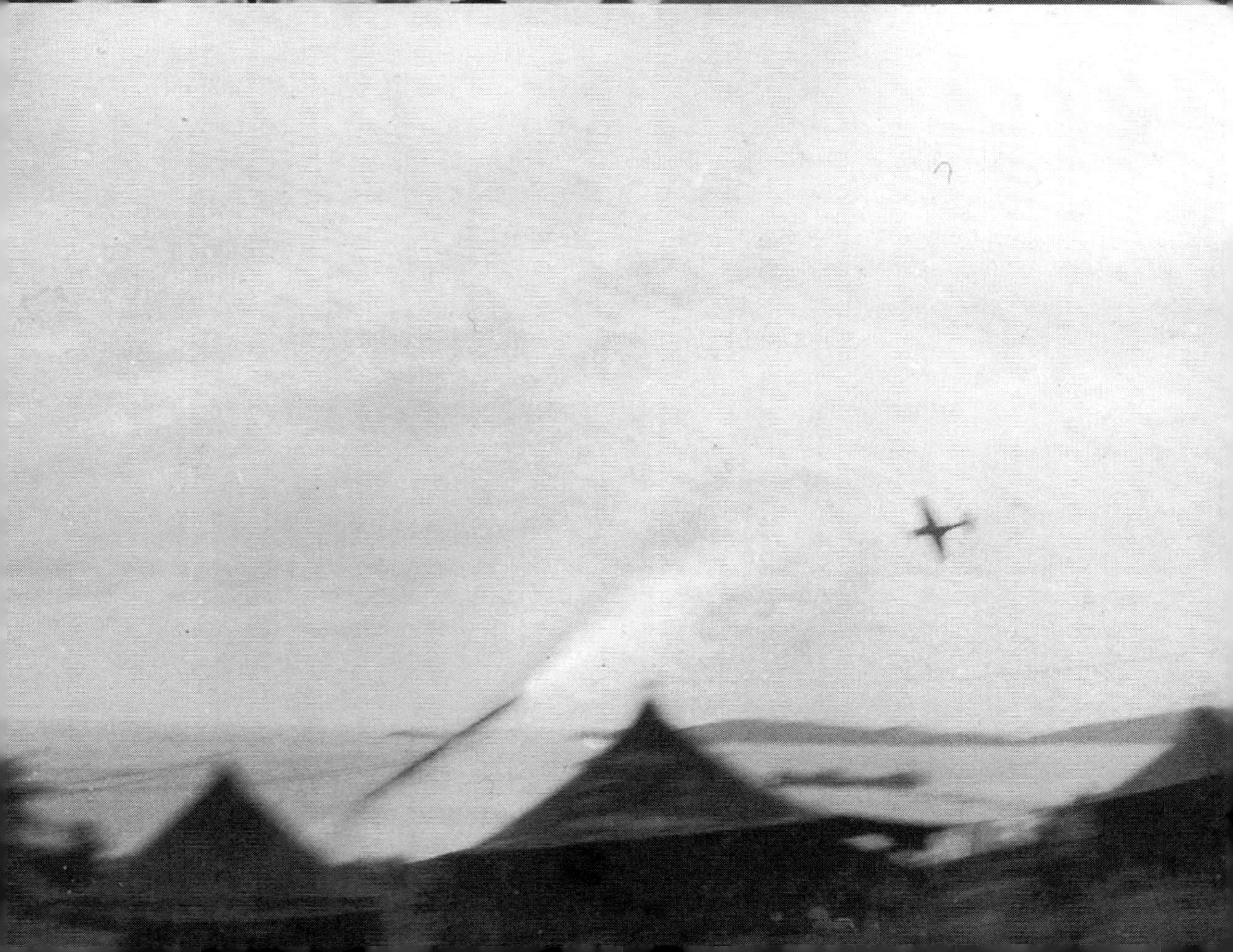

Sunday, January 21, 1945 This morning another Army fellow and I went with a bunch of Navy guys over to another ship to church. We got back in time for dinner, and what a dinner we had. Turkey, dressing, potatoes, pie, ice cream. The Navy sure has the edge on the Army when it comes to eating. The Army fellows on shore get only field rations.

Monday, January 22, 1945 Today I went on shore leave. Another fellow and I decided to do a little hitch hiking so we walked through town (Dagupan) to the Manila highway. There is a constant stream of trucks so we had no trouble catching a ride. This highway is of concrete and as good as any two lane highway in the states. We road to a small town about ten miles from Dagupan. We caught a ride on a kind of out of the way road to another little town. Neither of these two little towns were damaged to speak of by the war. After wondering around the second little town for a while, we stopped in the shade near a church to rest. A Filipino came along and started a conversation. I had bought a pair of slippers for Marian, of which he admired very much. After talking for a little while this Filipino asked us if we would like to have some bananas. Being we had had no dinner we quickly accepted. He told us to come along. So after walking about two blocks we came to his house. This house was quite small, being built entirely of bamboo, and thatch and elevated about five feet off the ground on bamboo poles. The inside of the house was spotlessly clean, having a sort of bamboo webbing for walls of each of the three rooms. This Filipino spoke English remarkably well, and after a short time we learned he as well as his wife were schoolteachers. A small table before us was set and two large bunches of bananas were brought in. Knowing only too well how short the Filipinos are on food we (even though pretty gaunt) held back on eating very many bananas. The conversation, as usual was about the Japs. He said his salary was 65 pesos a month, but this was no amount at all, since a hundred pesos was required to buy a small quantity of rice. When the Filipino gardens started producing vegetables, the Japs stuck a Jap flag in the garden and that meant "hands off." The Japs when suspecting a Filipino as being a guerrilla, would torture them by forcing them to drink water until they swelled up like a balloon and then laying them on the ground and jumping on their stomach. This school teacher told us that when he was in Manila shortly after the Japs took the city he was in a crowd of Filipinos, when a Jap came up and told them to bow their heads. For those not pleasing the Jap, he struck them over the head with a club. After talking a while we got up to leave. This Filipino's wife had wrapped the bananas up and gave them to us as we left. We walked over to the road we came in on and luckily we caught a ride clear back to Dagupan. We got on board the barge at 5 pm and came out to the 848.

Tuesday, January 23, 1945 This morning all Army fellows but seven, of which I am one, went on shore to work for a while. I feel I am rather lucky in getting to stay on the boat.

The war news is very good at present. The Russian Armies are sweeping across Poland and are now 150 mile from Berlin. In France Americans forces have succeeded in eliminating the last of the German bulge, by a gigantic air attack, which destroyed a German mechanized army. In Italy things seem at a standstill. No moves on either side. In Burma, Allied forces are driving towards Mandalay (C. Burma), twenty five miles away. In China allied forces have now opened a new supply road from India to Chungking, China.

American B29 super fortresses have in recent weeks increased the bombings of Japan. 45 raids have been made to date. The more recent raids have been made from Saipan, and the Mariana Islands. The Aleutian Islands and Alaska seem to be out of the war – no news from there for a long time.

Wednesday, January 24, 1945 I had rather planned on going ashore today, but changed my mind. I spent most of the day writing letters and trying to find some wood to make a box to send Marian's slippers home. Everything is going as well as ever here in the Philippines. The Americans are but a few miles from Clark Field, as of yet the Japs haven't put up any strong resistance. Only on our left flank in the mountains, just across the bay from here are the Japs resisting with any success. War ships here in the gulf are throwing shells into the beach and hills day and night. You can see puffs of smoke rise where the projectiles hit. In Europe, the Russians are but 150 miles from Berlin. Hitler has gone to the eastern front to personally conduct operations. The Americans on the western front are again making progress.

Thursday, January 25, 1945 I had planned going ashore today, but no shore leave was given as our ship pulled anchor and went over to the other side of the harbor to take on water from a water boat. We were alongside most of the morning, and at this point only about half a mile from the Jap position on shore. We could plainly see artillery shells bursting in the hills. The Japs have never fired their guns into the bay. I guess the only explanation of this is, that they would give away their positions. There is hardly anything for we Army fellows to do aboard ship. We loaf around most of the time. Once in a while we have to help unload supplies, but that is all. The latest news is that the Russians are 139 miles from Berlin. We had a show in the mess hall tonight.

Friday, January 26, 1945 The landing barge has discontinued coming out to our ship to take fellows on shore leave so consequently not so many get off the ship now, as a whale boat is the only other means of transportation and it will only hold a dozen or so. Today was just another routine day. I spent most of the time copying Jap and American press reports. I wrote Marian a letter and played Sgt. Quelen a few games of checkers. The Russians are still on the march and now in one sector but 125 miles from Berlin. Reports state the Germans are all but in a state of panic. Our forces here on Luzon have taken part of Clark Field and are still driving ahead without meeting any stiff Jap resistance. The same routine today. I guess it will be quite a while before this boat pulls out. I suppose not until our forces take Manila. Large numbers of supply ships are still coming in. I wonder what all those Japs over in the hills think of all the ships load of equipment that is coming in under their noses. I wonder if they hear any of their own propaganda. Conditions around the gulf are very quiet. In fact too quiet to make a fellow feel very comfortable. There hasn't been any Jap air craft over the ships in the gulf for the past number of days. At the present time is their best opportunity for raids, as the nights are clear and the moon is full. Our smoke screen conceals the ships to some extent, but I doubt, if very effectively at the present time. It is reported the Russians have inflicted 250,000 casualties on the Germans, as well as completed the trapping of 200,000 Germans in East Prussia. The Russians are 125 miles east of Berlin now. The Americans on the western front have erased all traces of the German attack into Belgium and are making gains into the Siegfried Defense Line (German defense line- Ardennes offensive.)

Sunday, January 28, 1945 I planned going to church this morning but it was to be this afternoon. After waiting around this afternoon we were told there were no services over at the ship to which we intended to go. I wrote a few letters this afternoon and spent the rest of the time in my bunk. Our forces are still driving ahead here on Luzon and have now captured Clark Field which has 13 first class air strips, as well as a large Army post. Our forces are now only 45 miles from Manila. American bombers have been bombing Corregidor Island (*C. Philippines – a POW camp for Russian, French, British, & American prisoners were held by the Germans.*) for the past two days. It is general opinion that our ship will go to Manila as soon as we have taken it.

Monday, January 29, 1945 Today is Sally's birthday. *(My dad's sister)* It is times like this that makes me realize everyone at home as well as myself are getting older. I have never gotten used to being away from home. I know I never will. It is nearly three years since I left. The latest rumor is that many of we fellows in on this operation will be sent home on rotation as soon as Luzon is taken. Rotation is like dreaming of something that is always just out of your reach. I think maybe I will see China before I do the United States. Right now we are only about 600 miles from the China coast.

Tonight two Jap planes came over the convoy here in the gulf. One of them was shot down. They say two Japs landed safely, but when our rescue boat came to pick them up they started to get nasty so they gave them the works.

Tuesday, January 30, 1945 Went on shore today. I didn't do much running around but went over to see some of my old friends. There was a little excitement while I was there. One of our A-20 light bombers came low over our heads not more than 500 feet high. As he went past we could see that one engine was dead. Just across the road about a quarter mile from us he dropped about 15 parachute bombs that exploded nearly all at the same time. Luckily no one was in the area where the bombs dropped. Filipinos and soldiers came running from all over. The G.I.s thought the plane had crashed and the Filipinos thought it was a Jap bomber.

I ate dinner over at an army camp nearby. The area is roped off to keep Filipino civilians out, but just across the fence a great number of Filipinos gathered with small cans and buckets to collect whatever food is left in the soldier's mess kits. After the soldiers are fed, the Filipinos line up and are given whatever is left. The Japs certainly starved these people to death.

From where I met my friends, to the camp where we ate dinner, the shortest route was through a cemetery. The Filipinos do not bury their dead in the ground, but in cement vaults a little larger than a regular casket on top of the ground. Along the front of the cemetery is a brick wall which in reality is a large vault. It is built some eight feet thick "honey combed" with vaults. The war has left its mark in this cemetery. This burial wall as well as many of the vaults in the cemetery have been broken open by shell fire exposing the remains of the buried bodies.

In the afternoon I went with one of my friends over to a Filipino's house to get his laundry. This was a much better house than other Filipino houses I have seen, built on poles, some ten feet from the ground. The entrance was on the ground level being a sort of small porch with a tiled floor. From there a wide stairs went up into the house. The inside of the house seemed quite modern, having hard wood floors and woodwork out and out. The floors were highly polished and everything neatly arranged. The windows were of a unique design. A certain kind of seashell ground down and highly polished until transparent, formed the pains. These were set into the frame work of the window in small two inch squares, making a sort of checker board design. These people, while down and out now, were at one time no doubt well fixed.

We learned that they owned a sugar mill which due to the enormous inflation, ceased to be at all profitable. After eating some coconut candy, given up, we went back to camp. It was rather late so I went back to the boat landing to catch the barge back to our ship.

Wednesday, January, 1945 The way I feel today I don't intend going ashore again for quite a while. A fellow gets pretty well worn out tramping around. One fellow on board this ship caught a ride and went over around the bay where the Japs are fighting. He said after seeing what our boys are going through he won't complain again about his work.

The Russians are still on the move, and now around 100 miles from Berlin, Germany. The Americans have taken a small portion of Siegfried fortifications. The American advance in Europe seems mostly at a stand- still now.

Here in Luzon another invasion force has landed at Subic Bay (C. Philippines) just above Bataan Peninsula (C. Philippines) Our troops advanced 11 miles inland before seeing a single Jap.

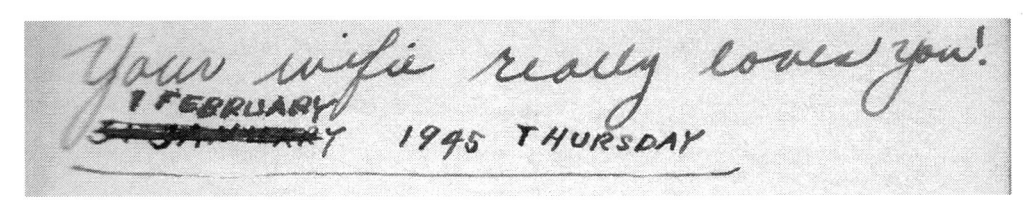

Your wife really loves you!
1 FEBRUARY 1945 THURSDAY

Thursday, February 1, 1945 I guess I will never get used to being away from Marian. Maybe one of these days rotation will come my way. I have tried to make the folks at home believe I am stuck over here for the duration. I think it best that way. The top line was written by Marian when she sent me this book. I am now watching the switch board which keeps me up until 11:30 PM every other night. "Juden" the fellow I have played checkers with quite often in the last number of months, and while we were stationed at Port Moresby, blew up today. I have always been able to beat him quite easily. He has always been a poor loser and I believe he has stuck to playing with me with a stubborn determination to get the edge on me. Lately I have been blasting him more than usual and today, after he had lost by a big margin in several games, he threw the checkers down and said he didn't like to play checkers with me. We exchanged a few hot words and then he got up and walked away. So that is that. I guess our ship won't leave here until our troops take Manila. Everyone expects Manila to be in ruins when we take it. Either the Japs will choose to make a stand there or burn the city before they leave. All of Clark Field is ours now and our troops are around 30 miles from Manila.

Friday, February 2, 1945 I just discovered I have been dating the last few days wrong. The fellows have rigged a diving board up on the fantail of our ship which we use when we go in swimming. I have been in the past couple of days and think I will go in everyday that I can. One fellow stands lookout with a rifle in case any sharks come around. Occasionally jelly fish come around when we are in swimming, and then we have to get out. A jelly fish has a sort of seaweed membrane on its body which if it touches you is very poisonous. The Russians are sure on the march. They are now 69 miles from Berlin. Here in Luzon the Americans are but 18 miles from Manila. American troops have made another landing south of Manila, meeting slight enemy resistance.

Saturday, February 3, 1945 Just another routine day aboard ship. I spent a little time working on an identification bracelet today. I tried making another bracelet for Marian but I ruined it. This evening it rained so a bunch of us took a shower out on the ship's fantail. The war news is of the greatest interest to us, as it gives us something of a "going home feeling." The Russians are now within 50 miles of Berlin, and as yet the Germans haven't checked their advance. It is expected the Germans will make a stubborn stand soon. Here on Luzon our troops are steadily closing in on Manila. Our forces now have the Jap army forces cut in half here on Luzon. Enemy forces in the south cannot assist the northern troops or vice versa. The Jap radio continues to pour out its propaganda. They don't elaborate on their false Luzon victories quite so much now, but are "ballyhooing" their China campaign to a greater extent.

Sunday, 4 February 4, 1945 This morning a bunch of us went to church over to a battle ship that is anchored a few miles away. This afternoon I worked on an identification bracelet I am making. It has been a little time now since my last mail. I guess we can't hope for any letters until after our forces move into Manila. Since our troops took Subic Bay, most of the ships have left. There is only a fraction of the number here now, that was here on invasion day. The war is still progressing as well as ever. The Russians are now but 50 miles from Berlin and steadily keeping up their advances. The Americans are pounding the Siegfried defenses, and have broken through in at a few points.

Monday, February 5, 1945 Things remain as quiet as ever, and there is very little for us to do aboard ship. It rained quite hard this afternoon so I took a shower out in the rain. Reports came through this afternoon that our troops have entered Manila. Tokyo is now saying that Manila is of little importance and the battle for Luzon is still to be fought. They are playing up the stand the Japs are making on our let flank across the bay from here, which was never one of our main objectives. The Russians are still advancing towards Berlin. They are now 46 miles away. We had a show on board tonight.

Tuesday, February 6, 1945 This morning we pulled anchor and went over on the other side of the bay for water. Another boat was tied along-side the Liberty ship that we were to tie up to, so we dropped anchor. At this point we were only about half a mile off the shore which is mostly controlled by the Japs. Artillery shells were bursting here and there up in the hills a short distance from the beach. It was quite late before we finally tied up to this Liberty ship. We were unable to get water, but we took on some supplies. Some of we Army fellows went aboard the Liberty and helped load boxes down in the hold. On this ship were many Americans who had just recently been rescued from a Jap concentration camp down near Manila. Some of the fellows talked to some of them. They told our fellows about how they had been treated and that the Japs promised that if the Americans came they would turn their machine guns on them. One of our fellows was told by one of these prisoners that they didn't receive much news, but over a period of time they succeeded in constructing a radio. They had to keep it hid all the time, which they did by passing it around among the prisoners. The main hiding place they chose was under the steps to the Jap general's quarters. The Japs tried for a long time to find this radio, but were never able to do so. With this radio the Americans were able to pick up an Australian station and once in a while an American [station] and get some idea on how the war progressing. However, this was on rare occasions, as the radio had to be on the move from one to the other or kept in hiding. The only other news they got was Jap propaganda. In September they saw the first American plane fly over the camp, and then they felt the Americans must be on the way back.

They didn't hold much hope of rescue, as the Japs had promised to kill them if that day ever came. This fellow said that when the rangers did arrive a Jap machine gun in a watch tower near-by was turned on the camp, but being there was a long drainage ditch near by the prisoners in that area took cover, and none of them were shot. A few rangers were killed at the main gate when they made their attack, but there were few casualities.

Wednesday, February 7, 1945 After the main water tanks had run dry the only water left was from a tank that hadn't been used only for laundry for a long time, and therefore not very much suited as drinking water. The ship's doctor put a double dose of chlorine in the water, which made it even worse, and many of the fellows are half sick from it. While our troops have taken the northern part of Manila the south part of the city is still in Jap hands. It is no surprise that the Japs are burning and blowing up many department stores, theaters, hotels, post office, banks, and power and water works, as well as looting private homes for whatever they can find. The Japs are intent on destroying as much of Manila as possible, before we drive them out, and just for the sake of destruction, not for any military reasons. In Europe the Russians are 35 miles from Berlin on more than a hundred mile front. The Russians are poised at the Odon River, which is the last natural barrier before a final plunge to Berlin. On the western front the Americans have succeeded in breaching the Siegfried Line at several points. At the Rhine River. the heaviest fighting is before Cologne (W. Germany.)

Thursday, February 8, 1945 The harbor is practically bare of ships now. All of them have left except a few war ships over on the other side of the gulf. We are on strict water ration now as it is hard to tell when we will be able to get anymore. The evaporators which are used to make fresh water from salt water are out of order, and being repaired. We get hardly enough water to wash in and none to bath in. Things are the same old routine here on board. Nearly all the fellows are paying close attention to the news lately, which we receive by radio from San Francisco. All of us are anxious for the Manila area to be cleared of the Japs, because as soon as this is accomplished we are to go down there. Our bombers are pounding Corregidor (C. Philippines) daily and it shouldn't be very long before it is neutralized. The latest rumor is that it may not be very long after Luzon is liberated, that Formosa or China will be invaded. Planes from our fleet air craft carriers have been pounding Formosa daily for quite a while now. Conditions remain as quiet as ever in the gulf. No Jap planes have come over in a long time now. Even though we have had it very easy as far as the Japs are concerned, the waiting for something to happen is nearly as strenuous as the real thing. There is heavy fighting still going on over across the bay in the hills. Artillery shells send up clouds of smoke in this area almost constantly. This battle field is but a short distance from the point where we landed from the L.S.T.

Friday, February 9, 1945 Nothing usual today. The same routine. The ship's water lines still have a lot of chlorinated water in them so the drinking water is still pretty bad. We heard that a lot of mail has arrived in the convoy that just came in last night. I still continue to write letters, which is sure a tough job. First a fellow's letters are limited by censorship – second, living in an area 180 feet long by 30 feet wide, doesn't give you much to write about, and third – not receiving any letters at all, I have little ambition to write.

Saturday, February 10, 1945 Today was inspection day and I worked most of the morning up until inspection, getting our quarters straightened around. The captain came through and everything seemed to be in order. I worked on the switch board this morning, which isn't much of a job, as we rarely get a call. The war news is still as bright as ever. The Russians have more or less slowed their drive on Berlin. The Russians seem to be working out a huge encircling movement which is now threatening Berlin, on more than a hundred mile front.

Sunday, February 11, 1945 This morning a bunch of us got in the whale boat and went over across the bay to another ship to church. Services were held out on deck, and most of the congregation was sailors, in fact I didn't see another Army fellow there besides myself. After getting back to our ship we had dinner. I spent part of the afternoon working on my identification bracelet. All the mail we heard about coming in was not for any of us on this ship. We had a show in the mess hall tonight.

Monday, February 12, 1945 Today I heard that Bernie Suitter has arrived. He was one of our team members that we left behind in the hospital at Hollandia, New Guinea. Tomorrow I hope to go over to the beach and see him. We were told that here after we will have our movies up on deck. This will sure be a lot better than the mess hall. Much more room and a lot cooler.

Tuesday, February 13, 1945 Today Carling Castelman and myself went on shore leave. The first thing I tried to do was find Bernie Suitter. I learned that he left early this morning to go down south, so I didn't get to see him. Castelman had a job to do that was next to impossible. He had a letter written by a Filipino that had been passed to a number of soldiers in his outfit, first starting somewhere in New Guinea. This letter was written to one of his family who lives in a small town a short distance from Dagupan. This Filipino's family hadn't heard from him for three years and this letter was to inform them he was OK and well. We hitch hiked to quite a number of little towns that took us most of the morning and part of the afternoon. Finally after quite a bit of trouble in getting rides we arrived in a small town called _____ *(my dad neglected to fill in the name of the town)*. After inquiring around we learned where these people lived which was a half mile walk. After a short time we got there and found we had the right place. These people invited us into their home, which was typical Filipino, being built of bamboo with thatched sides and roof. This house has about five rooms, the walls separating them being made of thin bamboo reeds. These people were overwhelmed at receiving this letter, and even though our time was growing short, they insisted that we have something to eat. In a short time the lady of the house had fixed us some fish, shrimp, rice, coffee and bananas. We ate in a hurry, and then bid them good bye, and started hitch hiking back. Luckily we caught a ride that took us back to Dagupan. When got back to the boat landing the barge was waiting for us. I was pretty tired so I went to bed early tonight.

Wednesday, February 14, 1945 Nothing much doing today. I laid around most of the time and wrote a few letters. There is still no mail for us. All of us are anxiously waiting the return of the 849, as on its trip to Leyte they were to pick up our mail. That ship should return any day now: all the men aboard worked after dark tonight unloading ship's stores from a barge.

Thursday, February 15, 1945 There was sure a big "row" today. It seems while unloading supplies last night, a box of peanuts and a dozen fountain pens were stolen. These were supplies for the ships P.X. This is one thing where this ship falls short. There always has been (as long as I have been aboard) a lot of steeling. Today things came to a head and the captain really put his foot down. The ship was searched from stem to stern for any stolen articles. Nothing was found, however. No doubt the guilty parties dropped the stuff over the side. The result of the whole deal is that the ship's store has been closed. Today Marian and I have been married three years, eight months. It has been a month since her last letter.

Friday, February 16, 1945 Early this morning we tuned in on "Radio Tokyo" to listen to their version of the news. They announced that at 7:30 A.M. carrier based air craft from our fleet had raided Tokyo air drones and military installations. Of course the Jap version of the attack was fatal with the inflicting of heavy loss to our planes. They stated that this was the first time light air craft had been used against the Japanese homeland. About fifteen minutes after the Jap announcement a news flash from San Francisco told of our attack against Japan.

> *Keep that twinkle in your eye!*

Saturday, February 17, 1945 Today was inspection day but being I worked from midnight until eight I slept most of the morning and didn't take part in inspection. News reports came through today that 30,000 marines have landed on the Bonin Islands, which are but around six hundred miles from Japan. The above entry from Marian. No mail yet.

Sunday, February 18, 1945 I didn't get to go to church today as I had to pull K.P. all day. It looks like the navy officers are taking advantage of we army fellows. There is now one army fellow and one navy, that has to serve chow. Even though there are but nine of we army fellows aboard, we still have to take half the load. American air born troops have now landed on Corregidor (C. Philippines) and it seems only a matter of time until we take it. The Japs in Manila are now backed up into a comparatively small pocket. Getting them out is a very difficult task, as the Japs have refused to release the large number of Filipino civilians in this area and our shelling are bound to kill many of them. Our troops now have full control of Bataan Peninsula, which was held so long by the Americans in the early part of the war. The war news from Europe is still encouraging; the Russian advance has turned mostly toward the north toward Danzig (N. Poland). It seems the purpose of the Russians [is] to cut off supply lines of the Germans, from their coastal ports. On the western front, American, British, Canadian and

French forces are still making gains through the Siegfried Line. In Burma the British are still making gains toward Mandalay (C. Burma). In China the Japs at some points are still advancing and along the old Burma Road the Chinese are on the march.

Monday, February 19, 1945 It seems that relations between the Army and Navy here aboard ship is beginning to tighten up to some extent. One Naval officer in particular resents the Army's presence aboard ship and would welcome a row. We Army fellows feel this K.P. deal isn't on the square, but we have all agreed to put up with it, as we still have a pretty good thing of it here on board. When it comes right down to a point, this is an Army controlled deal through the orders of General Aiken personally. This also doesn't set so good with the Navy, as our extended stay here in the gulf, the Navy feels is our fault, being we are in the Army. Went swimming today, and got my nerve and dove off a section of the bridge. It was pretty high for me [27 ft.] Had a show up on deck tonight. Had to stop it for a little while because of an alert. No Japs came over.

Tuesday, February 20, 1945 Castelman and I went on shore today. It was nearly noon before the L.C.M. came out. When we got to Dagupan we went down to a tent area where some of Castelman's friends were. We borrowed mess kits and went over to the chow tent which is a short walk through the cemetery. After dinner Castelman and myself got into a jeep with one of his friends and went down to the post office. While we were there I made an attempt at trying to get a line on where some of our mail might be, but it was the same as ever, no luck. After spending a little time at the post office, we decided to take a drive out to the air base. The road was fairly good, but rather rough from so many trucks traveling on it. A little ways from the road, just outside of town was a Jap Zero that had crashed. On out to the air base, which was but a few miles, we stopped and watched planes take off and land for a while, and then we came back to town. We drove back up to Castelman's friend's tent. Being I had to do a little looking around for one of my Navy friends, I went back up town and agreed to meet Cass at the boat landing at 4 P.M. I bought a pair of wood sandals for a friend who was on board ship, which cost him 18 pesos or nine dollars. This was sure an enormous price, but he wanted them so that was that. After this I stopped in at a small barber shop and got a haircut. This Filipino did a very good job but he was awfully slow. The price was one peso. I then walked up to the telecopy building where some of our outfit is staying to try and make a further check on our mail. To my surprise I learned that two sacks had just been sent out to the ship. I walked up to the boat landing where I waited for Castelman. In the meantime I traded some cigarettes for some Jap invasion money that some Filipino had. We sure had difficulty in getting a ride out to our ship. Not having any luck at this landing we had a Filipino take us across the river in a small boat over where some L.C.M.s were loading and unloading. After inquiring at nearly every boat in a long line, we finally found one that would take us down to the mouth of the river where the control boat was anchored. We felt our chances of catching a boat going out would be pretty good from there. Luck was with us though as the boat we were on was directed to go out into the bay, so we got back to our ship OK. This day really wound up with a bang. I received 14 letters, most of which were from Marian.

Wednesday, February 21, 1945 Nearly everyone on board received letters yesterday and all the fellows are in better spirits now. This was the first mail the Army or Navy aboard this ship had received in over a month. The tension between the Army and the Navy seems to have taken a back-seat for the time being. It looks like we will be stuck here in Lingayen Gulf (N. Philippines) for quite a while yet even though American troops have neutralized Corregidor (N. Philippines) and our ships are in Manila Bay.

Thursday, February 22, 1945 I was lucky in finding a spare cot down where our gear is stored away so I slept on deck tonight. There was a red alert for about forty five minutes, but no Japs came over. The moon is coming full and this is an opportune time for the Japs to come over. Today we pulled anchor and went over to the other side of the gulf and tied up alongside a large transport, and to our supplies. Our captain didn't have any luck getting any water, even though our ship's supply is getting rather low again. Had a show on deck again tonight. A bunch of fellows in a small boat started over from a Liberty ship to see our show. The water was rough and about halfway over their boat went down. Some of our fellows got in a whale boat and went over and fished them out. Today when our ship was going over to the other side of the gulf I saw the Liberty ship "Edwin T. Meredith." This ship was named after the founder of the company I worked for before the war, and where I hope to return.[49]

---

[49] My father did return to Meredith Pub. Co. where he worked until he retired after some 40 plus years.

Friday, February 23, 1945 Slept on deck again last night. Got a little cool before morning. Even though my regular bunk is much more comfortable than this cot on deck, I can still rest much better. Our quarters are so hot that it is nearly impossible to sleep in them at all after the sun has been beating down on the deck all day long. An air conditioning unit is being installed to cool the Army's quarters. Of course this is to be for General Aiken's benefit, but we Army fellows should get the benefit of it also. This is another thing that doesn't help Army/Navy relations. It is my guess that this unit will not be in operation until the General comes back.

Saturday, February 24, 1945 Inspection day today. I spent a couple of hours washing bulkheads and helping to clean up our quarters in general. It seems the tension between the Army & Navy fellows is dialing down: Went swimming this afternoon. Had a show tonight.

Sunday, February 25, 1945 I spent the day on K.P. today, which is a pretty tough job on Sunday. However, this gave me a priority on the ice cream and I had about all I could eat. Sunday dinner here on this ship is the equal to Thanksgiving dinners we have in the Army. Today we had roast turkey, & dressing, cranberry sauce, potatoes, corn, spinach, cherry pie, ice cream, and lemonade to drink. I was rather tired tonight, so I went to bed early. I neglected to mention the fact in yesterday's entry, that the twenty fourth marked the end of my third year in the Army.

Monday, February 26, 1945 We pulled anchor this morning and went over on the other side of the gulf to take on water from another ship. We were but a short distance off shore, and in this area the Japs are still putting up stiff resistance. Artillery action is exchanged constantly and we could see shells flashing up in the hills nearby. We returned to our original anchorage late this afternoon. The captain left early this morning to fly down to Manila to see Gen. Aiken. All of us hope that when the captain returns tomorrow it will be with orders to go to Manila. We are about the last ship left here that came in here on the invasion day.

Tuesday, February 27, 1945 I helped one of the Navy fellows take down a section of ventilator pipe today in preparation to installing the air conditioning unit. They say this air conditioning unit must be installed by the second. If this is true, it must not be long before the general will be back on board again. The captain returned this afternoon, but no one knows if we are to leave or not. Some think we will pull out on the second, but of course that is a guess. The last resistance has been eliminated in Manila. General Mac Arthur gave a speech from that city. B.29 and carrier based planes again attacked Tokyo. Hardly any Jap resistance was encountered. The Russian advance has slowed to some extent, with their forces consolidating in an encircling movement around Berlin. The Americans on the western front have advanced within 17 miles of Cologne (W. Germany) fourth largest German industrial city. Farther south, American forces are closing in on Saarbruken (NW Germany). Things seem to be more or less at a standstill in Italy. In Burma the British are still making gains toward Mandalay (C. Burma) against stubborn Jap resistance. In China, Chinese forces have succeeded in recapturing a former American Air Base. There was a show on deck tonight, but I had to watch the switch board so I didn't see it. It is a full moon now but no Japs have been around. The Jap air force must be a thing of the past here on Luzon.

Wednesday, February 28, 1945 The same routine as ever. There is a rumor going around that we may leave for Manila, March 2. We had a red alert tonight and some Jap reconnaissance planes came over. They stayed up very high and out of range of our "ack ack." I guess there is some mix up on our mail, as there was supposed to be some more on the way up from the Subic Bay

Thursday, March 1, 1945 We were informed today that the mail that was over on the beach for us was sent back down south because some officer who didn't know what the score was, as to our location. We were also informed the mail had once more headed back this way, and we should receive it tomorrow. We had another alert tonight. A Jap plane dropped some bombs over by the air strip and evidently hit a fuel dump as we could see the glow in the sky from a large fire. One of the ship's officers said that only about one ninth of the modern business district of Manila is now standing. The newer section of the city is in ruins. He said that the Japs, in destroying many of the large buildings, placed drums of gasoline on each floor, and then set fire to the buildings. Dead Japs are still laying around the streets of the old city section, where they made their last stand.

Friday, March 2, 1945 This morning we pulled up anchor and went over on the other side of the gulf, where we tied up alongside a repair ship, the remainder of the job of installing the air conditioning unit is to be done by them. At this location we were only about a quarter of a mile from the beach. Inland up in the hills, not more than two miles, the Japs are still well entrenched. There is the sound of artillery and the puffs of smoke where the projectiles hit. We remained tied along-side the repair ship all night. During the show that we had up on deck there was a red alert, which lasted nearly an hour. Reports were that there was a Jap plane flying twelve miles distance from our area. The Jap never came over our section of the gulf and we finally continued with the show.

Heading to Subic Bay

Saturday, March 3, 1945 We received definite word that we were to leave for Subic Bay and from there go on to Manila. The repair ship crew worked on the air conditioning unit until noon, and though the job is not completed they had to stop. We pulled away after chow and went out into the gulf where we joined a convoy of which we are to act as an escort vessel.

The ship Joe was on heading for Manila — the Japan

Sunday, March 4, 1945 The China Sea is very calm and our ship doesn't roll or pitch to speak of. All on board are enjoying this voyage very much, as we were very tired of laying around Lingayen (N. Philippines) Gulf for the past seven weeks. In the middle of the afternoon we arrived at Subic Bay. This is a small harbor compared with Lingayen Gulf, but would be twice as large as the harbor at Port Moresby, New Guinea. In some respects they are similar, as Subic Bay is closed in by mountains and hills, and closed in from the sea by a large island. The south shore of Subic Bay is the upper portion of Bataan Peninsula. I was on K.P. all day today.

Monday, March 5, 1945 Shortly after noon a bunch went on shore leave over to a small island which used to be Fort Weems, a Navy base and fortification guarding the entrance to Subic Bay. This island strong-hold was heavily fortified by the Americans before the beginning of the war, but at the time of the Japanese invasion of the Philippines they bombed this island fortress, at about this same time American and Filipino troops were retreating into the Bataan Peninsula. The Americans manning this fort abandoned it and with-drew into Bataan also. After the Philippines fell to the Japs, this island was not again put into operation by the Japs. They evidently felt quite secure in their new won territories. Only a small garrison of Jap troops were stationed on this island. Many of the long-range naval guns were removed and placed on the island of Corregidor, which guards the entrance to Manila Bay. As is typical of the Japs, everything was left just as it was when the Americans moved out. The Japs never bothered to clean up the wreckage of buildings and fortifications. Only the main gun installations that were undamaged by their bombings, did they man.

After reaching the island we went ashore. The pier is still in quite good repair, but everything else on this island, which is very small – about a mile wide by two miles long was total wreckage. There had been many nice buildings, such as the administration building, hospital, barracks, light plant, etc. All these were flat, just before the Americans returned to Subic Bay, our Air Force had given this island a royal plastering "1945 style" so all in all this island is quite a mess. Huge bomb [craters] are evenly spaced over nearly the whole island. The gun emplacements, while not all of them totally destroyed, were made useless by near misses.

The Navy fellows in our crowd were allowed to go only so far away from the beach, but being some of us were Army fellows we went on by the Navy "shore politics." On up the hill we came to the main gun emplacements. These defensive positions were – or had been – huge concrete structures half buried on the side of the hill away from the sea. The Naval guns were placed in concrete turrets on top of this structure, so that they were just above the crest of the hill, and commanded a broad view of the sea.

Many such gun emplacements were located along the high ground of the island, which was a low ridge that ran nearly its full length. All guns and ammunition of the island were all American made. Row upon row of ammunition magazines were filled with powder and artillery shells of all kinds. Some of these magazines had been blown up, but most of them were still in good condition. One fortification that we saw had evidently suffered a direct hit by a heavy bomb. The powder magazine had exploded and completely blown it out of the ground. All that remained was two guns on their concrete foundations on each side of a huge creator about forty feet across by thirty feet deep. Blocks of concrete four feet in diameter were hurled hundreds of yards.

During our walk around this area we were very careful as to where we walked, and we picked up nothing. It was a good spot for booby traps. About 3 P.M. we walked back to the dock to wait for our whale boat to come and pick us up. Being we had quite a little time to wait, we decided to go for a swim. The water off the pier was crystal clear. The clearest water I think I have ever seen. Even though it looked to be not more than six feet deep, it was actually twenty four. "Skipper" the ship's dog had quite a time in the water. He would jump off the pier and swim around until one of us helped him back up the ladder. Finally our whale boat came. We arrived back at the ship shortly after first chow, but in time for the last one.

There was sort of a mix up on our coming down here to Subic Bay. It seems our ship came under Navy orders as escort for the convoy, but the Army, to whom this ship is attached, didn't know anything about it. We now have to get further orders to proceed on to Manila. I sure hope we are not stuck here for a number of weeks, as we were at Lingayen (N. Philippines) Gulf. I saw a friend of mine today on the island. The last I saw or heard of him, he was in Hollandia (N. New Guinea).

Tuesday, March 6, 1945 Just a dull day aboard ship. Some of the fellows who didn't get to go over to the island yesterday, went over today. This evening we pulled anchor and went over to the water ship to replenish our supply. We have received our orders to leave for Manila at 4 A.M. tomorrow. They say the voyage to Manila will take but a few hours and we should be there by noon tomorrow.

Wednesday, March 7, 1945 When I awoke this morning we had been underway two hours. By the time I got up on deck the sun was just coming up and in the distance the island of Corregidor (C. Philippines) was just in sight. From the angle I was looking at it looked like a well raised pancake, with the Bataan Peninsula just to the left. Far across the bay to the right is Batangas Province (C. Philippines). Being we were acting as escort vessel, we "zig zagged" ahead of the convoy, from one side to the other. Due to this irregular course, at one time we passed within a short distance of Corregidor. I was fortunate in getting a view of the island through a pair of binoculars. You could see many of the islands fortifications, and many of them that had been knocked out by our Air Force recently. Just shells of many of the buildings were still standing on top of the island, and from this distance, many of them still looked to be in good condition. We could see the "stars and stripes" flying from a flagpole high on the island. Corregidor is shaped something like a "tad pole." The main part of the island seems to be nearly round with a narrow extending tail stretching in toward Manila Bay. The main part of the island must be something of a mile in diameter with the narrow section about three miles long. We were never as close to Bataan as we were to Corregidor, as we passed through the south entrance into Manila Bay. We were able to get a good visual of Bataan when we first approached the entrance to the Bay. Bataan to the most part is very mountainous, with two outstretching peeks rising about two thousand feet high, a short distance inland. For a stretch of about two miles leading down to the beach, closest to Corregidor, the terrain seems quite level. A Filipino on board told me that this was the point of the American/Filipino last stand on Bataan. This Filipino, one of a group, that came aboard at Subic Bay, and had been a guerrilla, talked in broken English, but was very interesting to talk to. He had been in the battle of Bataan and after it fell he escaped to Corregidor. When Corregidor fell, he was taken prisoner. He told of a six day march without food or water, to the concentration camp. Any soldier who dropped out of ranks from exhaustion was shot. At night they were made to squat or sit in small bunches, not allowing the prisoners enough room to stretch out. This Filipino said he was in the concentration camp three months until he escaped. Another Filipino said that he and his wife were in a different concentration camp about three miles apart, for the full time of the Jap occupation of Luzon, and he never was allowed to see her. Just to one side of Corregidor to the south is another small island fortress which is called *(Puerta Princesa – SW Philippines – my father didn't record a name for this island – I am assuming this is the island he is referring to.)* The Japs still hold this island, but it is no longer any good to them as our air craft bomb it continually. Our ship passed quite close to this island, being at one point about a quarter of a mile from its shore. After our convoy had passed by, a bunch of American dive bombers came over and one by one dove from high altitude toward a portion of the beach. We didn't notice these planes until the first bomb struck the island. Our first impulse was that these were Jap planes bombing our convoy. We sure had a ring-side seat watching our planes making their attack. Our bombers in a short time had made their first run. Flames billowed up in huge red balls and smoke covered most of the island. Our planes waited for the smoke of the first attack to clear, and then they repeated the same treatment in the next run. Three planes dove down one behind one another, dropping their bombs in the same area near the base of the cliff. These three planes had hardly flown clear when another of our planes came in toward the island, just above the water, strafing (to attack a position or troops on the ground with machine gun or cannon fire from a low flying aircraft.) With the three planes coming in high and the other coming in low, it gave you something of the idea of the old "football statue of liberty play." About 2 P.M. Manila came into view, as soon as we were close enough to see the outline of the business district along the water front, we could tell that all had been destroyed. One pleasant sight was 21 half sunken Jap ships over in one area of the harbor. We were told that some of the last Jap troops in Manila made their way out to these ships and tried to hide there. After dropping anchor we signaled over to the 849 that was tied up to the breakwaters over near the beach. They have some mail for us that will be brought out as soon as possible.

Thursday, March 8, 1945 Late last evening our whale boat returned and brought a couple of bags of mail. I received two letters, two greeting cards, and some air mail envelopes, and stationery from Marian. This is the first mail I have received for quite a while. All of us are anxious to go ashore but I guess it will be quite a while before we will. On the south side of the harbor there is still heavy fighting going on. You can hear the sound of artillery firing constantly. We had a show on deck tonight.

Friday, March 9, 1945 Nothing unusual today. Wrote a few letters and laid around up on deck. They have been painting our quarters, and wet paint is everywhere. Being our quarters are so small, all of us have a good share of this fresh paint on our clothes. Most of we Army fellows aboard this ship are eligible for rotation, and are anxious to get ashore to try and find out if anything is being done. Not much is ever done for you if you are not on the scene.

Saturday, March 10, 1945 Dave and Keller went on shore today. They are the first ones to get off the ship to go into Manila (that is the first Army guys). I guess tomorrow they are going to start giving regular shore leave to the crew. The sailors who go ashore have to dress in Army fatigue clothes, as sailors are not authorized shore leave yet. I won't get shore leave tomorrow, as I have to work K.P. all day.

Sunday, March 11, 1945 Over half of the Army fellows went on shore leave today. I worked K.P. all day, and that is about the full story. Had a show on deck tonight.

Monday, March 12, 1945 Went on shore today. Manila is in equally as bad a state as was told me by the other fellows. The entire business district is in total ruins. Only the shells of some buildings remain standing. Most of the streets have been cleared of debris, but most of the side streets are still clogged. Burial squads are still busy, as many Japs are still being dug out of the ruins. The sailor friend who I was with and I, took a walk over to the walled city. It is just across the river and is the scene of some of the heaviest fighting. This was the point of the Jap's last stand in Manila. We were not permitted to go inside the walled city, as there are still many "booby traps" and mines. The smell of the dead was sickening so we didn't stay long. We got back to the dock about 4:30 PM, where the whale boat was waiting to take us back to the ship. The dock area is in ruins with many sunken ships and barges near the docks. There were some letters for me when I returned to the ship tonight.

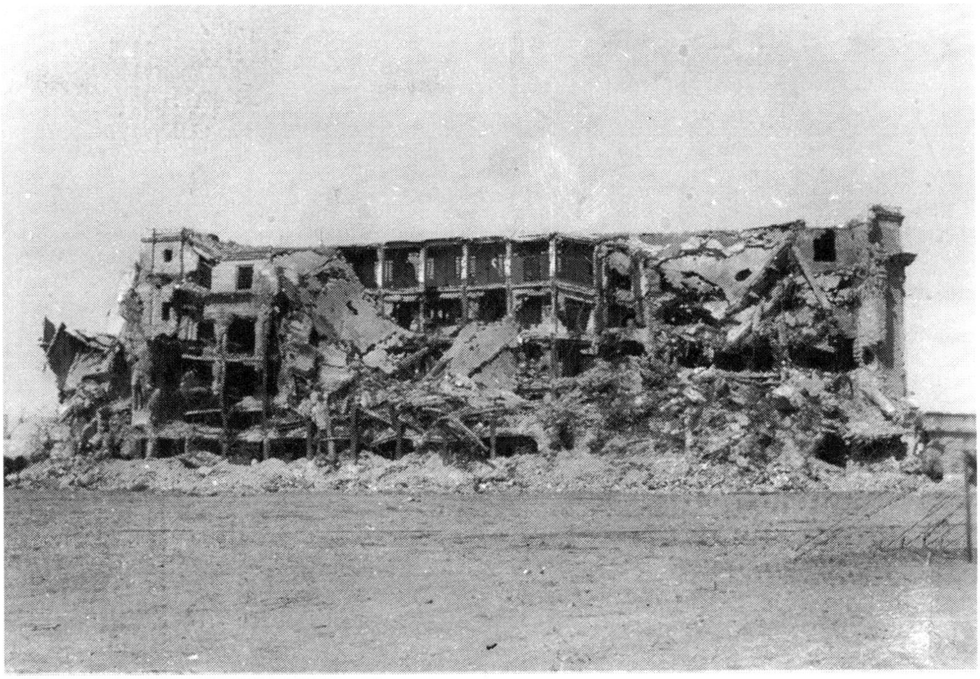

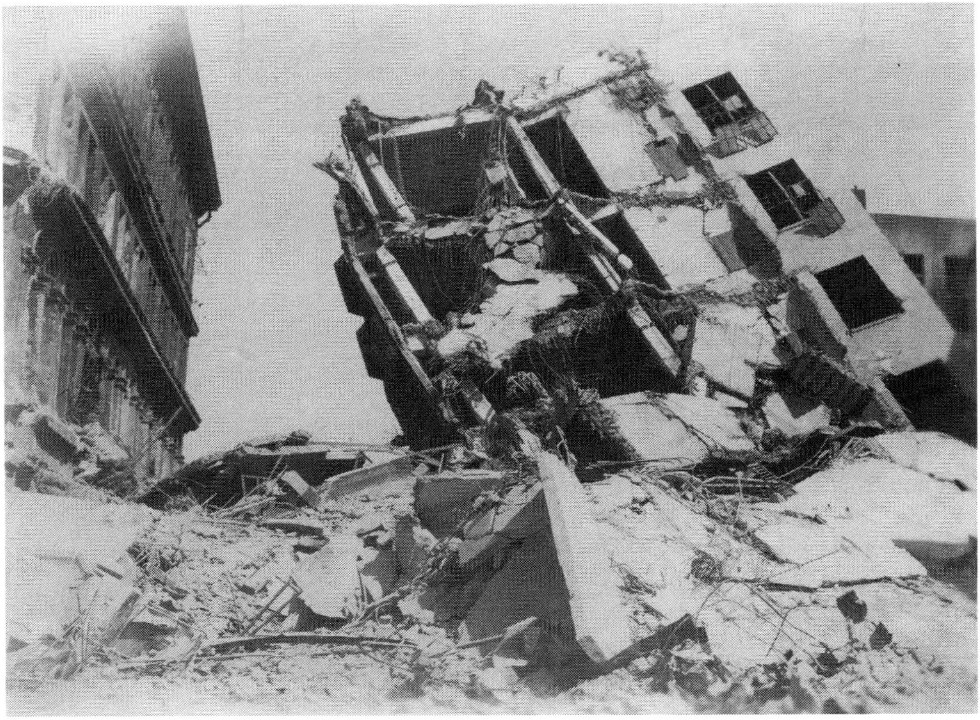

Tuesday, March 13, 1945 I am sure tired today from tramping all around Manila yesterday. One disagreeable thing about going on shore for the day is that it is difficult to get anything to eat. There are a few small cafes, but they are not at all clean, and prices are sky high. An egg sandwich is 3 pesos or about $1.50. Yesterday we had a sandwich that we brought along from the ship, and we bought a cup of coffee [.15 cents] I haven't felt so good all day.

Wednesday, March 14, 1945 I spent a pretty miserable night last night, continuously making trips to the toilet. I was in bed all day today with a temperature of 100 degrees. I don't know what made me so sick. It might have been the coffee I drank on shore, or it might have been the macaroni we had for supper. It didn't taste quite right when I ate it.

Thursday, March 15, 1945 I feel a little better today, but I still have a little fever and I am awfully weak. Laid around most all day and wrote a few letters. Marian and I have been married three years, nine months today. I wonder when her pictures will come.

Friday, March 16, 1945 Went on shore today with Keller, Dave, and myself. Caught a ride out to the transmitter station, which is quite a number of miles. When the Japs had control of Luzon, this was the location of one of their main propaganda stations in the far-east. The Japs didn't get a chance to destroy any of the antenna towers or buildings, so this is a pretty good set-up.

Upon our capture of the position, the Japs left a large transmitter behind, as well as a panel and switch board, which we are now using. We ate dinner at the transmitter station and then went over to the receiver station. A Chinese boy who owns a Packard Sedan took us over. He doesn't know how to drive so one of the Americans drives for him. There is quite a story connected to the automobile. During the Jap occupation, the Jap invasion money, while practically worthless, had a value of about fifty to one of regular Philippine pesos. Getting possession of Jap invasion money was quite simple. The Chinese boy convinced someone that his car was worth 15,000 Jap pesos, so he bought it.

This Chinese boy's next problem was to hide his car to keep the Japs from taking it from him. His solution was to put his car in the garage and then covered it with kindling and coke where he left it until the Americans came.

It was quite a little distance over to the receiver station. We passed by a former Jap air field, which we are now using as a light plane base. Wrecked Jap airplanes were all around the area, parked in back yards, anywhere to avoid detection from the air. I saw quite a few friends that had been in Port Moresby with me. We didn't spend much time here as we had to get back to the transmitters. One lucky break we had today, we succeeded in getting some clothing, etc. from the G.H.Q. supply. I got two duffle bags of which I was in bad need of as well as some pants, shirts and socks. A truck from the transmitter station took us back down to the dock where we caught a ride back to our ship in the whale boat.

Saturday, March 17, 1945 I am sure tired today from the trip ashore. I am still a little weak from the sick spell I had. The war news is still very favorable. The Americans are now through the Siegfried Line on the European western front. The Russians are making drives to the north around Danzig (N. Poland). The British in Burma are fighting in the suburbs of Mandalay (C. Burma). American troops have landed on Mindanao (C. Philippines) here in the Philippines.

Sunday, March 18, 1945 Frye, a sailor friend, and I went on shore leave today. We went over to look around for some gifts to send home. From our former observations, we were aware you can buy cheaper by trading cigarettes than by using money. Therefore we took a carton of cigarettes a piece. Merchandise and everything is outlandishly high. I bought Marian a handkerchief which cost me 3 pesos or $1.50. I bought the folks a small table scarf, which cost me two dollars. I priced a linen table cloth, napkins & doily set. This was 90 pesos or $45.00. And these Filipinos ask you a price like that with a straight face. We had some pictures taken at a sidewalk studio. These cost us 5 pesos or $2.50 for three prints that are not much good. We got back to the ship about 4 P.M.

Monday, March 19 , 1945 I started working K.P. today. One of the sailors who worked in the galley went A.W.O.L. so it left me with the job to do by myself. They had one guy for breakfast, but he took off. I got sore and told them I didn't know where the Navy guy had gone, but if he came back they could find me in the Army quarters. I got by the noon meal about the same way.

The afternoon things sure wound up fast. We were told to pack all our gear, as we are leaving the ship, since it is going on convoy duty. We loaded our barracks bags in the whale boat late this afternoon and were taken over to the dock. After quite a long wait, a truck arrived and took us out to the receiver station. We were issued cots and assigned to our tents.

Tuesday, March 20, 1945 We reported to the lieutenant in charge this morning. I asked to be assigned to C.W. but it is doubtful if I will get it. I will probably be assigned to teletype. Being the schedule hadn't been made up by noon we were given permission to go into town. Queen and I looked around until we found the Signal Center. It seemed we looked around most of the so called down-town district before we found it. The Signal center is in the Trade and Commerce building, one of the few buildings with little damage. We saw quite a number of our old friends. It seems the complete old gang has arrived in Manila. We also picked up a stack of mail for the fellows out at the receiver station. Of this bunch of mail there were nearly thirty letters for me. Marian's picture was included in one of them. I was sure glad to receive her picture. It is the first one I have received in quite a long time. We had quite a time getting back out here to the receiver station. We caught a ride but went the wrong direction and circled around and ended up but a few blocks from where we started. We finally got straightened out and got out to the station in time for chow. There was a show a short distance from here tonight. It was a stage show put on by the Filipinos. We went over and saw part of it, but the show wasn't so good, so we left. I was sure tired tonight. Today was Marian's birthday.

Wednesday, March 21, 1945 Went to work this A.M. I am not on C.W. as I hoped I would be, but am working teletype which keeps me pretty busy. This is a pretty fair camp and the chow, while as usual comes from a can, isn't so bad. We get fresh potatoes quite often, and once in a while, fresh eggs. One thing I miss is the ice water we had on the ship.

Thursday, March 22, 1945 Laid around my tent most of the day, and wrote letters. Some of we fellows went over to another camp tonight to a show, after which, I hit the hay. Our camp site, as present, is about eighteen miles from the Jap lines. We can hear the sound of artillery day and night. One of these days a friend and I plan hitch hiking out that way.

Friday, March 23, 1945 Stayed around camp again today. I wrote letters this morning and slept most of the afternoon. This evening a friend and I walked over to a bomb disposal dump that is near-by. There was a great amount of Jap mortar shells, hand grenades, etc. Went to work at midnight.

Saturday, March 24, 1945 Today the same routine. Stayed around camp, wrote a few letters and that is about all. This evening a couple of fellows and myself walked a short distance up the road. Off to one side was the wreckage of what once was a beautiful home. We stopped to look around a little bit. In one corner of this former residence was an abandoned Jap artillery gun placed behind a wall that had enclosed the entire place. On the back of the lot, the owner that was a Chinese family that were living in a garage. We talked to this Chinese man for quite a little while. He told us the Japs took over his home and turned it into a fort a short time before the Americans came. As the Americans forces closed in on Manila the Japs abandoned this place, but not until they had burned and blew up this Chinaman's house. This house, he said, was built about a year before the Japs invaded the Philippines, at the cost of fifty thousand pesos or $25,000 dollars. He had been the owner of a large box factory, but when the Japs came they took everything, and shipped all his machinery back to Japan. About a year ago, this fellow said his father was killed by the Japs, as they thought he was anti-Japanese.

Sunday, March 25,1945 Worked the day shift today. I am gaining a little speed on the teletype, but I still have a long way to go to get any ways decent at the job. I will be glad when my turn comes to go on C.W. We are supposed to work one week teletype and two weeks C.W. Wrote Marian a letter this evening and went to bed early.

Monday, March 26, 1945 Worked five to midnight tonight, and I really put in a night's work. There is a rumor going around, and the only thing good about it is, it is not official. The latest dope is that individual rotation is at an end and here after only rotation will be in effect as a unit. We all know no signal unit will be sent home. Also the latest dope is that the 832nd is being disbanded and the personal being put into other units, which to the most part, have been overseas but a short time. It looks like my only hope of getting home will be to what degree of luck I have of getting a furlough home for 30 days. If this rumor is true, I will for sure be on this side of the world at the war's end. I would like to think the war over here could be won a year after Germany falls, but I believe a fellow would make money by betting it wouldn't be. I know all this talk is rumor, but being away from home so long makes one a sucker to rumors. I sure felt low tonight.

Tuesday, March 27, 1945 Today a friend and I started on a hitch hiking tour. We caught a few rides that took us to a small town that was up near the front lines. Being we had on our suntan uniforms we could go no further than this little town. To go on up to the front a fellow must carry a rifle and wear fatigues. This town, as are all other inhabited places the Japs passed through, is in complete ruins. We met a warrant officer who was driving a weapon's carrier, who said that if we wished to go up as far as the artillery, the next time if we intend to go, to wear our fatigue clothes and bring our rifles and he would take us. Walked over to the hospital tonight to the show. This hospital also suffered from Jap destruction. While they didn't have time to completely destroy the buildings many of them were set on fire.

Wednesday, March 28, 1945 Was supposed to go to work at midnight last night, but no one woke me so I slept on through. Nothing was said so I guess I wasn't needed very much. The American Armies on the western front in France are sure going to town. There has been a news blackout for the past few days, but reports state the Rhine River has been crossed at several places. The present offensive is reported to be called "The Last Battle of Germany."

Thursday, March 29, 1945 Today a friend and I decided to take a little jaunt up to the front. We wore our fatigues and carried our rifles. I don't know what good a rifle was to me, the clip I had was empty. After quite a number of rides, we arrived out to some flat country at the foot of the hills where most of the fighting was taking place. This, at one time, had been a Jap air base. Here and there were the wreckage of Jap planes. We stopped long enough to carve off a couple of pieces of aluminum. In this area, were strewn hundreds of Jap trucks. Most of them were Chevrolets, and Fords, but a few of them were something hatched up by the Japs. We learned that things were rather quiet up in the hills, at present, so we decided to catch a ride that would take us a ways farther. A captain and lieutenant came along in a jeep and picked us up. The road, as we drove into the hills, became a mass of steep hills and winding turns. No one would have to doubt this was combat country, as every once in a while you could hear a shell whizz over our head, and a few seconds later explode on a hill a mile or so away, where the Japs are dug in. At this point we were traveling parallel to the Jap lines. Due to the rugged country, their lines varied from one to five miles away. As we drove along we passed a number of wrecked Jap tanks, guns and numerous trucks. We rode on up to a forward camp site, where we stopped. Here everyone was packing their equipment in preparation to move. It seems the fellows in this spot were catching a lot of artillery fire from the Japs, and at night it was too hot a spot to be in. Our forces keep up constant artillery fire, while the Japs never open up until after dark. The Japs make every effort to conceal their artillery positions. Unless our forces spot a Jap artillery position, and make a direct hit, they are almost impossible to knock out. The Japs dig tunnels in the hills, and in them, they place the artillery piece. In the daytime the entrance is carefully camouflaged, with the gun pulled inside the tunnel. At night the Japs wheel it out and fire until daylight. Our troops are making progress against the Japs, but at present it is rather slow. All camp sites are dug in. Soldiers sleep in foxholes. Parking places for jeeps and old trucks are large ditches dug out with a bulldozer. We stayed but a short time, as we caught a ride back towards Manila in a truck, which at this point was around twenty-five miles. It was late afternoon when we arrived back at camp. After chow I went to bed, as I was dead tired. A fellow brought in a bundle of around forty letters for me this evening.

Friday, March 30, 1945 I was too tired to read my letters last night, so I took them to work with me this morning, sat on a slow circuit and read them.

The latest rumor out is that the 848 is going on another operation and we fellows will be back on board in a short time. They say there isn't to be much excitement on this operation, and a lot of guys are anxious to go. I rather hope I am one of them. The more I move around, the better I like it. The time passes much faster.

American forces in Europe are still shoving ahead. Not many details are given, but one captured German general stated that no organized resistance remained before Berlin and he thought things would terminate there.

Saturday, March 31, 1945 Didn't do much today but lay around and wrote a few letters. Reports have come through that American troops have landed on Ryukyu Island (Japan) located between Formosa (Taiwan) and Japan and they are only some 300 miles from Japan. The "anty" on rotation is still going up. It takes around 40 months now. It is like trying to grasp something always just out of reach. I am glad I have withheld any information I have had as to my personal rotation status, to Marian and the other folks at home. No need to have everyone in on this race which can't be won. Today is Mom's birthday.

Sunday, April 1, 1945 Today is Easter Sunday. George Kellar and I went into town with the intention of going to church. However, it was rather late when we arrived, and not knowing just where to go, we didn't attend church.

We went down to the Signal Center where we saw Lieutenant Sparks. We asked him a lot of questions about the coming operation of which our ship is to take part. Only rumors have come through so far. Some say Borneo is the place, while others say Java. There are a lot of rumors as to how many and who will go aboard the 848. As for me, if I go O.K. if not it makes no difference.

At the Signal Center I saw a lot of my old friends. Nearly the entire old Moresby bunch is here in Manila now. From the Signal Center we went over to the building where the fellows have their mess and living quarters. We met one of George's old friends who decided to walk around with us. Being it was nearly dinner time we rested a little while and then borrowed a couple of mess kits and had chow.

The chow here was far superior to what we have been getting out to our camp the past couple of weeks. At our camp we have been living solely on dehydrated stuff, and bread, our only fresh food and no butter.

This afternoon we walked up around the University where most of the American civilians are at, and where they were confined during the Japanese occupation. From there we walked over to where a Chinese mansion was. The grounds covered easily a square block, which was a beautiful garden with pools, statues, fountains, and small Chinese shrines, here and there. The house was the most spectacular piece of architecture I have ever seen. The house was built on a typical Chinese style, with high peaked roofs and up swept eaves, and many stained glass windows. The house itself was from two to three stories. On one corner was a tall tower, possibly six or seven stories high with separate eaves extending at each story.

We were not permitted to go through the house, but were given the privilege of going up to the top of the tower. From here we could see all of the downtown district of Manila, but it was a view of complete devastation. Strange as it may seem, the area surrounding this Chinese estate was in complete ruins, but this place was untouched. The story told [to] me was that the Japanese Army and Navy both wanted priority on this mansion for their use but were arguing back and forth as to who should have it. Consequently, time passed by and in the end, it was too late for them to destroy.

After looking around a while we walked on down to where the main river bridge had once been. Here along this street most of the buildings escaped destruction [for] the most part, as our forces closed in on this district very rapidly and the Japs had little time for destruction. Among some of these buildings, still in tack, was a theater, which is as modern as many I have seen in the states.

Filipinos and soldiers were crowded around the entrance, as this theater opened yesterday. We fellows decided to go in, even though we had seen the show before.

We understand that this theater acquires its motion pictures through the U.S. Army. After we got inside we had to stand for a short time until seats were available. After getting out of the show we decided to drop in at some café for a little bite to eat. Each of us ordered an egg omelets affaire and a cup of coffee. We knew our pocket books were in for an awful beating, and so we were not surprised when the bill came to ten pesos or five dollars.

We then said "so long" to our friend and then headed up to the end of town where we could catch a ride back to camp. It was very late when we arrived, and boy was I tired.

Monday, April 2, 1945 Today was uneventful except I was very tired and worked all day. It looks like Germany can't last much longer. Germans by tens of thousands are surrendering as our forces push farther into Germany. No one seems very excited about favorable developments, but everyone is just waiting patiently for that important news flash.

Tuesday, April 3, 1945 This morning George and I went into town again to see Lieutenant Sparks. The boat deal is still pretty indefinite, and only rumors still prevail. We ate dinner at the Signal mess, and then went across the bridge into south Manila to look around, since we haven't been around this area to a great extent. This part of the city is the most modern, and formerly having many modern schools, government buildings, the post office, and many modern clubs and hotels. The destruction of many of these buildings, such as the government buildings, is the most complete I have seen yet. To the most part they are no more than ground cement and stone blocks.

In this district the stench of dead Japs covers the entire area. There is yet any number of dead Japs laying in destroyed buildings, and countless of them lay buried beneath pits of rubble where buildings once stood.

Not much can be done to dispose of them as these bodies are in such a state that they can't be handled. It is just a case of hot sun and time plus ants and bugs to dispose of them. In some places bodies of dead Japs float in maggot infested water that has filled basements and cellars of partially wrecked buildings.

We walked hurriedly through this district, and had we known the condition of things, needless to say, we would have walked a long way around. We stopped a short time at a former Army and Navy Club. This, at one time, had been a really beautiful spot overlooking the harbor. It had a large swimming pool behind the hotel like club house. The main portions of the building still stands, but it has suffered shelling and explosions. Here, while looking through this building, I got separated from my friends and [was] unable to find them. I walked alone back to the signal mess hall in town. On my way I passed the street car parking lot, which was full of hundreds of wrecked street cars.

A short time after arriving back to the Signal mess and quarters, George and his friend arrived. All of us took a shower, which was an unusual treat, as here the city water is turned on and you could use as much water as you wish. We ate supper and then caught a ride back out to our camp.

Wednesday, April 4, 1945 Luckily I had last night off and didn't have to go to work, as I was pretty much worn out from our trip to town. The latest rumors as to the coming operation that we are supposed to go on, now has it that the original bunch who was aboard are to go. All we can do is wait and see what happens. Went over to the hospital to a show tonight. Had an air raid alert, but no Japs showed up.

Thursday, April 5, 1945 Just a routine day today, and spent the day on a circuit. Wrote a few letters this evening.

Conditions still look very bright on the war fronts. Advances are being made on all fronts except China, and in that theater the Japs have launched an offensive into central China. On Okinawa Island where the American Tenth Army recently landed the Japs are now putting up stiff resistance from prepared defensive positions.

In Europe the American Armies are still on the march, and something like 150 miles from Berlin. The Russian forces are closing in on Vienna, (NE Austria). It is thought that a clean out victory in Germany will not be accomplished for quite some time, as the Germans may continue the end of the war with an underground movement.

Friday, April 6, 1945 Nothing eventful today. Stayed around my tent most of the day and wrote letters. This is sure the dry season of the year here on Luzon. I think it has rained but twice since I arrived in January.

Saturday, April 7, 1945 The same routine today. Reports came through that the Jap fleet engaged our fleet off Okinawa. The Japs again came out second best. They lost several cruisers, many destroyers, and the largest Jap battleship the forty thousand ton Yamato. It is estimated that the Japs lost one fourth of their remaining fleet, and any one of our larger tank forces can deal with the Jap fleet. It has become quite official that all the fellows originally on the ship will go back.

Sunday, April 8, 1945 This morning a bunch of we fellows went to a rooster fight. Our enthusiasm was at a high pitch as one of the fellows had a fighting cock that he intended to enter in the day's entertainment. After walking for about half an hour we arrived at the arena. This arena was just a small place surrounded by many old buildings and grass huts. The fighting pen was about the same size as a prize fight ring. Around the outside of the pen were bleachers for people to sit on. However, nearly everyone crowded around the pen its self.

When we arrived the fights were already in progress. Not being able to understand Filipino, we were amused at the yelling and hissing, as they made their bets on the fights. Rooster fighting in the Philippines is a national sport, and the training and raising of fighting roosters is similar to the breeding of racehorses in the U.S.

There is quite a lot of procedure in each fight. First the roosters are matched as to size, weight and height, by the owners. If they agree on a contest, they wait their turn to the fighting pen. During this time a special razor sharp knife is fastened on the leg of each rooster, and a small leather sheath is put on. These knives are about four inches long, ground sharp on the top edge, and needle sharp at the point.

The roosters are finally brought into the pen and then the betting starts. The ring masters call for bets from the crowd, and in case one rooster is the favorite, will offer odds. Usually the odds are fifty/fifty, as luck is ninety percent of the outcome. During the betting session, which last nearly half an hour, the roosters are built up to a rage. The owners hold their roosters letting them make passes at each other, holding them just out of reach. Finally the betting is finished by the ring masters and the roosters go through the last procedure before they fight. One rooster is brought within reach of the other. The eyes and most of the heads are being covered by the owner's hand. With only the rooster's ears protruding. The other rooster is allowed to peck once at each ear, which makes him "fighting mad." After this procedure is exchanged both ways, the small leather sheaths covering the knives are removed.

At this time the crowd is in an uproar trying or making last chance side bets. If a bet is made with the ring master inside the ring, ten percent of the winnings are deducted. Bets made outside the ring is winner take all or vice versa.

The roosters are allowed to peck each other a couple more times and then they are placed on the ground about six feet apart facing each other and released. The roosters feint a couple of times and then attack with their feet striking out in the air with the knife stabbing, cutting or missing the opponent. Many times, only one pass is made with both birds flying together, each striking a fatal blow, and then both falling dead. A fight usually last only about a minute. At the end of the fight the roosters' fighting days are usually over, also, as he is so cut up that the frying pan is his next stop. It is seldom a rooster escapes without a scratch. If a rooster lives through six victories he is truly a champ.

Most of the fights we saw were a bloody mess. It is hard to see why it is such a popular pastime anywhere. The soldier in our bunch was unable to get a match for his rooster so he didn't fight.

Tired tonight and not too hungry at suppertime.

Monday, April 9, 1945 Spent nearly all day today writing letters. Late last night I received four letters from Marian, which left me a little down hearted after reading them. This evening another fellow and I went over to a house that is a short distance from here. A Filipino colonel lives there and had a piano which he invited my friend over to play. This colonel was quite a young fellow who put you at ease at the first moment of your meeting. Never for a moment did he put forth the expected superior air.

Tuesday, April 10, 1945 Well today official orders came through including a list of fellows who are to go back aboard the P.C.E. 848 to go on a forth coming operation. We were relieved from work and told we would likely go aboard Sunday. Naturally there is a little tension among some of the fellows as to what the operation will be like, and what the outcome will be. As for myself, I am not much worried. I am not immune to fright, but I am just rather numb to most reactions. I am rather looking forward to going back on ship, as a few more months will go by quickly.

Wednesday, April 11, 1945 It is the same old Army. Never fails to be inconsistent. This evening we were notified that everything is off. The 848 isn't going. I guess she needs some repairs and won't be ready in time for the operation. The American Armies are sure going to town in France. The 9th Army is now only sixty five miles south west of Berlin. Went to a show tonight.

Thursday, April 12, 1945 Most of the fellows are rather disappointed about the ship deal, but we figure, what is – is best. I went into town today and went over across the river where the 848 is tied up. I went on board and saw a lot of my old friends. They say it will take a few weeks to put the ship back into shape. There is a rumor that we will go on board then. I stayed on board the 848 nearly all afternoon and had supper, which is the first decent food I have tasted since I came on shore. I drank as much water as I could hold. Not having cold water is another item I have missed greatly. George was informed today that he now has a new rating, which is T/3. It is just one of those things that is typical of the Army. George is a C.W. operator as are most of all of us, but he far comes up to the standard of most of the fellows, and there is an awful feeling among some of the guys. As for myself I have a similar feeling, but mine is entirely towards the army way of handling such matters. George, being a good friend of mine, told me he knew what the score was, but he had nothing to do with it. His name was put in for ratings along with a lot of the rest of us. It is my guess, George just happened to draw the lucky straw. It is the same old story. The rating you hold has nothing to do with your qualifications.

Friday, April 13, 1945 Word came through today that President Roosevelt died of a cerebral hemorrhage early this morning Philippine time. Fellows in our camp were not stirred much, or was much conversation carried on about it. News commentaries carried on about it throughout the day. I handled quite a bit of traffic today on the Leyte circuit.

Saturday, April 14, 1945 Went to town today and went over across the river and to the place the 848 is tied up. A sailor friend, (Frye) and I planned looking around the town today. Frye was unable to get off duty until 1 P.M. so I stayed aboard the 848 for chow, which was a very pleasant turn of affairs from my point of view. Frye and I walked around town quite a while. There was a certain little shop he wanted to find, but didn't know exactly where it was at, so we nearly tramped our legs off. Price control is in effect, and prices have come down to some extent, but things are still a ways out of reason. An egg sandwich still comes to .75 cents. I bought a silver ring with an opal stone today, which was surprisingly cheap. I got out to camp too late to get paid. I will see if I can go out to the transmitter station tomorrow and get paid. We had our first really hard rain tonight.

Sunday, April 15, 1945 The same routine as usual today. Had fresh meat for dinner today, which was quite unusual. Our chow was pretty good today, but in the past few weeks all of us have been losing weight. I loaned one of my friends my mess kit today. He didn't bring it back, and when I went over to the kitchen after it my knife, fork, and spoon were gone. I hated losing them as it was the set given me when I came into the Army, three years ago. Marian and I have been married three years and ten months today. I received a stack of letters today. My mail seems to be coming through a little now.

Monday, April 16, 1945 Routine day today. This afternoon I went down to the waterfront where I met Frye. The 848 was not in her usual place, but over by pier 7 anchored a few hundred yards off the dock. I met Frye when he came over with the Liberty party in the whale boat. We walked around a while, went out around Santa Tomas (C. Philippines – POW camp). We stopped in at one of the cleaner cafes' where we had an egg sandwich and a cup of coffee. Total cost in American money $2.30. A fellow sure can't afford to go to town very often. With these Filipinos there seems to be two distinct classes. The upper class who are educated and live as most Americans, understanding the situation of the Philippines and anxious to cooperate. The other class regards the arrival of the Americans as an opportunity for them to cash in on the American's generosity, and are after but one thing and that is American's dollars. Inflation of the Filipino peso is fifty percent of the reason for high prices, but the Filipinos want as many American dollars as possible before their money comes to the prewar standard. At present, the American dollar on the average will bring a commodity which cost the Filipinos but fifteen cents before the war. Frye was late getting back to the ship and will probably catch restriction.

Tuesday, April 17, 1945 This morning I was awakened and told to pack and be ready to leave in fifteen minutes. I threw my stuff in my duffle bags, loaded it on a truck and in a short time the eight of we fellows were ready to go. Our new quarters are now down near the former business district across the river in the former water works building. This building is a large square structure four stories high, being built with each floor overlooking this court as sort of a balcony. This building didn't escape being damaged, but it is in better repair than most of the others in this vicinity. There are no other buildings around here, they are all flat. This building, while being burned as well as shelled, being of concrete and stone structure withstood the beating quite well. The building while still in pretty rugged condition, is now the place where we work. Our new camp is quite a little distance from the water works building. About a twenty minute walk if you don't get a ride. It is located in an area of about a square block, surrounded by a high fence. This place at one time, must have been a park or something, but was used by the Japs as a motor pool. The place, right at present, is more a junk yard than anything else. Luckily there weren't so many fellows in camp, and there were plenty of vacant tents, so we didn't have to put a tent up. There is no mess hall here and we eat at the 52nd, which is just across the road. I dread to think what this place will be like when the rainy season comes. Probably two feet under, as this area doesn't seem so well drained, and it is very flat. Being that but a few of us came here from the receiver station today, we had to work an extra long shift, from noon until midnight.

Wednesday, April 18, 1945 We had to go to work early this morning and work all day. Some of the other fellows moved into camp last night. We are still rather short- handed on help. Maybe some more will come in, in a few days.

Thursday, April 19,1945 Worked again all day today. The actual work we are doing isn't so bad, but this Army's efficiency B.S. sure gets you down. It makes no difference how much experience a fellow has, there is always someone at your neck. There was a show tonight, which I went to.

Friday, April 20, 1945 We got an extra fellow on our shift today, so I got the day off. I walked over to the docks to catch a ride out to the P.G.E. 848. Luckily a small landing boat was just coming into the docks from the 848 so I road back out with them. I knew Dave Castelman and Charlie, the only Army fellows left on the 848. I also know some of my sailor friends. Frye, one of my Navy friends who was over on leave the other day when we were on shore, is restricted to the ship. I talked to him quite a while. I ate supper on the ship and then caught the landing boat back over to the dock. There are still a few Japs laying around. I saw one as I crossed a small field today. He had been in the sun quite a while as there wasn't much left. The stench from the dead is nearly gone now, which brings an improvement to one's appetite. When I got back to camp tonight a bunch of new guys had moved in, and among them was an old friend of mine from New Guinea, Bob Larson. He hadn't seen the town so we walked around a while tonight.

Saturday, April 21, 1945 Worked again all day today on the first shift. This evening after work I took a little walk over to a cemetery that the Japs had turned into a fortress. The manner in which this cemetery was constructed probably lead the Japs to use it for this purpose. It is an area covering possibly four square blocks, surrounded by a high stone wall. This wall was so constructed that it acted as a burial place with hundreds of vaults in its construction. On the inside of this cemetery was another similar wall going around, inside the area included by the outer wall. At intervals, an archway through the inner wall led to the center of the cemetery, where there was a large Muslimism. This building, which must be hundreds of years old, was used as a barracks by the Japs. Reed mats, tin cans, and all kinds of rubbish covered the one large room. The floor contained vaults, which were marked by receptacles of various sizes of flat marble slabs. When the American forces closed in and this Jap strong point was under siege, the Japs, in order to gain a place of safety from our mortar fire and artillery, broke open the vaults in the walls, removed the remains and they, themselves, crawled in. About eighty percent of these vaults had been used for this purpose.

Sunday, April 22, 1945 Worked again today. This camp we live in is becoming "G.I." to the "nth" degree. A detachment of 832nd guys, just up from New Guinea has moved in. I am 832nd, but I am in Det.x so that rather sets me apart from this bunch, which makes me very happy. I think less of the 832nd than ever. I met Herring, a friend of mine, who is from Iowa, and an old Port Moresby tent mate of mine. Just about all of the old bunch is up here now. Quite a number of fellows are here who arrived from the U.S. a little over a month ago. One of them is in my tent. I sure keep him busy with amusing questions.

Monday, April 23, 1945 Above item from Marian. According to G.I. procedure I should have been home a long time ago, but the G.I. system of doing things paints a different picture. I have the misfortune of being in a group of fellows who all are so called "old timers." The quota each month (if there is a quota) is very small – not beginning to affect the larger number of fellows eligible to go home. So the result, the overseas time requirement is constantly moved ahead. When this plan was brought into effect, it was tooled up as the "18 month plan" a number of more months, "the two year plan" then came the "30 month plan". It now stands at 36 months, but I hear it is to be 40 in a short time. It is my guess, when the war's end is at hand. The "name" rotation will be dropped, and the war is nearly over, and we will all go home together "sort of thing" will take place. Just another day today.

Chin up! & Hurry Home!

23 APRIL 1945 MONDAY

Tuesday, April 24, 1945 Our shift changed over to midnight last night, but I didn't have to go to work, as I had the night off. The war in Germany seems to be reaching its climax. The American forces are rapidly advancing towards Berlin. Elements of the 9th Army are now but 17 miles away. General Patton's 3rd Army has cut across southern Germany and is now in Czechoslovakia. The Russian offenses against Berlin is in full swing and they now occupy many of the suburban districts. Hitler has broken Marshal Von Rumstead to a Private. I have an idea some of us may be going on another operation before long. Perhaps a hot one.

Wednesday, April 25, 1945 This afternoon a friend and I went up to the water works building to see Capt. McKenny. This friend, who I just met a few days ago, is Master Sergeant Bob Lawson, and he has known McKenny, since they came overseas together. I have known McKenny for about two years, first having him as an officer at Port Moresby. Bob wanted to ask McKenny about what he will do in the future. Went to work at midnight. Working a circuit is sure a tough job, with these new overseas guys at receiver station bucking their heads off.

Thursday, April 26, 1945 Had tonight off but stayed in camp, saw the show just across the road, and wrote a few letters. The war in Germany is progressing as usual and it broke as if their surrender would come at any time. The Russians are in the heart of Berlin, fighting the Germans in the streets and subways. The Russians and American forces have joined cutting Germany in two. The American forces have stopped their advance approximately 17 miles from Berlin. The Russian Armies have surrounded Berlin and now hold two thirds of that city. Jap resistance here on Luzon is rapidly being broken, and their forces eliminated. The stiff resistance of the Japs in the mountains approximately 25 miles from here is no longer a major operation, and only an estimated 500 starved Japs remain. Fighting on Okinawa is slowly going to our favor, but for a time it seemed a question.

Friday, April 27, 1945 Today I had to make a trip to our signal officer's office. I knew what he wanted before I went in. This radio discrepancy business. He told me I had ten procedure violations against me, and that was the quota set to be eligible for a visit to him. About all the Sig. officer said was that he knew it seemed rather silly, but this business was some colonel's idea, and he had to tell me to watch my procedure. This whole thing has little to do with regular radio operating, only that to be as G.I. about it as they want you to be. You can remember only one thing, and that is correct procedure at all times, whether you can pass traffic or keep contact with your station or not. From now on I am only after a clean slate in operating procedure, which means to forget what I have learned in the past two years, as well as two and a half year of experience. A rumor is out that Germany surrendered?

Saturday, April 28, 1945 The same routine as usual today. Tonight at ten P.M. the Co. 1st Sergeant came in and run us out of our tent to go on a detail. We had the job of loading a bunch of teletype machines on a truck, and then unloading them over at another building. We didn't get back until 11:30 P.M. "Oh Boy" this Army! The Russian Armies now occupy nine tenths of Berlin. General Patton's 3rd Army is near the Austrian border. There are rumors of surrender by the Germans but it is only natural, at this time. It is generally believed that unconditional surrender by the Germans is at hand.

Sunday, April 29, 1945 Nothing new today, had to work five until midnight so I didn't get to see the show tonight. Allied forces in Italy are advancing rapidly and cutting German resistance to pieces. The Russian forces now occupy most of Berlin.

Monday, April 30, 1945 For the past couple of weeks I have been taking the "trick chief's" job, when he has a day off. The trick chief job in the station here is quite simple. You are left pretty much alone by the officers and everything runs quite smooth. The latest rumor going around is that fellows overseas, over two years, and who have five combat stars, will, after the surrender of Germany, be sent back to the states, and discharged. "Boy" I wonder where this "bologna" gets started.

Tuesday, May 1, 1945 Reports came through today that Hitler is dead. No details were given on how his death occurred. It might be a hoax to try and hide him.

Had a pretty tough day at work today. I worked a circuit attempting to contact the P.C.E. 849, who I finally got in the middle of the afternoon. The P.C.E. 849 is on the invasion of Borneo. I was supposed to go on this same operation aboard the 848, but she wasn't in condition for this operation due to generator trouble.

Up until the time I established contact with the 849 there was an assortment of colonels, captains, lieutenants breathing down my neck. Those who could acquire a receiver turned in on my frequency. You would think they were the ones in this invasion. At first the Signal Officer complained as to the procedure we were using in attempting contact. I told him the procedure I was using was strictly G.I. and if I did any different there was a guy monitoring my circuit, just waiting to cut my throat. The Signal Officer told me to forget about procedure and he would take responsibility.

Wednesday, May 2, 1945 The war in Germany is rapidly drawing to a close. All German troops in Italy have surrendered. The Germans have asked the Americans and British for unconditional surrender, but didn't include Russia. The Germans are trying all the fast tricks they know. There isn't much of a government left in Germany. Each of Germany's fighting units that are left are completely their own governing power. Admiral Karl Doenitz, successor to Hitler has told all Germans troops to continue the war.

General Gerd von Rundstedt who was reported to having been broke to a private by Hitler, has been captured by the American Seventh Army. "Tokyo Rose" broadcasting from Tokyo Japan, is stating the plan on which Japan will be victorious over the American Armies. She says General Patton's mechanized army will be taken care of by the Japanese Air Corp's special attack squadrons. She didn't mention what would be done about the attack of the rest of the American Forces as well as the British, and perhaps the Russians, and all the rest of the world powers who want to pitch in.

There is a rumor going around that a message from the 849 stated that they had been hit by mortar fire and two men were killed. I don't give rumors much consideration, but just the same there are a lot of my old buddies on that ship. I have 32 months overseas today.

Thursday, May 3, 1945 A Manila daily paper came out today with big red headlines. *"Germany Surrenders unconditionally"* a heading at the bottom of the sheet told how our 7th Army was making gains. The reason for such a misleading headline seemed to be an opportunity for the sale of a few more papers. It seems the general attitude of the Filipinos is not so much to clean their city up, but to capitalize on the occupation of the American soldiers.

After experiencing the unscrupulous means most Filipinos are using to get American dollars, I am becoming more convinced each day that the fate of the Philippines is of little interest to me. The Philippines look to two things: their independence, and what the U.S. can do to put them back on their feet.

Friday, May 4, 1945 The P.C.E. 848 is back from Subic Bay. Repairs have been completed on her generators and she is ready for the next operation. Rumors going around are we will go around the end of the month on some kind of an operation. I say we, as I guess, I would go back aboard the ship with the rest of the bunch.

I went out to the 848 this afternoon. I stayed over for the show tonight and then came back over to the pier in the whale boat around 10:30 P.M. Getting back to camp was quite an experience, as it was dark as pitch and walking along the streets where many man hole covers are missing made me feel as if my next step would find me at the bottom of the river. I finally got to one of the main streets, caught a ride up town, and then another ride back to camp.

Saturday, May 5, 1945 News came through today that all Nazi Armies in Denmark and Holland have surrendered. In Norway, the Germans also have laid down their arms. The German resistance left Czechoslovakia.

One of the fellows told me about two Japs who were caught about two blocks from our camp yesterday. One Jap shot himself. The other one tried to get away and was shot. On the average about nine Japs a day are picked up here in Manila. Went to a show tonight at the State Theater in town.

Sunday, May 6, 1945 I hung around camp nearly all day today. I wrote a few letters. Trying to get caught up on all that — I am so far behind.

This afternoon I decided to go out to the 848. I got over to the dock about 5PM and had quite a little wait, as the whale boat didn't make a trip until six. During this wait, the wind started to blow and it rained a little. The water in the bay got pretty rough. The captain of the 848 had invited two Chinese girls and two Chinese men to visit the 848 and to them the whale boat ride was quite an experience. Being I had the night off, I stayed aboard the 848 all night.

Monday, May 7, 1945 I got back to camp rather early this morning, as I had to pick up my laundry. This afternoon I went up town to the Red Cross for a while. I stayed until around 4 PM and then came back to camp.

Tuesday, May 8, 1945 While at work I received the news that Germany has finally officially unconditionally surrendered to the United States, Great Britain, and Russia. This official news was no surprise to us as the German's surrender has been the headline on almost all Philippine news papers here in Manila for a week. Went out to the ship this afternoon. There were a number of news paper and some building magazines that Marian sent me in the ship's mail for me.

Wednesday, May 8,1945 Went out to the ship this afternoon. One of my sailor friends and I went on shore liberty. A general warning has been put out to all Army personal that a large number of Japs are filtering into Manila, disguised as Filipino civilians. Most of we Americans are unable to tell one from the other. A Filipino soldier can spot one of them a mile away. Seven Japs the other night tried to blow up one of the bridges that crosses the Pasig River.

Thursday, May 10, 1945 It is but two days since the surrender of Germany, and everyone is talking about getting out of the army. Rotation has been forgotten and demobilization is the main subject. Everyone is counting up the number of points he has. According to the plan a soldier must have 85 points to be eligible for discharge. A soldier's points are determined by the length of time he has spent in the Army and extra points added for each month overseas. 1 point at home per month, and 2 points a month for overseas duty. 5 points are given for campaign stars, and extra points awarded for decorations.

This whole business reminds me of the rotation plan in its early days when it was called "The eighteen month plan." (It is now nearly the forty month plan). Demobilization will go the same route. Just as sure as the sun comes up in the morning it will work the same.

Friday, May 11, 1945 Received six letters from Marian today, and at work tonight started answering them. Getting back to camp from the five to midnight shift, in case you miss the bus, is quite a "deal." During the Jap scare around Manila, many "trigger happy" G.I.s have shot Filipinos and anything that walks.

When we have to walk back to camp we sing, whistle, anything that sounds American. We have more reason to be afraid of the G.I.s than the Japs. Had tonight off, and went to hear the Manila Symphony Orchestra.

Saturday, May 12, 1945 Nothing new today, the same routine as usual. The chow here in camp is improving a little. We are getting fresh meat occasionally. I never saw a bunch of cooks who could so thoroughly ruin what good food we do get.

Sunday, May 13, 1945 Today is "Mother's Day." I intended going to church this morning, but being I had to relieve for noon chow I didn't go. This afternoon I wrote a letter to my mom and also Iva. We had a heavy rain tonight and our tent area is a sea of mud. Many of the fellows are moving out.

Monday, May 14, 1945 Nothing unusual today, except I met a lieutenant who is from Des Moines. He left the states in February and was at home for Christmas. Read in the paper that supplies are already on their way from Italy to the Pacific.

Tuesday, May 15, 1945 Today Marian and I have been married three years, eleven months. One of my Christmas packages arrived today from Marian, which took the place of an anniversary gift. This is Christmas package number two, I have received. My mail is coming through somewhat on schedule now. I have received a number of letters only fifteen days old.

Wednesday, May 16, 1945 This morning I took my citation certification up to 52nd headquarters to have it entered in my service records. I think this will be good for five points. I tried to get a line on the point system as to what points I might actually have, but everyone is pretty much in the dark about it. The same routine today.

Thursday, May 17, 1945 It has been raining nearly all week, and our camp is one sea of mud and water. Many fellows have moved out of camp without permission from the orderly room and rented rooms here and there which costs nearly a month's pay.

I bought some pictures today of some of the ruins of Manila. These pictures cost quite a bit of money, but having no camera this was the only way I could get them.

Friday, May 18, 1945 Same routine today. Went to the show over at the 52nd tonight. Haven't received any letters for a number of days now.

Saturday, May 19, 1945 Received two letters from Marian today as well as one from Aunt Effie. They were dated May 1 & 2. I answered these letters on the midnight shift tonight. The job I had of assistant Trick Chief was taken over tonight by a Master Sergeant. He is getting paid for the responsibility so he might as well take it.

Sunday, May 20, 1945 Went to church this morning with two of my tent mates. Before church we stopped in at the Red Cross and got in the Coke line for a couple of Coca Cola drinks. This evening Bob Larson and I took a walk on over in south Manila. I had never been over in this district before. It is similar to most of the area of Manila south of the Pasig River. Pretty well beat up by the retreating Japs.

Monday, May 21, 1945, This afternoon I went down to the water works building and signed my application for the demobilization plan. I have an official 91 points. I have 39 months in the Army of which I am credited with 32 months overseas. Overseas time counts two points, regular Army time at home counts one point. I have four campaign stars, Papua Campaign, New Guinea Campaign, Southern Philippines Campaign, and Luzon Campaign. Each of these awards gives me five points. I also have a citation but this is of no point value. Eighty five points are required to be eligible to make application for discharge. Points earned up until May 12 this year are all that is counted.

On June 27 the war department is to make the final decision, and determine what the final score for eligibility is. If a fellow gets by this round, then round three comes up which determines whether or not you are essential.

While many fellows look with high hopes to getting home, I think this whole business is a build up for an awful let down for most of them. Our desire to return home, rather dulls our ability to accept reasons for not being able to get back.

Tuesday, May 22, 1945 Routine day today. The weather has cleared and our camp is somewhat dry again. I caught a bad cold during last week's wet spell. My mail has been coming through fairly regular, and maybe at last I will receive a few recent letters for a change. I received a Des Moines Register news paper today that took 14 months to reach me. I received a Christmas package from the folks, the first one from them. Went to the show tonight.

Wednesday, May 23, 1945 Not much doing today. The war here in the Pacific seems to [have] slowed down to a great extent, since the end of hostility in Europe. The battle for Okinawa is still going on, and is a pretty tough one. Our forces are making gains very slowly and it will without a doubt be a couple of months before we capture the whole island.

Thursday, May 24, 1945 In the letters I have recently been receiving from Marian she mentions the discharge plan and how I rate with it. The best thing to do is to keep all the folks at home as much in the dark as possible. In this way my hopes will only be crushed, as I suspect they will be. Work as usual again today.

Friday, May 25, 1945 In a short time the other camp that we are to move into will be ready. They say we will move out of here in another week. I think the new camp will be much better, as it is on higher ground. It has been freshly graded though, and will be very muddy when it rains. Nothing unusual today, went to the show tonight.

Saturday, May 26, 1945 Messed around camp all day. This afternoon a friend of mine in the orderly room told me to "scram" that they were looking for a detail and had their eye on our tent. I took off and went up to the Red Cross where I finished writing some letters. Went to work at midnight tonight.

Sunday, May 27, 1945 I got off the midnight shift this morning and went to bed. It was so hot in our tent that sleep was impossible, so I got up and went to church with two of my tent mates. I stayed around the tent this afternoon and tried to get a little rest. This evening I went to the show at the 52nd.

Monday, May 28, 1945 Worked the day shift today, and received a few messages for a change. This evening Bob Larson and I went up the street to the G.H.Q. area where they have a P.X. In this P.X. they have a large store of goods, supplies items that we could never hope to get. They have an ice cream fountain, cola, serve American style hamburgers. All this is for G.H.Q. only. Bob and I hung around outside until Bob was lucky in borrowing a pass from one of the G.H.Q. guys. Bob went inside where he borrowed another friend's pass, and I got in on that one. We took full advantage of everything they had. This whole set up is the usual run of Army fairness.

Tuesday May 29, 1945 We were told today that we are to move to the other camp tomorrow so we packed most of our stuff so we will be ready. I didn't have to work tonight so I went to the show with the fellows.

Wednesday, May 30, 1945 We sat around most of the morning waiting for our turn on the truck to take our stuff up to the new camp. After noon chow we dropped our tent, rolled it up, and threw it on the truck. Smitty and I went along with the tent to pick out a tent site, and Marty and Howse stayed to load the rest of our junk on the next load. We were lucky in finding a pretty good spot for our tent, being the end tent in one of the rows. Our tent will be a little cooler than the others. We spent the rest of the day getting straightened out.

Thursday, May 31, 1945 More fellows moved into camp today. As yet the mess hall equipment is at the old camp, so we have to ride back and forth in the truck to our meals. I got a little inside dope from one of my friends in the orderly room, that the first Sgt. and others are in trouble with the Filipinos black market control, on the matter of distributing food supplies. I wonder if this has anything to do with some of the bad chow we have been getting.

Friday June 1, 1945 Worked the day shift today, and was lucky as most of the fellows in camp had to pull detail. This evening Marty and I went down to the "Engineers" to see a movie.

Saturday, June 2, 1945 I left camp early this morning after nearly getting caught for detail. I only made my get away by ducking through a bunch of tents and going out the back way. I met one of my friends on the street and he told me the P.C.E. 848 was in, so I headed over toward the docks. I had a little trouble locating her, but after looking around a while I spotted the 848 whale boat, and they came and picked me up and took me around to pier seven where she was tied up, unloading some cargo. I went aboard and spent most of the afternoon talking to the fellows. In the meantime the 848 pulled away from the pier and went over to another location where she dropped anchor. This evening Frye, Castelman, and myself went to town. There wasn't much to do. We went up to a dance a while and then went over to the Red Cross. Being I don't have to go to work until tomorrow at 5 PM, I decided going back out to the ship and stay all night.

Sunday, June 3, 1945 Slept pretty well last night, on a mattress for a change. For dinner today we had fresh roast turkey & dressing, fresh potatoes, peas and bread and butter. We were to have ice cream but a bunch of sailors the other night got in bad with the commander, over on the beach, so to get back in his good graces, the ship gave the commander the ice cream we were suppose to have had today. About the middle of the afternoon I caught the whale boat and went back to camp. I was lucky in going over to the ship, as there was a bunch of packages there for me. A number of the fellows got stuck with restriction to the ship for telling the commander to "Blow it out his —-!"

Monday, June 4, 1945 It looks like the point system is going to work for some of the fellows. Fellows in our outfit with 100 or more points have been relieved from duty and will soon go home. Nothing unusual today, the same routine.

Tuesday, June 5, 1945 Worked at the station today. This evening Smitty, another fellow and I went up to the Red Cross to the dance. We were there plenty early, and found a good place to sit down near the dance floor. At 7 PM the orchestra arrived and at 7:30 they played the first number. The hostesses were not there yet so the crowd just listened to the music. After a short time, Smitty and I decided to go get a drink and went over to where the cold drink counter was. There were no cups there as yet so Smitty and I went down stairs. After getting a drink, Smitty and I started back up stairs. However, an M.P. was at the foot of the stairs, and said we couldn't go up. We argued with the guy for a while, and told him we had just come down for a drink, and left one of our buddies up there. The M.P. said one of us could go and get our friend if we wanted to, so I told Smitty to go ahead. My only alternative was to go back to camp, and as thoroughly disgusted as I was, going back to camp seemed like a good idea. The Red Cross is run as much like the army – as the Army is. When the day comes that I can forget the Army, I will also forget the Red Cross donations.

Wednesday, June 6, 1945 Today marks one year since Allied troops landed in Europe. Things seem to be rather quiet here in the Pacific. Our forces have broken Japanese resistance on Okinawa, and it appears that the island will be completely ours in another week or so. Chinese forces in China are making extensive gains against the Japs. The Japs seem to be transferring their troops to the Manchuria border where they expect an attack from the Russian forces. As for the American, British, and Chinese forces, they prefer that the Russians do not enter into the Pacific War, as the Russians, in such an event would expect to gain territories in the Pacific also.

Thursday, June 7, 1945 Nothing unusual today, laid around camp most of the time and wrote a few letters. This evening I went down to the 52nd to see a show. Then to work at midnight.

Friday June 8, 1945 Slept part of the morning and got up for early chow. Laid around this afternoon and tried to get a little more sleep. This evening I went up to the Red Cross to take another stab at going to the dance. I got there plenty early, and this time I didn't go back down stairs to get caught in their elimination system. It was rather late when the Filipino hostesses arrived. As far as I was concerned, the dance didn't give me much pleasure, so I found a writing room off to one side and wrote Marian a letter. Arrived back at camp rather early.

9 June, 1945, Saturday The same routine today. Many fellows who have over a 100 points have left to go home. They say next month they will take many more in the 90 bracket. Boy I feel as if I will go nuts waiting to see what happens. If this going home deal should blow up this time and I come to realize, as I have in the past, that I am stuck for "many – many" months more – that is something I can't think of.

Sunday, June 10, 1945 I had a pleasant surprise this morning. I heard that Bill Pandolfi was in camp, and in a short time I located where he was at. The last time I had seen Bill was in Port Moresby. He is one of my closest friends, and with whom I went on two furloughs to Australia. Bill and I took a walk up town and spent most of the time shooting the breeze about old times. Bill decided moving in with us.

Monday June 11, 1945 Worked at the station all day. We now have contact with the 848, which is on an operation in Borneo. This evening Bill and I went out to see the stage show "Oklahoma." We first went out to the receiver station where we borrowed a couple of chairs. We arrived over at the show grounds in good time and found a pretty good place to sit that was fairly close to the stage. The show started and was about through the first act when it started to rain. In a short time the rain was coming down in sheets. Bill and I had our raincoats with us, but as hard as it rained they were of little use. We gave up the idea of seeing the show and started back to the receiver station. The road was muddy and much of the way we had to wade in water knee deep. When we arrived at the receiver station we were well soaked. We were lucky in one respect, as a messenger was going to town in a jeep, so we rode back with him. I had to go to work at midnight.

Tuesday, June 15, 1945 Today is my birthday, my thirty second. Slept most of the day. Bill and I sat around and talked about last night's difficulties. Received a badly beat up Christmas package today. Couldn't tell who it was from. Went to the 52nd to the show tonight.

Wednesday, June 16, 1945 Worked at the station on the day shift today. This evening I decided to take another try at seeing "Oklahoma." I couldn't persuade Bill to go along so I went alone. I found a good place to sit and saw the entire show, and managed to get back to camp dry. This afternoon I signed a slip in the mess hall putting down the number of points I have for my priority on going home. There were 27 on the list with 85 or more points and with the 91 that I have, I am about half way up the list.

This was taken about April 25. Since I don't have but 1 print of these, Honey, will you return these 3 to me after you are thru looking at them. Notice how pretty Deana is in this picture. (How do you like "our" suit.) Your wife looks like an old maid; doesn't she!

Thursday, June 14, 1945 Today is dad's birthday. There are quite a number of important days this month. Coming up tomorrow is my wedding anniversary. Quite a number of fellows with 100 points and more have gone home. There are rumors a lot more may be sent home next month, and this will include fellows in my standing. However, no one seems to know what the score is so all I can do is sit and wait. I have no confidence in my prospects of getting home. It could be in a month and not for another year. The way the Army has of doing things, the latter is more likely correct. When I do get home it will be by a lucky break, not because any system worked.

Friday, June 15, 1945 Today is my fourth wedding anniversary. Of these four years Marian and I have had but 8 months together. A Filipino came into our tent today and I bought a pocket book to send to Marian. Worked until midnight tonight.

Saturday, June 16, 1945 This afternoon Smitty and I took a walk over to the old walled city. The M.P.s wouldn't let us go in so we walked around and found a hole where we went inside. Everything is totally destroyed except an old church, which was built in 1599. This is the oldest church in the Philippines. How everything around it could be so flat, and this church practically undamaged, is a mystery to me. The decomposed remains of many Japs still lie around here and there. You see parts of leg bones and so forth in nearly every pile of dirt that has been swept up. The walled city is the original Manila and founded by the Spanish over three hundred years ago. It covers an area of about a mile wide by a mile and a half long. In recent years many modern buildings had been built there. The streets are very narrow and more like allies than anything else. Received some packages from home today, two from Marian and one from the folks. These packages were beat up to some extent, but all the items, except the edibles were OK. I was happy to find a camera and some film enclosed in one of the packages. The other articles such as socks etc. from the folks will come in handy.

Sunday, June 17, 1945 Had to work today; otherwise I would have gone to church. Many of my old friends who are in the 52nd sig. B.V. have gotten ratings. One month they were made T/4 and the next month T/3. I have had my rating over two years and fellows in the same outfit or formally 832 haven't a chance of promotion since we are on teams that have no R.O. (rating schedule).

Monday, June 18, 1945 Nothing out of the ordinary today. Borrowed a pass from one of the G.H.Q. guys and went down and had some hamburgers and cola at their P.X. this afternoon. The main topic of conversation is still this "going home" business. I wish they would keep still so all of us could rest in peace.

Tuesday, June 19, 1945 Nothing doing much today, except it rained pretty hard, which it has been doing every day the past week. Our camp is getting more G.I. everyday. We can't walk around the camp without a cap and must be in correct uniform at all times. The time isn't far off until we have to start saluting officers.

Wednesday, June 20, 1945 Nothing much doing today. This evening Bill and I took a walk up town. We walked around up past the Times Theater and thought we might see the show, but what was playing, we had already seen, so we went down to the Red Cross, got a cold drink and then came back to camp. It rained quite a bit again tonight.

Thursday, June 21, 1945 This morning I learned that a bunch of my old friends came back from Borneo. This afternoon I saw some of them when they came down to camp. As I have imagined all along, this demobilization business is becoming not only screwed up, but prospects of dying a customary "Army death". It is rumored that many fellows eligible to return home won't make it for another year. The way I figure things stand with me. If I don't get home in another month, I won't make it another year. What with the impending operations which will freeze all other movements, the need they say [is] for replacements shipping deficiencies. Today is the longest day in the year. All of "em" are damn long as far as I am concerned.

Friday, June 22, 1945 Today Marty and I were supposed to report for company detail but being it rained and the fact we have a new first sergeant, who more than likely doesn't have the old roister to check upon, we just stayed in our tent. We had a show in our mess hall tonight.

Saturday, June 23, 1945 Heard the PCE 848 is in port. One of my sailor friends, Frye, called me up and he and another fellow came down to the camp tonight. We messed around town for a while, and then went out to the ship where I stayed all night.

Sunday, June 24, 1945 Stayed aboard ship all day today, as I don't have to go to work until tomorrow morning. All the crew is anxious to know if they are to go on an operation in the near future. Personally I hope I go back aboard and go on another invasion, rather than sit around here in Manila where the G.I. B.S. is getting thicker all the time. I become more certain everyday that my going home is — well – who knows?

Monday, June 25, 1945 Worked the day shift today. This evening took a walk up to the Red Cross. Walked over past the Times Theater with the thought of maybe seeing the show. There was a string of G.I.s two blocks long, so we came back to camp.

Tuedays, June 26, 1945 Met my sailor friend, Frye, up town this evening. We sat around and talked a while. I got back to camp around 10pm as I had to be at work at midnight.

Wednesday, June 27, 1945 Slept most of this morning. This afternoon Bob and I borrowed a G.H.Q. P.X. pass and went down and had some cold coke, etc. Had a show in our mess hall tonight. Another "bailey bridge" has been put into service across the Pasig River. This one replaces the "Quezon Bridge" that was destroyed along with the others.

Thursday, June 28, 1945 The demobilization plan is going the same route as rotation. Reports have come out that men with 90 to 100 points need not plan on return to the states before, after the first of the year. The big talking point on the point system was that it was to be handled on an individual score basis, but at the least in this theater it has fallen into a quota set-up, which is discharge back to the states by unit quota. There are yet many men around, in some units with over 100 points, while men in some of the other outfits have gone back to the states with 95 points and less. I don't know when my moral has been lower.

Friday, June 29, 1945 Things are the same routine. Took a walk up through town this afternoon with Bill. Rizaul Ave. is improving all the time. New stores are being built and much of the trash has been cleaned up. The only commodities to be bought at any of these stores is souvenirs, and all these at an outrageous price. Manila is more of a midway than anything else.

Saturday, June 29, 1945 Went over to the 848 this afternoon. Being I get tomorrow off I stayed on board tonight. I wrote Marian a letter and read some that came today. Marian's letters are coming through quite regular now.

Sunday, July 1, 1945 Frye, Sprinkle, (two sailor friends) and I went on shore this afternoon. We came over here to camp and hung around our tent for a while. We went up to the Red Cross where we sweated out a long line to get a cold drink, and then went on up Rizaul Ave. where we stopped in at a theater where a Filipino stage show was playing. My two friends went back to the ship and I came back to camp, getting to bed a little past 11 PM.

Monday, July 2, 1945 Today marks my thirty forth month overseas. Lately my moral has been so low that I have been about half sick. It looks like the demobilization plan has fallen through like everything else does. So I have spent 34 months over here, I could spend that much more time, and it would make little difference to the Army.

Tuesday, July 3, 1945 Today Bob Larson went to the hospital with an attack of malaria. I hope to go out and see him tomorrow. Nothing out of the ordinary today. Had some training motion pictures in the mess hall this afternoon.

Wednesday, July 4, 1945 Today was Independence Day. It was just an ordinary day here. This afternoon some of we fellows hitch hiked out near the Filipino president's palace, where there is a swimming pool. This is the first fresh water I have swam in since leaving home. To work at midnight.

Thursday, July 5, 1945 Slept this morning, and then hitch hiked out to the hospital to see Bob this afternoon. He is feeling much better now. He told me he might be able to get me an officer's traveling bag at the P.X. there. I got back to camp in time for supper, after which I wrote some letters and then went to the show with the fellows.

Friday, July 6, 1945 Went out to see Bob again this afternoon. He succeeded in getting the traveling bag for me, and I brought it back to camp with me. I took the sewing machine needles up town with me this evening and sold them to some sidewalk merchants for 24 pesos. Twelve dollars for two dozen is bad.

Saturday, July 7, 1945 Nothing out of the ordinary today. A lot of brass around the Signal Center are sure making our work miserable. The way they are clamping down, a fellow might get a bust for nothing at all. You don't hear so much about demobilization anymore. All you do hear is "bitching." Nearly everyone is disgusted and disappointed with it, beyond words. It isn't coming close to being fair, as it seems to be a scramble with some units coming out better than others. One of my friends who has 92 points, because his service records are in Leyte, is on orders to go home. Only fellows with 100 points attached to this base have gone home from here.

Sunday, July 8, 1945 Frye wanted me to come over to the ship for dinner but being I had to work I couldn't make it. Things are sure a mess at the station. We don't know from one day to the next what wild dream some officer will think up next.

Monday, July 9, 1945 The regular routine today. Saw some training films in the mess hall this afternoon. Boy what won't they think of next? The chow has been fairly good lately. We have been having fresh potatoes, and we occasionally, also fresh eggs for breakfast. Rained hard tonight so we fellows stayed around our tent. We keep pretty dry except for the little rain that blows in the side, and sprays through the top.

Tuesday, July 10, 1945 This afternoon a bunch of we fellows got on a truck and went out to the swimming pool near the president's palace for a swim. However, when we arrived there the pool was being drained for cleaning, so we came back to camp with no swim. Tonight Bob and I went hitch hiking, and took a ride out Rizanl. We stopped off and took a walk through part of the Chinese cemetery. It was rather dark so we didn't see much of it. I hope to go out and take some pictures one of these days. Arrived back in camp around 10 PM. and went to bed.

Wednesday, July 11, 1945 Worked all day today. There is a rumor going around that an investigation is to be made into this demobilization business around here. Received three letters from Marian today. Mail service has been pretty good lately. It has been raining every afternoon now for the past two weeks.

Thursday, July 12, 1945 Today Smitty, Bill, Bob, and I went up to the Red Cross where we had some coffee. While we were standing drinking our coffee we noticed a camera laying there. Bob picked it up and we took it up to the desk. Bob asked how long they would keep the camera in case the owner didn't call for it. They said one month and then they would turn it into the quarter master. All of us felt that in case the camera wasn't claimed it should go to the finder, and we told the Red Cross worker we felt that in the event the rightful owner wasn't found, there was no reason why the quarter master or someone attached to that unit should have it. We left the desk and took the camera with us intending to try and find the owner ourselves. We walked up stairs and was standing near a post when a couple of fellows came by. I heard one of them say something about a camera. I called them over and one of the fellows was the one who had lost the camera. We told him about the quarter master deal, and he said he didn't blame us for not turning it in.

Friday, July 13, 1945 Today Smitty, Bob, and I went hitch hiking. We went out near Quezon City, then on out Rizaul Ave. to north Manila. We arrived back in camp in time for chow. I went to bed early tonight as I was sure tired.

Saturday, July 14, 1945 Another ordinary day. I have little heart in keeping up this diary any longer, writing letters home is a task. I am trying to accustom myself to one thought, and that is my return home won't be until the end of the war. Many of Marian's letters contain paragraphs asking about my prospects on demobilization, but the way things stand it is better I don't say anything one way or another.

Sunday, July 15, 1945 Marian and I have been married four years and one month today. We always have remembered the fifteenth of each month as an important date since we have been married. I worked the midnight shift last night and attempted sleeping a while this morning, but it was so hot all I could do was lay in my bunk and sweat.

Monday, July 16, 1945 Today Ed our chief operator came over to our tent with a form for me to fill out. It was a check on when I had my last rating on my present duties (present and past) I guess this is recommendation #5 coming up for another rating. I hardly think anything more will be heard from it.

Tuesday, July 17, 1945 The war against Japan is going into high gear. Our planes, both Army and Navy, are over Japan nearly at all times. Our war ships are now sailing up and down the coast of Japan, shelling at close range Japanese war industries located near the coast. Nothing unusual today, same routine.

Wednesday, July 18, 1945 This afternoon Smitty, Bob, Bill, Marty, and I took some pictures. We took a walk up town and I left the film to be developed. It will be a miracle if any of these pictures turn out. This is the roll of film I had to rewind on a 120 spool and I had a lot of trouble doing it. Went to work at 5 PM.

Thursday, July 19, 1945 This morning Smitty and I took a walk over through the walled city. It is unbelievable the change that has taken place in this area. Army engineers have gone in with stream shovels, bulldozers, and trucks, and are clearing away the rubble and wrecked buildings. When the army finishes what was formerly the walled city – it will only be a huge vacant lot, with only the old 15th century church standing. This church was the only structure not totally destroyed in the walled city. Most of the wall remains standing, but there are huge gaps blasted in it here and there. We spent a little time going through the old church. It is in fairly good condition and surprisingly modern in architecture. The surrounding gardens, etc. of the church have been destroyed. All that remains of this area is numerous small rooms and passages with much of the roofs and side caved in. After spending a little time here we went on over to the new YMCA snack bar that is off towards the edge of the walled city. We bought a couple of cokes and hamburgers, and then came back to camp. Thirty such snack bars are to be constructed throughout Manila for the G.I.s. This should put something of a damper on the "get rich overnight" restaurant owners around Manila.

Friday, July 20, 1945 Not much out of the ordinary today. Received a fruit cake in the mail from Marian's Uncle Linn, even though it had been en-route ten months, and it was crushed to 50 percent of its original thickness, this fruit cake was really delicious. Worked the day shift today. Went to the show tonight.

Saturday, July 21, 1945 This morning Smitty borrowed the lieutenant's jeep and Smitty, Bob and I went out touring around. It started to rain and we saw a

Filipino woman, and two girls trying to get a ride. Since we had no place in particular to go we took them home. We visited with them a while and then came back to camp. They were very grateful for the ride, and invited us to come back and see them.

Sunday, July 22, 1945 Bob who is working in the orderly room told me I had been recommended for a good conduct ribbon. He also informed me of something I never knew. The one day that I was AWOL after I had been in the Army but 5 weeks at Camp Crowder is marked up in my service record. One day more or less in the Army after four years doesn't make any difference one way or the other. My mail from home is slowing up a bit. Maybe it will pick up in a few days.

Monday, July 23, 1945 Last night and today was clear. This is the first rainless day we have had in over a month. Worked the day shift today, and saw a bunch of training films plus the regular show tonight. We sat for nearly four hours with some of the training films being on malaria control, how to put up a mosquito net, how to wash a mess kit. "OH BOY @#&$"

Tuesday, July 24, 1945 This morning Smitty, Bill Mac, Marty and I went up town to get the pictures I snapped the other day. Surprisingly as it may seem all of them but one came out OK. We messed around town a while and then came back to camp for noon chow. This afternoon Bob and I went over to the YMCA recreational center and went for a swim. It seemed quite odd that a swimming pool could be found undamaged on the second floor of a building full of shell holes, and partly destroyed. This evening I went down to G.H.Q. P.X. with Bob, where we smuggled ourselves in and had a coke and hamburger. Went to bed rather early.

Wednesday, July 25, 1945 Nothing unusual today. I went through my barracks bags and sorted out a lot of stuff I intend to send home. If ever the time comes that I do get to return home I don't want to have a lot of extra junk to carry. Slept before going to work at midnight tonight.

Thursday, July 26, 1945, Slept this morning after getting off the midnight shift. This afternoon Smitty, Bob, Mac and I went over to the snack bar near the walled city. All we fellows in our tent get along swell. Bob is rather imposing at times but quite easy to get along with. I don't think there is another tent in our camp where the fellows hang together so thoroughly as we do. Our working schedules permitting, we go to town together, to chow, look after each other's mail, and go to the shows together. We really have the family spirit in our tent.

Friday, July 27, 1945 Worked the day shift today. Boy things are sure in a muddle as far as our set up is concerned. A number of troops have arrived here from Europe, and there seems to be more soldiers from down south coming to Manila also. The G.I.s are so thick in town you can hardly walk through. Fellows wishing a cold drink at the Red Cross must stand in a line a block long. What snack bars there are, conditions are the same. The sidewalk merchants on Rizaul Ave. are really drumming for business, at the usual high prices. Rizaul Ave. is quite cleaned up of rubbish and many quite attractive stores have been opened.

Saturday, July 28, 1945 This afternoon Smitty, Mac, Marty and I went over to the snack bar near the walled city. We sweated out the line for a coke and hamburger and then decided to go up to the Red Cross. It and the snack bar near-by, were so crowded we didn't try to buck the line, so we came back to camp. Went to the show at G.H.Q. tonight.

Sunday, July 29, 1945 Mac and I went to church at G.H.Q. this morning. This noon Bob and I got into a pretty heated argument. He is a fairly nice guy, but he has to be told off once in a while. Shortly after chow I went up to the orderly room to get shots. I had to take the works this time – cholera, tetanus, typhoid, plus a smallpox vaccination. About tomorrow when all this serum hits me I will be in bad shape. This afternoon Marty, Mac, Bob, and I went over to the YMCA and smuggled our way into the swimming pool. I didn't stay in very long as my arms are getting stiff from the shots. I now have a shift of my own, and went to work at 5 PM.

Monday, July 30, 1945 I laid in my bunk nearly all day today as I am sure feeling punk from the shots I took the other day. Marty told me a pretty hot rumor today, one that I wish I hadn't heard. In a few days, fellows with 96 points will be sent home, and at the end of August fellows with 90 to 96 points are to be put on orders to go home. According to this I might be home for Thanksgiving and Christmas. Give me strength if things fall through this time also.

Tuesday, July 31, 1945 I was rather feverish last night and because I kicked the cover off, I caught a bad cold. I am so horse I can hardly talk. I went to work today, but Ed, our chief operator looked after things for me. I spent the day in my bunk.

Wednesday, August 1, 1945 Today they issued campaign ribbons, overseas bars, etc. I received a Asiatic Pacific Ribbon, four Campaign Stars, and six overseas Hash Marks. I also received my Citation Ribbon. There is still a lot of talk going around about this going home business. If things should work out for me this time, it is possible I could get home for Christmas.

Thursday, August 2, 1945 Rained a little while today and cooled things off a bit. I still feel pretty punk from the cold I caught. Today is the 35 month mark for my overseas service. Worked five to midnight tonight. This job is sure a joke as far as anything to do, and it makes us wonder how long we will have it.

Friday, August3, 1945 Went up town today and bought a few gifts to send home. Rumors of the good kind are still going around, and their origin seems quite authentic. Orders are to be cut in a few days down to 91 points for fellows to be sent home by the end of the month. Whether or not 91 is included, I am not sure, but anyway, even if fifty percent of this rumor is correct, it shows some sort of effort is being made to get the fellows home.

Saturday, August 4, 1945 One of my friends off the 848 came over to camp this afternoon. The ship arrived in port yesterday. As soon as I get the chance I am going out to see the fellows. Rumors about this going home business still are going around and a good percentage of the fellows are taking it 100 percent. As for me, I can't help but fall for it even though I know I shouldn't. Bob, one of my tent mates, who has 79 points, and as things stand, not much chance of getting home this year, has in his mind, I think, decided to make a try at a medical discharge. The section eight kind, or in other words, mentally unbalanced. For the past two mornings, when Bob gets out of bed, he asks we other fellows if we heard those airplanes landing in the street? Anyone of us knows he is putting on an act. He is crazy alright, for thinking he can fool a bunch of doctors who make mental cases their business.

Sunday, August 5, 1945 (*written in red ink*) This is the first red ink I have used and I am using it now as this is all I have at the moment. Yesterday afternoon I got paid, and salted it away in my soldier's account. It rained all day today and nearly all night. This evening, just as I was getting ready for bed I heard someone call me from outside. I went out to see who it was, and standing on the outside of the fence, was what I thought was a Filipino boy. I went over to see what he wanted. However, it turns out to be a girl. She said she had just gotten in from the province, and had no place to sleep that night. She said she was the only one of her family left, that the Japs had killed all the others. I don't know what she thought I could do. I guess she saw me sitting on my bunk from the street. Anyway I told her how to go up to the Red Cross, the only place I could think of to send her.

Monday, August 6, 1945 I am really going off the deep end on getting home now. Today the headlines in the paper stated that half of the 150,000 men eligible to return home will leave by the end of this month. Orders are supposed to go down, inclusive of 91 points, if everything works. I should just get under the wire. I took some negatives up town this afternoon to have some prints made of the 848. I don't know what's the matter with me, but I still feel pretty lousy. Maybe I have had a little touch of fever. If I don't feel better tomorrow I guess I will go on sick call. It would be really "H" though to land in the hospital, and miss going home this time.

Tuesday, August 7, 1945 Worked at the station all day today. On one of our circuits we received an S.O.S. message from a plane that had gone down into the ocean. I never heard if they were rescued or not. The first atomic bomb was dropped on Hiroshima, Japan. This bomb, weighing but 400 pounds, caused 2000 times as much destruction as the six-ton British Block Busters. No photographs have yet been taken of Hiroshima, as a cloud of dust and smoke still cover the area. It is thought that nearly the whole city was wiped out. It has become official now that in a few days we are to receive our orders to return to the states.

Wednesday, August 8, 1945 Went over to the 848 today. Castelman and I went to town for a while. Being I had to go to work at midnight I was back in camp at 9:30. There isn't much to do but walk around town anyway.

Thursday, August 9, 1945 Reports came out today that Russia has declared war on Japan and have started an advance into Manchukue (Japanese Puppet State). The second atomic bomb has been dropped on Japan. Another ultimatum has been sent to Japan to surrender or be destroyed.

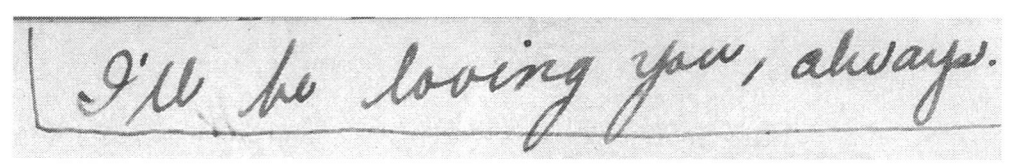

At the top of this page my mother has written:, "I'll be loving you, always.

Friday, August 10, 1945 Today has been the kind of day that could only happen in the Army. One of the greatest extremes of disappointment and happiness. To start with, this morning I was on my way over to the 848, and waiting on the dock for the whale boat. When the 848 whale boat came over, Lieutenant Sparks, was aboard and told me all of we old members of the 848 were to go back aboard, to go on another operation. The story I got when arriving at the 848 was that we are to go to Okinawa in a few days, and there stand by with the intention of going on to Japan when they surrender, which is expected shortly. I ate dinner on board the 848 and then came back to camp to pack my stuff. Bill Pandolfi is also to go aboard the 848. In the middle of the afternoon we said good-bye to Smitty, Mac and Bob, and loaded our stuff on a truck that brought us out to the transmitter station where we are to stay until we leave. All we fellows who were expecting our orders to return home really feel down in the dumps. This evening Bill and I went to town. With part of the money I had saved for going home, I bought a few souvenirs to send home. Bill and I went down to camp where I got my laundry and then, since there was nothing else to do, we started hitch hiking back to camp. While we were standing beside the road trying to get a ride, a truck came by loaded with fellows who were yelling, "The war is over – the war is over." In a little while we could hear shots from all kinds of small arms going off. Whistles started blowing, and a search-light started sweeping across the sky. Bill and I decided we would go back to town and see what was going on. Filipinos and Americans were going wild. Signs were torn down and liquor stores were broken into. Bill and I decided the best thing for us to do was to go down to our old camp and not take any chances of getting run under or shot up town.

We learned that this surrender report had not been confirmed. It was broadcast from the Japanese news agency that they were notifying Switzerland that they would except the Allied surrender terms, providing they could keep their emperor.

After being encased in the conditions of war for so long the realization that the war is, or nearly is over is an indescribable feeling. One that I have never – or could ever have again. This 848 operation may fall through yet, and perhaps I can still get home for Christmas.

Saturday, August 11, 1945 Bill and I arrived out here at the transmitter station a little before eight this morning. The lieutenant stopped in and said that more than likely, if Japan officially surrenders – in a few days we will probably go aboard the 848 and go to Japan. We have turned in a clothing list to be issued winter clothing.

I received three letters from Marian today. In a round-about way she expressed her disapproval on my procedure about my returning home prospects. Again, I am glad I have given her no encouragement. Stayed around camp all day.

Sunday, August12, 1945 Stayed in camp last night and saw the show. This morning we were told to pack our stuff and get ready to go aboard the 848. Bill had gone to church and so I packed his junk also and loaded it on the truck. Just as we were ready to pull out Bill arrived back at camp, so he made it by the skin of his teeth. We got aboard the 848 around 2 PM and spent the rest of the day getting settled. None of we Army fellows were permitted shore leave tonight. It made little difference to me, as I am pretty tired tonight. Saw the picture show on deck.

Monday, August 13, 1945 This afternoon we pulled anchor and went out in the harbor to take on water, and oil. We thought perhaps we would leave tonight, but our orders were canceled. I guess our sailing depends on negotiations made as to the Jap expectations of our peace terms. The Allies have returned the Jap peace offer with alterations as to our Allied Supreme Commander having complete control of the Japanese Empire, until such time as the surrender terms are carried out and Japan is dismembered as a power capable of staging war.

Headed to Okinawa - Peace Treaty or an invasion?

Tuesday, August 14, 1945 We remained tied alongside the tanker all night [then] pulled away and dropped anchor in the middle of the morning. The lieutenant gave us our instructions as to our future duties this morning. In case Japan surrenders we are to go to Japan and act as communications back to G.H.Q. Manila until more permanent facilities can be installed. In case no peace terms go through we will go to Japan, but with an invasion force. We are to go first to Okinawa before going to Japan. We pulled anchor around five PM and got under way. They say we should arrive at Okinawa in three or four days.

Radio report came through tonight that Japan has accepted our peace terms. However, this is not official as yet. No one aboard is much concerned about this voyage, only the possibility of running into a typhoon up around Okinawa. There has been some bad ones in recent weeks.

Wednesday, August 15, 1945 The skies were clear and the sea calm today as we proceeded along the coast of Luzon. Reports came over the radio this morning that Japan and the Allied powers have agreed on unconditional peace terms and hostilities have ceased. General Mac Arthur has been appointed Supreme Allied Commander of Occupation Forces. Only the signing of the peace treaty remains to complete the official end of World War number Two. Even though hostilities have ceased, we still sail under full war cruising conditions. Who knows, maybe the Japs are trying to pull a fast one. " Another" Pearl Harbor."

Thursday, August 16, 1945 Just a routine day aboard ship. The sky is clear and the sea continues to be calm. We rounded the northern tip of Luzon this afternoon and headed in a northeasterly direction. The Japs still don't seem to consider the war as being over. Many Jap planes are still being shot down as they attempt to fly over our fleet. The Japanese Emperor is to fly to Okinawa and then on to Manila to sign the peace treaty. It seems we can notice the weather getting a little cooler as we go farther north.

Friday, August 17, 1945 The sky was clear again today but the ocean was a little rough, and the ship pitched and rolled to some extent. Not having been at sea for a time I feel a little woozy, as do most of the G.Iers aboard. More Jap planes are being shot down as they continue to attack our fleet. Emperor Hirohito.[50]

Saturday, August 18, 1945 We arrived here at Buckner Bay, Okinawa shortly past midnight. However, we didn't attempt to enter the bay until day light and spent the time cruising around the outer harbor. It is easy to see what an advantage the Japs had in defending this beach. The harbor, being nearly a half circle is overlooked by a ring of hills that rises nearly from the beach. No one seems to know how long we will be here. I guess we will move on to Japan as soon as the surrender negotiations are completed. Japan still seems to be stalling and they are still attacking our fleet, and aircraft. General Mac Arthur has informed the Japanese government to send their peace delegation to Manila without delay.

Sunday, August 19, 1945 Today we pulled anchor and went over to an oil ship where we took on fuel. I guess we will be here but a short time before we go on to Japan. The Japanese envoy of fifteen Japanese officials arrived at Manila late this afternoon. A conference was called soon after and carried on until 3 AM. The Japanese officials came with sailors and pistols, but were not permitted to take them to the conference room with them. The Japanese envoy were given a turkey dinner with all the trimmings. A lot of Army, Navy, and Marine battle scared victims will enjoy hearing that!!!! Today the Navy fellows were informed of a point system for discharge. A number of fellows on board are eligible, and the captain is taking action on their release. Frye, one of my Navy friends is eligible for release.

Monday, August 20, 1945 I spent the day as mess cook (K.P.) we Army fellows have to take turns at this job. The Navy sure gets things done. My friend Frye and some of the other Navy fellows are to go aboard a troop ship tomorrow

---

[50] Born 1901 (-1989) – came to power in 1926 – was supposed to be a descendent of the sun god, but had to admit this was not true after Japan lost the war.) Has informed the Allies that there would be a little delay in his signing the treaty. It looks like the Japs haven't had enough yet.

to go home. Why can't the Army show a little sign of organization like that? I guess surrender negotiations are still going on. At least the Japanese envoy has not as yet returned to Japan. General Jonathan Wainwright *(1883 – 1953 – Survived the Bataan Death March – was held in a POW camp in Manchuria – was with General MacArthur on the USS Missouri when the peace treaty was signed)* has been rescued from a Jap prison camp in Manchuria. He was Officer in Command when Bataan and Corregidor fell to the Japs in the early part of the war. According to rumor we might get under way tomorrow. If plans work out as planned, we are to have a teletype circuit to the battleship Missouri. We are supposed to go long side her and unload some equipment in the near future.

Tuesday, August 21, 1945 A bunch of we fellows got shore liberty this afternoon. We caught a ride in a weapons carrier and the driver, being a regular guy, took us on sort of a sight-seeing tour. We traveled over sort of a back road to Naha, Okinawa, the largest city on the island. This city was formerly about eighty thousand, but little of it remains standing now. There are some remains of what had been a number of modern buildings. On our way to Naha, we passed through many small villages that had been totally destroyed. The country that we saw was very hilly and many cliffs and bluffs overlooked the valleys all of these the Japs made the most use of, constructing fortifications where ever possible. The Japs had also taken advantage of the many tombs that were built around the countryside, turning these into fortifications. The Okinawans didn't seem to construct a central place such as a cemetery for burial of their dead. Each family had their own tomb built on their property. I sure take my hat off to the Americans who had the job of dislodging the Japs from this island. Got back to the ship around 5 PM. Managed to snap a few pictures today. (Little does my dad know that one year from today he will become a "daddy."—I will arrive)

Wednesday, August 22, 1945 We pulled anchor this morning and went over to take on water. However, we no sooner got tied up than we received orders to pull out. Outside the harbor the ocean was really rough. Our ship rolled and plunged, the bow going completely under some of the time. My sea legs only stayed with me a couple of hours. I managed to eat dinner, but I lost it over the rail soon after. Boy am I sick. Nevertheless, I had to stand my radio watch. The only thing I could do was lay on the deck with the headphones around my neck. We are now on our way to Tokyo.

Thursday, August 23, 1945 Today wasn't quite so rough, but even so our ship is rolling around enough so that many aboard are sick. The only way I can keep anything on my stomach is to lay in my bunk. TOO SICK TO WRITE MORE!

Friday and Saturday, August 24 and 25, 1945 Today and yesterday is the worst it has been. The ocean is a mass of mountainous waves. Our ship is being tossed around like a cork. About half the sailors, as well as we Army fellows are sick. Many of the dishes in the galley are getting broke. We are maintaining radio contact with two other ships. The only way I can work my shift is lay on the deck of our radio room with the head phones around my neck. We arrived at the position of the rendezvous, where we fell into position with a convoy. We are now 250 miles east of Tokyo. We learned today that we are not to go into Tokyo until Tuesday.

Sunday, August 26, 1945 Last night it was so rough I could hardly keep from falling out of my bunk. The past few days has got me on the "ragged edge." I never felt so sick, run down, weak, and worn out in my life. Bill is about the worst off of any of us. He hasn't eaten at all hardly in the past four days or has gotten out of his bunk. I have been too sick to have been able to keep my diary up on a day-to-day basis. News item today stated that fellows with 85+ points would be home by November.

Monday, August 27, 1945 The ocean calmed to quite an extent today, and this evening I began to feel like myself again. I ate this evening's meal without having to rush out again, due to my weak stomach. I wrote Marian a letter this evening, the first since leaving Okinawa. Our mail isn't going out anyway. Our convoy made up of some forty ships is now headed toward Tokyo Bay at six knots. We are due to arrive tomorrow morning.

Tuesday, August 28, 1945 Late yesterday afternoon a Jap submarine, about forty miles ahead of us, notified a destroyer of our convoy that they wanted to surrender. A crew was selected from several ships, who went aboard the submarine.

At 8:30 A.M. I got my first glimpse of Japan. Through my binoculars you could see the faint outline of Mount Fuji. It was noon until we were well within the outer Tokyo Bay. This is about forty miles from the inner bay and Tokyo. So far, the several small islands that we came near were not very scenic, but rugged, with a moderate amount of vegetation here and there. After arriving at the position where we dropped anchor, we were then about a mile offshore. There were many factories and small village areas located along the coast. There are many war ships of all types laying at anchor that arrived yesterday or today. All ships have discontinued gun watches and full war cursing conditions while at anchor. We had a movie topside tonight.

Wednesday, August 29, 1945 I slept quite a lot better last night. I am over the spell of sea sickness that most of us went through during our voyage from Okinawa. This morning we could plainly see Mount Fuji rising in the distance high about the surrounding country. Clouds have kept it hidden from view to the most part. I didn't get a chance to get a picture this morning as I didn't have any of my 620 film rewound to fit my 120 camera. Perhaps tomorrow I might get a picture.

We pulled anchor early this morning and got underway. As we passed through the mouth of inner Tokyo Bay, a cruiser passed us and took over patrol with a destroyer. Far up ahead the destroyer was dropping some depth chargers. A midget

Jap sub was evidently prowling around the area. This morning the Jap submarine that surrendered yesterday came into the harbor. I managed to get a snapshot as it passed by. They say this is the first Jap sub to surrender.

Thursday, August 30, 1945 This morning troop transports, and L.S.D's pulled to within about a mile of the beach in preparation to the initial landing of Marines to take over Japanese defense positions, and naval installations. In the hills just back of the beach white flags are flying, marking the position of the Japanese coastal guns. These were marked in such a way so that our forces would know their location.

Many formations of Navy fighters and dive bombers, as well as formations of B.29 bombers flew over the landing area. While watching these operations from the deck of our ship, we listened to an account of it from San Francisco. This operation went off like any invasion, only without the shooting.

Friday, August 31, 1945 This morning, early, we pulled anchor and went over to the ship Teton to take on water. We were alongside until shortly after dinner, and then got under way and went up the coast to a new anchorage spot. At this point we were but a short distance offshore, and near- by a Jap battleship. From what I can learn, it is the Kongo, the only Jap battleship left that is in halfway decent repair at all. It was rainy and foggy all day today, and I spent little time out on the deck. I still didn't get a chance to take a picture of Mount Fuji. Our work in our radio station is picking up to some extent, and with the now existing eight stations in our one "High Command" net things are in quite a turmoil. Our work schedule is quite irregular. Sometimes we are on four hours and off four, while we might work eight hours and have off eight. Had a show in the mess hall tonight.

Saturday, September 1, 1945 Today was quite an eventful day for us. Around noon we pulled anchor and went into dock at Yokohama. Our ship was no sooner tied up than the fellows started jumping over the side onto the dock. There was no sign of a Jap to be seen anywhere around the dock, warehouses, or dock area. About half the fellows off the ship started on a little tour of inspection in and around the warehouses that were unlocked. We rummaged around through piles of junk here and there. We found many boxes containing travel folders of United States and Canada. These the Japs must have acquired just before the war started. One group of fellows found a book containing diagrams of many of our war ships. Some of the guys found souvenirs quite worth- while, such as drinking tumblers that had pounded engraved bronze vases, and candle holders. A bunch of us finally went for a walk up around General MacArthur's headquarters. Around this area of Yokohama are a number of Jap soldiers and police. It is disgusting, the false attitude the soldiers and police put on. All of them break their arms saluting any American soldier that passes. Whether the Jap soldiers be a private or an officer, they all salute. From the opinion I gathered, their attitude is one of defeat, but being what they are, they would stab us in the back and start another war tomorrow if they had the means to do it with. After talking to some of the Air Born Troops, they said that all of Yokohama is absolutely dead. Nearly the entire population has gone to the hills. Due to Japanese propaganda, the people believe they would be tortured and killed by the Americans. The Japanese soldiers, to some extent, show signs of fear when Americans walk in their direction. Soon after we returned to the ship, she pulled away from the dock to make room for some L.S.T.s to unload. We pulled away from the dock a short distance and tied up to a barge. A short distance across the inlet where we are now at is a Jap aircraft carrier that was evidently sunk by our planes. Most of its stern is under water.

Sunday, September 2, 1945 Today officially brings to a close World War Two. Today is "V.J. Day." At approximately ten A.M. the Japanese officials signed the peace document aboard the Battleship Missouri. This morning around eight A.M. ceremonies got under way over at the dock, which is about three hundred yards from where we are moored. Three destroyers were alongside the pier for the purpose of convoying General MacArthur, Admiral Nimitz, and Admiral Halsey to the Battleship Missouri. We could see most of the ceremony from the deck of our ship. Soldiers were lined up in ranks along the pier, while sailors aboard the destroyers, dressed in whites, stood at attention. After a short time, the destroyers pulled away from the pier, while the band played "Anchors Away" and many other military numbers. Today marks my third anniversary overseas. Prospects of returning home very soon seem to be pretty nil and were further dampened, when Gen. Aiken gave a speech aboard ship tonight. He congratulated the personal on the part they had played aboard the 848 in the conclusion of the war. He said, also, that we would be aboard for quite a while yet. This was a hard pill to swallow, as many of us were hoping to be home by Christmas.

Monday, September 3, 1945 Moral of the Army fellows aboard ship is pretty low with the prospect of staying around Tokyo Bay for what will no doubt, be for several months. Yokohama has been placed out of bounds to all service men, except those assigned to duty. All we can do is stand on the deck and look at the waterfront. Some of our friends who we are working with by C.W. radio, back in Manila, have told us, that many of the guys have, or soon, will go home. Marty, my old tent mate, who had 91 points, the same as I, have gone home. Some of my old friends who arrived overseas a month later than I and with five less points, are on orders to return home. General MacArthur made

P.C.E.R 848 Ship I was on. 3rd ship into Tokyo Bay when peace was signed

Joe C. Hightower

General MacArthur 3rd from L.
General Jonathan M. Wainright 4th L.

the statement that (and I quote) "No man is essential to the Army below a Brigadier General." We have often read news reports and listened to communiqués, stating, that under the point system, an individual will be taken care of on an individual basis. A number of Army jobs have been classified as essential, but our type of work, or speck numbers [job classification number, mine is 777] was not on the list. I wonder if the people back home know what goes on inside the Army Whirlpool. I know they don't. This morning our ship pulled over alongside a transport to take on water. We remained tied up most of the day. This evening when we pulled away we came over to a different place in the harbor to moor our ship. The position, where we are now, is near the Yokohama shipyards. From here we can see cargo ships that were under construction. Moored in the bay are two other ships with completed hulls, but with the super structure still unfinished. These ships are similar to many of our cargo ships, but not as large. Off to one side of the shipyards is a half sunken Jap air craft carrier, that had evidently been sunk by our air force. The stern shows signs of having been hit with heavy bombs.

Tuesday, September 4, 1945 Some of the fellows were given shore leave today over at a small area near one of the docks. Here, three hospital ships are tied up, and nearby along the dock is a half sunken Japanese aircraft carrier. Evidently the carrier was attacked by our planes while tied up by the pier. Being I had to work this afternoon I didn't get to go ashore. Maybe I will get to go over tomorrow. Most of we fellows are feeling pretty much down and out about our chances of going home. At our request, Lieutenant Sparks (our C.O.) made up a message and I sent it by C.W. to Manila. This was a message asking for relief for we fellows and action to be taken to send us home. I guess I look on the pessimistic side of most everything, but I suppose nothing will come of this message. I hear Bernnie Suiter, back in Manila got another stripe.

Wednesday, September 5, 1945 This morning I went over on the beach with one of our lieutenants and T/36T Keith Davidson after a couple of super pro receivers. We had to talk our way past the M.P.s at a bridge, in order to go over to the warehouses where the 232nd sig. sev. Bn. Is located. We acquired our two receivers and were lucky in getting a ride with them back to the dock in a jeep. Transportation is sure at a minimum. The only trucks available are the ones commandeered from the Japs. Half of these will hardly run, and the rest is considered common property by whatever American unit can steal a truck from the other. When we got back to the dock our whale boat wasn't there yet, and we had quite a while to wait. I walked over to one of the hospital ships and there met a sailor who had been a prisoner of the Japs. He said he could talk for hours on the atrocities the Japs had committed, but we more than likely wouldn't believe him, and anyway that was one thing he wanted to forget. Of the time I spent talking to him, hardly a minute passed that he wouldn't break off the conversation and say that he could hardly believe everything had come true. He said the past five months were much easier for them, as the Japs must have realized they could not win the war. This sailor looked quite healthy, but you could tell he had gone through a period of partial starvation.

Went on shore liberty this afternoon. We were taken over to the small area by the hospital ships. Most of we fellows spent our time going through the half sunken Jap aircraft carrier that was near the dock, a short distance from the hospital ships. This Jap carrier was pretty heavily damaged by our aircraft. The fantail was mostly blown away. The forward part of the ship was gutted by fire and due to what had been wooden bulkheads, the flames must have spread all over this area of the ship. This Jap carrier is sure a flimsily constructed ship compared to our carriers. It appeared to only have the bare necessities required to house the crew and enable this ship to exert the duties of an aircraft carrier. It seemed to leave an impression of shoddiness, lack of refinement, and simplicity. The simplicity part of this carrier might tend to be an advantage, but I think it only existed because of the Jap's lack of a high level of craftsmanship. By estimation I judge this carrier to be, perhaps, 500 feet long by 80 feet wide.

The whale boat came after us around 5 P.M. and we returned to the 848. This evening Col. Eddy came aboard and lieutenant Sparks, our commanding officer asked him about we fellows with better than 90 points, going home. Col. Eddy really gave our Lieutenant a lot of encouragement for us. He said that he would see that we were relieved and in perhaps two weeks we would be on our way. All of we fellows feel pretty good about our prospects. It looks like Christmas at home.

Thursday, September 6, 1945 Got to go on liberty again this afternoon. I messed around the Jap aircraft carrier and took some pictures, then I walked over to the other side of this small area, which is sort of a peninsula, stretching out in the bay. Nearby, in a small Jap shed I found a number of Japanese post cards. I talked to one of my old friends back in Manila by C.W. tonight. Nearly all the fellows with 85 points are either on their way home or orders are being cut for them. Fellows as low as 75 points are also to be sent home.

Friday, September 7, 1945 I could have gone ashore again this afternoon, but instead I stayed on board and sorted a lot of my stuff over so I can send as much of my stuff home as possible, so I won't have it to carry with me.

Saturday, September 8, 1945 Many of we fellows were in for a big letdown today. After things were looking so bright as to our going home, the whole thing came back at us in reverse. Col Eddy evidently just shuffled the thing off, and we received a lame excuse from some major over on the beach. Our C.O. aboard ship tried to make arrangements so that we could leave here and go directly aboard a transport that is returning to the states. However, the answer was no. It seems there is some regulation as to first going to a casual camp, and at the present time there isn't any, and we were informed it would be a good while before one was built. I never felt so crushed in all my life, and many other fellows aboard this ship feel the same way. We were also told that there are personnel here to replace us. We fellows have decided that at first possible chance we are going to find an inspector General and see if we can get something done. Our lieutenant told us in an unofficial way that he thought this would be the wise thing to do.

Two sailors in fifteen minutes notice, were taken off this ship and put aboard a transport to go to the U.S. today. The end of book four.[51]

---

[51] My father had five separated diaries—this is the final one of the five.

Sunday, September 9, 1945 I don't know when I have felt more depressed than I have the past few days. Tomorrow, six of we fellows are going over to see the Inspector General and see if something can be done about us getting home. Not a one of us feel we have anything to lose by seeing the I.G. Since Col. Eddy is giving us the run-around anyway, we might as well give him a reason for giving us all this B.S. The Inspector General is about the only recourse an enlisted man has to settle his problems, outside the Red Cross. This is the only means you have of going over the head of some of the big shots, when they give you a rough deal.

If you put your point across to the C.O., the officer, or officers responsible for your complaint catch heck. Win or lose, you are behind the eight ball with the brass hats who gave you a bad time. In our case if we get to go home- fine and dandy, if we don't, what happens won't make any difference to us anyway.

Went over to the beach this afternoon. Some of we fellows walked over where there had formally been a Jap coastal gun emplacement. All the guns had been removed and only the turrets remained. In the immediate vicinity was an underground network of military installations for a large number of troops. Found a Jap ammunition box that I intend using to send some of my stuff home in.[52]

Monday, September 10, 1945 Shortly after dinner six of us went over to Yokohama to see the Inspector General. By two fellows carrying guns we were permitted to go into the city proper. We first went to see the I.G. of the Eighth Army headquarters, but being we are of the Sixth Army, and detached to G.H.Q., we couldn't get anything done there. A major, who seemed to be a pretty good fellow, and wanted to help us, informed us of another office to go to. Here we saw a colonel and after telling him our story we had little hopes of accomplishing very much. He was an old Army man, and one of the types who considers your home in the Army, whether here or in the U.S. However, he said he would look into the matter, and he took the data we had written out. We gave him Colonel Eddie's and another major's name, who are directly responsible for our delay in getting home. We fellows don't feel we accomplished much today. In fact, we are probably worse off than before. We will probably hear from Colonel Eddy and he isn't going to be very happy.

Tuesday, September 11, 1945 I don't think anyone could feel any lower in spirits than I do today. I guess each one of us has the same personal opinion.

---

[52] Many of my dad's "souvenirs" I have acquired. This is one of them.

I am worked up to the point where I can hardly sleep and am about half sick. Working our C.W. to Manila doesn't help matters much either, as the fellows talk back and forth, and learn all the dope down there. Most of the bunch we left behind in Manila are on their way home, and orders are being cut on fellows down to 75 points will go home in another month. No one had better ever try and tell me the point system is fair. Not only has it turned out to be a farce with me personally, but this is the case with thousands stuck over here in the Pacific. We hear many comments on demobilization from Senators and Congressmen. Some say it stinks, other advocate making it even worse.

Wednesday, September 12, 1945 Worked this morning and this afternoon, packed the box I have to send home. The sailors here on board are up in the air about the revised demobilization plan that will make many of them eligible to return home. We are still standing by to go on up to Tokyo. As rumors go, we should leave soon.

Thursday, September 13, 1945 This afternoon a sailor friend and I went over on the beach. Since I had borrowed a 45 automatic from another friend, we were permitted to go outside the dock area. We walked down the street a number of blocks, crossing over many small bridges. We finally came to what seemed to be a main boulevard. We walked on across this street up another where a large number of civilians were coming from. After walking a few more blocks we arrived at a railroad station. All trains arriving were electric at this station. The whole area that we had seen since leaving the docks was completely destroyed by firebombs dropped by our B29 bombers. This railroad station was no exception. Station installations were nearly completely destroyed. With crowds, equaling those of any large railroad station, and only three low walls left of the men's restroom, we were surprised at the nonchalant attitude, as the Japs still were using this former building. We also saw some steam trains, of which were all narrow gage, and looked to be about the same gage as Australian trains of similar gage. The Japanese coaches were very similar to American, except built on a much smaller scale. I took some pictures today, but as has been the case, nearly every day, since we arrived, it was quite cloudy. We arrived back at the ship at 5:30 P.M. Saw the show on deck tonight.

Friday, September 14, 1945 We received some news today that was really encouraging. Our service records were taken over to headquarters, which is on board the communications ship "Teton" for the purpose of checking them for our qualifications to go home. We are supposed to be on our way home by the twenty sixth of this month. I wonder what I will be looking forward to after the twenty sixth?

Saturday, September 15, 1945 This afternoon a group of around eighteen of we soldiers and sailors with two officers in charge went on a little sightseeing tour of Yokohama. The first thing we did was to stop a streetcar which we all piled on. We rode out away from the business district a couple of miles and then got off all along the route, nearly the entire area was burned out by the fire bombs our bombers had dropped. We decided to walk around through a residential district, which was, by appearance, a lower-class neighborhood. Nearly all the houses are very small. From what we could see, these houses seemed very clean. The floor of the house was built up above the street level, perhaps two feet. The Japs, upon entering, would take off their sandals, and either sit or kneel on the floor of their house. The only walls that separated the main room into smaller rooms, seemed to be of a thin material. We were able to see into these houses quite easily, as most of them had large openings in the front. The streets winding around through the neighborhood was hardly larger than small alleys. After looking around a while, we came to where there was a temple. Knowing that the Japanese have a special sort of religious belief, and not wishing to infringe on their religious beliefs, we asked some Japanese nearby, if we could look around for a little while. Very few Japs we have met can speak English, so we have to use our best sign language on them. At the entrance to this temple, I attempted to take a picture even though the sky was cloudy and there was hardly enough light to take snap shots by. After leaving this neighborhood we walked through a sort of community shopping district. We went into a store that sold mostly different kinds of vases, cups, and saucers, etc. I bought one rather large vase, and would have bought many more, but with the one, I was quite loaded down, having to carry my camera also. We finally caught a streetcar back to the city, and then walked down to the waterfront where we caught our whale boat back to our ship. I wrote some letters home tonight. Marian and I have been married four years, three months today.[53]

After our long delay, tomorrow we are to go up to Tokyo. The P.C.E. 848 has been up there nearly a week now. We were supposed to go to Tokyo at the time, but we have been handling a large amount of traffic to Manila, and our

---

[53] As previously noted – my folks were married only 8 months when my dad left.

orders were delayed. This evening some of the sailors came back to the ship in a Jap harbor patrol launch that they had found over near the pier. The engine in it doesn't work so good, but with a few adjustments it should be OK. The sailors plan to take this launch up to Tokyo tomorrow.

Sunday, September 16, 1945 This morning at eleven A.M. we left Yokohama Harbor, sailed out past the fleet and headed up the bay to Tokyo, a distance of thirty-five miles. All along the coast, between Yokohama and Tokyo was a solid area that had formally been one of Japan's main industrial areas. Our B-29 bombers did a good job here. While we were still far out in Tokyo Bay, and approached the dock area, our ship was required to come in near the docks through a narrow channel marked by buoys spaced every few hundred yards apart. The main harbor area was partially enclosed by what appeared to be unusual small artificial islands. The P.C.E. 849 and another small patrol vessel were tied up at the pier, and our ship pulled in just behind them. Ours is the third U.S. ship to tie up here at Tokyo. The ship "Teton" also came up here to Tokyo today but being a large ship and drawing twenty-four feet of water, she was unable to come alongside the pier as the water was too shallow. This afternoon we were given liberty. Around twenty-four soldiers and sailors and two officers were in our bunch. Ginga Ave. one of Tokyo's main streets is not far from this dock area, so by stopping a Jap truck we rode up near the center of the business district in a short time. After looking around a short time all of us filed on board a streetcar and road farther into the center of the city. Transportation facilities seem to be in normal conditions, but Tokyo is certainly in bad condition as far as the effects of our bombing on the business and industrial areas are concerned. Seldom in the center of a business district, did we see an undamaged building? In this area there were large plots of ground, many acres, some of them, where once there had been modern buildings, but now are vacant lots filled with rubble. We fellows finally decided to get on a subway train and ride out into the suburbs. We soldiers have made it a practice to get our transportation for nothing. When getting on a streetcar, we just get on. When we wish to get off, we tap the motorman on the shoulder. The regular fare is the equivalent to one cent American money. The street cars and subways are much smaller than those in the U.S. but being the average Jap is quite small in stature, their transportation facilities are adequate for them. After getting off the subway, we walked around for a time, and then decided we had better start back to the ship. We stopped a Jap truck and motioned to the Jap driver, which way we wanted to go. The Jap didn't seem too happy about having to drive clear back across Tokyo, but we didn't mind about that. After the Jap let us out by the docks, we gave him a package of cigarettes and a few yen, which was probably more money than he had made all day, and then he was all smiles. Had a show on deck tonight. Unless a fellow puts on a jacket you sure get cold sitting through a show. We can notice that the weather is getting colder all the time. As to our demobilization point rating, we have been given a new point rating of points gained since May 12. I now have 98, having gained 7 more points. There is some talk that we may be given an additional 5 points for being in Japan before the peace was signed.

Monday, September 17, 1945 Being I had to work today I didn't rate liberty. However, this morning I got away from the ship for a short time to try and find a box to send some stuff home in. This afternoon some sailor went out and came back with a three wheeled motorcycle. I guess how they got it wouldn't be rated as just borrowing. The sailors are still talking and planning on their prospects of going home under the new point system the Navy has. It rained a little bit tonight.

Tuesday, September 18, 1945 This morning three other fellows and I took a walk down around the docks. About all there is, is row upon row of warehouses and most of them empty. We went into one warehouse that was formerly a Jap signal supply depot. There were untold quantities of radio equipment. Nearly all of it was of low-grade stuff, and according to our standards, out of date. A few items of their equipment showed a high standard of workmanship.

This afternoon Bill and I went on shore liberty together. Our plans were to buy a few souvenirs to send home. The Japs won't take American money, and as yet the Army hasn't come out with the invasion money, so we had to devise another means to get a few yen. Cigarettes are about the only alternative, and you can get thirty yen or the equivalent of two dollars a package for them. As far as the Army is concerned, selling any Army issued is illegal, but selling cigarettes is a common practice around here, and nothing has been done about it.

Bill and I bought a few pictures, etc. and then caught a streetcar back to the dock area. A couple of sailors came back to the ship today with another motorcycle. The P.C.E. 849, who has now moved over to another mooring position, gave a 35 Chevrolet Sedan to our ship – the officers got this.

Wednesday, September 19, 1945 Last night the tail-end of a typhoon blew through this area. Our ship was tripled moored with extra lines. Being tied up to the dock, and inside the breakwater, the storm had little effect on us. A small boat with fifty men aboard sank out in the bay last night. Forty of them were rescued. This morning our C.O. Lieutenant Sparks called all Army fellows out on the fantail and gave us a talk. What he told us was both good and bad. He said that this ship is on the alert for another assignment and might leave anytime. However, all fellows with 80 points or more are to be taken off and go to a casual camp, possibly in a couple of days. I wonder if we will be "Shanghaied" again? Our getting off in a couple of days is supposed to be another promise of Col. Eddie's. I wonder what will happen this time.

This morning our ship pulled out of the harbor, and we went down to Yokohama to take on oil and supplies. The sky was clear, and for the first time since I arrived, I got my chance to snap a picture of Mount Fuji. My picture taking days are just about over, as I am just about on the last of my film. We didn't pull clear into the dock area of Yokohama, but tied up along-side a tanker a number of miles away. While we were taking on oil and getting supplies, the captain of our ship was informed of a troop ship that was going back to the states, so all the sailors eligible for discharge were told to pack their gear and prepare to leave on fifteen minute's notice. These sailors didn't get off in Yokohama, but will go back up to Tokyo. Our ship arrived back at Tokyo about sun-down.

Had a show on deck tonight and I about froze watching it.

Thursday, September 20, 1945 Didn't rate liberty today so was on board ship all day. I spent most of my time packing a box to send home today. "Boy" what a job it is to get this stuff ready. The fourteen sailors left the ship today to go home. Why can't we Army fellows get results like that, instead of promises? The bunch of fellows I came overseas with have gone home, and none of them had as many points as I have.

The ship "Teton" that we have worked in conjunction with has received orders to return to the states on the twenty sixth. All signal equipment has been put out of operation and is to be taken off the ship.

Friday, September 21, 1945 Had to work this afternoon so I got no liberty today. Our main W.T.A. circuit has been closed down and now we have only the W.T.A. [Manila} and the WVLO [Okinawa] net circuit and the high command net circuit left. We only stand by on the high command net, and with traffic practically nil, we have little to do. Our teletype and VHF circuits have been closed down. The communications ship, Teton, which is the largest of the ships used for this purpose, and weighing around 8,000 tons, has closed down all circuits and are removing all communication gear, as on the twenty forth she is to sail back to the states.

Saturday, September 22, 1945 This morning I worked over in the warehouse that we fellows are fixing up into a gym. A couple of sailors are making two baskets, and the rest of us are marking, and painting lines on the floor for a basketball court. This afternoon I went with a couple of soldier friends of mine to see a Japanese civilian about buying cameras that he had to sell. My two friends got two nice cameras from him, and Monday, this civilian said he would have a couple of more, so I told him I would come and probably buy one of them. We walked around to several camera shops where my friends got a few accessories for their cameras. We caught a ride back to the ship where we arrived around 4:30 PM. The fellows were playing basketball, but I was too awfully tired to play. Went to bed early tonight.

Sunday, September 23, 1945 Today our radio station closed down, and now all is secured. Our duties aboard this ship have come to an end. We also learned today that our service records have been flown to Manila to be checked over, so we may be given orders to return to the states. We are in hopes that perhaps orders to return home may be sent back with our service records. This afternoon Bill and I went sight- seeing.

We took a walk over to the Imperial Palace grounds, and the House of Peers, the equivalent to our U.S. capitol. The Imperial Palace grounds appear to be in two areas, the inner grounds, and the outer palace grounds. Both of these areas are surrounded by a high stone wall and skirted by a moat. All persons may enter the outer grounds, but only a very few persons actually ever enter the palace and palace grounds proper. The Japanese, who pass through the outer palace grounds, stop at the main entrance to the inner grounds and bow toward the Emperor's palace. While we were standing by this main entrance, two high priests walked up to the edge of the mote that surrounds the inner grounds and carried out a Japanese religious ceremony. They made a lot of noise by beating on a couple of drums. I don't know why they do this, I had my camera along and took a number of pictures.

From here we took a walk up to the Diet Building, or House of Peers. This was nearly six blocks in distance. On one side of the street was the moat and high stone wall surrounding the Emperor's palace this apparently had been untouched by our bombs. On the other side of the street, all was burned out by our bombings. The Diet Building that is on this side of the street was about the only building in this area that was not destroyed. It was undamaged. The Diet Building is not as large as one might suppose. Our state capitol, I believe, is larger.

We walked around to the visitor's entrance, where a Jap guide took us through the building to the Diet Chamber. Looking down from the balcony this assembly was very impressive, with the different colored drapes and the red plush seats in a semi-circle. Above the speaker's bench was a small compartment with a gold chair of which was occupied by the Emperor when the House was in session. It was quite dark in this assembly, with only light entering through a large skylight. Even though, under such conditions, taking pictures was nearly impossible with my type of camera. I took a half minute time exposure in the hope I might get a color picture of this chamber. The sky was quite overcast when I got outside, so I didn't attempt to take a picture of the Diet Building.

We walked down to the main part of town where we caught a ride out near the dock area where our ship is anchored. I am really tired tonight.[54]

Monday, September 24, 1945 Well today is or I mean was supposed to be the day we were to move off this ship to go to a casual camp in preparation to going home. With the faith we have of such promises, none of us had our bags packed or made any preparation to leave. This afternoon two friends and I went to see the fellow about the camera he was to get for me. This civilian had two cameras. One of them was sort of a cheap affair, and not so good. The other was a small German 127 folding camera that seemed like a good buy for 400 yen, so I got it. My friends and I then walked over to a camera shop where I bought a few accessories for this camera. We then walked around through some of the stores in the hopes of seeing something worthwhile to buy. However, nearly the same condition is coming into existence that usually occurs with a large number of souvenir hunting G.I.s. The price[s] on items are going sky high even in American money.

Arrived back to the ship around 5 P.M. We have put the movie screen up in the recreation hall where we will now have our shows

Tuesday, September 25, 1945 This morning the "Teton" pulled out and is underway, headed for the states. As far as we could learn, no Army fellows were

---

[54] The House of Peers was the upper house of the Imperial Diet under the Constitution of Japan. In effect from 1889 to May of 1947.

aboard her. I guess the Teton is to go to Guam where she will pick up a few hundred sailors. We fellows on our ship are now attached to 1st Co. H.Q.s 4025, so I don't know if anything much will be done with our service records in Manila – (just another Army game to keep us overseas). We were told that likely we will receive five points for being in Japan before the peace was signed. My point score, in that case, now stands at 103. Of course, the point system is dead. All they have to do is bury it. Went looking for Souvenirs again today but didn't have much luck.

Wednesday, September 26, 1945 Some of our fellows went ashore today to check on the going home prospects. At our orderly room, which is now on shore (L ca HQS. 4025) they said our service records were back from Manila and no action had been taken on them. Not only this but nothing in sight was being done here. The rumor going around is that General Aiken does not intend to release any Signal Corps men from this area for some time yet. The fellows who are supposed to relieve us are on the beach doing detail, while we are just sitting here on this ship with top point scores, doing nothing. This evening three first Calvary soldiers came on board for supper. They said they have 75 to 80 points, and they have orders to leave to go home tomorrow. I guess we fellows are going to make another trip to the I.G. even if it probably won't do any good.

Thursday, September 27, 1945 Our C.O. here aboard ship informed us today that things are really starting to pop. Lieutenant Colonel Eddy, as well as General Aiken are in pretty hot water in their neglect in returning any Signal troops to the states. So many Signal Corps soldiers with high point scores have been going to the Inspector General's office as well as many G.I.s writing home, and their folks writing to their senators, that now a little action is being taken. We were told that our service records are being checked again in Manila, and we can expect orders to go home in a short time. We were on edge all day. Today as the ship has been ordered to return to Manila and is to leave tomorrow morning, Lieutenant Sparks looked nearly all day for Colonel Eddy to authorize our leaving the ship, so we won't have to sail with her. Col. Eddy got in touch with our C.O. this evening and said "By all means, get us off the ship before it sails." We packed our bags and are to leave in the morning. Played basketball this afternoon and am sure tired tonight.

Friday, September 28, 1945 This morning after breakfast we started carrying our gear off the ship and loading it on a truck. Being the ship is to go to

Manila they will have to get rid of the collection of transportation they have collected. One of the soldiers got one of the automobiles, they gave me the motorboat, but since I would have no way of taking care of it, and I hope that I may go home, I gave it to another sailor who was stationed on a ship nearby. We are now stationed in the Finance Building, which at present must house some three thousand G.I.s. This building is five stories high and is nearly two blocks long and the same distance wide. There are many units with separate mess halls, orderly rooms, supply departments, etc. Our living quarters are in a large room or more correctly a hall on the main floor. The mess hall where we eat is on the fourth floor, but with elevator service we don't have any stairs to climb. This evening we saw a teletype copy of fellows submitted for orders to return to the states that was sent to Manila. This list comprising of soldiers of 80 to 100 or more points, from the 232 and 4025 Signal Service outfits contained around 150 or more names. Of the enlisted men, my name is fourth from the top. It is rumored we should leave here in not more than a week. In a building this large and so many G.I.s, they sure saw us coming. Five of our guys are on K.P. tomorrow. Received three letters from Marian, one from the folks this evening.

Saturday, September 29, 1945 Five of our fellows who were to be on K.P. [were not] on hand this morning, and had to make a trip to the C.O. He gave them five extra days. This morning and this afternoon I got out of the building as soon after chow as possible, as I didn't want to get stuck on detail. I went down to get some more film for my camera, of which I have now collected thirty roles that I intend taking home with me.

Sunday, September 30, 1945 Went to church up in the auditorium this morning. This afternoon Dave, George, another fellow and I went for a walk. By late afternoon we had walked around the Emperor's Palace grounds, which is quite a number of miles. We took snap shots of points of interest on the way. Wrote a letter and went to bed early tonight.

Monday, October 1, 1945 The weather is getting cooler all the time. At night I have to sleep under both my blankets, plus my jacket thrown over me. The only shower is out in the court, and the water is ice cold. This is the only means we have of taking a bath. Three of we fellows caught a ride out by Ueno Park, this morning. *(Ueno Park – est. 1889 – in the Ueno District of Taito, Tokyo Japan. Today a large park with museums, a zoo, and known in the spring for its* *cherry blossoms)* We stopped in at a large department store where I bought a book and a couple of folders. We then got a ride on a truck to the place we buy film, where I got a few more rolls. We got a ride on another truck and got back to our quarters in time for chow.

This afternoon another friend and I caught a ride back out near Ueno Park. We walked around through a nearby neighborhood where evidently not many Americans had been before. These Japs are the most curious people I have ever seen, if you stop anywhere for a few minutes the Japs all flock around you. Most of them ask for gum, chocolate, and cigarettes. They will give you twenty yen for approximately $1.30 for perhaps 5 sticks of gum and the same price for a small bar of chocolate.

While we were walking along a narrow street a Japanese fellow, speaking very good English, asked us to come into his store. There he showed me a couple of Japanese dollies. He agreed to let me have one of them for five packs of cigarettes, so I made the deal. How I am going to lug all this stuff home is more than I know.

When I stepped out of the store, I didn't see "Scotty" or my friend around anywhere. I heard him yell at me and there he was, standing in the second story window of a house nearby. He told me to come up stairs, so, I not seeing any other means of entry, went up a ladder. I guess these Japanese people were quite surprised to see me enter their home through the upstairs window. Before going inside as is the Japanese custom, I took off my shoes. In this room, which was about fifteen feet square, were reed mats covering the floor. The only furniture was a small low table about twelve inches high. Everyone sat on cushions laying around the floor. The American speaking Japanese, who proved to be in the import business, also came in and he rather acted as an interpreter for Scotty and I. The master of the house was in the manufacturing business of different novelties, etc. He was interested in our opinion of a lamp shade he intended to manufacture as a souvenir for the Americans. He was quite pleased when we told him he should be able to sell a lot of them. When the lady of the house came into the room, she bowed low a couple of times and then sat down. One of the daughters made us a special kind of tea, which was a brilliant green, whipped into sort of a foam. It tasted something like tea, but mostly like boiled grass. We were then served some pickled peaches, which were quite tasty. The lady of the house showed us a couple of dolls they had and finally when we had to leave, the dolls were wrapped up and given to us. These Japanese people, I am sure, are of the class that dislike war as much as the average American family and have little to do with the starting of the recent one. The English-speaking Japanese gentleman said that the devastation caused by the earthquake years ago did not in the least, equal the damage done by our bombers. It was nearly dark when Scotty and I left this house. One of the small boys of the family directed us to the railroad station where we caught a train to the Tokyo station.

Tuesday, October 2, 1945 Stayed around quarters all day today in preparation to moving. Late this afternoon we loaded our gear on a truck and moved to the new building, the "San Shine" building. *(A.K.A the Sunshine Building, one of Tokyo's tallest buildings)* Our bunch is being split up and we managed to have only five of us in one room together. We are in room 416 on the fourth floor, and our quarters are quite ideal, having many windows, and plenty of room for all of us. There are sixteen of us in our room, but this room really consists of two as number 418 is an entrance also. Our room was evidently an office formerly, as there are many flat top desks piled up in here. Many of we fellows have placed one of these desks near our bunk for our personal use. The main floor of this building is something like a spacious hotel lobby, but built with many show windows along the main corridor. Besides a wide stairway there are five elevators built in a semi-circle. Our mess hall is in the basement where there was formally a restaurant. As for our chow, it is terrible. For dinner we had bully beef mixed with sauerkraut, string beans, and dry bread. Went over to the Daiichi Building to a show tonight. *(This building was also General MacArthur's headquarters and is still a part of Tokyo's skyline today.)* Fellows in the Signal Center say that our orders should be in either today or tomorrow. Perhaps my returning home isn't so far off. Overseas 37 months today

Wednesday, October 3, 1945 The captain in charge of this outfit is really a character. He will put a notice up on any post, and if you don't happen to see it, it is just too bad, you catch company punishment. He put a note up on the elevator door of to the effect, that no one is to leave the building. Nearly all of us use the stairs, but luckily one of the guys told us about the note so we stayed around the building.

Took a number of pictures from the roof this afternoon. This evening we heard some darn discouraging news. A Master Sergeant told us that no orders were being cut on us, that it seems there is a dispute as to who is, or what outfit is to make out the orders to send us home. Consequently, we just have to sit. We fellows are just about set to make another trip to the I.G.

Thursday, October 4, 1945 This afternoon about a dozen or so fellows who have 90 points and above went over to see the I.G. They submitted a list of all ninety points and above men in a formal complaint as to our being held. The I.G. acted as if he would do something about it. Things are sure in a muddle with the Signal Corps here in Tokyo. This outfit we are in requests our orders to return home to be made out in Manila. The 4025 in Manila want to get out from under all responsibility and have us transferred into the eighth army, so that the eighth army will have the responsibility of getting us home. While they are wrangling back and forth, we just sit.

Friday, October 5, 1945 Rained all day today. Soldiers in the Quartermaster First Cavalry, and Air Corps, have left to go home, down as low as 70 points. It is our misfortune to be in a really screwed up outfit. There are around twenty-five soldiers not assigned to any job in particular with ninety points and above. I am of the opinion that the I.G. department doesn't care what becomes of us eight. We were told that we had a good cause for coming and seeing the I.G. and something would be done to get us home, but that is as far as it goes. The latest rumor and this is our only source of information, which has been quite reliable, being from our friends in the Signal Center, is that we are to be transferred into the Eighth Army, in which case we would be out of here in 48 hours. I guess there are miles of Army red tape connected to this move, and we will sit many more days or weeks until it finally goes through. This afternoon some of we fellows went to see a Japanese state show at the Takarazuka Theater. This theater is a short distance from here and its name is inscribed in large Japanese characters, such as:

東京寶塚劇場

The admission was nine yen which from Japanese standards is quite high. This theater is one of Tokyo's best though, and at this theater the best state talent in Japan appears. The first act was a Japanese spiritual dance. The music was furnished by ten Japanese musicians crowded on a platform on the stage. No modern musical instruments were used. A type of two stringed banjos, whistlers, and small drums that they beat with the palms of their hands furnished an oriental type of music. The actor doing the dance depicted a story by the actions of the dance and different costumes. At the start of this performance the dancer appeared in a white kimono. With the aid of a Japanese attendant, always present on the stage at different intervals, would help the dancer disrobe from one Kimono to the other. All this was done as a part of the dance. The change from a dull colored Kimono to a brilliantly colored one would evidently mean either happiness or sorrow. In the box seat where we were seated was an American women news correspondent gathering information for an article. With her was a Japanese interpreter who told her the trend of events on stage. Therefore, we also gained the meaning of the stage performance. This spiritual dance represented a rich girl who married the man she was not in love with and at the end of the dance, which lasted about twenty-five minutes, the dancer went through actions of torture, and this represented the husband killing her. We were told that the person doing this dance was actually a man. The hairdo he wore was very elaborate and his face was colored chalk white. Either that or he wore a mask. We couldn't quite tell. The other three acts of the program were of a more western type of entertainment but was all spoken or sung in Japanese. On the rest of the program was a ballet number called the "Blue Danube" done by about twenty-five girls. There was a Japanese actor (Japan's most popular) and a Japanese girl singer, who had a top-notch position in entertainment circles. Two of the numbers she sang were "south of the Border" and "Fennec u lee Fennec u Lau" This show lasted nearly all afternoon, we did not get out until after four. When I got back to our quarters we learned we are to go on guard tonight. I was quite fortunate and was only on from 8 P.M. until midnight.[55]

Saturday, October 6, 1945 Another fellow and I went out near Ueno Park this afternoon to shop around. In a small store I bought some more silk (?) to take home, I also managed to relieve a Jap of his Jap flag, with the aid of a pack

---

[55] The Takarazuka Theater was and still is the home of Takarazuka Creative Arts. Built in 1934, torn down in 1998, and rebuilt in 2001.

of cigarettes. We heard today that the Eighth Army has turned thumbs down on taking over our outfit. If that is true as things stand now, I guess we are stuck for quite a while yet.

Sunday, October 7, 1945 When I got up this morning the sun was shining and the sky was very clear. For the first time in many weeks the clouds that usually hid Mount Fuji were not there, and Fuji was plainly visible. I took my camera and went up on the roof where I took a couple of pictures. This afternoon a friend who still has possession of the automobile he acquired after the 848 left for Manila, drove a friend and I out to the zoo, where we took a few pictures. Most of the animals have been disposed of by the Japs during the war to cut down on the food they were fed. In a number of cages and pens were hogs, chickens, and horses. Went to the show tonight.

Monday, October 8, 1945 We learned today that our orders are on their way up from Manila, where they were finally cut. However, due to the bad weather conditions the plane bringing our orders to Tokyo was grounded at Okinawa. The chow is improving to a slight degree, but it is still pretty punk. Wrote letters tonight and went to bed early.

Tuesday, October 9, 1945 This morning John Dillon, the fellow who has the Jap automobile, and some more of we fellow went out for a drive. Actually, there is a decided question whether we legally can use this car. John has a paper authorizing him to drive this car, made out by the ship's officers. John is to take care of it until the ship returns. We drove out near Ueno Park, where we stopped in at the small store where we do most of our trading to see if he had any more silk. We heard today that our orders have arrived, and we should get ready to leave here in a few days. A bunch of Air Corps Signal fellows left today who have 70 points. Went to the show on the eighth floor of our building tonight.

Wednesday, October 10, 1945 Over at the Signal Center all fellows with 70 or more points have been relieved from their jobs in preparation to being sent home. The Air Corps fellows who left the other day came back from the casual camp, as the place is full. They won't take anyone with less than 89 points. Perhaps we fellows will have something of a break. This morning I was over in the park, and I struck up a conversation with a young Jap college student. He could talk very good English, and we had no trouble understanding one another. We asked questions and exchanged ideas on many subjects. He asked me such questions as "What does the United States expect from Japan?" "If I thought U.S. and Russia would go to war?" We exchanged ideas on "Japanese and American customs." I asked him his opinion on Japanese suicide tactics, and he with vigor said that was a wonderful way to die. I pointed out to him that actually this type of warfare was not good strategy and had aided in the defeat of Japan. He argued with me on the strategy idea, but dying for one's country was so glorious that it over shadowed its lack of strategy. I asked him if he thought Japan could win the war after Russia came in and Germany was defeated. He said many Japanese felt in their hearts they would not win, but they were afraid to say so for fear of the secret police. He said they had a certain amount of faith from their religious beliefs, that the Japanese are God's chosen people and he would find a way for them. I asked him why Pearl Harbor had been attacked in such a manner. He said the people were told the American Navy was ready to attack them. He told me that the first Doolittle raid by B-25 bombers was a surprise to the Japanese, that the air alert didn't sound until twenty minutes after it was over. He said the planes came in very low, and not until after they had gone did they realize they were Americans. He said very little damage was caused. This Japanese fellow, from the impression I gathered, seemed happy the war was over even though Japan had been defeated. He was all out for Japan but realized the war lords had kept them in the dark. This fellow was filled up with Japanese tradition. I believe he really thinks Japan is God's chosen people, and he steadfastly believes that women are the weaker sex both physically and mentally, and therefore should take a backseat. If what he says is true the colleges and schools are principally for the men. The women are to only be wives and raise families. When a boy is born everyone is happy, but a girl is a disappointment.

Thursday, October 11, 1945 It has been rainy and cold most of this week, and I have a bad cold as the result of it. We heard today that our orders have not yet arrived, as all planes have been grounded due to the bad weather. The Army newspaper "Stars and Stripes" is full of news about fellows going home and gives encouragement to fellows with low point scores. Most G.I.s in this area are at a loss as to knowing who this newspaper information is meant for. As what the newspaper contains is certainly contrary to the actual state of things. Actually, only a few thousand men (4000) or two shiploads have left with homeward bound troops to date, which is the extent of the demobilization plan in Tokyo and Yokohama. The paper states that next month 40,000 are to go home, but of persons concerned no faith is put into this propaganda. Went over to the Tokyo theaters this afternoon and tried to take some pictures of the stage show. Not being much light, all my pictures were under exposed.

Friday, October 12, 1945 Rained all day today. I spent part of this morning washing some of my clothes. The captain in charge of this outfit is really going wild. He says we are now in the Peacetime Army, and we are to be soldiers. He says he will court martial a fellow for any reason or slight deviation from the regulations. We no longer can have a clothesline in our room. How we are to dry our clothes through this rainy weather seem of no concern of his. There is no other means of getting your laundry done, and a bath is off by a wash basin. The Red Cross is now open here in Tokyo and is located in a former Banker' Club building about five blocks from here. Went to the show on the eighth floor this evening.

Saturday, October 13, 1945 Today the sun shone bright all day. All of us are feeling in better spirits as we feel sure our orders should come through today. This morning Bill, John, and I went in John's car to get some film for our cameras. This afternoon Bill and I took a walk up to the Diet Building where we took some pictures. We also went inside to the House of Peers assembly chamber where we took some pictures. These pictures did not turnout so good though, being under-exposed. Bill and I stopped in at the Red Cross and had some coffee before going back to our quarters.

Sunday, October 14, 1945 Today has been another nice day. Walked around the park for a while this morning. Stayed around our quarters this afternoon and wrote letters. No news came through about our orders today. I guess, being today is Sunday, all offices are closed. Went to the show on the eighth floor tonight. Today we heard that no orders have been sent from Manila, and there is no intention that they will. As far as any action being taken to send us home, things seem at a stand-still. We fellows sat around our room most of the morning not saying much of anything. We are at a complete loss as to what we can do. We were informed by some other fellows that the I.G. won't hardly let you in his office anymore. Some of our fellows have written home telling their families of conditions, and asked them to contact newspapers, inform congressmen, etc. of the absolute disregard of soldier's eligibility to return home, and failure to do anything about it. So far, I have refrained from informing anyone at home of existing conditions with me, as I don't wish to get them up in the air if I can help it. As a last resort perhaps, I will ask Marian and the others if there is anything they can do. This evening a bunch of we fellows ate over at the Imperial Hotel. Army Recruiting office has been opened. That is one G.I. line you can fall into anytime and be first.

Tuesday, October 15, 1945 Stayed around my quarters this morning. This afternoon got on a truck and went out to a stadium where Danny Kaye and Leo Durocher are putting on a show. The show was fairly good and I managed to get a few pictures. It has been several weeks now since my last letter from Marian, or any of the other folks. Today Marian and I have been married four years and four months. Today all soldiers are supposed to start wearing O.D. or winter uniforms.

Wednesday, October 16, 1945 Washed out some of my clothes today. Being the weather has been rainy and cold the only place we have to dry them is in our room. The C.O. put out an order barring all clothes lines in the rooms. What he expects us to do is beyond my imagination. We were told today that the restaurant for enlisted men over at the Imperial Hotel has been taken over for officers, so that is the end of that. For enlisted men who come into Tokyo on pass, they either have to bring some food with them or go without, as there are now no restaurants in Tokyo for enlisted men. This evening some of us went down to the Red Cross. While we were there we saw a "Stars and Stripes" newspaper reporter and we proceeded to tell him the facts about our demobilization prospects. He seemed very interested and said he would look into the matter. George Heller, our representative, went to see the I.G. today, but was given little satisfaction. I guess we are just stuck.

Thursday, October 17, 1945 Perhaps I should write to the folks at home and give them the facts about the run around we are getting on going home. Pressure from the home front is the only thing that will get the Army to take any action at all. This afternoon Bill and I walked down Ginza to a number of department stores. Before coming back to our quarters, we stopped in at the Red Cross for some coffee. Saw a movie over at the Dai Ichi Building tonight.[56]

Friday, October 18, 1945 Today in the "Stars and Stripes" newspaper there was an item about we fellows in regard to the neglect of sending us home. Stayed around our quarters all day.

---

[56] The Ginza area is still Tokyo's largest shopping area. The Dai Ichi Building was General MacArthur's headquarters.

Saturday, October 19, 1945 I guess I have the dates in this book mixed up a little! A "Stars and Stripes" news reports interviewed me today for an article on Demobilization, as to how many points I have, time overseas, what results gained by trying to get home, etc. The reporter said perhaps this news item would be printed back in the states. Some of we fellows went to the Red Cross this afternoon. We heard that 8th Army is to cut orders on us but have no official confirmation. Saw a Japanese Stage show over at the Dai Ichi Building tonight. Japanese girls dressed in very colorful kimonos danced some of their customary dances.

Sunday, October 20, 1945 We heard today that our orders will be ready by 4 P.M. At 4P.M. a swarm of fellows went over to GHQ and asked when the orders would be ready. They were informed the orders would be ready at 5 P.M. and tomorrow morning they would be distributed. My name should be on those orders.

Monday, October 21, 1945 This morning one of the fellows said the orders were down in the orderly room. I went down to see about it, and sure enough of the enlisted men I am fourth from the top of the list – at long last, I have my orders for returning home. Receiving our orders doesn't necessarily mean I will leave for home right away. We yet have to go to the casual camp and be processed. After that we may spend considerable time waiting for transportation.

Loading up to begin our journey home

Tuesday, October 22, 1945 This morning we reported to the dispensary to take shots. Since I was pretty much up to date on receiving shots, I got by this morning with only taking one, a typhus shot. This afternoon we packed all our gear and assembled on the main floor to wait for trucks to transport us to the 4th replacement depot. The 232 Signal service Battalion fellows also quartered in this building –(this morning) were given Japanese war souvenir of pistols, carbines, etc. Our outfit is also entitled to receive these souvenirs, but it has to be taken care of by your company headquarters. As usual nothing was done. Getting home is all that matters with me anyway. At 2 P.M. we loaded our stuff on a truck and after a short delay our truck convoy of 18 trucks got underway. We traveled out Ginza, and on to Yokohama, a distance of 20 miles. All along the route from Tokyo to Yokohama, the area once crowded with industries was completely burned out, the result of our B-29 raids. We drove on through Yokohama and over a rough country road nearly 25 miles to the 4th replacement depot, located at Zama. *(A United States Army Post.)* This camp was formally the main Japanese Army Center of Japan or in other works the "West Point" of Japan. In our convoy was Signal troops of the 232 and 4025. As soon as our truck arrived at our destination the officers in charge of the 232nd arranged quarters for these troops. As usual nothing was done by the officers of our outfit, and we stood out in the lot for over an hour until a 1st sergeant took it upon himself to pick up a few orders from the fellows and went to the office to fix things up. By the time we were settled in our quarters it was 8 P.M. We were told that we would have supper at 9 P.M. after which a sergeant gave us a clothing check, which is the first of the routine of different inspections made before our return to the states. No one knows just how long we will be here, but things seem favorable for a rapid return the U.S.

Tuesday, October 23, 1945 This morning we were marched over to the auditorium where we listened to talks on the routine we were to go through in preparation to our return to the U.S. After this we marched over to supply where shortages in clothing were issued. After dinner we marched over to another building where our service records were checked over. I was told I would receive my discharge at *(in this entry my dad has left this part blank.)* After reporting to the medics and receiving a shot for influenza, we were through for the day. We have heard that several ships are due in at Yokohama in a few days. It is anyone's guess how long we may be here though. Wrote to Marian tonight.

Wednesday, October 24, 1945 This morning we marched over to the auditorium to hear a talk on the "G.I. Bill of Rights" also a talk on what to expect when we return home and adapting ourselves to civilian life again. This afternoon our clothing, etc. was checked for duty clearance back into the U.S. After this I went down to the finance office where I changed over some of the Australian, Duty New Guinea, Filipino, and Jap money to American Green Backs. This was the end of our U.S. bound formalities and now orders can be cut for our shipping orders. There was a slight earthquake this afternoon that caused our barrack to vibrate to a small extent.

Thursday, October 25, 1945 This morning early, we were told to stay around our barracks, as at 10 A.M. there was a possibility that we might be called to leave. However, we were not called, and we spent the day within a close distance of our barracks. We had to do latrine detail this morning. The usual amount of griping was missing over such a disagreeable job, as everyone is in high spirits, due to our prospects of returning home. This afternoon some of we fellows went down to the gym and shot baskets for a while. We spent the evening by going to the show.

Friday, October 26, 1945 At 2:10 A.M. the C.Q. woke me up and told me to pack my stuff and be ready to leave at 2:30 A.M. I got dressed and threw my stuff in my duffle bag and carried my gear down in front of the Administration Building. Don Jenson, and I were the only ones of our group called to leave. We thought at first we might be going to get air transportation, but discovered the reason for our being called at such an early hour was that all fellows supposed to go to Fort Leavenworth, are to board the ship in one group. I was rushed around so much this morning that I didn't have time to say goodbye to anyone.

We stood in the lot in front of the Administration Building until 4 A.M. when finally, a group of trucks came and the fellows started loading up. By this time there must have been close to 300 soldiers. After a short ride of about ten minutes, we arrived at a railroad station and got on board a passenger train standing by. The coaches of this train were quite similar to those of American trains, only much smaller. Two persons were all each seat would hold.

We were informed that this train ride would last around three and a half hours. We were quite sure we were going to Yokohama, a distance of not more than 30 miles, but not until we got underway at 4:30 A.M. could we realize why it should take us such a long length of time to travel such a short distance. First, we traveled west for nearly an hour. Then, after changing engines and switching over on another line, we then traveled east for a time. By this time, it was around 7 A.M. and whenever our train would stop for a short period, Japanese men women and children gathered, and the soldiers of our train would throw them candy and sugar, that we had left from our K-ration packages.

At around 10 A.M. our train arrived at Yokohama. After unloading our gear on the platform, and waiting a short while, trucks came, we loaded our luggage and were taken to the dock where our ship was moored. We fell in line as our names were called and proceeded to walk up the gang plank. We were taken down four decks to our assigned quarters (compartment D-4) and assigned bunks. There are probably 100 of us in our quarters, which makes it rather crowded, but even so we are quite comfortable. In our compartment is a drinking water cooler that is on at all times.

By 12 noon we were quite settled and we were taken to chow. No mess kits or mess cups are needed, as we eat off of trays, which are washed by a dishwasher.

For dinner we had fresh ham, fresh potatoes, peas, celery, bread, fresh butter, and coffee. We not only had all this good food, but all we could eat.

UP UNTIL 6 p.m. only the 400 of us who came aboard this morning had arrived, all told, they say, that the rest of 3000 soldiers are to come aboard tonight. It is reported the ship is to be ready and will sail tomorrow morning. After chow tonight, which was another meal we used to only hear about, of roast beef, fresh potatoes, pea & bean salad, bread and butter, and all we could eat, Don Jenson and I went up on deck and wanted to see if our bunch of fellows would be among those coming aboard. We watched until after dark. Finally, I saw Keith Davison standing in line down on the dock. He told me that the other fellows would come aboard after a while. I saw Bill Pandolfi, and then some of the others. With our entire old bunch together, the voyage will be even more pleasant. "It is hard to realize that I am really on my way home."

Saturday, October 27, 1945 Just after breakfast, our ship the "U.S.S. General Heintzelman" was swinging away from the dock and we headed out to sea for Seattle, U.S.A It is said weather permitting we should reach port in 10 to 11 days. All day long our ship forced its way against a very strong wind and a rather heavy sea. This ship is quite large though and hasn't so far rocked around very much. I believe I will make this voyage without getting seasick. My tour of duty aboard the P.C.E. 848 should help.

All of us are quite in the dark as to what we are to do when we reach the states. I intend to call Marian as soon as possible. I will have to wait and see what – where – and when of transportation out of Seattle (?) Where to (?) time of arrival at Fort Leavenworth, if I go there (?) I hope perhaps to meat Marian in Kansas City, but I will have to wait and see how things work out.[57]

---

[57] My own thoughts, at this point in my own ten year plus journey in documenting my father's entries, I am sitting here with tears in my eyes and feeling an overwhelming sadness. My father sacrificed over four years of his life, fighting for the freedoms, this country has been blessed with. My dad and mom were separated for nearly five years, after only eight months of marriage. He was thin and malnourished, had to have extensive dental work done, and sent home with only a short talk on adjusting back to civilian life. If you have read this account of a "soldier's time spent in Hell", if you have read every entry from day one, perhaps I have brought about an awareness of how difficult this war was on our WWll Veterans. No modern-day luxuries for communicating with loved ones, no modern facilities for taking care of such amenities, as laundry, shelter from the elements, the "chow", the living conditions, and dealing with the environment of the jungle, not to mention the "system" that so many times let them down." And the most amazing part of all "WE WON THIS WAR."

Sunday, October 28, 1945 The sky has been clear and the sea calm all day and our ship must be making good time. It is said our course will take us within 50 to 100 miles of the Aleutian Islands.

I attended church services this morning. So far I haven't been on any details. Fellows have been put on K.P., guard, and clean up details, all around me, but so far so good. As we go farther north the weather gets cooler.

Went to the show held up on deck tonight. There are three movies shown on topside at the same time, so you have a fair chance of seeing one you like. However, the number of troops on board out-number the amount of available space for the show, so you have to be there very early. Went to bed early tonight. Set our watches ahead one hour.

Monday, October 29, 1945 Clear skies and calm seas still prevail, and our ship is still plowing along at 18 knots. Whenever up on deck, you have to wear plenty of clothing as it is quite cold now. The voyage is becoming rather monotonous. Nearly a hundred percent of the conversation aboard is about getting home and the variety of plans each fellow has. Good home cooking is one of the main topics.

Our compartment (D-4) is now on the end of the chow schedule, which is not so good. Usually very little food is left when we get the call to go to chow. However, you hear very little "bitching" as everyone has but one thought in mind, and that is getting home. Stayed up rather late tonight and washed out some socks, and underwear.

Tuesday, October 30, 1945 The days are really dragging now and even though the weather is still clear and the seas calm and our ship is making excellent time, it seems as if we are hardly moving. It is said that if conditions prevail we should arrive in Seattle in less than 11 ½ days, as is the time designated. The weather is much colder now than when we left Yokohama, and a fellow, even though dressing as warm as possible can only stay up on deck a short time. I have caught a little cold of which I am trying to hold down without getting more. Went to bed early tonight. Set our watches ahead one hour.

Wednesday, October 31, 1945 Today was just another routine day. Spent quite a little time up on deck today, even though it was very cold. This afternoon the sky clouded over, and for a short time a few flakes of snow fell. This is the first snow I have seen in over three and a half years.

Our compartment is getting farther up the chow schedule, and we eat earlier and get more to eat than we did. Our ship is making as good time as ever. In a 24-hour period we cover better than 430 miles

Thursday, November 1, 1945 Today went as usual with our ship still making excellent progress. At 8 A.M. we were within 115 miles of the island Amatignak, an island also of the Aleutian chain *(is in southwestern Alaska)*. We were within 130 miles of an island known as Amchitka, also of the Aleutian Chain. *(Amchitka is the most southern point of Alaska)*. At 6:25 A.M. we crossed the 180th meridian, or International Dateline, therefore at midnight tonight the time will be set back 24 hours and tomorrow will again be November 1st. At 7 P.M. this evening we passed the halfway mark of our voyage.

Thursday, November 1, 1945 Today, again, Thursday as yesterday we crossed the 180th Meridian, or the International Date Line. During the night we ran into bad weather and today our ship is rolling and pitching through rough sea. Everyone stayed below today because of the salt spray flying across the decks. Better than half the troops on board are laying in their bunks, seasick. Anyone who is well enough to go to the head, if able to endure the condition of the place, caused by vomiting G.I.s can stand the sea at its worst. As for myself I have little appetite and have missed breakfast and dinner today. By staying in my bunk, I have worked the necessity of a mad dash to the head, which at this distance would be a losing race.

Friday, November 2, 1945 Still rough today, but not quite as bad as yesterday. I ate dinner today. The rest of the time I spent in my bunk. They say we should arrive at Seattle Monday night.

Saturday, November 3, 1945 The ocean has calmed to a great extent, and I am feeling more like myself again. I ate all three meals today and spent some time up on deck. I am still in the dark as to what procedure we will go through when we reach port. All we know is that we will be taken to a camp somewhere in Seattle where we will spend perhaps not more than a day before being sent on. I guess I will be sent to Fort Leavenworth, Kansas. It doesn't seem possible I am nearly home. Maybe I can arrange to meet Marian in Kansas City. Will have to wait and see how things go.

Sunday, November 4, 1945 The ocean was quite rough today, and a strong wind blowing, however both the sea and the wind are working in our favor, as our ship is traveling with them. As of 8 A.M. this morning we have only 615 miles more to go and we should sight land tomorrow morning. They say going through the straits and into Puget Sound on to Seattle, a distance of 135 miles, will probably take 8 hours, as we will travel at reduced speed. Had an excellent dinner today, but being our compartment is on the end of the schedule now we didn't eat until nearly 3 P.M.

Monday, November 5, 1945 At 11 this morning I saw my first glimpse of the U.S. at around 1:30 p.m. we entered the straits of Juan de Fuca off cape Flatttern, a distance of about 131 miles from Seattle. all afternoon our ship cruised along amid the scenic splendor of pine covered slopes and snow covered mountains in the distance. Around 8:30 this evening we came into the harbor at Seattle. Never in my life have I seen a more beautiful or impressive sight than that of Seattle. All the lights of the city, marking its patterns throughout the surrounding hills, and valleys neon lights of different colors and buses, and automobiles made me realize that here would be the life that was lost in Manila, Tokyo, Yokohama, etc. and of which never existed in New Guinea. My coming home has finally come true. Our ship anchored in the bay tonight and is to dock at 8 a.m. tomorrow.

This is the last entry my father made in his journals. As the "story" goes, my father called my mother when he got off the ship in Seattle. She has stated, that when she heard the phone ring at work (Meredith Pub. Co) she knew it was her husband, and she "floated" to the phone, and heard his voice for the first time in over four years. They met in Kansas City, at the Muehlebach Hotel on November 19, 1945. I was born on August 21, 1946. ☺

I have deep regrets that I never asked my father more questions or even asked him to share this with me while he was still alive. There were times when we would sit together, with a world globe, and he would show me the routes he had taken from Camp Crowder to Tyler Texas, to San Francesco, and, south from there out of San Francesco Bay. He would take me through his entire travels, never sharing the horrors, miseries, and the extreme loneliness and despair of his journey. Never once did I hear my mother, or my dad complain about their time away from each other. I did hear comments made by both of them about "fellows" who could have gone, but found an excuse to stay home. These "fellows" were not respected by either one of them.

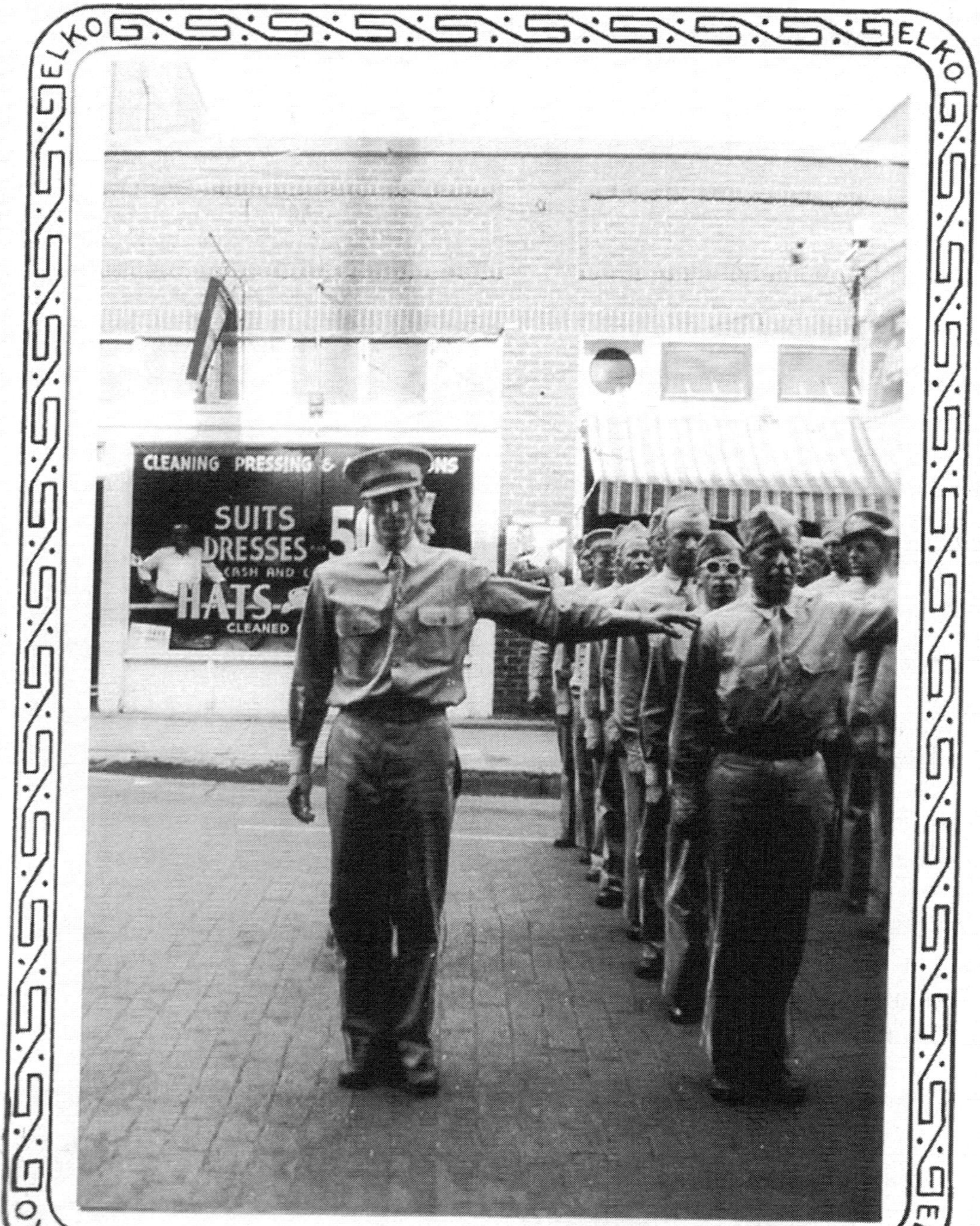
ELKO
CLEANING PRESSING &
SUITS
DRESSES
CLEANED

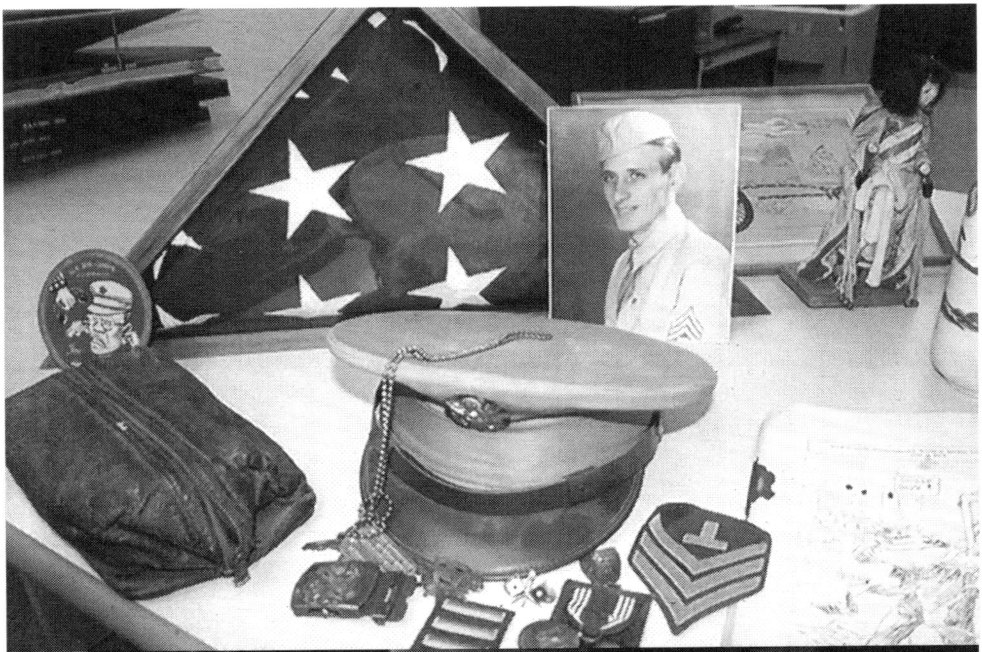

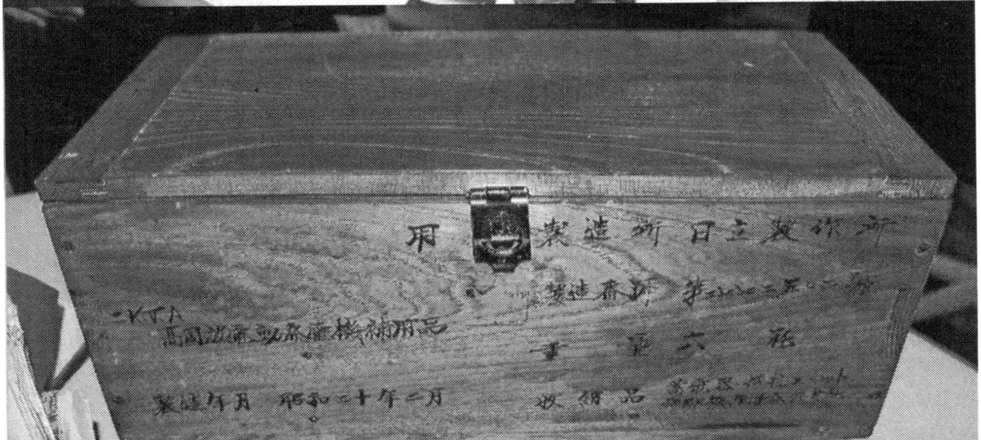

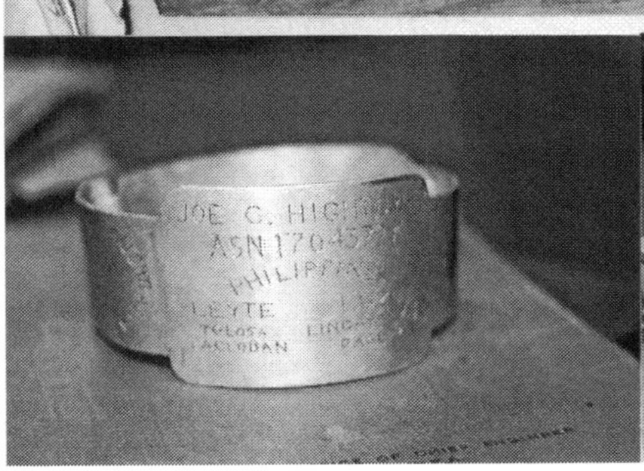
LEYTE

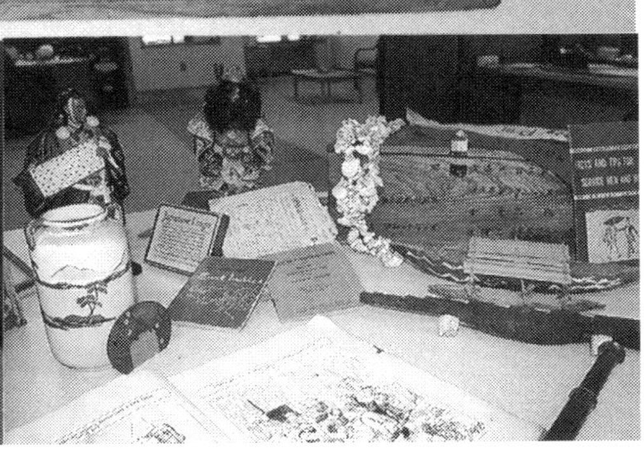

Biographies

Joseph Carl Hightower (1913-1998)

Joe was born in Carlisle, Iowa, in 1913. He lived most of his life in Des Moines, Iowa, where he retired from Meredith Corporation in 1978 after forty-one years as a Pressman (printer). He was a Journeyman Pressman and a member of the International Pressman's Union. He was married to LaVerne Marian Hightower. Mr. Hightower served abroad in World War II for three years, nine months, and fourteen days. These diaries offer the details of his service and end the day of his return.

Marijo Starnes

Marijo Starnes was born in Des Moines, Iowa, in 1946 to Joe and Marian Hightower. She resides in Colo, Iowa, with her husband Jeffrey Starnes, a retired corporate pilot. Marijo retired from her career as a dance teacher after running her studio, Marijo Bickel-Starnes School of Dance, for over three decades. She has three sons: Joe Bickel, her father's name-sake Joseph Carl, stepson Chuck Bickel who assisted in transcribing and digitizing the diaries and photographs Mr. Hightower wrote and photographed, and stepson John Starnes.

CHARLES BICKEL

Charles Bickel was born in Des Moines, Iowa, in 1971. He helped Marijo, his stepmom, proofread the journals, digitize pages, and restore Joe's photographs. He resides in Elkhart, Iowa with his wife Kathy Bickel, a scientist at the USDA.

He is a painter, curator, illustrator, and writer. In his youth he studied painting under the tutelage of Dimitar Krustev (1920-2013). In the late 1980s he studied Graphic Design at Des Moines Area Community College, and he later studied Fine Art and Spanish at Drake University.

Charles was one of the original members of the Santa Ana Artist Village in the 1990s where he curated and created art in his studio and showed in local California galleries. He has published writings, has a corporate collector of his paintings, and has published illustrations. The Iowa Gold Star Military Museum in Johnston, Iowa, purchased one of Bickel's paintings in 2020.